THE ECONO[illegible]

This book proposes a selection model for explaining cross-national variation in economic voting: Rational voters condition their economic vote on whether incumbents are responsible for economic outcomes because this is the optimal way to identify and elect competent economic managers under conditions of uncertainty. This model explores how political and economic institutions alter the quality of the signal that the previous economy provides about the competence of candidates. The rational economic voter is also attentive to strategic cues regarding the responsibility of parties for economic outcomes and their electoral competitiveness. Theoretical propositions are derived linking variation in economic and political institutions to variability in economic voting. The authors demonstrate that there is economic voting, and that it varies significantly across political contexts, and then test explanations for this variation derived from their theory. The data consist of 165 election studies conducted in 19 different countries over a 20-year time period.

Raymond M. Duch is University Professor of Quantitative Political Science at Oxford University and Professorial Fellow at Nuffield College. Prior to holding these positions, he was the Senator Don Henderson Scholar in Political Science at the University of Houston. An authority on the application of formal theories and quantitative methods to questions in comparative political economy, public opinion research, and democratization, his research has been published in the leading journals in political science, including the *American Journal of Political Science*, the *American Political Science Review*, the *British Journal of Political Science*, and *Political Analysis*. Among his award-winning articles are "It's Not Whether You Win or Lose," which won the 2001 Robert H. Durr Award for analysis in quantitative methods, and "The Global Economy, Competency, and the Economic Vote," which won the Best Paper in Political Economy Award in 2006. Professor Duch is an Associate Editor of the *American Journal of Political Science*. He is also the author of *Privatizing the Economy: Telecommunications Policy in Comparative Perspective* (1991).

Randolph T. Stevenson is Associate Professor of Political Science at Rice University in Houston, Texas. His professional research applies quantitative and formal approaches to questions of comparative political behavior, party competition, and cabinet government in parliamentary democracies. Professor Stevenson's research has been published in the leading journals in political science, including the *American Political Science Review*, the *American Journal of Political Science*, the *British Journal of Political Science*, *Social Choice*, *Electoral Studies*, and *Political Analysis*.

POLITICAL ECONOMY OF INSTITUTIONS AND DECISIONS

Other books in the series

Alberto Alesina and Howard Rosenthal, *Partisan Politics, Divided Government, and the Economy*

Lee J. Alston, Thráinn Eggertsson, and Douglass C. North, eds., *Empirical Studies in Institutional Change*

Lee J. Alston and Joseph P. Ferrie, *Southern Paternalism and the Rise of the American Welfare State: Economics, Politics, and Institutions, 1865–1965*

James E. Alt and Kenneth Shepsle, eds., *Perspectives on Positive Political Economy*

Josephine T. Andrews, *When Majorities Fail: The Russian Parliament, 1990–1993*

Jeffrey S. Banks and Eric A. Hanushek, eds., *Modern Political Economy: Old Topics, New Directions*

Yoram Barzel, *Economic Analysis of Property Rights*, 2nd edition

Yoram Barzel, *A Theory of the State: Economic Rights, Legal Rights, and the Scope of the State*

Robert Bates, *Beyond the Miracle of the Market: The Political Economy of Agrarian Development in Kenya*, 2nd edition

Charles M. Cameron, *Veto Bargaining: Presidents and the Politics of Negative Power*

Kelly H. Chang, *Appointing Central Bankers: The Politics of Monetary Policy in the United States and the European Monetary Union*

Peter Cowhey and Mathew McCubbins, eds., *Structure and Policy in Japan and the United States: An Institutionalist Approach*

(Continued on page following index)

THE ECONOMIC VOTE

How Political and Economic Institutions Condition Election Results

RAYMOND M. DUCH
Nuffield College, Oxford University

RANDOLPH T. STEVENSON
Rice University

CAMBRIDGE UNIVERSITY PRESS
Cambridge, New York, Melbourne, Madrid, Cape Town,
Singapore, São Paulo, Delhi, Mexico City

Cambridge University Press
32 Avenue of the Americas, New York, NY 10013-2473, USA

www.cambridge.org
Information on this title: www.cambridge.org/9780521707404

First published 2008
Reprinted 2012

A catalog record for this publication is available from the British Library.

Library of Congress Cataloging in Publication Data

Duch, Raymond M., 1953–
The Economic vote : how political and economic institutions
condition election results / Raymond M. Duch, Randolph T. Stevenson.
p. cm. – (Political economy of institutions and decisions)
Includes bibliographical references and index.
ISBN 978-0-521-88102-9 (hbk.) – ISBN 978-0-521-70740-4 (pbk.)
1. Voting – Economic aspects. 2. Elections – Economic aspects.
I. Stevenson, Randolph T. II. Title. III. Series.
JF1001.D825 2008
324.9–dc22 2007026982

ISBN 978-0-521-88102-9 Hardback
ISBN 978-0-521-70740-4 Paperback

Dedicated to my parents, Duke and Shirley Duch

R. M. D.

Dedicated to Rick Gritz

R. T. S.

Contents

Preface

As our friends, families, and colleagues will attest – and bemoan – this book has taken almost eight years to complete. The ultimate product has little in common with the initial idea that we intended to explore, which was examining the extent to which the impact of the "real" economy on political behavior is mediated by its representation in the electronic and print media. We got side-tracked with the question of whether there was, in fact, an economic vote and whether it varied across contexts in any significant fashion. And then we decided we needed to come up with a theory to explain this contextual variation.

Our treatment of the economic vote in this book is a significant departure from much of the comparative economic voting literature. One of its novel aspects is that it takes seriously the importance of writing down a rigorous theoretical model of the vote decision and of precisely how context conditions the importance of economic evaluations in the voter's preference function.

We hope our readers will appreciate that this has been an ambitious project both in our effort at developing a theory of the economic vote and in our determination to assemble and analyze the appropriate data for testing these theoretical hypotheses. We could not have accomplished these tasks without generous support from a number of funding institutions and academic institutions. Most importantly, we benefited from a National Science Foundation grant (#SBR-0215633) that enabled us to undertake the ambitious data collection and analysis.

We also extend our sincere gratitude to our home academic institutions. They have been particularly supportive and patient – the University of Houston, where Ray was based for much of the project, as well as Nuffield College, Oxford University, where he has spent the past year, and Rice

University, where Randy is based. The initial work on this project occurred while Ray, at the generous invitation of Dave Brady, was a visiting scholar at the Graduate School of Business, Stanford University.

We both owe a particular debt to our advisor, Bingham Powell, who, whether he likes it or not, is responsible for our commitment to a truly cross-national approach to explaining the economic vote. He has also been extremely supportive of the project and provided helpful comments. We are also indebted to Jim Alt who, very early in the project, took some time out from his busy American Political Science Association (APSA) schedule to have coffee with us. In his inimical fashion, he posed the obvious question: "Guys, why do you think anyone would be interested in this?" And then, of course, Jim proceeded to suggest precisely what questions about comparative economic voting are important and interesting. His early, very critical review of the manuscript proved particularly helpful. Michael Lewis-Beck has been wonderfully supportive of our project, and we have benefited tremendously from the wisdom of the "dude's" many years studying the comparative economic vote. An early, and premature, APSA roundtable discussion (2005!) of the book "manuscript" provided invaluable insights at an important juncture in its development. In addition to Jim Alt, Michael Lewis-Beck, and Bingham Powell, we thank the additional roundtable participants Rob Franzese and Jonathan Nagler (and Doug Hibbs, who provided detailed comments *in absentia*). And, as we finally completed the manuscript, we were particularly heartened by the positive reaction we received from Steve Ansolabehere, who had just assumed the editorship of the Cambridge University Press *Political Economy of Institutions and Decisions* series.

We would like to acknowledge and thank the participants of seminars at the University of Houston (2002), Princeton University (2004), Université de Montréal (2004), New York University (2006), the European University Institute Conference on Contextual Effects in Electoral Research (2006), the Nuffield Politics Seminar Series (2006), Washington University (2006), the European University Institute Conference on Electoral Forecasting Models (2007), University of California, Los Angeles (2007), not to mention the participants on the countless panels at the annual meetings of the APSA and Midwest Political Science Association where we presented various versions of book chapters. Among the numerous participants at these venues who provided insightful comments we thank Ken Benoit, Geoff Evans, Mark Franklin, Mark Kayser, Orit Kedar, Michael Marsh, Harvey Palmer, Meredith Rolfe, Josh Tucker, Wouter van der Brug, Cees van der Eijk, Lynn Vavrek, and Guy Whitten.

This project has involved the analysis of many public opinion surveys, and we are indebted to the various national and international entities that have funded these studies and made them widely available to the public. These include national elections studies that were initiated in the United States in 1948 but have since spread to most developed democracies in the world. Our study would have been impossible without the rich, comparative electoral data that are available in the Euro-Barometer Studies and in the studies that make up the Comparative Study of Electoral Systems. We hope this book and the findings we report here are testimony to the importance of continuing these and similar efforts at providing comparative electoral behavior data.

As a result of the proliferation of national election studies and multination electoral surveys there exists an abundance of voter preference data. The challenge was collecting all of these data and getting them into a format that we could use to estimate the models that are the foundation of the empirical work in this book. And to estimate properly specified models employing these very diverse voter preference studies, we undertook an extensive review of the electoral behavior literature related to each of the 19 countries in our study. These data collection and cleaning tasks and detailed reviews of the electoral behavior literature were completed by our graduate students, to whom we are truly indebted. Accordingly, we thank Jeff May, Beth Miller, Chandru Swaminathan (our IT "guru"), Jessy Tyler, and Toshi Yuasa. We and our graduate students were also assisted by Guillermo Useche Gonzalez and Federico Orozco during our data-gathering efforts in Spain – we thank them for their help.

Much of the creative efforts and the more tedious data work associated with this project took place at Ray's home, Le Tournié, in France. We and our graduate students owe a debt of gratitude to Crisanto Hernandez, who so competently managed the practical, day-to-day details of these research meetings. And finally, a special thanks to Scott Parris at Cambridge University Press, our editor, who at an early stage in the gestation of this project responded so positively to our efforts and continued to encourage us over the lengthy time it took us to complete the manuscript.

1

Introduction

It is virtually a universal belief among politicians, political commentators, and even voters that elections are referenda on the economy. Politicians fill their speeches with economic rhetoric; political commentators generate endless streams of economic analysis, and high-paid consultants base their statistical predictions on little else. The extent and depth of this belief is revealed most starkly when it appears to have been violated. When incumbents win despite a bad economy or lose despite a good one, we observe in the postelection hand-wringing a concerted search for *ad hoc* explanations that preserve the more fundamental belief that the economy matters. Perhaps voters' perceptions of the "real" economy were distorted; foreign policy issues may have overshadowed its effects; or, maybe, ineffective campaign strategies undermined the expected economic vote.[1] Ultimately, however, in most elections, the economy is thought to be determinate.

Popular beliefs, of course, are not social science laws and exceptions to economic determinism are easy to find, even if they are often explained away as idiosyncratic. More generally, the systematic empirical work on economic voting, conducted in most of the advanced democracies over the last thirty years, reveals not a universal law of economic voting but, rather, a conditional one. Economic voting *is* very likely widespread and often important; but, its magnitude and nature across elections is almost certainly variable (Duch, 2001; Lewis-Beck and Stegmaier, 2000, 2006). There are limits, however, to the guidance the extant empirical literature can give us. The description of economic voting that it provides across countries and over time is at best a sketch. In some countries and in some

[1] Examples in which each of these three excuses were prominent are the 1992 U.S. presidential election, the 2002 German Parliamentary elections, and the 2000 U.S. presidential election, respectively.

periods, there are simply no data with which to describe the economic vote. In other cases, data exist but awaits a systematic analysis. In many other cases, the published estimates of the extent and nature of economic voting are simply not comparable to each other.[2] Overall, the vast amount of data relevant to economic voting in the world's advanced democracies has not yet been leveraged to describe variation in economic voting across countries and over time. Consequently, one of the major goals of this book is to provide a more complete and reliable description of the magnitude and nature of economic voting across a large number of countries (eighteen) and a long time period (1979–2001). With this goal in mind, our study for the first time reliably compares the extent and nature of this economic vote across a large number of cases, confirming that the economic vote is both widespread and variable.

If our description of economic voting reveals a conditional law, we do not yet know its conditions. Why was the effect of the economy so pronounced in the 1980 American presidential election and so surprisingly absent twenty years later? Why is it consistently more important to the electoral fortunes of British prime ministers but not their Dutch counterparts? Why, in short, does economic voting vary as it does? The second goal of this book is to answer these questions. We do this by offering a theory of how different political and economic institutions condition the economic vote and by testing hypotheses drawn from our theory. Our explanation is built on a long tradition of theoretical work that suggests economic voting is the result of instrumentally rational voters trying to use their votes to achieve the best possible economic future.

Within the family of rational choice explanations of economic voting, our contextual theory is a generalization of the competency model of rational retrospective economic voting that has been used informally by many scholars and formally by theorists studying political business cycles in the United States (e.g., Alesina and Rosenthal, 1995). The competency model suggests that rational voters condition their vote on the incumbent's record of economic performance because this is the optimal way to identify and elect competent economic managers under conditions of uncertainty. Our generalization of this model explores how political and economic institutions alter the quality of the signal that the previous economy provides about the competence of candidates. Thus, both the rationality of voting in the competency model and its focus on the voter's

[2] This murkiness is because much of the empirical literature consists of independent studies produced by researchers working with very different data and methodologies.

desire for competent economic management lead to a set of theoretical propositions (and empirical hypotheses) that link variation in economic and political institutions to variability in the economic vote.

Overall, our contextual theory of rational economic voting provides a rigorous theoretical foundation for generating hypotheses about the kinds of political and economic contexts likely to condition the economic vote. Furthermore, our empirical map of economic voting provides the raw material for testing these hypotheses. In the rest of this chapter, we preview the potential usefulness of these contributions both to the study of comparative political behavior and to the understanding of specific elections, review the theoretical and empirical work that motivated the project and that define its contribution, describe the general theoretical approach that we take to explain economic voting, and give an overview of the organization of the rest of the book.

ECONOMIC VOTING IN RECENT ELECTIONS: THE IMPORTANCE OF A COMPARATIVE PERSPECTIVE

Although the main goal of this project is to produce a set of theoretically driven empirical generalizations about the nature and sources of economic voting in different contexts, we hope that it will also help us to better understand (and predict) the role of the economy in specific elections. Our premise, however, is that a proper understanding of specific elections requires that they be viewed in a comparative perspective. As an illustration, this section briefly compares two recent German and Italian parliamentary elections (held in September 2005 and May 2006, respectively) and asks what we can learn about them (and similar cases) from the kind of comparative analysis offered in the chapters that follow.

Economic performance leading up to the elections in both Germany and Italy had been quite poor. Despite turning in slightly improved performance over previous years, the 2005 German economy still grew by only a percentage point in real terms and unemployment rates were persistently above 10 percent. Similarly, real GDP in Italy actually contracted in 2005, while the country registered the lowest level of working-age employment in Western Europe (58 percent).[3] Furthermore, as Figure 1.1

[3] Just before the Italian elections, *The Economist* noted, "But the biggest difference from the past is that the economy over which Mr. Berlusconi has presided has done so badly. Last year GDP growth was near-zero; this year's forecast has just been cut from 1.5% to 1.3%. Italy deserves its title as the new sick man of Europe. It is in far

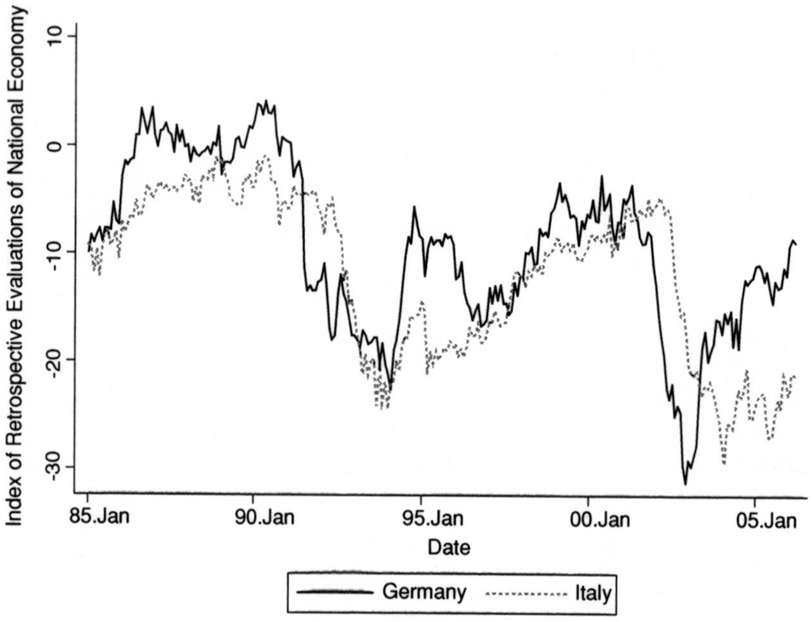

Figure 1.1. Retrospective economic evaluations for Germany and Italy.

shows, voters were clearly aware of these trends. Public sentiment about the economy dropped precipitously in both countries after 2001. But German sentiment rebounded before the 2005 election, whereas Italian sentiment remained at historically low levels as the 2006 election campaign began.

Before the elections, pundits argued that these records of economic performance would result in a strong rejection of the incumbents.[4] As it turned out, however, the German SPD trailed their CDU/CSU challengers by less than a percentage point (34.3 percent and 35.2 percent, respectively) and Italian Prime Minister Berlusconi's incumbent coalition

worse shape than Germany or France. And the pressing need to find a cure for that sickness means that the outcome of next week's election matters" (*The Economist*, April 18, 2006, 28).

[4] Some representative (English-language) headlines: "Economy to dominate German election" (Deutsche Presse-Agentur, August 22, 2005); "German election boils down to jobs, economy" (Associated Press, September 18, 2005); "As Germans look toward national election, economy remains key issue" (Associated Press, September 11, 2005); "German jobs the focus of tight poll race: Unemployment and welfare state dominate election campaigns as Europe's economic miracle turns sour" (*The Guardian*, September 9, 2005).

garnered 49.7 percent of the popular vote compared to the 49.8 percent obtained by Prodi's alternative center-left coalition. As a result, and in stark contrast to preelection commentary, discussion of the economy was essentially absent from most of the postelection analyses offered by the press.

But did the economy play an important role in these elections or not? To answer this question definitively, we need a statistical analysis that estimates the impact of the economy on the election while controlling for other influences. Furthermore, because our interest is in exploring these specific elections, we need individual-level measures of economic perceptions and vote choice.[5] We conducted surveys previous to both elections (see Chapter 6 for details) that included these data (as well as relevant controls) and were able to produce estimates of the importance of economic voting in each case.[6] These estimates reveal that, contrary to the impression that may have been created by the relatively strong performance of the incumbent parties, voter perceptions of economic performance in fact played an important (and perhaps decisive) role in both elections. In both the German and the Italian elections, our estimates indicate that the prime minister's party (the SDP and Forza Italia, respectively) would have gained between 6 and 7 percent of the vote had perceptions of the economy improved moderately.[7] Furthermore, it is likely that this increase in strength would have been enough for both incumbent parties to retain the prime ministry.

So what can we learn from estimates such as these? First, they provide a much clearer picture of whether, and to what extent, economic voting was actually important in a given election. Accordingly, they can help correct misconceptions about the role of the economy in specific elections that are typified by the journalistic accounts of the recent Italian and German elections. Of course, this is not new. Social scientists have been producing well-specified statistical models of individual-level vote choice and economic voting for many years. What is different about these examples, however, is that they were produced using methods that allow

[5] Alternatively, one could examine the role of the economy in a single election using aggregate data at the regional level.

[6] These were produced using the methods described in Chapter 2. However, they are simply intended as illustrations here and they are not included in the data used in the rest of the book (they fall outside the time period covered in our data). Details about the data and the specific models estimated are available at http://www.nuffield.ox.ac.uk/economicvoting.

[7] We define "moderately" in Chapter 2.

us to systematically compare them to one another.[8] Thus, based on our estimates, we can confidently assert that economic voting was about as important in the 2005 German election as it was in the 2006 Italian one.

Should we expect to see very similar levels of economic voting in these two countries? And if so, why? Perhaps the similar levels of economic voting result from some fundamental and general characteristic of individuals that applies to all voters across contexts, even those as different as Italy and Germany. Norpoth (1996a) may be correct in asserting that economic voting is "hardwired into the brains of citizens." Alternatively, and much more likely, these cases may be similar because of corresponding similarities in context. What might these be? Well-motivated answers to this question must await the theory and analysis in the rest of this book. However, one possibility that has been suggested in the previous literature is that the distribution of policy-making power among incumbent parties was similar in the two cases: the German SPD and Italian Forza Italia were both dominant parties in their respective ruling coalition governments. Thus, voters interested in punishing an incumbent party for poor economic performance faced a roughly similar challenge in identifying whom to blame. Although this may or may not in fact be the appropriate explanation, it illustrates the importance of comparable estimates of economic voting across elections and national contexts. Having estimates of the magnitude of the economic vote from multiple elections – admittedly in this example only two cases – is what leads to speculation about the interaction between the economic vote and the structure of power sharing across parties. No analysis of a single election could hope to produce a similar insight.

These two elections are even more informative when viewed comparatively. Specifically, as we show in Chapter 3, the typical size of the economic vote over the last two decades in Germany was about 5 percent, whereas in Italy it was about 2.5 percent.[9] This comparative perspective makes it clear that although economic voting in the 2005 German election was only slightly more important than usual, in the 2006 Italian election it was dramatically so. Again, a great benefit of being able to make this (somewhat richer) empirical conclusion is that it stimulates us to ask why. What has happened to cause Italians in 2006 to weight

[8] Indeed, the whole point of the first part of this book is producing, for the first time, a large set of comparable estimates of economic voting at the individual level.

[9] That is, a moderate worsening of economic perceptions decreases the prime ministerial party's vote by about 5 percent.

the economy as heavily in their vote as Germans usually do? It is certainly not difficult to think of ways that the electoral situation in Italy has become more similar to that in Germany over the last decade. In contrast to most of the postwar history of Italy, there is now real electoral competition between two well-defined governing alternatives. As a result, Italian votes now matter in the choice of governments at least as much as German votes do. Such changes in the electoral context may well alter the weight that voters give to retrospective economic performance in their vote choice.

This comparison of historical economic voting in these two cases leads to a more general question: Why it is that the economic vote is typically higher in Germany than in Italy? Indeed, extending the basis of our comparison again, we can see that the typical magnitude of German economic voting places it in the middle rank of the Western democracies (higher than Italy, Belgium, and the Netherlands, for example, but less than the United States and the United Kingdom). Thus, our question becomes not just why is the German economic vote typically larger than the Italian one, but also why does it rank in the middle more generally? Understanding why Germany ranks as having an average amount of economic voting will provide insight into the dynamics of the 2005 elections.

Our intuition is that the German economic vote ranks as it does because it has a mix of contextual features that both raise and lower levels of economic voting. Specifically, we have already noted the potentially positive effect that real electoral competition over alternative cabinets can have on economic voting. Furthermore, such healthy competition has been typical of the German case throughout its history and so may be one of the enduring features of the German context that contributes to a fairly large economic vote. However, other factors may well keep economic voting below that of some other countries. For example, a number of institutional features disperse policy-making authority in Germany: a long history of coalition cabinets, a strong federal system of government, and a moderate amount of corporatism. Again, it may be the case that the dispersion of power in Germany reduces the importance that economic performance can play in German voter's decisions – at least in comparison to the highly concentrated distribution of policy-making power in more unitary and noncoalitional systems like that in the United Kingdom. Other explanations for Germany's mid-ranked level of economic voting may be its similarly mid-ranked level of trade dependence. It often has been suggested that voters in countries whose economies are more dependent on international trade are less willing to hold domestic politicians accountable for outcomes (that are not of their making). If this were so, we would expect German voters to be less willing than, for example, American voters to hold politicians accountable for poor performance but more willing than voters in more trade-dependent countries such as the Netherlands or Belgium.

Our speculations about economic voting in the recent Italian and German elections illustrate a central theme of this book: to understand the role that the economy plays in these, or any given election, or to make predictions about its role in future elections, we need to be able to place the voting decision in a comparative context. This does not mean describing everything that is unique about an election but, rather, identifying those features of the context that help explain systematic variation in the economic vote. This, of course, can only be done by building a reliable map of economic voting across countries and over time and by identifying the kinds of contextual variables that condition the economic vote. In the rest of this book, we attempt to accomplish these two tasks. Of course, both our theorizing and our empirical work builds on (and responds to) the literature on economic voting as it has developed over the last forty years. Thus, in the next sections we review the academic work on economic voting that has created both the need for this project and the opportunity for it to be accomplished.

THEORETICAL FOUNDATIONS OF ECONOMIC VOTING

This book explores differences in the way voters condition their vote choice on the economy in different political and economic contexts. Consequently, our theoretical effort begins with a model of the individual voting decision that explains why the economy, or at least perceptions of the economy, matters for the vote. A number of theoretical developments are critically important to our model-building efforts. First, early in its history, the economic voting literature adopted the notion that instrumentally rational individuals make vote choices based on their utilities for competing parties. Second, efforts to specify how economic evaluations enter into the voter's utility function resulted in two modeling approaches: sanction and selection models of vote choice. Third, these sanction and selection models have been adapted to explain how context conditions the economic vote. Finally, if economic voters are rational, then developments in the literature on vote choice imply that strategic context should be one of the factors that condition the economic vote. We now briefly explore the development of these theoretical traditions and how they contribute to our rational model of retrospective economic voting.

Economic Evaluations and the Voter Utility Function

For the most part, the economic voting literature treats voters as instrumentally rational actors. Downs (1957) introduced the notion that individuals make vote choices based on their comparison of expected utilities for each of the competing parties. The notion of voters as utility-maximizing political "consumers" was a significant deviation from widely accepted explanations for vote choice that borrowed from the social-psychological literature (Berelson et al., 1954; Campbell et al., 1960). But it was Kramer's (1971) efforts to "test the Downsian rationality hypothesis" by exploring the link between economic outcomes and U.S. election results that inspired early economic voting research.[10] Kramer in effect argued for the importance of economic well-being in the voter utility function introduced by Downs. Fair (1978) took this argument a step forward by providing a formal statement of how economic performance enters the voter utility.[11] This was an important theoretical advance because it established a foundation for modeling vote choice from a rational utility-maximization perspective that included economic well-being in the utility function. We follow in this tradition. The notion that voters rationally derive expected utilities for competing political parties and that these determine their vote choice is a central feature of our contextual model of the economic vote.

Fair's (1978) effort, though, highlighted theoretical controversies as to exactly how the *economy* enters into the voter's utility function. As Fair emphasizes, theory is a necessary guide in determining how the economy enters into the utility function. Are voters narrowly retrospective and motivated primarily by a sanctioning reflex, which is suggested by the early Kramer (1971) findings? Or do voters gather more extensive information on past economic outcomes in an effort to assess how competing potential governing "teams" might perform in the future, a selection perspective hinted at by Downs (1957) and Stigler (1973)? Both perspectives

[10] That is not to say that the link between the economy and elections had not been explored. In fact, Kramer (1971) does a nice job of summarizing the early efforts in this regard.

[11] As Hibbs (2006) points out, this contribution was also important because it derived an aggregate-level vote equation from this individual-level utility function that could be estimated empirically.

share a model of individual decision making in which instrumentally rational voters are maximizing a voter utility function. The sanctioning perspective has been widely adopted in much of the economic voting literature to date. Although it is much less widely employed in the literature, we will argue that the selection model has advantages for incorporating context into explanations of the economic vote.

The Sanctioning Model (aka the Moral Hazard Model)

The early pathbreaking work of Kramer (1971) and Fair (1978) suggested that vote choice was shaped by the recent economic performance of incumbents rather than by comparative assessments of how competing parties might perform if elected. They concluded that the economy entered into the voter's utility function in a simple fashion: punish poor performance and reward good outcomes. V. O. Key's widely quoted characterization of the economic vote seemed well founded: "Voters may reject what they have known; or they may approve what they have known. They are not likely to be attracted in great numbers by promises of the novel or unknown" (1966: 61). Fiorina's (1981) classic work, *Retrospective Voting in American National Elections*, provided a more general expected utility model of voting that included economic evaluations.[12] And although both retrospective assessments and future expectations of the performance of incumbents (and challengers) figured prominently in Fiorina's models of the vote decision, Fiorina argued that future expectations are, for the most part, simple extrapolations from current trends. This provided further support for the retrospective sanctioning perspective. Hence, early in the history of economic voting, this sanctioning model of voter behavior– either explicitly or implicitly – became the workhorse of models linking the economy and vote choice.

One of the attractions of this stark punishment model was that it demanded relatively little of the average voter, which tended to comport with early empirical findings regarding the political sophistication of the average citizen (Converse, 1964). But did this narrow focus by the voter on retrospective economic performance constitute rational behavior? Should we not expect rational voters to undertake a more comparative assessment of the likely performance of competing candidates, both incumbents and challengers, if elected? Barro (1973) and then Ferejohn (1986) showed

[12] Fiorina stopped short of providing a formal model in which retrospective economic voting emerged as rational behavior.

how retrospective economic voting could be a fully rational voting strategy by building on the notion that candidates, like firms, are motivated by the maximization of rents. Voters, according to this model, are confronted with a moral hazard problem when deciding on voting for the incumbent versus opposition parties. They argue that if voters do not sanction economic performance, they risk signaling to incumbents that poor economic performance would be tolerated and, hence, invite rent seeking on the part of self-interested political candidates. In this model, voters are not engaging in the comparative assessment of utility income streams from competing political candidates – rather, they simply establish a threshold performance level and reelect incumbents that satisfy this requirement and punish those that do not (Ferejohn, 1986). This leads to the *sanctioning* feature that characterizes most accounts of the economic vote. It is the concern with reelection in the future that motivates incumbents to avoid shirking their responsibilities. They anticipate that voters will sanction them if they underperform. And, to maintain the credibility of this threat, voters punish incumbents at the polls when retrospective economic performance is substandard.

Adopting this sanctioning perspective on rational voting had important implications for the specification of economic voting models. Pure sanctioning models of the economic vote are decidedly retrospective – voters entirely discount candidate promises (so these do not enter into the utility function) and only pay attention to economic performance over the course of the incumbent's recent tenure in office. Expectations about future economic outcomes are not necessarily precluded from shaping voter preferences but, again, they simply reflect information about past economic outcomes.

The Sanctioning Model and Context. Ferejohn's (1986) formalization of the sanctioning model provided the micro-foundations for the simple vote choice rules that were articulated earlier by Kramer (1971). An interesting puzzle, though, is why sanctioning varies across contexts. Why are incumbents in some countries, for example, punished or rewarded with greater intensity or frequency than is the case in others? Why might the moral hazard incentives vary from one context to another?

Sanction models of the economic vote require that voters have retrospective information about the performance of the macro-economy and that they punish or reward incumbents in a fashion that credibly signals to candidates the electoral costs of shirking or rent seeking. Context can matter in these models because signals of the incumbent's responsibility for macro-economic outcomes may be more "noisy" in some contexts as opposed to others (Fearon, 1999; Ferejohn, 1986). Hence, conventional sanction models of economic voting often explain variations in sanctioning behavior in terms of variations in levels of information (e.g., Powell and Whitten, 1993).[13]

Hibbs (2006) has pointed out that Kramer's (1983) famous "error-in-variables" conception of economic evaluations can be used to model contextual variations in the signal-to-noise ratio regarding incumbent economic performance. If the politically relevant portion of economic outcomes is small, then usual survey measures of economic evaluations in the voter's preference function will contain considerable error. Hence, a particularly complex governing coalition situation or a context where relatively large exogenous shocks affect the macro-economy would likely reduce the extent to which voter's economic evaluations reflect the politically relevant portion of economic outcomes. As Hibbs (2006) demonstrates, higher levels of error in the measure of economic evaluations will have a downward bias on its coefficient in a voting equation. Hence, contexts in which the politically relevant portion of macro-economic outcomes is small – reflected in relatively high measurement error when overall economic evaluations are used – will be those that have a low correlation between economic evaluations and vote choice.

The Selection Model (aka the Competency Model)

Selection models of economic voting stipulate that the vote decision entails more than a simple reward–punishment response to economic outcomes. They suggest that instrumentally rational voters are motivated by the desire to select the most competent candidates – that is, voters use information about economic outcomes to assess the future competencies of competing candidates. Selection models were not unfamiliar to the early economic voting scholars. Voters in Downs's model are future-oriented and compare the platforms of contending candidates, logic that more closely resembles a selection as opposed to a sanctioning model. Likewise, Kramer (1971) viewed voters as future-oriented but unwilling to spend the resources to assess future promises. Rather, again echoing Downs,

[13] There is also a coordination issue – voters need to agree on what constitutes a threshold of "bad" economic performance. This could also be the basis for contextual variations in the magnitude of economic voting in a sanctioning model (Ferejohn, 1986).

Kramer assumed that rational voters rely on the retrospective economy to inform them about the likely actions and economic success of future incumbents. Stigler's (1973) famous critique of Kramer also adopted the selection perspective but pointed out that voters should be uncertain about how much the previous economy should tell them about the competence of incumbents: "Per capita income falls over a year or two – should the voter abandon or punish the party in power? Such a reaction seems premature: the decline may be due to developments beyond the powers or responsibilities of the party" (1973: 164). However, Stigler also recognized that with knowledge of the role incumbents play in shaping policy, rational voters might be able to tease out of economic outcomes those fluctuations that are related to the actions of incumbents and those that are not. Consequently, they might use this information in a prospective fashion to "... determine which party is on average more likely to maintain a high and steady rate of growth of income" (Stigler, 1973: 165).

Although this early work clearly pointed the way toward a rational model of economic voting based on the selection of competent politicians, informal models left many questions unanswered; for example, could it be rational for voters to use the previous economy to infer competence, if politicians had incentives to manipulate the economy for electoral gain? Answers to these kinds of questions have had to await the development of the rational expectations literature in economics and its expression in the study of political business cycles.

The development of rational expectations theories provided the theoretical tools for developing formal selection models of the economic vote. Rational expectations treat forward-looking decisions in the same rational fashion as static decisions, particularly in terms of how individuals use information. This implies that individuals do not make systematic (or repeated) mistakes in forecasting the future.[14] Their expectations about future outcomes should be conditioned on reasonable "models" of the "variables" and functional relationships that have historically generated such outcomes. Rational expectations theories essentially associate the same rationality assumptions with forecasts that are typically linked to static decision making. This implies, for example, that policy makers could have no permanent or predicable impact on economic outcomes because they would be anticipated by rational economic actors (Alesina, Roubini, and Cohen, 1997).

[14] Begg (1982) presents a comprehensive description of the rational expectations revolution in macro-economics.

Building on these advances in rational expectations theory, Cukierman and Meltzer (1989) and Rogoff and Sibert (1988), independently proposed the notion that governments differ in their competence in handling the economy and that information about their competencies plays a critical role in vote choice. By observing economic outcomes, voters become informed about the competence of an incumbent and use this information in their vote decision. Persson and Tabellini (1990) and Alesina and Rosenthal (1995) developed models that explicitly incorporated rational expectations and very nicely drew out the implications of rational expectations and competency assumptions for the economic voting model. Because voters in these models are fully informed about the incumbent's policies and anticipate their impact on subsequent performance, only unexpected shocks to the macro-economy can have any impact on their voting decisions. And these shocks can be either exogenous shocks – unrelated to the policy action of incumbents – or they can be competency shocks – unexpected outcomes that can be associated with incumbent initiatives.

The Selection Model and Context. The signal-extraction problem that confronts voters in selection models is to determine the extent to which observed shocks to the macro-economy are the result of incumbent competency. The usual variance (perhaps reflected in historical fluctuations) in shocks to the economy may provide the voters with information that allows them to make rationally informed assessments of the extent to which shocks to the economy are the result of incumbent competence rather than nonpolitical exogenous factors. To the extent that historical fluctuations in the macro-economy are more likely to have resulted from competence shocks rather than nonpolitical shocks, voters will weight current shocks to the economy – such as an unexpected change in real GDP growth – more heavily in their vote decision.

Hence, context could impact economic voting in selection models because the relative magnitudes of exogenous and politically relevant competency signals vary systematically across different economic and political contexts. This potential has certainly been recognized (e.g., Scheve, 2004), but both the theoretical and empirical implications of this kind of contextual variation have yet to be fully explored. The model we offer in this book identifies the contextual implications of the selection model by assuming that the relative weight of electorally and nonelectorally accountable decision makers in economic policy making directly impacts the variance of both political (e.g., competence) and nonpolitical (exogenous) shocks on the economy. Consequently, political and economic institutions that impact this ratio should have a direct influence on the quality or strength of the competence signal that the economy provides to voters. For example, our theory suggests that voters in economies that are highly integrated into the global economy will recognize that economic policy making is weighted toward nonelectorally accountable decision makers and so rationally conclude that exogenous factors play an important role in producing macro-economic shocks. Accordingly, we predict that economic voting will be higher in countries with closed economies.

Strategic Voting and Context

Rational models of economic voting should clearly reflect the strategic incentives introduced by features of the electoral system and the nature of contention among the competing candidates. Just as voters have rational expectations about economic outcomes, they also should have rational expectations about the relative electoral strength of competing candidates (Cox, 1997) and the impact that their vote can have on the postelection distribution of policy-making power. If rational voters believe that their vote can have no impact on who makes policy, then they should not worry too much about identifying which politicians are competent or about sanctioning underperformers. Although this observation is hardly new, the fact that models of economic voting have been developed largely in the context of American two-party elections (in which strategic incentives are muted) has limited work on this potential source of contextual variation in the economic vote.

Of course, the notion that voters respond strategically to electoral institutions, and to the nature of contention among competing parties, follows directly from our assumption that voters are instrumentally rational (Gibbard, 1973; McKelvey and Ordeshook, 1972; Satterthwaite, 1975). One of the key insights in this literature is that rational voters will take into account whether their vote makes a difference in who wins or who loses elections and who gets into government. The usual understanding is that rational voters should not "waste" their vote on candidates who are sure to lose, but the same logic also applies to parties or candidates who are sure to win. More generally, our theoretical generalization of the strategic voting logic (to cases in which there are multiple parties and coalition cabinets) explores how characteristics of the "distribution of contention" for policy-making authority shape the incentives for strategic voting.

These strategic considerations have important implications for our contextual model of the economic vote. We anticipate there will be frequent situations in which an individual's vote will have little impact on the postelection distribution of policy-making authority (because the same parties will get into government for all plausible electoral results); hence, economic evaluations will play a minor role in voting in such elections.[15] Our decision to treat voters as being instrumentally rational and our desire to explore the implications of this model in diverse political contexts dictates that we account for the impact that different strategic voting incentives, arising from different political contexts, may have on the extent and distribution of economic voting.

The Overall Message from Theoretical Developments in the Literature

Our reading of the theoretical literature on economic voting produces two clear messages about how contextual explanations of economic voting should be shaped. First, the underlying individual-level theory of voting upon which the model is based should incorporate the assumption of instrumental rationality and thus the model should produce hypotheses about how different strategic contexts impact economic voting. Second, the existence of two quite different explanations for instrumentally rational economic voting in the literature (sanction versus selection models) makes it imperative that any contextual theory be explicit about which explanation is being invoked and what implications of the theory flow from that choice. In the theoretical chapters in Part II and Part III of this book, we propose a contextual model of rational economic voting that explicitly adopts the selection approach to understanding the motivation for rational retrospective economic voting at the individual level. In Part II, we explore the empirical implications for context that follow from this choice, and in Part III, we generalize the model so that it reflects strategic voting incentives.

[15] A number of scholars have pointed out that contextual variation in strategic voting incentives can affect the voter's utility function such that some factors or issues matter in vote choice in one context versus another. Myerson (1993, 1999), for example, demonstrates that under Duverger's law for plurality voting, in which parties compete on ideology, strategic voting considerations can lead voters to vote for corrupt candidates despite their preferences to minimize rent seeking and despite the fact that there are candidates with compatible ideological positions who lack the rent-seeking baggage.

EMPIRICAL EVIDENCE OF AN ECONOMIC VOTE

As this discussion indicates, theoretical efforts have for the most part focused on results that explain, in general (although with the U.S. political context in mind), why economic evaluations shape the vote decision. The early empirical work on economic voting – much of it dominated by the U.S. case – focused on establishing that, in fact, economic evaluations motivated vote choice. And, over time, there has been an impressive increase in the number of empirical studies of economic voting conducted outside of the U.S. context. A brief review of this empirical work on economic voting serves several purposes. First, the U.S. empirical evidence in particular, but also results for a number of other national contexts, provides a strong foundation for the general claim that there is an economic vote. As the time series of voting studies in the United States have lengthened and as the number of non-U.S. voting studies have proliferated, the empirical puzzle that motivates the book emerges: existing empirical findings suggest that the economic vote is quite unstable both cross-nationally and also over time, even within the U.S. context. Accordingly, we now review the empirical findings from the U.S. case on which much of the case for economic voting is made and then examine the cross-national findings that provide the empirical puzzle addressed in the remainder of the book.[16]

The United States

When taken together, the large literature on economic voting in the United States unambiguously confirms the existence of a robust empirical connection between the economy and vote choice in the American case. Three different strains of research, each initiated in the 1970s, contribute to this consensus.

Mueller's (1970) classic study of presidential popularity introduced one important line of inquiry: estimating the economic vote based on aggregate-level models of presidential popularity that employed, typically, monthly readings of public approval of the chief executive with objective measures of economic performance as the independent variable (typically the actual rates of unemployment, inflation, or real GDP change).

[16] The empirical literature on economic voting has benefited from a number of excellent reviews (the most recent by Lewis-Beck and Stegmaier, 2006) and we will not attempt to replicate these efforts here. Rather, our goal in highlighting just some of the works in the vast empirical literature on economic voting is to explain how our work adds to what has already been done.

Although the detailed specification of these presidential popularity functions has been the subject of some debate, almost all estimates of presidential popularity functions confirm that the economy is a significant factor driving presidential popularity (e.g., Beck, 1991; Norpoth, 1985). Furthermore, the various estimates tend to agree (roughly) on the magnitude of the effects. For example, Muller's original estimate was that presidential popularity declined by about three percentage points for every percentage point rise in unemployment (Mueller, 1970: 29). Norpoth's (1985) results for inflation and unemployment are similar. He calculates that the overall change in the popularity of Nixon, Johnson, Carter, and Ford that was caused by changes in unemployment and inflation was 5.5, 2.5, 4.4, and 4 percent, respectively. Although there is disagreement about the exact set of aggregate economic indicators that should appear in presidential popularity functions, there is little disagreement that *some* set of aggregate economic variables predicts changes in approval and that the overall impact of usual changes in these variables is to move popularity in the range of between three and ten percentage points.

A second avenue of empirical inquiry examines how actual election outcomes depend on objective economic outcomes. One of the first and most influential of these studies was by Tufte (1978), who provided evidence that the economy plays a predominant role in American presidential elections. Although based on only eight data points, his evidence was striking and simple: in presidential elections from 1948 to 1978, the relationship between annual real disposable income and the vote of the president's party was practically a straight line. This simple but powerful picture resonated with subsequent researchers who, using more data and refined models, confirmed Tufte's original finding (e.g., Bartels and Zaller, 2001; Erikson, 1990; Hibbs, 2000, 2006).[17] Importantly, this confirmation was not limited to the *existence* of economic voting in the aggregate data but also extended to estimates of the *magnitude* of the economic vote in U.S. presidential elections. Specifically, a 1 percent change in annual real disposable income produces a two- to four-percentage-point increase in support for the incumbent presidential party. These results are consistent with the magnitude of economic voting effects found by the studies discussed earlier, which focused on presidential popularity rather than the vote.

Early aggregate-level research on the economy and elections in the United States also explored congressional contests. Kramer's (1971)

[17] They find that the "Bread and Peace" model proposed by Hibbs (2000) performed particularly well.

influential analysis of U.S. congressional elections from 1886 to 1964 was the first to establish that change in real disposable income over the course of the election year predicts the success of the president's party in congressional elections. This result was subsequently championed by Tufte (1975, 1978) with more recent supporting evidence from Jacobson and Kernell (1983), Lewis-Beck and Rice (1992), and Kiewiet and Udell (1998). However, unlike the results for presidential elections, this finding has been challenged by a number of scholars who failed to find a significant relationship in aggregate data (e.g., Alesina et al., 1993; Erikson, 1990; Marra and Ostrom, 1989). Nevertheless, the bulk of evidence seems to argue for the existence of economic voting in congressional elections, although the relationship is almost certainly weaker than in presidential elections.

The third strain of empirical economic voting research traces its intellectual roots to Key (1966), who explored the impact of popular assessments of incumbent performance on the actual voting decision. Similar early efforts to use individual-level survey data to explore economic voting specifically relied on questions that asked voters about their "personal financial situation." However, the later (and most enduring) individual-level evidence for economic voting in the United States has come from questions that ask respondents about general business conditions or the country's "economic situation." Fiorina (1981) conducted an important early analysis of these survey data, in which he demonstrated that economic perceptions of the national economy significantly impact vote choice in U.S. elections (both presidential and congressional). And soon thereafter, Kiewiet (1983) confirmed Fiorina's conclusions with more data and more elaborate statistical specifications. Furthermore, he demonstrated that assessments of general economic conditions play a more important role in shaping vote choice than pocketbook evaluations (i.e., perceptions of one's personal financial condition). Fiorina's and Kiewiet's empirical conclusions quickly entered into the lexicon of American political science and, with some relatively minor qualifications or extensions, have withstood extensive scrutiny (some notable examples are Alvarez and Nagler, 1998a, 1998b; Duch et al., 2000; Markus, 1988, 1992).

Unlike aggregate studies of economic voting, which are most useful for estimating a single, average magnitude of economic voting across elections, individual-level survey data, if available for several different elections, can be used to construct (and compare) estimates of the magnitude of economic voting in each election. Kiewiet (1983) was somewhat of a pioneer in this respect because he explicitly estimated economic voting for a number of different American election studies (for the period 1958 to 1980). Given the relatively small number of election surveys in his sample (only four of the presidential election surveys included national economic evaluations), he was limited in terms of the over-time comparisons he could make. Nevertheless, he was able to highlight and propose explanations for the average difference between congressional and presidential elections. (Consistent with the aggregate results described earlier, he found economic voting to be relatively weaker in congressional elections.) As the number of these U.S. individual election studies has increased with time, scholars have become increasingly interested in using them to compare the magnitude of the U.S. economic vote from one election to the next. Fiorina et al. (2003), for example, evaluate the magnitude of the presidential economic vote and speculate as to why it varies from election to election.

Despite the many individual-level studies of economic voting that have been done, there is no clear consensus in the American literature on the appropriate methodology for characterizing the magnitude of the economic vote at the individual level. Kiewiet used one approach, Fiorina another, Alverez and Nagler (1998b) still another. As a result, individual-level estimates of the magnitude of economic vote for presidents in the United States range broadly from election to election. For example, Kiewiet reports that a typical change in economic perceptions moves the electoral support of the incumbent by 13 percent (Kiewiet, 1983: 35). In contrast, Alvarez and Nagler's (1998b: 1360) estimate is close to 38 percent.[18] The lack of a uniform methodology for calculating the magnitude of the economic vote from survey data means we do not know if estimated differences reflect real variation in the size of the economic vote or whether these differences are simply artifacts of the different methods for calculating them.

Overall, the economic vote has been subject to extensive scrutiny in the U.S. context and the effort has borne some important insights.[19] Voting for the U.S. president is strongly influenced by economic performance. At the aggregate level, we have precise estimates of the effect of various economic aggregates on the presidential vote and on presidential approval. At the

[18] The Kiewiet (1983) result is based on moving economic evaluations for an "average" voter from "worse than a year ago" to "better than a year ago"; the Alvarez and Nagler (1998b) result is based on moving national economic evaluations from worse to better.

[19] In 1990, Erikson (1990) concluded that the relationship between economic performance and the vote is probably the most widely accepted hypothesis about voting behavior and elections – here, he was obviously referring to the U.S. case.

individual level, results reinforce the importance of national economic evaluations on the presidential vote, although estimates of its magnitude vary significantly. Nevertheless, there is no consensus on how to assess the magnitude of the economic vote, and its election-to-election variation, based on the results of individual-level election studies.

Non-U.S., Single-Country Studies

Given the overall strength of the empirical results in the United States, one might expect to find similarly strong evidence for economic voting in other developed democracies. However, an examination of the country-specific studies of aggregate and individual-level economic voting suggests considerably more variation than is the case in the United States. In many countries, we find weak empirical evidence for economic voting. This is particularly true at the aggregate level although, even with individual data, the evidence is negative or mixed in a number of countries. Thus, although we do not disagree with Lewis-Beck and Stegmaier's (2000) conclusion that evidence of economic voting can be found in much of the developed world, in almost no country is there anywhere near the level of consensus or confidence that characterizes the American literature. What this means, of course, is that it is difficult to use the country-specific literature on economic voting to make anything but the grossest comparisons of economic voting across countries or (for most countries) over elections within countries.

The country-specific studies of countries other than the United States come in the same three flavors as those employing strictly U.S. data: aggregate studies of the economy and government popularity; aggregate studies of the economy and electoral returns; and individual-level studies of economic perceptions and vote choice.

Goodhart and Bhansali (1970) provided the first aggregate study of popularity, demonstrating that the popularity of British governments was strongly influenced by movements in the aggregate economy. However, this result came under almost immediate criticism (e.g., Frey and Garbers, 1971; Miller and Mackie, 1973). And although more recent aggregate work tends to support the existence of economic voting in Britain (Clark and Stewart, 1995; Clark et al., 1997; Sanders et al., 1987; Whiteley, 1986), dissenting voices have, to some extent, persisted (Chrystal and Alt, 1981; Norpoth, 1987). Likewise, analyses of aggregate popularity and vote functions in other countries showed considerable variability. Most estimates for France exhibited strong aggregate economic effects (Hibbs and Vasilatos, 1981; Lafay, 1977; Lewis-Beck, 1980), although there have been exceptional studies suggesting no relationship (Lecaillon, 1981). The estimates for Denmark were initially negative and later mixed (e.g., Nannestad and Paldam, 2000; Paldam and Schneider, 1980). Kirchgässner (1991) found evidence for the impact of employment on the popularity of German governments before 1982 but not after. Frey (1979) examined the fate of incumbent parties over sixty-seven years in Denmark, Norway, and Sweden and found mixed results. Similarly, Madsen (1980), in a careful study of aggregate popularity in Denmark, Norway, and Sweden, found no evidence for economic voting in Denmark and Norway but did find evidence for Sweden.

More generally, in the 1970s and 1980s, the pattern of results from aggregate-level, single-country studies of economic voting in developed democracies (outside the United States) reveals a great deal of variability. The evidence for an aggregate-level relationship is stronger in some countries than in others, but in no case do we find the kind of strikingly simple aggregate level pattern of data that Tufte reported for the United States.

Individual-level analyses of economic voting in countries outside the United States were slow to emerge because of the relative paucity (before the mid-1980s) of individual-level surveys addressing the economic voting question. However, the few individual-level studies that were done in the 1960s and 1970s did confirm the existence of individual-level economic voting beyond the U.S. context. For example, based on their study of the U.K. electorate, Butler and Stokes (1969: 392) concluded that "The electorate's response to the economy is one under which voters reward the Government for the conditions they welcome and punish the Government for the conditions they dislike."[20] However, as more individual-level studies were undertaken in other countries, a message similar to the aggregate-level country-specific studies began to emerge – the extent and nature of economic voting at the individual level was highly variable. For example, although support for economic voting at the individual level was forthcoming in France and Britain, Miller and Listhaug (1985) found little evidence for individual-level economic voting in Norway and neither did Bellucci (1985) for Italy. Likewise, Nannestad and Paldam (1997), in contrast to most other results, found evidence that personal economic conditions were more important to Danish voting than evaluations of the national economy.[21]

[20] As cited in Lewis-Beck (1988: 34).

[21] This result, however, has been challenged by Hibbs (1993) and Borre (1997).

The scholars who reported negative results or discovered evidence for unusual forms of economic voting were keenly aware of how these findings differed from expectations (stemming from the U.S. consensus) and so almost always tried to attribute them to unique features of the country's political or economic context. For example, by the early 1980s, Italy had experienced almost forty years of Christian Democratic rule (and so no true alternation of power). This distinguished it from most of the other Western democracies and, according to Bellucci (1985), may have depressed the Italian economic vote. Likewise, Miller and Listhaug (1985) speculated that the weak individual-level economic effects they found might be explained by the fact that Norway's economy is so heavily influenced by international economic trends. It might be the case, they argued, that voters in Norway recognize that their government has little responsibility for economic outcomes and so do not consider economic performance to be important for their vote decision. Similarly, Nannestad and Paldam (1995) suggested that Danish voters hold the government accountable for their personal economic circumstances because the extensive Danish welfare state created a connection between government policy and personal economic circumstances that did not exist in many other countries.[22]

Overall, an important result of this variability in the evidence for economic voting across countries was that it encouraged scholars to speculate about the kinds of differences in domestic politics and national economies that might drive differences in economic voting across contexts. However, as Lewis-Beck and Eulau (1985) and Lewis-Beck (1988) have both emphasized, one can get relatively little leverage on the question of how political and economic context impacts economic voting by comparing the results of a relatively small number of studies that also differ dramatically in the statistical models used to produce the estimates of economic voting. Thus, the country-specific literature provides only very crude evidence of whether economic voting exists, or does not, in particular survey contexts. Instead, a better estimation of cross-national economic voting requires a more coordinated effort to produce comparable estimates – a task taken up by Lewis-Beck and a small number of others.

[22] Lewis-Beck (1983) previously suggested this explanation for his results about the importance of personal financial circumstances in French economic voting. And Pacek and Radcliff (1995) provide evidence of this argument employing aggregate-level data.

Cross-National Comparative Studies

By the early 1980s, large-scale cross-national survey projects were becoming more common – examples included the first wave of the twenty-two–nation World Values Survey in 1981 and the initiation of the nine-country EuroBarometer series in 1974. Taking advantage of these developments, in 1984 Lewis-Beck conducted the first cross-national individual-level study of economic voting, with evidence from five countries. His main conclusion was simply that economic voting is widespread in developed democratic contexts (Lewis-Beck, 1988). However, he also demonstrated that directly comparable estimates of the magnitude of economic voting from different countries reveal considerable cross-national variance. Furthermore, the estimated variation appeared to follow a pattern that he interpreted as consistent with the traditional reward–punishment logic for economic voting. Specifically, his evidence showed that the more parties included in the cabinet (e.g., Italy's five-party cabinet versus Britain's single-party cabinet), the smaller the impact of the economy on the voter's decision to vote for or against the cabinet parties. This pattern, he argued, might indicate that as the cabinet became more complex, voters found it difficult to attribute responsibility to specific incumbent parties and so could not reward or punish optimally.

Lewis-Beck's evidence of variability in economic voting and his tentative explanation captured the imagination of students of comparative political behavior. However, the lack of suitable comparative survey data forced these scholars to turn back to aggregate-level data to pursue this comparative project further. The resulting analyses typically estimated the relationship between fluctuations in macro-economic indicators (usually unemployment, inflation, and real income) and change in vote share for the incumbent governments across a large sample of elections from multiple countries. Unfortunately, however, the aggregate approach has proven largely disappointing as a way to identify robust relationships between context and the economic vote. Specifically, some influential large-scale studies have simply found no widespread evidence for economic voting in the aggregate data. For example, Paldam (1991) analyzed electoral data from seventeen countries over the postwar period and found little evidence of economic voting in any country. Although, like Lewis-Beck, he hinted that the explanation for his weak results might lie in cross-national differences in the nature of governing institutions, his evidence did not really produce enough statistically detectable variation in economic voting for him to speculate as to the nature of these influences.

Some other cross-national aggregate-level results have detected more economic voting than Paldam did (using different statistical models and, in general, smaller samples). However, the nature and magnitude of the estimated economic voting effect varies significantly from one study to the next. For example, Lewis-Beck and Mitchell (1990) examined aggregate data on twenty-seven elections in five European countries and found that rates of unemployment and inflation do affect the vote for governing parties. However, Chappell and Veiga (2000) analyzed an expanded sample of European countries over a longer time period and found that none of the usual economic indicators had an impact on incumbent party vote share (although they did find that change in inflation rates *relative* to the European average had a significant correlation with vote share). Some of these differences in results certainly reflect differences in the elections sampled and model specification; however, one is hard-pressed to have much confidence in the robustness of the economic vote in the aggregate cross-national data if the result is so sensitive to the particular sample of countries employed or the precise model specification.

Responding to the negative and inconsistent cross-national aggregate results, Powell and Whitten (1993) suggested that the impact of economic evaluations on vote choice might interact with institutional context. Powell and Whitten (1993) developed a measure of institutional "clarity of responsibility" that measured the extent to which political institutions allowed incumbents to diffuse responsibility for economic outcomes.[23] The results from their analysis of 109 elections led them to conclude that "the greater the perceived unified control of policymaking by the incumbent government, the more likely is the citizen to assign responsibility for economic and political outcomes to the incumbents" (Powell and Whitten, 1993: 398).

This clarity of responsibility argument and result resonated positively with many scholars of comparative economic voting and spawned a literature identifying different contextual influences on economic voting in aggregate data. Some of these studies took clarity of responsibility itself

[23] Their index of clarity of responsibility combined measures of the following institutional characteristics: voting cohesion of the major parties, the extent to which legislative committee systems accommodated opposition party power sharing, bicameralism, coalition governments, and minority governments.

as a starting point – trying to extend the result to different samples of elections or to different dimensions of clarity. The results of these efforts, however, have been mixed. Chappell and Veiga (2000) analyze 136 European parliamentary election outcomes for the period 1960–1997 and find evidence that inflation (relative to European averages) shapes vote outcomes but find no support for the clarity of responsibility argument. Royed, Leyden, and Borrelli (2000) specifically challenge the robustness of the Powell and Whitten result claiming that there is little support for the clarity of responsibility argument – in fact, claiming that economic voting is higher for coalition as opposed to single-party governments. Although Palmer and Whitten (2003a, 2003b) have rigorously rebutted the Royed, Leyden, and Borrelli claims, it is hard to avoid the conclusion that the aggregate evidence for clarity of responsibility, like the aggregate evidence for cross-national economic voting in general, is fragile. A clue that the source for this fragility may lie in the use of aggregate electoral data (rather than in the weakness of the underlying relationship itself) comes from Anderson's (1995) application of the clarity idea to monthly popularity data rather than electoral data. Although he worked with only five countries, his empirical analyses indicate quite conclusively "...that more responsibility in the government results in the economic variables having stronger effects on party support" (Anderson, 1995: 210).

Almost all of these efforts that followed Lewis-Beck's five-nation study focused on aggregate-level electoral and economic data. One conclusion that can be drawn from this evidence is simply that the economic vote varies from election to election and from country to country. It is certainly not absent as Paldam's (1991) aggregate study suggested, but neither is it universal (Norpoth, 1996a). More important, given that there is variation in economic voting from election to election, the cross-national literature has begun to identify the correlates of that variation. This search, however, has been hindered for the most part by reliance on aggregate data and less-than-robust evidence.

Scholars have recently, though, begun to heed Lewis-Beck's suggestion that a fruitful effort to explain cross-national variation in economic voting is more likely to result from individual-level data on people's economic perceptions and vote choices rather than on aggregate-level data about electoral returns and economic performance. Hellwig (2001) analyzes a pooled sample of nine individual-level election surveys and includes contextual measures of both economic context (economic interdependence) and the institutional variables employed by Powell and Whitten (1993).

He confirms the important role that political institutions play in mediating the magnitude of the economic vote and also provides evidence of a similar mediating role for economic variables such as the extent to which national economies are integrated into the global economy. Tucker (2006) examines how the political context of post-communist transitions can condition the nature of the economic vote in these new democracies. Van der Brug et al. (2007) examine voter preferences for parties competing in European elections in fifteen countries over three different time periods. Accordingly, with a total of forty-two different electoral contexts, they are able to test institutional explanations for individual-level variations in the economic vote. They conclude that the economic vote is not very large in general and, to the extent that it does exist, it is restricted to contexts in which there is high clarity of responsibility.

The Overall Message from Empirical Developments in the Literature

The empirical literature on economic voting that has developed over the last four decades makes it clear that economic voting is both pervasive and variable. However, the real extent of economic voting and the nature of its variability has often been obscured in the comparative literature by an over-reliance on aggregate data and the incomparability of individual-level studies conducted by different researchers pursuing different priorities and using different methods. What is needed, and what we attempt to provide in this book, is a description of economic voting across countries and over time that is constructed from individual-level data in a way that makes meaningful comparison possible. Fortunately, this goal can now be achieved – because over the last twenty years a large number of national voter-preference surveys and cross-national survey projects have been undertaken. Furthermore, the content of these surveys reflects a broad consensus on the basic factors motivating voters in the Western democracies – so that a more or less standard battery of survey questions appears in many of these voter preference surveys. Many surveys include, for example, questions about the voter's perceptions of movements in the national economy. These developments make it possible (as we demonstrate in Chapter 3) to develop a description of economic voting at the individual level that is both comprehensive and comparable across elections in different countries and at different times. We hope that this will serve as a foundation for identifying the elements of the political and economic context that condition the economic vote.

A CONTEXTUAL THEORY OF RATIONAL RETROSPECTIVE ECONOMIC VOTING

Our assessment of the comparative work on economic voting suggests an empirical direction that focuses on the analysis of individual-level surveys and a theoretical approach founded on rational models of individual vote choice. Because our goal is to explain contextual variation in the economic vote, we have adopted insights from the theoretical literature that we think will best explain how voters incorporate information about the political and economic context to condition their economic vote. Specifically, our contextual theory of the economic vote builds on two traditions in the theoretical literature that we reviewed previously.

First, we concur with the likes of Cheibub and Przeworski (1999) and others (Fearon, 1999, for example, in the same volume) that a selection model rather than a traditional sanctioning model is a promising theoretical approach for explaining cross-national variation in economic voting. Although one can gain considerable insights into contextual variation in economic voting by adopting a moral hazard approach, we believe a more persuasive theoretical case can be made that the vote decision is motivated by selection (as opposed to simply a sanctioning motivation). Fearon (1999) has shown that selection incentives overwhelm sanctioning incentives when models of electoral selection and electoral sanction are combined formally. Specifically, when voters perceive any relevant differences between candidates in an election, it is rational for them to vote over those differences rather than to try to use their vote to discipline incumbents.

Second, rather than relying (as much of the current comparative literature does) on differences in voter knowledge about political and economic context (i.e., their level of "clarity") to drive expected differences in economic voting, we assume voters are rational and have complete information about the political and economic context. Moreover, because voters are rational, they use all of this information in making their vote choice. This implies that voters have rational expectations regarding the macro-economy – they use all available information about the current and retrospective performance of the economy in order to anticipate future economic outcomes under different potential incumbents. It also implies that voters have rational expectations about likely electoral outcomes and, hence, vote strategically. Accordingly, our contextual model of rational economic voting is a selection model in which voters have rational expectations regarding economic outcomes and also vote strategically.

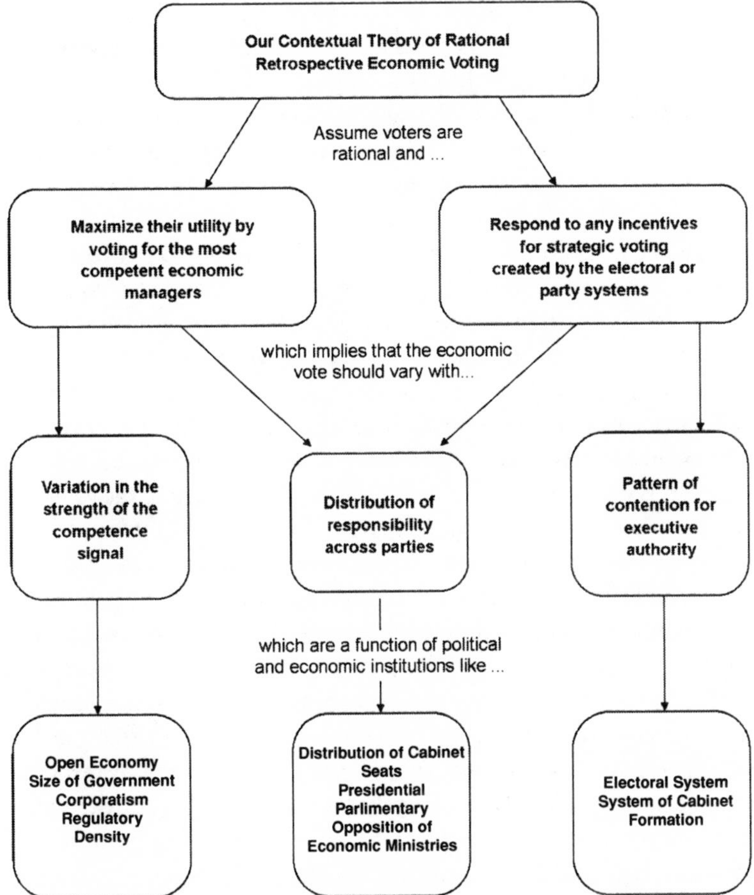

Figure 1.2. Overview of the theory and its implications.

Figure 1.2 provides a simple overview of the theory as well as the empirical implications that emerge from it. The first part of our contextual theory of rational retrospective economic voting (described and tested in Part II) provides a rational selection model in which voters maximize their utility by voting for the best economic managers (ignoring strategic voting incentives). In this model, movements in the previous economy enter the rational voter's utility function for each party weighted by a "competency signal" that ranges from zero to one, depending on how much information about that party's competence economic fluctuations actually contain. The model assumes rational expectations on the part of voters so the economic outcomes associated with different incumbent parties are fully anticipated. Consequently, economic growth depends only on the natural rate of economic growth plus unanticipated shocks. These shocks, however, consist of both an exogenous component and a component that depends on the incumbent party's competence (and is persistent over time). Consequently, rational voters can use retrospectively observed economic performance to infer the competence of incumbent politicians or parties.

Specifically, in this model, voters can observe shocks to the macroeconomy but cannot observe the mix of exogenous and competence components that comprise these shocks. Voters do, however, know the variances of the distributions of these different kinds of shocks and so are able to solve a well-defined signal-extraction problem that produces a competence signal. This competence signal is simply a weighted value of economic performance (or perceptions of performance) in which the weight varies between zero and one and is minimized when the variance in exogenous shocks is very large relative to the variance in the competence of politicians. In the full model, this competence signal enters the voter's utility function for each party and so the theoretical variation in the competence signal provides exactly the kind of potential contextual influence that we are trying to identify in this project. When it is near zero, there will be little economic voting because the exogenous influences on the economy are so great that the rational voter can glean little information about the competence of politicians from its usual fluctuations. Alternatively, when an economy is insulated against exogenous shocks (i.e., the variance in these shocks is quite small from period to period), observed movements in the economy would be relatively informative about the competence of politicians and so important in the vote choice of rational voters.

Two kinds of empirical implications flow from this part of the model (i.e., the selection logic that leads to the competency signal): those that say how the size of the competency signal itself should change with changes in the historical variation in the domestic economy and those that suggest how institutions that provide more or less political control of the economy (e.g., the openness of the economy) should impact the size of the competency signal.

The second part of the theoretical model is described and tested in Part III. It begins with the voter utility function implied by the selection model (i.e., one that includes the previous economy weighted by a competence signal) and – once we generalize the model to more complex political environments (that create strategic voting incentives) – adds an analysis of strategic voting to the utility function. That is, we ask: If the voter's preferences for parties are determined by the utility functions implied by the selection model, which party would actually be preferred if the electoral system (and system of executive selection) creates complex strategic incentives? And, how do these incentives then impact the likelihood of an economic vote? Our answers to these questions are built on McKelvey and Ordeshook's (1972) formal model of strategic voting in multiparty contexts. We generalize this logic to account for cases in which multiple parties compete in elections and executive authority may be shared among several parties. This generalization leads to implications about how the pattern of party competition impacts economic voting.

In addition, our analysis of strategic voting incentives interacts with the logic of the selection model to produce implications about the way that variations in the distribution of administrative responsibility among members of the incumbent government will alter the strength of the competency signal and thus the strength of economic voting. In general, the implications of the model in this regard are the same as the implications from previous arguments about the incumbent or status quo distribution of policy-making responsibility (e.g., from the clarity of responsibility literature) – that is, as responsibility is more widely shared across parties, economic voting will be weaker. Furthermore, because any individual incumbent party has a greater share of responsibility, economic voting will be a more important influence on that party's electoral performance.

ORGANIZATION OF THE BOOK

The book is divided into three parts. Part I focuses primarily on defining what we mean by an economic vote; providing a detailed discussion of how the economic vote is measured; and building a comprehensive map of the variation in economic voting across eighteen countries, over twenty-two years, and across 678 parties. In Chapter 2, we develop a number of different conceptual definitions of economic voting that correspond to the various ways economic voting has been used in the literature (and in our theory). These include the economic vote for the chief executive, the economic vote of the government, and the volatility of the economic vote, among others. Next, we describe a four-step procedure for measuring these concepts using individual-level data from 163 different electoral surveys (drawn from eighteen countries from 1979 to 2001). In brief, our procedure generates measures of economic voting by first estimating a separate multinomial statistical model of vote choice for each of the 163 electoral surveys. The estimated parameters from these models are then used to produce measures of the general economic vote for each party in an election, which we define as the change in support for each party if the distribution of economic perceptions in the sample shifts by a given amount. Changes in predicted values calculated from the statistical model are a rather direct measure of this concept and so, for each of the 163 surveys, the procedure produces a measure of the extent of economic voting for each party. Finally, by combining these estimates in various ways, we can produce measures of the different conceptions of economic voting mentioned previously.

In Chapter 3, we use these measures to construct an empirical map of the variation in economic voting across the Western democracies over the last two decades. This map unambiguously confirms Lewis-Beck's assertion that economic voting in the Western democracies is widespread and forcefully contradicts the most pessimistic assessments emerging from cross-national aggregate studies (e.g., Paldam, 1991). More important, it clarifies the nature of the cross-national, over-time, and across-party variation in economic voting and suggests a number of empirical puzzles for our theory to solve.

To evaluate the quality of the map of economic voting that we have produced and to test hypotheses that come out of our theory, we build statistical models designed to explore the sources of variation in our map of economic voting. Chapter 4 reviews two strategies for doing this, both of which we use in the remainder of the book. One strategy is to pool the data from the 163 individual-level surveys and then estimate hierarchical multilevel models in which we use interaction terms to look for suspected contextual influences on the extent of individual-level economic voting. An alternative two-stage strategy takes the estimates that we have already used in Chapter 3 and makes them the "dependent variable" in second-stage analyses exploring the sources of their variation. Both strategies typically generate similar estimates of contextual effects (Duch and Stevenson, 2005). However, most of our empirical work uses the two-stage strategy, largely because it allows informative visual representations of the results, which greatly simplifies reporting and interpretation and lets the reader visualize the relationships in the data to a far greater extent than is possible with the one-stage models. Nevertheless, for the sake of robustness, we also report (when appropriate) results from one-stage hierarchical models.

Chapter 4 also asks whether the variation in economic voting that is revealed in our empirical map is an artifact of differences in the 163 statistical models used to produce them. Using a variety of empirical strategies, we rule out a number of possible artificial sources of variation in our estimates, including differences in question wording across surveys, differences in the "fit" of the individual-level models, differences in the timing of the surveys relative to the election, differences in the list of control variables included in the different models, differences in the applicability of the assumptions underlying the statistical model itself, and endogeneity in our measure of economic evaluations. Overall, we conclude that the variation in our map of economic voting is not the result of the specification of the individual-level models used to estimate its 163 different data points.

Part I leaves the reader with a comprehensive description of the contextual variation in the economic vote that our theory of rational economic voting will explain. Part II presents the foundations of our contextual theory; it develops the competency-signaling component of the theory; and it presents empirical tests of the hypothesized impact of political and economic contexts on the economic vote. Chapter 5 develops a selection model of the economic vote that incorporates competency-signaling arguments that, as we have seen, have significantly influenced rational-expectations models in the political economy field. We build on Alesina and Rosenthal's (1995) model of rational retrospective economic voting in which rational voters try to select competent economic managers from the set of parties competing in the election. Voters assess competence by observing past economic performance and using this to sort out what portions of macro-economic shocks are a result of political competency as opposed to exogenous factors.

Chapter 6 explores two of the assumptions of the model developed in Chapter 5 – that voters have a sense of the magnitude of normal variation in their economies compared with others and that they understand the extent to which their economy is subject to exogenous influences that domestic politicians cannot control. Given the considerable skepticism that students of political sophistication have about the knowledge of the average voter, and because there was little empirical work available to give us confidence in these assumptions, we collected two data sets that can be used to explore what information about economic variation is available to voters (i.e., coding of economic information in more than ten thousand newspaper front pages) and what they actually know about the extent and sources of variation in their economies (an original survey conducted in six countries). The results indicate that a great deal of information about economic variation is available to voters and that knowledge about the comparative level of economic variation in their economies is surprisingly widespread and sensible.

Once it is established that voters have information about variation in economic outcomes, Chapter 6 also explores whether perceptions of differences in the extent of economic variation before elections actually lead to differences in economic voting, as the theory predicts. The results suggest that national differences in the variation in shocks to their macro-economies are sufficiently large that they could signal the economic competency of incumbents. Furthermore, the chapter provides evidence that economic voting responds to these macro-economic signals as hypothesized by the theory.

Chapter 7 examines how institutional and structural features of the domestic macro-economy affect the voter's signal-extraction efforts. Our competency theory predicts that as the ratio of decisions affecting macro-economic outcomes by nonelectorally accountable decision makers to those by electorally accountable decision makers declines, the overall competency signal will rise and vice versa. The competency signal will be lower in an open economy because the ratio of nonelectorally accountable decisions (many originating with decision makers outside of the country) to elected electorally accountable decisions will be higher than in an economy less open to global influences. As a result, economic voting should be lower in open economies. Paradoxically, a more expansive state sector increases this ratio of nonelectorally accountable decisions to electorally accountable decisions and, hence, undermines the magnitude of the competency signal. Contexts with fewer statist institutions – lower government expenditures as a percent of GDP, the absence of central wage-bargaining institutions, and limited government regulation – have higher levels of economic voting.

Part III explores how the economic vote may be conditioned by the structure of electoral competition, the nature of postelection bargaining over the distribution of executive authority among parties, and the distribution of policy-making authority among incumbent parties. In Chapter 8, we begin by generalizing the rational-selection model of individual-level economic voting from Chapter 5 to contexts in which there are multiple parties competing for election and where executive authority may be shared among several parties. This generalization shows that in political contexts in which policy-making authority is widely shared, the rational voter's ability to extract an informative signal about the competence of any one party declines. Furthermore, because multiparty competition and shared executive authority necessarily introduce incentives for strategic voting, both the extent to which different parties are competitive in the contest to obtain executive authority and the extent to which elections matter in this contest should be important contextual influences on economic voting.

Chapter 9 explores whether variations in the distribution of policy-making responsibility among parties currently in government conditions the economic vote. We find, as the theory predicts, that parties with a greater share of the status quo distribution of administrative responsibility have a greater share of the economic vote in a given election. We also demonstrate that as the distribution of policy-making responsibility is shared more equally among the parties in an election, retrospective economic evaluations will be generally less important in the vote choices of voters.

Chapter 10 examines whether patterns of governmental contention influence the distribution of the economic vote among parties. We find that economic voting is more important to the support of opposition parties that are members of more competitive, alternative governments than it is for other opposition parties that are not. We also find, consistent with our theory, that economic voting is smaller for incumbent parties that are members of competitive, alternative cabinets than for incumbents who are not. For example, as predicted by the theory, a prime ministerial party that is a member of each of the several different cabinets that have any real chance of forming clearly receives a weaker economic vote.

Our generalization of the selection model to political contexts, in which coalitions usually form, assumes that voters understand the likely outcomes of the coalition process and how their votes can impact this process. Chapter 10 also presents preelection survey data from Norway, Denmark, and Sweden, showing that voters in these countries have accurate perceptions of the likely outcomes of the coalition-formation process (and how they are likely to differ with different electoral outcomes). We conclude that voters in these relatively complex coalitional systems have the information they need to cast strategic votes with as much confidence as any British or American voter who decides to abandon a hopeless third-party candidate.

Each of the empirical chapters in Parts II and III explores how a particular set of contextual variables impacts the economic vote. An equally important task for comparativists, as Franzese (2003) has nicely pointed out, is capturing the higher-level interactions among contextual or institutional settings. For example, we expect the competency signal to be relatively strong in political contexts where administrative responsibility is concentrated (e.g., a single-party majority government). By contrast, if domestic economic outcomes are shaped entirely by global economic trends, beyond the control or influence of incumbent governments, we would expect the competency signal in such a context to be extremely small. Thus, concentrated administrative responsibility is a necessary – although not a sufficient – condition for economic voting to occur. Given the clear interactions between different contextual variables that are implied by our theory, our final chapter begins to explore how different contextual factors interact to shape the economic vote.

PART I

Describing the Economic Vote in Western Democracies

2

Defining and Measuring the Economic Vote

In this chapter, we explain what we mean by phrases such as "there is more economic voting in one election than in another" or "one party has a greater economic vote than another." We begin this task with a discussion of our conceptual framework for understanding voting in general and then tackle economic voting specifically. Once our concepts are clear, we then move on to measurement issues and ultimately describe our empirical strategy for mapping the variation in economic voting across countries and over time.

A CONCEPTUAL MODEL OF VOTING

We will take the act of voting to be a discrete choice. Discrete-choice situations suppose that a decision maker chooses from a finite set of alternatives that are mutually exclusive and exhaustive. In democratic elections, vote choices can be represented by this structure. Voters are allowed to choose one party or candidate, to abstain, or to cast a blank ballot; and these alternatives are limited to those who are on the ballot at the time of voting.[1] Given this structure, we also assume that whatever cognitive processes the individual may use to make this choice, the overall process of decision can be *represented* in the following way:

1. Each alternative in the choice set has some "value" to the individual, and this value is a function of variables that vary over alternatives, as well as variables that do not vary over alternatives but are characteristics of the individual making the choice. For example, a variable that

[1] Any more complex electoral system (e.g., systems that allow voters to cast two votes) also can be represented as a discrete-choice problem – with an appropriate definition of the choice set (e.g., all the combinations of ways that a voter may cast two ballots).

would vary over alternatives is the voter's perception of her ideological distance from each candidate. In contrast, the voter's subjective assessment of the economy would not vary over alternatives.

2. The individual's value for each alternative includes a random element. This randomness is usually thought of as arising from the researcher's ignorance of all the variables that contribute to individual choice (Train, 2003: 21). However, it could also arise from an inherent randomness in the value function.
3. Individuals choose the alternative that has the highest "value."

Given the first two assumptions, we can represent the voter's *value function* for each alternative j as[2]:

$$V_{nj} = g(x_{nj}, s_n) + e_{nj} \; \forall j \tag{2.1}$$

where n indexes voters, x_{nj} are characteristics of alternatives, s_n are characteristics of the voter that are constant over alternatives, and e_{nj} is a random term. In this notation, the third assumption simply requires that the voter will vote for the party or candidate, j, with the highest value function, given x_{nj}, s_n, and e_{nj}. One important implication of this framework is that the vote choice must be defined in terms of the probabilities of voting for each alternative. Accordingly, the "vote" is not a single observed ballot but rather an unobserved vector of probabilities that sum to one over the alternatives. As a number of recent contributions to the literature suggest, this has important ramifications for the estimation of vote-choice models in multiparty contexts (Alvarez, Nagler, and Willette, 2000; Blais et al., 2004). Furthermore, this has important implications for how we conceptualize economic voting that go beyond simple issues of estimation and that have not been fully articulated in the economic-voting literature.

CONCEPTUALIZING ECONOMIC VOTING

Given our understanding of voting as an individual discrete choice, any definition of *economic* voting at the individual level must posit some relationship between a person's perception of the economy and the probability of casting a vote for each of the available parties or candidates in an election (we call these probabilities the voter's "support vector" or just her "support"). The task of building a conceptual definition of economic

[2] This notation and the basis for much of this discussion rely on Kenneth Train's (2003) excellent treatment of the general subject of discrete-choice models.

voting is to specify the nature of this relationship. The previous literature is full of possibilities. For example, much of the empirical literature conceives of economic voting as any decrease (increase) in support for the chief executive that results from worsening (improving) economic perceptions (e.g., Lewis-Beck, 1988). Powell and Whitten (1993) conceive of economic voting similarly but focus on changes in support for the governing coalition as a whole. In contrast, Stevenson's (2001) "luxury good" model conceives of economic voting as any decrease (increase) in support for leftist parties (whether incumbent or not) when economic perceptions are improving (worsening).

As these examples make clear, there is no single concept of economic voting that is appropriate for all purposes. The appropriate concept depends on one's theory or (in the absence of a clear theoretical guide) how the concept is to be used. In this book, we have two empirical goals: we want to describe patterns in economic voting across countries and over time; and we want to test hypotheses about the impact of political and economic context on economic voting that are drawn from a specific theory. These different purposes sometimes call for different concepts of economic voting, so we present and compare multiple concepts of economic voting in this chapter. We begin by describing a very general concept of economic voting and then discussing how we operationalize this concept. Next, we discuss other (more restrictive) concepts of economic voting and how they can be measured.

The Most General Concept of Economic Voting

The most general concept of economic voting that is consistent with the discrete-choice framework discussed in the last section (and that maintains some relationship between economic perceptions and support) simply defines economic voting as any change in a voter's support for parties that is caused by a change in economic perceptions.[3] We call this *general economic voting* to distinguish it from other more narrow concepts of economic voting discussed in later sections. Notice that, consistent with the discrete-choice framework, *general economic voting* is a vector of changes in the probability of voting for each party in an election. If all elements

[3] This is formally true. If we define a set of all changes in support that are caused by a given change in economic perceptions, the most general definition possible would "count" all these changes as economic voting, whereas every other definition necessarily excludes some elements of this set from its count.

of this vector are zero, we say that there is no economic voting, whereas if some element is nonzero, we think of this voter as an economic voter in this general sense.[4]

This clearly differs from most conceptions of economic voting because it is neither directional nor incumbency oriented (e.g., *worse* perceptions lead to *decreases* in support for incumbents but not for opposition parties). However, because this general concept captures *any* possible connection between changing economic perceptions and electoral support, it provides a benchmark for defining other concepts of economic voting, which necessarily exclude some of these connections. Furthermore, if we can successfully operationalize this general concept, we can use this measure to construct measures of any other concept of economic voting that we choose. Thus, our first task is to build a measure of *general economic voting* that is applicable to a diverse set of countries and time periods. Once we have achieved this, we return to the task of defining more restrictive conceptions of economic voting.[5]

Measuring General Economic Voting

Producing a measure of *general economic voting* is complicated by the fact that the theoretical quantity we want to measure (the economic vote) is a *causal effect* (i.e., it is the impact of one variable on another) and

[4] Indeed, because *general economic voting* is the most general concept of economic voting, if all elements of this vector are zero, there can be no economic voting under any definition of economic voting.

[5] A final definitional issue concerns our focus on individual vote choice as the basis of our conceptual definitions. Economic voting is an individual-level phenomenon. It is only when individuals condition their votes on their evaluations of the economy that economic voting can occur. This theoretical basis of the individual-vote decision is why our language has been (sometimes laboriously) in terms of changes in support that a voter assigns to different parties rather than changes in the aggregate vote of those parties. However, despite the impression this language may have made, we are not be interested in explaining differences in economic voting among individual voters. Rather, we focus on a single average (or otherwise typical) voter in each population we study and try to explain variation in economic voting among these average voters. This has two implications for the terms we use and the inferences we make. First, if we focus on the general economic vote of a single average voter in some sample of voters, then the changes in vote probabilities for this average voter can be equated to changes in the expected vote shares of parties. Thus, instead of referring to economic voting as "changes in support of an individual voter that are the result of changing economic perceptions," we often drop references to the individual and instead discuss economic voting as an aggregate phenomenon – that is, the change in the vector of expected party vote shares as a result of changes in economic perceptions.

so cannot be observed directly. Instead, a measure of this effect must be estimated from data on the two variables that comprise the relationship (vote choice and economic perceptions). The information that we use to produce measures of *general economic voting* comes from surveys of 163 different national populations in eighteen Western democracies from 1979 to 2001.[6] Because each of our surveys is based on a large sample from the relevant population, we can use statistical models to produce the necessary estimates (as well as measures of our uncertainty about them). Of course, there are many different statistical models that one could use. For example, a particularly simple method would be to estimate economic voting in each population from the bivariate correlations between economic perceptions and vote choice in the corresponding survey. By comparing these correlations across populations, one could characterize the strength of economic voting across countries and over time. Correlation analysis, however, is not the best way to estimate causal effects because it does not account for the influence of other variables that can confound the relationship and bias the estimates.

More generally, in choosing an estimation method, we should strive to produce estimates of economic voting that reflect its true value in the population. In statistical terms, we seek to produce *consistent* estimates of the economic voting in each population.[7] In the statistical models that we use to produce our estimates, consistency is only achieved when one specifies the components of the statistical model correctly (i.e., they match the true process that generated the data). This means including the correct explanatory variables in the statistical model, choosing a probability distribution that correctly characterizes the random components of the process that generated the dependent variable (i.e., an individual vote choice), and correctly specifying the functional relationship between the explanatory variables and the dependent variable.

Clearly, consistent estimation is an ideal and is never achieved in practice. Indeed, because we never know the true process that generated the data, we can never know for sure if we have a correctly specified statistical model. Still, we do not come to the process of model-building unarmed. We can use logical constraints to rule out many possible specifications (e.g., a variable that can only have positive values cannot be generated

[6] Each survey randomly samples the national population of adults at the time of the survey. In some cases, the sample had to be weighted to account for nonrandom oversampling of some groups in the population.

[7] An estimator is consistent if it converges to the true value of the quantity being estimated as the amount of data used to produce the estimate increases.

by a random process that sometimes results in negative values). We can use our knowledge of the substantive problem (e.g., Which explanatory variables are likely to be important?) and we can ask if the model produces estimates that conform to what we know (e.g., we would question a model that generated estimates implying that leftist political orientations increased the chances of a conservative vote).

In this book, we produce our estimates of *general economic voting* for an average voter in each of the 163 sampled populations from carefully specified statistical models of individual voting behavior. In specifying the components of these models, we have been guided by the vast literature on voting behavior in general, the country-specific literatures on voting, and a growing body of work concerned with the particular statistical problems associated with estimating vote-choice models. The 678 estimates obtained from these models (one for each party in the 163 populations) are the numbers that we use to characterize the strength of economic voting in each population. We describe the four-step process we used to produce our estimates of general economic voting in each survey.

Step 1: Obtaining Comparable Vote Choice and Economic Perceptions Questions. The first step in obtaining comparable estimates from different surveys is to identify those surveys that ask respondents about their vote choice and their perceptions of the economy. Because questions are not asked in exactly the same way in each survey, we need to make judgments about the degree of difference in question wording that is tolerable across surveys. Too high a tolerance will hurt the comparability of the resulting estimates, but too low a tolerance will unduly limit the number of surveys from which we can glean evidence. Fortunately, however, there is a remarkable degree of consistency in the question wording for vote-choice and economic-perception questions across surveys and, where differences do exist, they are seldom idiosyncratic. Rather, there are usually only two or three ways a given question is asked and so there is almost always a group of surveys that asks questions in the same way. Hence, with enough cases of each type of question wording, we can do secondary analysis to look for any systematic impact that the differences have on our estimates. For example, if there are two ways in which the vote-choice question is asked and this difference matters for our analysis, then we should see some systematic difference in our estimates of economic voting generated from one question type versus the other. We review the questions that were used for vote choice and then turn to economic perceptions. We reviewed more than three hundred candidate surveys for inclusion in this study and 163 were judged to have sufficiently comparable questions on vote choice and economic perceptions.

VOTE CHOICE. Three types of vote-choice question were used in our sample of surveys. In each type, the question asks about a vote in a single election. We did not, for example, use surveys that only asked respondents to identify the party to which they felt closest (e.g., the early Italian Eurobarometers). The three kinds of questions we did use differed in two ways: (1) in their temporal relationship to the election for which the vote applied, and (2) in their treatment of nonvoting. With respect to the first issue, surveys conducted directly after elections simply asked respondents to report their vote choice in the preceding election. In contrast, those surveys that were conducted just before an election asked respondents for their vote intention in the upcoming election. Finally, surveys that were not proximate to an election asked the voter about a hypothetical election: "If there were a general election tomorrow, which party would you support?" There is a large literature on the strengths and weaknesses of these different kinds of questions in measuring vote choice; however, the key question for our analysis, addressed in Chapter 4, is whether these differences introduce systematic biases into our estimates of the strength of economic voting.

The second difference in the vote-choice variable concerns the treatment of nonvoting. All of the surveys we used allow the voter to express whether they did not vote or did not intend to vote. Furthermore, most allow the voters to indicate they cast, or would cast, a blank ballot. These studies differ in how they determine whether the respondent did not intend to vote. In many surveys, the option of nonvoting is simply included along with the other parties in the vote-choice question. In others, however, a two-question format is used in which the respondents are first asked whether they voted (or intended to vote) and only then for whom they voted (or intended to vote). While this is a readily apparent difference in the way the vote-choice question is asked in different surveys, it is unlikely to be consequential, because we decided to ignore nonvoters in our analysis.[8] The important point is that in all our studies, voters were

[8] In many of the individual-level models we analyzed, we had difficulty finding a parsimonious set of variables to include in the model that could consistently predict nonvoting. Even when such efforts were fruitful, these factors did not often overlap with the variables that predicted which party one voted for, and so including them in the models meant adding a large number of extra parameters to the equation (for each variable included, we had to estimate as many parameters as parties in the election minus one).

allowed some way to express that they either did not vote or did not intend to vote.

ECONOMIC PERCEPTIONS. Each of the 163 surveys used in the analyses in this book asks respondents a question of the following general form:

"Looking back over the last year, would you say that the economic situation in [name of country] has gotten much better, somewhat better, stayed the same, somewhat worse, or much worse?"

The key elements of this question are that it is retrospective, it refers to the national economy, and it is about *change* in the economy rather than its absolute level (i.e., the economy is good or strong). For a survey to be included in our study, we required that it include an economic-perception question with these three elements. However, other less fundamental deviations – such as whether the retrospective evaluation was over a year or two years and whether the question had three, four, or five response categories – were tolerated. We do not expect these deviations to be consequential but, as with the vote-choice question, we investigate this expectation empirically in Chapter 4.

Practical constraints dictate the adoption of the retrospective version of national economic evaluations because this question, by far, outweighs prospective evaluations in the elections surveys conducted over the past thirty years. This, of course, is not by chance but rather reflects the theoretical importance of the retrospective model of the voter's economic reasoning beginning with Key's (1966), *The Responsible Electorate*, and the micro-level findings in the United States of Fiorina (1978, 1981) and Kinder and Kiewiet (1979, 1981). Moreover, recent evidence that the economic voter, in fact, forms prospective expectations of economic performance in evaluating incumbents emphasizes that these prospective evaluations are dependent, although not exclusively, on retrospective assessments of economic conditions (Duch and Stevenson, 2007; Erikson, MacKuen, and Stimson, 2000; MacKuen, Erikson, and Stimson, 1992). Because the purpose of this book is not to determine the relative importance that voters accord retrospective versus prospective assessments in evaluating the macro-economy, we focus exclusively on retrospective national evaluations. And although we do not go so far as to accept Down's (1957) suggestion that the two evaluations are identical, we believe that prospective assessments incorporate considerable retrospective information. Hence, calibrating the magnitude of the economic vote based on retrospective assessments is parsimonious (in the sense that it captures a key information input into prospective evaluations), consistent with the dominant theoretical work in the field, and meets our practical data constraints. Finally, the general model of rational economic voting that we develop implies retrospective economic voting – not prospective voting – and so it is variation in this type of voting that we hope to explain with the theory.

Step 2: Identifying Control Variables. As we pointed out earlier, to improve the consistency of economic-vote estimates, we specify our vote-choice models with variables that control for the impact of other important factors shaping voter preferences. This increases our confidence that our estimates reflect the true relationship between economic perceptions and vote choice in the population to which the relevant survey applies. For each survey, we identify the appropriate control variables from the voluminous comparative and country-specific literatures on voting behavior. There is considerable consensus in these literatures regarding what concepts to include in our models. First, the literatures in the different countries usually point to the same kinds of variables as important determinants of the vote. Second, because the scholars who have written the voting literatures in each country are usually the same people who design the surveys, measures of these basic factors are usually included in election studies.[9]

In general, three theoretical traditions provide the foundations for most empirical models of voting (Alt and Chrystal, 1983; Dalton, 2002; Dalton and Wattenberg, 2000; Evans, 1999b; Franklin et al., 1992; Miller and Niemi, 2002). First, the sociological tradition identifies class, urban/rural residence, religion, region, language, and race as important predictors of vote choice (Alford, 1963; Lijphart, 1981; Lipset and Rokkan, 1967; Rose, 1974; Zuckerman, 1982). These variables capture the voter's position within the cleavage structure of society so that in countries with different cleavage structures, different subsets of these variables will be important. For example, linguistic cleavages are important in Canada and Belgium and thus are included in our Canadian and Belgium models; but, they are unimportant in France and, hence, excluded from the French analyses. Of course, a number of these socioeconomic variables will be common to virtually all of the model specifications. This is the case with age, income, religiosity or church attendance, gender, occupation, and education.

[9] Although the same concepts (e.g., age, religion, education, left-right self-placement) are usually included in different election studies, the specific measures used to capture these concepts are often not the same.

Second, expected utility theorists and students of issue-voting argue that voters make choices based on the expected policy implications of electoral outcomes (Downs, 1957; Kedar, 2005b). This tradition emphasizes the importance to the vote decision of the spatial distance between voter issues preferences and those of contending parties and coalitions (Alvarez and Nagler, 1998a; Enelow and Hinich, 1984; Niemi and Weisberg, 1992). In contexts with unidimensional political competition, this can be captured by the position of the voter and the parties on a left-right scale. In contexts with multidimensional competition, one must measure the positions of voters and parties on different policies.[10] Accordingly, we included in all of our models a measure of voter placement on a left-right scale (or liberal-conservative scale, in the U.S. case).[11] In addition, we frequently include a measure of policy preference. For example, in many of the countries in our sample, we included respondents' attitudes toward the European Union (EU). For the individual national election studies, or non-European studies, we included policy measures appropriate to each election (The North American Free Trade Agreement [NAFTA], for example, in the case of the 1988 Canadian election).

Finally, the influence of the Michigan school, particularly in the United States, points to the importance of the direction and strength of partisanship as an explanation for vote choice (Campbell et al., 1960; Fiorina, 1981; Miller and Shanks, 1996). However, the distinctiveness of partisanship and vote choice has been challenged in many countries (Borre, 1984; Budge et al., 1976; Butler and Stokes, 1969). There is a lively debate about the role of partisanship in voting in some country literatures such as Canada (Clarke, Kornberg, and Wearing, 2000; Clarke and Stewart, 1996; Stewart and Clarke, 1998) and Britain (Budge et al., 1976). Accordingly, with the exception of the U.S. models, we exclude partisanship from the vote-choice models. Nevertheless, because of this lack of consensus (even among scholars working in one country), we produce extensive secondary analysis to determine if our estimated variation in economic voting across countries hinges on the decision of whether to include a measure of partisanship in the vote-choice model (see Chapter 4).

Most empirical analyses of voting behavior populate their models with variables derived from these three traditions and, as we noted earlier,

[10] There is a large literature that demonstrates that voters across the Western democracies use a single left-right dimension to summarize contemporary policy debates (e.g., Fuchs and Klingemann, 1989; Inglehart, 1984; Klingemann, 1979).

[11] In a handful of studies, this measure was excluded because it was not included in the survey instrument.

most election studies include one or more measure of many of these concepts. Furthermore, the appropriateness of variables from each of these three traditions in each of the Western democracies has been debated in the country-specific literatures on voting behavior. Consequently, we make no effort in this book to critique or improve on the individual-level models of voting that these literatures have produced but rather rely on their collective wisdom to guide our selection of appropriate "control variables" for each election study we analyze. Because we have 163 individual-level models, it was not possible to include the details of each specification here. However, this information, a codebook, and the estimated coefficients for each individual-level model are available online at http://www.nuffield.ox.ac.uk/economicvoting.

It is also important to understand that nothing requires that the "control variables" appropriate to vote-choice models in a given country or election be the same as in other countries or elections. Although it could be that all the determinants of voting behavior are universal, this is unlikely, given the diversity of influences identified in the country-specific literatures.[12] Rather, although there does seem to be a core set of factors that are important to vote choices in all Western democracies, there also are other factors that vary in importance both across countries and from election to election. Furthermore, even when the same concepts are important influences on vote choice across our cases, there is no guarantee that the measures of these concepts used in specific surveys will be identical.

Given this variability in the likely determinants of vote choice from election to election, a practical question about the specification of the vote-choice models is whether using different control variables in each model will compromise the comparability of our measure of economic voting. As long as including different control variables (e.g., a linguistic variable in Canada but not in France) is necessary in order to ensure a properly specified model, and the rest of the model is specified correctly, then the resulting estimates of economic voting will be consistent and so comparison of the estimates among models from different contexts will be meaningful.

Step 3: Estimating the Statistical Models. Once we have decided on the variables to be included in the model for each individual survey, we

[12] For another illustration of the extent to which these variables vary in their importance for vote-choice models across different national contexts, see Franklin et al. (1992).

estimate a multinomial logistic (MNL) model of vote choice. The MNL model is well suited to the task of estimating a discrete-choice model of voting because it allows one to estimate the probability that the voter chooses each of the available parties and to see how this distribution of support changes when perceptions of the economy change. These models have an advantage over binomial models because they do not force us to artificially treat multiparty elections as a contest between incumbents and opposition parties. Indeed, consistent with the concept of *general economic voting* that we use these estimates to measure, the MNL model does not even require that we define incumbency previous to the estimation.[13]

An often-used alternative to the MNL model is to estimate a set of binomial logistic regressions, one for each party in the election, in which the vote choice for each party is recorded as either being for a party or against it. The estimates from these models will not obey the constraint that estimated choice probabilities sum to one across alternatives and actually require one to estimate a larger number of coefficients than the MNL model – that is, for nine independent variables and five parties, one would estimate fifty coefficients (and only forty with the MNL model). Still, for purposes of comparison with the MNL model estimates, we have estimated these models and have found no significant differences in the general pattern of results.

In later sections, we introduce estimation procedures based on pooling the data. However, these models do not allow us to produce estimates of the *general economic vote* for each survey (as defined earlier) because these models demand that we define the choice set similarly across the studies to be pooled (i.e., we can estimate a pooled model in which the dependent variable is a vote for or against an incumbent but not when it is for or against each of the available parties – which differ from survey to survey). Thus, pooling the data is not a useful alternative to separate

[13] Of course, there are disadvantages as well. The most often discussed disadvantage of the MNL model is that is assumes independence of irrelevant alternatives (IIA) (Alvarez and Nagler, 1998a; Greene, 2003). This assumption – that the addition or removal of an alternative will not change the relative selection probabilities of existing choices – seems clearly false for voting models (i.e., a new socialist party should take a higher percentage of votes from the older socialist party than from the conservatives). However, this naïve interpretation forgets that the assumption applies *conditional* on the variables included in the model. As Train (2003) points out, ultimately, a well-specified choice model that accounts for the major factors driving choice will achieve conditional independence of the errors in the value functions, which is equivalent to having IIA hold. In Chapter 4, we estimate choice models that do not assume IIA (i.e., the multinomial probit model) and demonstrate that, in fact, the estimated-vote probabilities are virtually identical.

estimation of the *general economic vote*. It will prove useful, however, for exploring variation in more restrictive concepts of vote choice. Thus, we defer discussion of pooled models until after we define these concepts.

Step 4: Using the Estimated Parameters to Estimate Changes in Support. Once we have obtained estimates of the coefficients of well-specified vote-choice models, we still need to construct measures of the substantive impact of changes in economic perceptions on the average voter's vector of party support.[14] To do this, we use the estimated coefficients (and variance-covariance matrix) from the model to produce predicted changes in support for each survey respondent when economic perceptions change by a given amount. We also produce appropriate measures of uncertainty around these predicted changes.[15] Next, we average the predicted changes in support over the sample to get an estimate of the average *general economic vote*.[16] This procedure has the advantage that one can present a single summary measure of *general economic voting* for each case; but, even more important, these estimates are a much better representation of the true magnitude of *general economic voting* in the population than is choosing the average individual, as is often done (see Train, 2003, for a discussion of the advantages of averaging over the sample in reporting results from discrete-choice models).

Finally, all our estimates of economic voting rely on the same "given change" in economic perceptions. This change is a move in each respondent's reported economic perception one unit in the direction of a

[14] Given that the MNL model is nonlinear, the coefficients themselves do not reflect the substantive effects. Furthermore, because we have different (and different numbers of) parties in each of the 163 estimations, the coefficients on the economic-perceptions variables will not be directly comparable across cases, although the substantive effects (given a well-specified model) will be.

[15] More specifically, we set the independent variables in the model to the values for the first individual in the sample and calculated the impact of a given change in economic perceptions on that individual's vector of vote probabilities. We then repeated this procedure one thousand times and, in each replication, we drew the parameters used to calculate the prediction from a multivariate normal distribution with the mean vector and variance-covariance matrix equal to the estimates from the model. This resulted in a distribution of estimated general economic votes for each individual. We then repeated this whole exercise for each individual in the sample and obtained summary measures by averaging over the sample. All the simulations were produced using the Clarify package in STATA version 8.0 with a minor modification to produce results in a useful format.

[16] Likewise, we average over the distributions of predictions across respondents to get an average over the sample of the distribution of changes in support (and so confidence bounds on the average point predictions).

worsening economy.[17] If the voter's perceptions were already at the worst category, we left them where they were.[18] This represents a reasonable shift in the distribution of economic perceptions based on their variability in our 163 surveys. We also calculated the opposite change in which each voter's perceptions get one category better. Comparing the results from the two measures reveals no asymmetry in economic voting – the size of the economic vote is the same in both cases (although with opposite signs).[19]

We have now described how we estimate the change in party support resulting from a unit deterioration in economic perceptions. This gives us 678 estimated economic votes, one for each of the parties in our sample of 163 voter-preference surveys. For example, in the 1985 Dutch survey, this procedure produced estimates of the changes in support for the CDA, VVD, Left, D66, Calvin, and the PvdA parties of, respectively, −.055, −.029, −.007, .016, .015, and .061. Likewise, in the 1997 British survey, the estimates were −0.056 for the Conservatives, .053 for Labour, and −.004 for the SDP/Liberals. These estimates can be used to construct a variety of measures of the economic vote corresponding to particular concepts. We discuss a number of these in the next section.

DEFINING AND MEASURING OTHER CONCEPTS OF ECONOMIC VOTING

As the British and Dutch cases illustrate, our estimated changes in support will vary in a number of ways depending on the nature of the party system and they will include parties both in and out of government. Hence, on

[17] We always code economic perceptions into a three-point scale indicating whether the economy got better, stayed the same, or got worse, over the previous year.

[18] We also have produced estimates of economic voting when all respondents' perceptions move from the neutral perception to the worse perception.

[19] When one considers that the distribution of economic perceptions varies considerably in different surveys, sometimes being skewed to the right and sometimes to the left, this result means the estimation method must be choosing different coefficients for different distributions of perceptions in order to "enforce" symmetry (i.e., the best-fitting models have no asymmetry in predicted values). One result of this is that alternative ways to define a "meaningful change" that are often used but that are not conditional on the distribution of economic perceptions (e.g., setting each voter's perceptions to the neutral category and moving them one category better or worse) must create asymmetry *by definition*. Furthermore, the result calls into question previous studies that have diagnosed asymmetry in economic voting by comparing coefficients on dummy variables for "better," "neutral," and "worse" perceptions. If symmetry in economic voting as we have defined it is an underlying feature of the true model, but the distribution of preferences is skewed in different ways, the estimation must produce different coefficients for these dummy variables in order to achieve symmetry in the substantive impact of economic voting.

their own, these vectors of changes in party-vote probabilities cannot easily be compared. For example, was there more economic voting in the British as opposed to Dutch case? In order to answer that question or, more generally, to compare the extent of *general economic voting* across elections in which different numbers of parties compete, we need concepts that summarize the "size" or overall amount of electoral change that is represented by the *general economic vote* vector. Furthermore, our theory will demand a concept of economic voting that reflects an asymmetry between incumbents and opposition parties. There are a number of possibilities that have different advantages and disadvantages, which we now describe.

Volatility of the Economic Vote

One possible summary measure of the economic vote is based on the familiar concept of "electoral volatility" that has often been used by scholars interested in the electoral stability of modern electorates (e.g., Bartollini and Mair, 1990). This concept captures how much electoral change occurs from election to election. It is calculated from observed changes in party-vote shares by summing the absolute value of the change in vote share for each party (from one election to the next) and then dividing by two. The resulting number is the amount of the electoral support that "changed hands" from one election to another. We can produce an analogous concept for *economic* voting by applying the formula for electoral volatility to the *general economic vote* (which is, after all, just a vector of changes in support over parties). The result is the *volatility of the economic vote* (or just *volatility*) and is just the amount of electoral support that "changes hands" as a result of a given change in the distribution of economic perceptions. We can operationalize this concept by applying the standard formula for electoral volatility to our estimates of the *general economic vote*. Specifically, we sum the absolute values of the estimates of the *general economic vote* for each party and divide this number by 2.

The concept of the *volatility of the economic vote* is illustrated in Table 2.1 along with our concept of *general economic voting* and some other concepts of economic voting that we discuss in this section. The table presents three hypothetical cases in which three or four parties are competing (we ignore nonvoting). In each case, the columns provide a set of hypothetical changes to each party's initial support that results when the voter's economic perceptions worsen, holding all other influences on the vote constant. Thus, these columns are the *general economic votes* defined previously.

Table 2.1. *Illustrating Different Concepts of Economic Voting*

	Changes in Support Due to Worsening Economic Perceptions		
	Case 1	Case 2	Case 3
Socialist (PM)	+0.05	+0.025	−0.05
Liberal (Cab Partner)	−0.03	+0.025	+0.025
Christian Democratic	−0.02	−0.025	+0.025
Conservative (Cab Partner)	–	−0.025	–
Volatility of the Economic Vote	0.05 tied	0.05 tied	0.05 tied
Economic Vote of the Chief Executive (changes "in the wrong direction" set to zero)	0 tied	0 tied	−0.05 most
Economic Vote of the Chief Executive (changes "in the wrong direction" included)	+0.05 least	+0.025 middle	−0.05 most
Economic Vote of the Government (changes "in the wrong direction" set to zero)	−0.03 middle	−0.025 least	−0.05 most
Economic Vote of the Government (changes "in the wrong direction" included)	+0.02 middle	+0.025 least	−0.025 most
Mean Economic Vote of the Government (changes "in the wrong direction" set to zero)	−0.015 middle	−0.0083 least	−0.025 most
Mean Economic Vote of the Government (changes "in the wrong direction" included)	+0.01 least	+0.0083 middle	−0.0125 most

Note: "Most" refers to the most economic voting and similarly for other rankings. Larger negative numbers indicate more economic voting.

Just looking at the *general economic vote*, it is difficult to compare the overall level of economic voting in these three cases. However, when we calculate the *volatility of the economic vote*, we discover that the amount of electoral support that changed hands because of the economy is the same for each case. Thus, the magnitude of the *general economic vote* is the same in the three cases, though its distribution across parties differs.

The *general economic vote* and its aggregate, *volatility of the economic vote*, provide an upper bound to the amount of economic voting that can be found in a given case. This occurs because these concepts "count" *any* change in support that results from a change in economic perceptions as part of the economic vote. However, Table 2.1 also illustrates other concepts of economic voting that differ from *volatility* because their definitions exclude some changes in support that are included in the *general economic vote.* As an example, although the *volatility of the economic vote* is the same in the three cases in Table 2.1, the other concepts would lead to a different conclusion. The point here is that when we are comparing economic voting from one case to another, our conclusions regarding the relative ranking of cases may depend on the particular conceptualization we choose. Consequently, we describe several alternative concepts of the economic vote and identify the one most appropriate for our theory.

Economic Vote of the Chief Executive, Cabinet Parties, and the Opposition

The concept of economic voting that is most often used in empirical work is the *economic vote of the chief executive.* We define this concept as any decrease (increase) in support for the party of the incumbent chief executive that is caused by worsening (improving) economic perceptions.[20] Similarly, we define the *economic vote of a cabinet party* as any decrease (increase) in support for a cabinet party that is caused by worsening (improving) economic perceptions. The *economic vote of an opposition party* is similarly defined as any increase (decrease) in support for an opposition party that is caused by worsening (improving) economic perceptions. Unlike our definition of *general economic voting*, these definitions are explicitly directional and so require us not to "count" as economic voting any changes in support that are not in conceptually consistent directions (even if these changes are due to changing economic perceptions). To see why this is important, consider the *economic vote of the chief executive* for the cases in Table 2.1. *Volatility* is the same in all three cases, but the *economic vote of the chief executive* differs. Furthermore, we get a different ordering depending on how we "count" changes in support for the chief executive that are inconsistent with the definition given previously. For example, in cases 1 and 2, worsening economic perceptions lead to an increase in support for the prime minister; however, the definition of the *economic vote of the chief executive* applies only when worsening perceptions result in declining support.

Given this, what might cases "in the wrong direction" mean? If we apply the conceptual definition of the *economic vote of the chief executive* rigorously, the only thing these examples tell us is that economic voting is absent in cases 1 and 2 – they say nothing more about its magnitude.

[20] By "incumbent chief executive" we mean the party that was chief executive at the time of the survey or election to which a survey refers.

Indeed, the information about the extent of the *economic vote of the chief executive* is exactly the same as it would be if the change in support had been zero. Consequently, in trying to sort out "how much" economic voting there is from case to case, it would be appropriate to set those that are "in the wrong direction" to zero. This accurately reflects their status with respect to the conceptual definition we are using and removes the impression that positive values of the *economic vote of the chief executive* somehow indicate less economic voting than would a value of zero. Looking again at the table, this understanding leads us to the conclusion that the *economic vote of the chief executive* in both of the first two cases is properly considered zero, whereas for the last case it is –.05.

Although this conclusion is consistent with our conceptual definition of the *economic vote of the chief executive*, when we turn to measuring the concept we must recognize that the relationship between support and economic perceptions is not observed directly but rather must be estimated in each case. This raises the possibility that estimates "in the wrong direction" can provide information that is usable (and interpretable) within our conceptual definition. Specifically, such estimates may arise as a result of estimation error, even though the true relationship (that we cannot observe) is consistent with the concept. Indeed, we are increasingly likely to produce such estimates when the true relationship is closer to zero. Thus, conclusions like "the *economic vote of the chief executive* should be seen as larger for case 2 than for case 1" can have a sensible interpretation if one understands that such statements assume (1) that the true relationship conforms with the conceptual definition (i.e., it is zero or negative) although the estimates do not; and (2) the estimation method is likely to produce larger inconsistencies the closer the true level of economic voting is to zero.

In the end, because our empirical analysis of contextual variation in the *economic vote of the chief executive* relies on estimates, we chose to include all the estimates in our maps of variation in economic voting (and in other analyses) even if they are "in the wrong direction" and to treat those estimates that are farther from zero (in the wrong direction) as indicating increasingly less economic voting (interpreted as a greater chance that economic voting for the particular case is zero).[21] As it turns

[21] An alternative strategy would be to constrain the models that produce the estimates to only produce estimates that are consistent with the conceptual definition. If the constraint is wrong because the theory that produced the concept is wrong, then the model will not fit the data well and the underlying theory and concept should

out, we are quite confident of this interpretation because the estimates of the *economic vote of the chief executive* described in the next chapter produce very few results in the wrong direction, and those that are in the wrong direction are close to zero, which suggests strongly that they are, in fact, a result of estimation error.[22] Similar observations apply to the *economic vote of a cabinet party* and the *economic vote of an opposition party*.

Economic Voting of the Government

Another concept of economic voting that has been used in previous empirical studies is the *economic vote of the government*. This concept is similar to the *economic vote for the chief executive* but places different restrictions on the elements of the *general economic vote* that "count" as economic voting. Specifically, it is defined as any decrease (increase) in support for the incumbent party or parties that is caused by worsening (improving) economic perceptions. Clearly, this reduces to the definition of the *economic vote of the chief executive* with one incumbent party but may produce different levels of economic voting when there is more than one incumbent.

Although this concept is often used with little discussion of its meaning and measurement, there are at least three sources of ambiguity in the concept that limit its usefulness. The first is the definition of incumbency. Few theories of economic voting are precise enough to dictate a single appropriate concept of incumbency. For example, the traditional reward–punishment explanation for economic voting has voters attributing responsibility (and punishment) to incumbents for bad economic performance but is silent about which parties should be considered incumbent.[23]

be rejected. We do not pursue this approach here because, correctly or not, many other scholars view such constraints in empirical models with suspicion (Did we somehow cook the results?). Of course, if this really mattered to our substantive conclusions, we would spend the time necessary to convince readers that this is an appropriate strategy. However, as it turns out, there are so few estimates "in the wrong direction" that it does not matter to our substantive results which of these methods we choose.

22 Of course, future researchers examining other samples (e.g., in developing countries) may well find many more inconsistent estimates. If the number of these is large, then it becomes less and less plausible that the true relationships are actually consistent with the definition provided here, and so the utility of the concept itself (and the theories from which it arises) should be questioned.

23 Indeed, even in the relatively simple American case, this ambiguity has spawned an empirical literature that tries to resolve the question by testing whether

The situation only gets worse when many parties participate in government, where minority government is possible, and where opposition parties play an important role in policy making.

The second conceptual ambiguity that arises in defining the *economic vote of the government* concerns the rule for aggregating the economic vote for each party in the cabinet into an economic vote for the government as a whole. There are at least two immediately plausible options for defining the concept: the *economic vote for the government* could be the sum of the *economic vote of the cabinet parties* or the average economic vote over these parties.[24] Again, theoretical discussions in the empirical literature that have used this concept provide little guidance in making an appropriate choice, although the measurement convention seems to be to sum the economic vote for each party (e.g., Powell and Whitten, 1993). Although this choice does not seem to reflect a theoretical commitment to a particular conceptual definition, it could certainly matter empirically.

The final ambiguity that arises in defining the *economic vote of the government* is closely related to the one we identified for the *economic vote of the chief executive* – it asks how we should include changes in support for cabinet parties that are in the wrong direction in the summation that produces the aggregate economic vote. In this case, however, a close adherence to the conceptual definition does not give us any guidance because the definition is about an aggregate (though it would suggest counting as zero any *sum* that was in the "wrong direction"). Our discussion of how to count changes in support in the "wrong direction" for chief executives applies directly to the economic vote of each cabinet party that goes into the summation for the *economic vote of the government*. Again, there is no conceptual justification for including these errant changes in the summation; however, because they are estimates, they may only be in the wrong direction because the true values were close to zero (but in the right direction). For chief executives, we were reassured that interpreting wrong-signed estimates as caused by estimation error was reasonable because in our data there were few estimates of *economic voting for the chief executive* in the wrong direction. However, in the case of the *economic vote of a cabinet party*, we have many more wrong-signed estimates

economic voting is apparent when one focuses on different plausible incumbents (e.g., American governors, Representatives, Senators, or the president (Leyden and Borrelli, 1995; Lowery, Alt, and Ferree, 1998; Peltzman, 1987).

24 We also could consider a weighted sum or average over the government parties, where the weight is the relative influence of the party in cabinet.

and so we are correspondingly less comfortable, assuming they arise as a result of estimation error.[25]

The issues we have raised about the concept of *economic voting for the government* should give us pause. There was certainly no universally applicable resolution for any of them and, taken together, the various plausible ways the different ambiguities could be resolved leads to a large number of plausible definitions of *economic voting for the government*, each of which could be used as the basis of an empirical study.[26] Thankfully, however, there is no real need to tolerate such ambiguity in the study of contextual variation in economic voting. Specifically, as we show in the next chapter, focusing on the *economic vote of the chief executive* rather than the *economic vote of the government* is seldom consequential substantively.[27] Furthermore, when parties other than the chief executive are of interest, rather than aggregate the economic votes of several parties, one can simply focus on the economic vote of the parties individually (defining an appropriate concept specific to these parties). This greatly reduces the problem of defining incumbency and avoids the aggregation problem entirely. Furthermore, it presents few additional methodological difficulties and provides much more detailed information about the pattern of economic voting across parties. This is the strategy that we pursue in Chapter 9 in which we reveal that the extent and consistency of economic voting for cabinet partners is very different from that of the chief executive. This difference underlines further the wisdom of avoiding aggregating the economic vote of multiple cabinet parties in studying contextual variation.[28]

[25] As was the case with individual parties, one could similarly define an economic vote for the opposition as a whole, which would face the same issues with aggregation.

[26] Given these problems, we avoid the use of this concept in the rest of the book. However, in the next chapter, we do compare it to the *economic vote of the chief executive*. Thus, for that purpose, we follow convention and identify incumbents as those parties that hold cabinet seats, use the sum of the economic votes of the cabinet parties (rather than their average), and include "wrong-signed" estimates in the sum.

[27] Clearly, for a large subset of cases – one-party governments – these are equivalent, but (as elaborated in Chapter 9) even when the economic votes of other governing parties are aggregated along with that of the prime minister, their economic votes tend to be very small relative to that of the prime minister. Therefore, although the two measures *could* differ considerably, in our sample they do not.

[28] This caution applies both to the procedure of aggregating estimated economic votes for parties as we do here and the more common procedure of aggregating each individual respondent's vote over government parties (i.e., coding a 1 if the voter voted for a government party and 0 otherwise), and then using this individual-level

SUMMARY

In this chapter we have tried to delve somewhat more deeply than is usual into the conceptual definition of economic voting and to make plain the tradeoffs between different conceptual choices. This attention to definitional issues is absolutely necessary for studies, such as this one, that must compare the magnitude of economic voting across cases. As we have seen, different definitions of economic voting can easily lead to different orderings of cases when size comparisons are necessary. Of course, it is an empirical question whether these definitional differences turn out to be practically important for understanding the pattern of variation in economic voting or for exploring the sources of this pattern. Nevertheless, our conceptual discussion does lead us to favor some measures over others. Specifically, the theory that we present in Chapters 5 and 8 clearly calls for a definition of economic voting that is directional in the usual way (i.e., economic voting is any decrease [increase] in the vote of incumbent parties that is caused by worsening [improving] economic perceptions and vice versa for nonincumbents).[29] Thus, when our theory calls for consideration of the economic vote of a particular party, we use the *economic vote of the chief executive*, the *economic vote of a cabinet party*, or the *economic vote of an opposition party* rather than the general economic vote.[30] Likewise, when our theory calls for consideration of the general level of economic voting in an election rather than for a particular party, we should rely on directional measures. Thus, we seldom use the volatility of the economic vote because it "counts" any change in the support of parties as a result of changing economic perceptions as an indication of economic voting. Likewise, the various problems with the concept of *the economic vote of the government* lead us to rely on the *economic vote of the chief executive* as our usual summary measure of overall economic voting in an election.

With some examples from our sample of surveys, we can illustrate the consequences, for the ranking of cases, of adopting different concepts of the economic vote. Table 2.2 presents estimates for the *economic vote of the chief executive*, *economic vote of the government*, and *volatility of the economic vote* from the 1983 German and the 1985 Dutch surveys.

variable to estimate a single model of economic voting for the government as a whole.

[29] The various versions of the theory are quite specific in providing appropriate definitions of incumbency, so there is no ambiguity of the kind mentioned herein.

[30] Although not mentioned earlier, the last of these is defined analogously to the others.

Table 2.2. *Two Examples of Alternative Measures of the Overall Economic Vote*

	Germany 1983	Netherlands 1985
Economic vote of the chief executive	−0.08	−0.055
Economic vote of the government	−0.058	−0.084
Volatility of the economic vote	0.085	0.091

What is particularly interesting here is that each of the measures suggests a different conclusion regarding the ranking of the two cases. The *volatility of the economic vote* suggests that the two cases have similar levels of economic voting: .085 for German and .091 for the Netherlands. The other two measures suggest exactly the opposite ranking of the two cases: in the case of the *economic vote of the government measure*, the Netherlands has a much larger economic vote (−.084) than Germany (−.058). By contrast, the *economic vote of the chief executive* measure ranks Germany with a much larger economic vote (−.08) than the Netherlands (−.055). Although it is an empirical question (addressed in the next chapter) whether this type of reversal is a more general problem, it illustrates the need for careful theoretical justification of the particular concept of the economic vote employed for estimating contextual effects. The next chapter reports our initial description of contextual variation in the overall economic vote, which is measured by the *economic vote of the chief executive*. Subsequent empirical chapters use some of the other concepts, again depending on the particular theoretical issue being addressed.

3

Patterns of Retrospective Economic Voting in Western Democracies

The analyses of the 163 surveys described in the previous chapter generate a wealth of data: a total of 678 economic vote measures for 113 political parties in eighteen countries over a twenty-two–year period. As we pointed out in the Introduction, the theoretical and empirical focus of this book is on explaining contextual variation in the economic vote, as defined in the previous chapter. Before proceeding to these efforts, we address two particularly critical empirical tasks in this chapter. First, is there a significant and pervasive economic vote in advanced democracies? Second, is there significant contextual variation in the economic vote that is sufficiently interesting to justify a book-length treatment?

The first question we posed is not simply rhetorical. There is considerable skepticism as to the importance of economic voting (a recent statement is Cheibub and Przeworski, 1999). If, as some would argue, economic voting were apparent in only a small number of countries or elections, or if it were wildly inconsistent in direction and magnitude, then there would be little reason to try to understand how contextual factors might affect it. Part of this skepticism concerns the importance of economic evaluations relative to other influences on the vote. Again, if economic evaluations have a much weaker influence on the vote than other factors, then our time would be better spent studying contextual variation in those factors. Readers can probably anticipate the answers to these questions. The evidence presented in this chapter indicates that economic voting of the usual kind (i.e., incumbents are hurt by a poorly performing economy) is pervasive in the advanced democracies. Indeed, the size and pervasiveness of economic voting estimated here should put an end to any speculation about the importance of cross-national economic voting. Furthermore, at the end of this chapter, we show that economic voting is not only important in many different contexts but is also among the most important influences on the vote in any given context.

The economic vote may be pervasive but, as we establish in this chapter, it varies quite significantly across contexts. An important goal of this chapter is to demonstrate that this contextual variation in our particular measure of the economic vote conforms to the patterns of variation noted in the previous literature (albeit for limited samples of cases). And, indeed, the comparison of our contextual variation with those in the literature provides strong face validity for our measure of the economic vote. Our description of contextual variation in the economic vote in this chapter also serves an important theoretical purpose. Our measurement strategy and the relatively large size of our sample of voter-preference surveys allows us to provide a much richer description of contextual variation in the economic vote than has been the case in the previous literature. This allows us to highlight patterns of variations in the economic vote that have never been examined in the previous literature. Economic voting varies across countries; it also varies over time, or from one election to the next, within countries; it varies across political parties (controlling for their governing status), but also the economic vote of parties varies over time. These patterns of contextual variation in economic voting that we graphically depict in this chapter are the foundation for our theoretical and empirical efforts in the rest of the book. They provide the clues as to what features of the political and economic context voters likely use to condition the magnitude of their economic vote.

MAGNITUDE OF THE ECONOMIC VOTE AND ITS VARIATION

In the previous chapter, we pointed out that there are good conceptual reasons for focusing on the *economic vote of the chief executive* as a measure of the magnitude of overall economic voting. Most important, and unlike the *volatility of the economic vote*, it is appropriate for testing *directional* theories of economic voting (in which only some changes in electoral support are "counted" as economic voting). It also avoids the need to aggregate (in essentially arbitrary ways) the economic votes of incumbent parties. In this section, we demonstrate that patterns of variation in the magnitude of the *economic vote of the chief executive* are quite consistent with the existing economic voting literature – again, providing assurance that our measurement strategy is sound. Furthermore, the contextual variations in the economic-vote magnitudes point to interesting patterns of variation, the explanation of which is the subject of subsequent chapters.

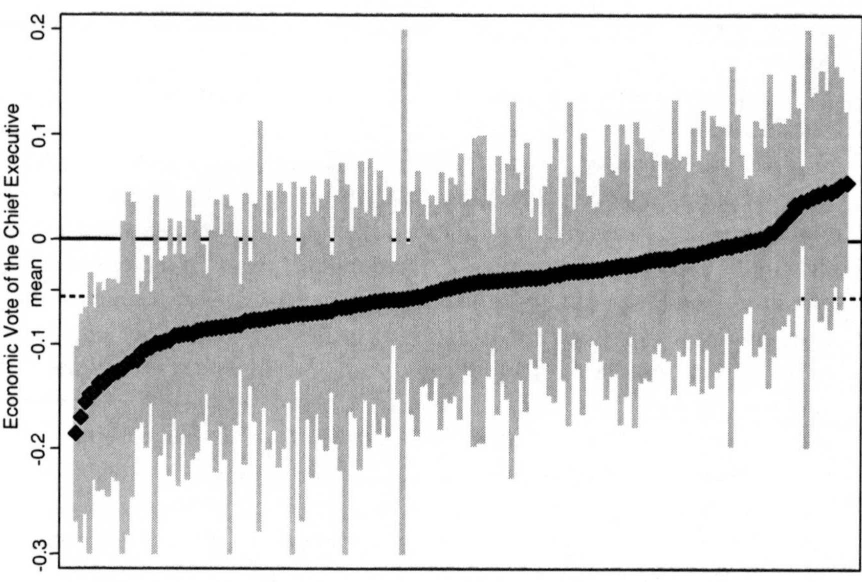

Figure 3.1. Confidence bands for economic vote of the chief executive.

We begin with Figure 3.1, which orders our estimates of the *economic vote of the chief executive* from largest on the left to smallest on the right (there are 163 estimates here corresponding to each of the voter-preference surveys in our sample). The line rising from the lower left to upper right quadrants of the graph represents our point estimates of the *economic vote of the chief executive*, whereas the vertical bars represent 95 percent confidence intervals around each point estimate. Recall that given our measurement strategy, a larger economic vote is one in which the party *loses* more support as economic perceptions worsen. Thus, larger negative values indicate more economic voting. The *economic votes of the chief executive* range between about −20 percent to about 8 percent with a standard deviation of 0.04. Approximately 90 percent of the estimates are negative and about 50 percent are less than −4.5 percent. The average *economic vote of the chief executive* is −5 percent and is represented by the horizontal dashed line. These simple distributional plots indicate that ruling parties are punished as economic perceptions worsen. A moderate decline in perceptions of economic performance typically results in a 5 percent drop in support for chief executive parties.

The magnitude of this result is consistent with the historically modest electoral volatility found in most elections in established democracies. For example, in their analysis of ninety-three parliamentary elections, Powell and Whitten (1993) estimated that the average single-party majority government – the equivalent of our chief executive party – lost 3.6 percent of the vote. Our estimated *economic vote of the chief executive* of 5 percent is certainly consistent with such a finding. In contrast, estimated levels of economic voting that deviate significantly from these modest levels are not really plausible. Hence, reports in other studies of typical shifts in support of 30 or 40 percent of the vote because of changing economic perceptions are probably not representative of the kinds of changes that actually occur. These inflated economic vote magnitudes likely result from reporting substantive effects for nonrepresentative individuals or for massive shifts in perceptions that do not reflect typical changes in economic evaluations.[1]

Clearly, our estimated shifts in support are substantively important. The median economic vote magnitude is about 5 percent, and one can easily identify elections in which swings in support of this order determined winners from losers.[2] Nevertheless, Figure 3.1 indicates that if one were to base an assessment of economic voting on a single election study, one might conclude that the economic vote is not significantly different than zero. The advantage of working with a large number of diverse surveys is that we can examine not just the statistical significance of each study separately but also can consider the total density of the 95 percent confidence intervals for all of 163 estimates of the economic vote (the gray area in Figure 3.1). If the density of the confidence intervals was equally distributed above and below the zero line – or if it was concentrated above the zero line – we would reject the notion of an economic vote significantly different than zero. In fact, we find that over 70 percent of the density of these intervals falls *below* zero. The picture, then, leaves little doubt that there is a consistent cross-national economic vote that hurts incumbents who preside over a period of worsening economic perceptions. Furthermore, Figure 3.1 indicates that drawing conclusions regarding the magnitude of the economic vote from one – or even a small number – of voting studies is likely to be misleading, given that any one

[1] Lewis-Beck (1988: 84), for example, reports substantive effects in the range of 16 to 54 percent, which are based on changing scores on all his economic variables from neutral to a position of discontent.

[2] The recent U.S. presidential elections electing G. W. Bush are an obvious case in point. Lewis-Beck (1988: 86) also points to the 1974 and 1981 French presidential elections, in which the margin of victory was significantly lower than 5 percent.

study has a good chance of generating point estimates that are not statistically different from zero in typical sample sizes.[3]

This finding is the first comprehensive evidence of economic voting at the individual level across a large number of countries and over an extended period of time. These results are important because they lay to rest any reservations about the generality of economic voting in the Western democracies. Cheibub and Przeworski (1999), for example, have raised questions about the economic vote, noting that, with some relative minor exceptions, "... economic performance does not affect the survival of heads of democratic government even during the years that elections are held" (Cheibub and Przeworski, 1999: 237). Our findings suggest that these and other (Paldam 1991) reservations about the prevalence of economic voting in developed democracies are unfounded. In addition, our results provide rigorous support for comparativists who have found economic voting at the individual level, although based on survey results from a small sample of countries (Anderson, 1995; Blais et al., 2004; Lewis-Beck, 1988). Hence, economic voting is alive and well and pervasive, at least in developed democracies.

Contextual Variation

We have established that there is an economic vote and that it varies significantly. Let's now explore the patterns of contextual variation in the economic vote. Again, our overall objectives here are twofold. One goal is to establish that the patterns of contextual variation in our measure of economic voting are consistent with the results of other comparative economic voting studies. A second objective of this exploratory data analysis is to flag patterns in the data that raise interesting puzzles to which we will return in subsequent chapters.

Recall that the estimates for our economic vote are derived from 163 individual voter preference surveys (from eighteen countries and over a twenty-two–year period) and that estimates from each of these specific surveys are the unit of analysis for our second-stage estimations. Hence, the total variation in economic vote summarized in Figure 3.1 can be broken down into three different components: country-, temporal-, and

[3] To be clear, we are arguing that even in cases in which economic voting for the chief executive is small – so that a typical sample of one thousand respondents is not enough to distinguish the small effect from zero – the larger view proposed by Figure 3.1 should give us comfort that economic voting in this case really is there.

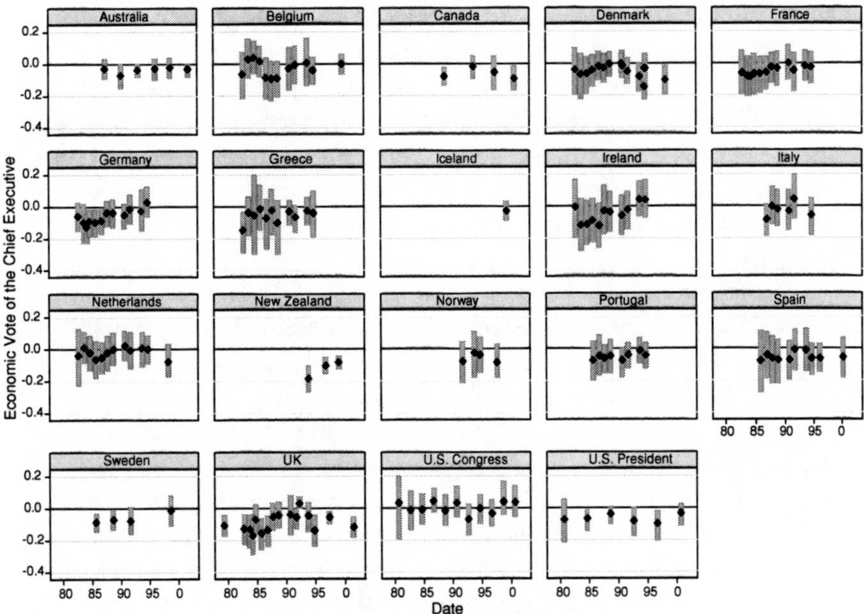

Figure 3.2. Economic vote of the chief executive by country and voter survey.

survey-specific variation. Variation in average economic voting from country to country is simply the economic vote for each country averaged over all of the years in our sample. Variation in average economic voting from year to year is the economic vote in each year averaged over all countries in our sample. What remains is survey-specific variation, which is variation not captured by the country- and time-specific effects.

Figure 3.2 provides some insight into these components of this variation by organizing the *economic votes of the chief executive* and their confidence intervals from Figure 3.1 according to country and survey date. We can, for example, identify country differences in the graph: We find an identifiable group of countries in which the *economic vote of the chief executive* is usually close to zero: Italy, the Netherlands, and U.S. congressional elections, for example. We also can identify a cluster of countries in which the *economic vote of the chief executive* is very high: the United Kingdom, U.S. presidential elections, Ireland, New Zealand, and Spain. But what Figure 3.2 highlights, and much of the literature tends to underplay (an exception is Nadeau et al., 2002), are the interesting patterns of variation within each of the countries. Ireland and Germany, for example, seem to have decreasing levels of economic voting throughout our sample period, which of course could be a temporal trend (which is shared with the other countries in our sample) or the result of survey-specific effects (e.g., changes in the perceived competitiveness of the incumbent coalition parties). But before we assess the relative importance of these different components of economic vote variation, let us look more closely at each of these individual country results, which are in themselves quite informative.

The variations in the economic vote in each of the individual countries in Figure 3.2 are quite consistent with other findings in the comparative economic voting literature; at the same time, they point to interesting puzzles. The U.S. results are a case in point of the results lining up exactly as the literature predicts. Specifically, the extensive literature on economic voting in the United States has consistently found a strong economic vote in presidential elections (Erikson, MacKuen, and Stimson, 2002; Kiewiet, 1983) while indicating a much weaker impact of the economy in congressional elections (Alesina and Rosenthal, 1995; Erikson, 1990; Keech, 1995). Our results are consistent with both of these expectations: U.S. presidential elections produce high levels of economic voting, compared to the other countries in our data, whereas we show almost no economic voting for the party of the president in congressional elections. It is also interesting (and encouraging) that the modest negative spikes that do occur in the congressional economic vote series (i.e., years of larger economic voting) correspond with presidential elections, which is again what the U.S. economic voting literature would predict. The relatively weak levels of economic voting in the 1988 and 2000 presidential elections are also consistent with other findings and speculations that the economy should play a less important role in elections when there is no sitting U.S. president (Nadeau and Lewis-Beck, 2001; Norpoth, 2002). And the relatively high levels of economic voting in the 1992 and 1996 presidential elections are consistent with other analyses of these elections (e.g., Alvarez and Nagler, 1995).

The United Kingdom, as most would expect, also ranks as having a relatively high level of economic voting but this clearly varies. During much of the 1980s, the economic vote for the party of the prime minister was extremely high, in the −10 to −15 percent range, whereas in the 1990s, the economic vote was much closer to −5 percent. This is consistent with other efforts to measure the magnitude of the British economic vote. For example, Evans (1999a) documents the relatively weak impact economic evaluations had on vote choice in the period 1992 through 1995. And Blais et al. (2004) found that the 1987 election in Britain generated a particularly high level of economic voting, dropping to relatively low levels in the 1992 and 1997 elections and then picking up again in the 2001 election. Readers will note in Figure 3.2 that this is precisely the pattern of results that we obtain. One explanation for this pattern that we explore in more detail in Chapter 6 is that the economic context differed significantly between the late 1980s and 1990s, which may have affected the importance of the economy for vote choice in the United Kingdom.

We see a similar pattern in the German case with economic voting declining over the sample period. Again, economic context is a plausible explanation here. This decline could be the result of a significant improvement in inflation performance during this period; this would be consistent with Anderson's (1995) argument that inflation has been a key economic variable driving the economic voting in Germany. But changes in the German political context offer an equally plausible explanation. Note that until 1986, the German economic vote is in the neighborhood of −10 percent and it drops rather significantly to −4 in 1987. The 1987 election was a watershed election; it marked the transition of Germany from a three- to a four-party system with the Green Party polling an equal number of votes as the FDP (roughly 10 percent each). By complicating the strategic voting considerations and the alternative coalitions that could replace the incumbent Kohl government, this may have moderated the economic vote.[4]

The Italian case is also suggestive, although based on only one observation, that dramatic changes in the party system can affect the magnitude of economic voting. Consistent with the common wisdom on postwar Italy (Bellucci, 1991), we find almost no economic voting (although 1986 is an exception) before the electoral reforms of 1993. We do, though, find a very large economic vote in 1994, which was the first election under the new election laws of 1993 that provided for single-member districts and was the catalyst for subsequent majoritarian trends in the Italian party system.

At least superficially, the French results seem to confirm arguments regarding the impact of cohabitation on economic voting in that country

[4] Our 1987 measure of the economic vote is based on a EuroBarometer survey that was conducted in November 1987. Hence, voters are responding to a more complex political landscape that had been in effect for approximately ten months when the EB survey was conducted (the 1987 German election occurred in January).

(Lewis-Beck and Nadeau, 2000). Note that the magnitude of the French economic vote ranges between −6 to −8 percent before 1987 (the first full year of cohabitation) but then falls rather precipitously to around −3 percent in 1987 and 1988. It recovers to around −5 percent in 1991 but then falls again during the next period of cohabitation, 1993 and 1994. We revisit this variation in French economic voting in our discussion of government responsibility and the economic vote.

Spain is another interesting case in which levels of economic voting are a rather constant 5 to 7 percent over most of the time period in our sample. The exception is 1991 and 1993, when we see the economic vote drop to essentially zero. Part of the explanation may lie with the recognition by voters that Spain was feeling the effects of a European recession – which by 1991 was beginning to take a serious toll on the Spanish economy – over which the González government had little control. Our theoretical results, discussed in later chapters, suggest that voters likely discount the importance of economic outcomes in their vote decision when these outcomes are seen as resulting from exogenous factors beyond the control of incumbent governments. The 1993 economic vote also could have been influenced by the narrow election victory for the González government that forced the Socialists to govern in a minority with the parliamentary support of the Catalan nationalists. Again, we argue in subsequent chapters that as policy-making responsibility is shared more equally – which would be the case with a minority as opposed to majority government – economic voting will decline.

Our results for Spain are at odds with the excellent set of historical accounts of Spanish economic voting described in Maria Maravall and Przeworski (1998) and Fraile Maldonado (2001). Both accounts focus on post-Franco Spanish democracy and show the size of the economic vote (particularly the retrospective economic vote) increasing as the Socialist government aged (it was initially elected in 1982 and replaced by the People's Party in 1996). We, in fact, find little variation in the economic vote with the exception of 1991 and 1993, the tail end of the Socialist reign, when, contrary to these historical accounts, we find very little economic voting.

Other country results exhibit similarly interesting patterns of temporal variation. In Belgium during the early 1980s and much of the 1990s, there is essentially no economic voting, but during the second part of the 1980s, the economic vote is actually quite large. The 1993 economic vote in Canada declines rather precipitously relative to the 1988 election, which is consistent with Alvarez et al. (2000) although not with Blais

(2004).[5] Our finding might not be entirely unexpected given that the 1993 election represented such a radical meltdown of the Canadian party system. The economic vote in Ireland has a remarkably linear and negative trajectory, moving from having a rather large economic vote in the early 1980s to having no economic voting by the mid-1990s.

Overall, the pattern of variation within countries that is revealed in Figure 3.2 is both encouraging and intriguing. It is encouraging because, with the possible exception of the Spanish case, it conforms to what we already know about the magnitude of economic voting in those few cases in which explicit temporal comparisons of economic voting are available or for which a "common wisdom" has otherwise emerged. And it is intriguing because it reveals patterns of variation that on their face look like they could have systematic causes. As we have already pointed out, some of the largest temporal changes in economic voting occur during equally dramatic periods of political and economic change. Furthermore, much of the estimated temporal variation in economic voting within countries is "smooth." That is, the estimates for any country are not fluctuating up and down from year to year but seem to trend up or down in somewhat longer cycles – as if they are responding to systematic forces rather than simple randomness.[6] We can gain further insights into these variations by examining the individual components of the variation in the economic vote described earlier. Specifically, by aggregating the estimates from Figure 3.2 within countries, we can get an ordering of the average economic vote for each country and compare our ordering to other work. Likewise, by aggregating within years, we can examine the secular changes in economic voting that may apply across countries and benchmark them in a similar fashion.

Cross-National Variation

Figure 3.2 suggests that countries vary in their overall level of economic voting. In order to put this in better perspective, Figure 3.3 provides a box-plot of each country's *economic vote of the chief executive* over the sample period. The median country in this sample is Canada, with an

[5] Our comparisons with Blais et al. (2004) are with respect to their Table 2 (p. 526), which employs a method of estimating the magnitude of the economic vote that is most similar to ours.

[6] There is a significant correlation between adjacent surveys within countries (a positive regression coefficient of .35 in a bivariate regression of *the economic vote of the prime minister* and its "lag," t = 5.25).

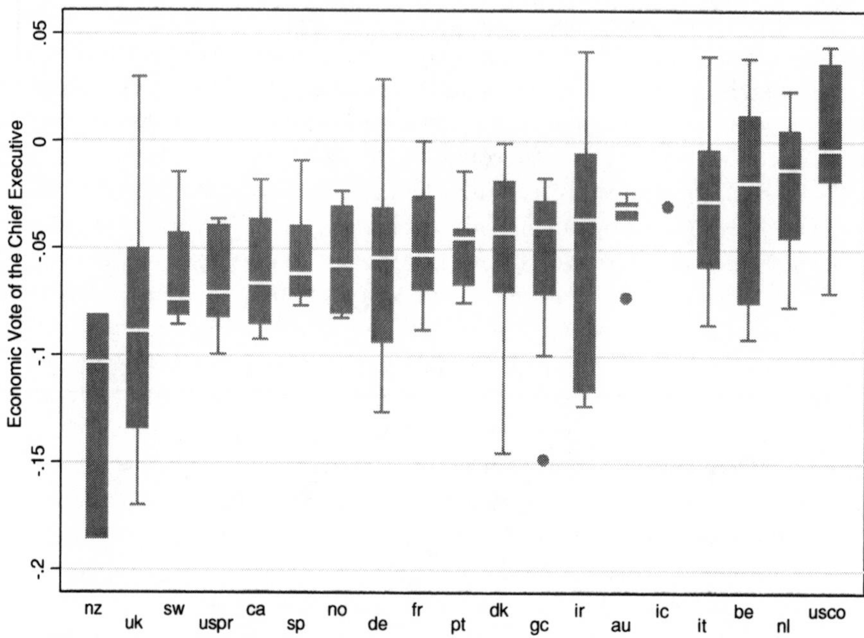

Figure 3.3. Magnitude of the economic vote by country.

economic vote of the chief executive of about −5 percent. And the pattern of cross-national variation is consistent with what we know from previous work. A case in point is Lewis-Beck's (1988) classic study that measures cross-national differences in the economic vote, based on individual-level surveys. Our rank ordering of countries in terms of the average magnitude of the economic vote is precisely the same as those in Lewis-Beck's analysis (from highest to lowest: Britain, Spain, Germany, France, and Italy). The fact that Britain ranks as having the highest level of economic voting (next to New Zealand) is consistent with Anderson (1995), who finds that Britain unambiguously has the highest level of economic voting in his sample of five countries. The low ranking of the Netherlands and Denmark also fits with Anderson (1995) findings. Our rankings are also roughly consistent with the ranking of the eight-nation study conducted by Nadeau, Niemi, and Yoshinaka (2002): the United Kingdom has the highest magnitude in their results; France and Germany rank second, which is consistent with Figure 3.3; and in their estimates, Italy, the Netherlands, and Belgium have the lowest economic vote magnitudes, again consistent with our findings. Our rankings of Denmark and Ireland, by contrast, do not correspond with theirs.

The United States has been the focus of much of the empirical work on economic voting, which, for the most part, suggests relatively high levels of economic voting in the country (Alvarez and Nagler, 1995; Kiewiet, 1983). Our results in Figure 3.3 tend to confirm this general expectation: the median economic voting score for U.S. presidential elections is about −6 percent and falls slightly above the median level of economic voting in our sample. Note though that the variation in U.S. economic voting is significant, rising to as high as −10 percent in 1996 but falling to almost zero percent in the 2000 election study. And as we pointed out earlier, the U.S. results for congressional elections support the conventional wisdom – the median economic vote in U.S. congressional elections ranks as the lowest case of economic voting in our sample (but note again that there is considerable variation among these elections).

In short, for those cases in which previous work provides some expectation about the likely pattern of cross-national variation in economic voting, our measures are consistent with these expectations. This should, of course, increase our confidence in the overall patterns of variation described in Figure 3.3.

Overtime Variation

A number of the individual countries examined earlier exhibited clear temporal trends in the level of economic voting – the declining levels of economic voting in the United Kingdom, Ireland, and Germany are a case in point. Some in the literature suggest that the developed democracies share a common temporal trend in the economic vote. Anderson (1995: 35), for example, identifies a positive trend in the economic vote and suggests that it is the product of the government's increasing role in the economy, which he argues raises the voters' sensitivity to economic performance. Anderson's (1995) results suggest that there might be an asymmetric period effect whereby economic voting is moderated during particularly good economic times (in his case, pre-1973) and exaggerated during difficult times (again, in his case, the post–oil crisis). Others have argued that global economic convergence should reduce overall levels of economic voting because national governments have declining control over economic outcomes (Alesina, Roubini, and Cohen, 1997; Alvarez, Nagler, and Willette, 2000). Political factors also have been suggested as a possible explanation for trends in economic voting. Kayser and Wlezien (2005) argue that economic voting is negatively related to levels of partisanship and, hence, declining levels of partisanship in Europe over the 1976–1992

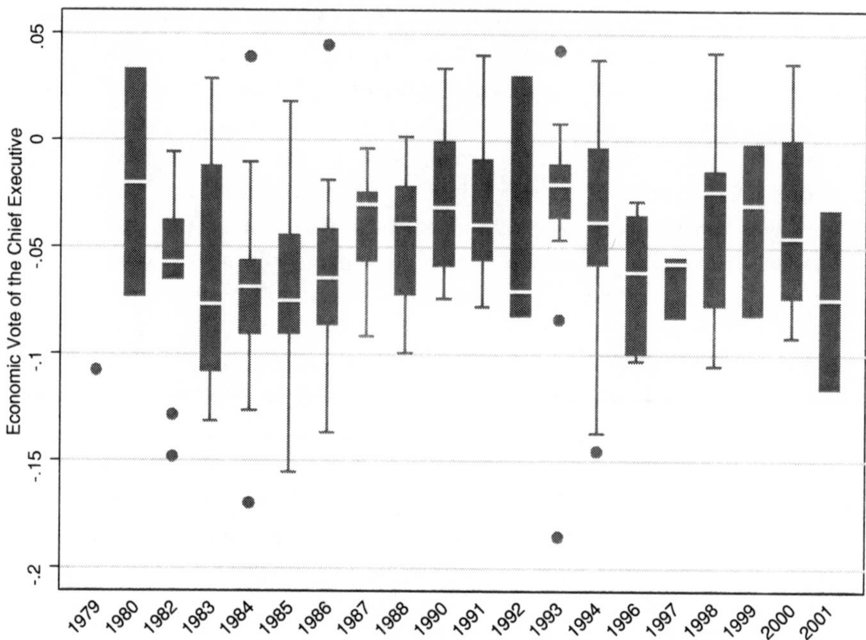

Figure 3.4. Magnitude of the economic vote by year.

period have resulted in an increase in the economic voting. They speculate that the opposite has occurred in the United States, where they point out that partisanship appears to be rising. Clearly, there are conflicting views of the precise nature of recent trends in economic voting. Our relatively large sample of economic-vote magnitudes can provide some insight into the veracity of these claims regarding trends in the economic vote.

Figure 3.4 allows us to assess visually whether there is any overall trend in the economic vote. In this figure, we present box-plots of the economic vote in each of the years of our sample. By now, it should not surprise readers to see considerable country variation in the magnitude of the economic vote in any particular year. Judging by the median vote in each year, there is some evidence that in the pre-1990 period, the typical *economic vote of the chief executive* was larger than in the post-1990 period. In the period 1990 through 2001, seven of the eleven years had median economic votes of less than −5 percent. In the period 1979 to 1989, three of the eight years had median economic votes of less than −5 percent. Hence, to the extent that there is any temporal trend in economic voting, it appears to be declining moderately.

Are these temporal variations in the economic vote consistent with the economic voting literature? Claims that the global economies are converging and that this should in turn reduce the magnitude of economic voting (Alvarez, Nagler, and Willette, 2000) might be consistent with the fluctuations in Figure 3.4.[7] Arguments such as those of Kayser and Wlezien (2005) that presume rising economic voting in developed democracies are problematic because the case for increasing economic-vote magnitudes seems unlikely given the results summarized in Figure 3.4. The decline in economic voting (i.e., trending toward zero) is particularly obvious between 1984 and 1990, which is part of the period in which Kayser and Wlezien (2005) argue the economic vote should be rising.[8] And Anderson's (1995) claim that the economic vote tends to be exaggerated during particularly bad economic performance might be consistent with our finding that economic vote is moderately declining over the sampled period. Clearly, there is no consensus in the literature regarding temporal trends in the economic vote. Accordingly, our evidence of a moderately declining economic vote would seem to be consistent with some of the arguments in the literature but obviously challenges others.

The Components of the Variation in Economic Voting

Our visual inspections of the economic vote confirm that there is contextual variation of a nature that poses some interesting puzzles. What is not entirely clear from these graphical displays is precisely how this variation is apportioned among the three different components described earlier. How large is the temporal variation relative to the cross-national variation? And is there any significant residual variation that is survey-specific? Understanding these relative magnitudes is important because they provide a guide to the theoretical variables that are likely to have the highest explanatory payoffs. One convenient way to do this is to estimate a variance components model in which we partition the economic

[7] Although the year 2001 seems to call into question this argument, it should be noted that there were only two voter surveys in our sample from this year – the United Kingdom and Australia – and, hence, this particular time point is not particularly informative when assessing temporal trends in the data.

[8] The Kayser and Wlezien (2005) analysis includes EuroBarometers extending back to 1972, whereas our analysis begins in 1979. Nevertheless, this trend is quite unlikely given the declining pattern of economic voting that we observe between 1980 and 1990 in our data. Kayser and Wlezien (2005) analyze only a subset of the countries in our sample, but most of them – the United Kingdom, Germany, Ireland, and France – exhibit declining economic voting in our analysis.

vote for any particular case into four additive parts: an overall mean, a country-specific effect, a time-specific effect, and a residual effect that is particular to the specific case. By treating the last three of these effects as random draws from appropriate zero-mean distributions, we can estimate the respective variances of these distributions and so get an indication of how much of the total variation in the economic vote is accounted for by differences in country means, differences in temporal means, and factors associated with specific surveys.[9] This is useful because it will immediately tell us whether explanatory variables that are constant within countries, constant across countries, or variable over time and across countries are most likely to account for the total variation in economic voting that we observe.

Our estimate of the total variation in the *economic vote of the chief executive* across all cases is .066.[10] Thirty-one percent is accounted for by variation in country means, 13 percent by variation in yearly means, and 56 percent by survey-specific variation. To put it another way, if we could identify variables to account for 100 percent of the variance in economic voting, then we would expect slightly more than half of the explanatory power to come from variables that vary from survey to survey (e.g., the extent of electoral competition, clarity of responsibility, and many others), slightly less than a third of the explanatory power to come from variables that vary across countries but are relatively constant over time – at least for the time period covered in our data (e.g., trade openness, size of the government sector, and number of parties in competition), and about 13 percent from variables that are constant across countries but vary over time (e.g., secular trend variables).

This section demonstrated that the *economic vote of the chief executive* is a reasonable measure of our concept of economic voting – at least insofar as its magnitude and variation are quite consistent with existing findings in the literature. We pointed to a number of interesting patterns in this variation that we hope to explain in the subsequent chapters. And,

[9] These numbers come from a variance components model (estimated using Stata 9.0's xtmixed function) in which the dependent variable is the *economic vote of the chief executive*, there are no covariates in the model, and the grouping of observations is by country and by year. Specifically, we assume $y_{it} = \alpha + \mu_i + \tau_t + v_{it}$, where α is the mean of y_{it}, μ_i is a random effect for country i, τ_t is a random effect for year t, and v_{it} is the remaining survey-specific effect. The estimates reported in the text are simply the estimated variances of the three different error components. The method is described in Goldstein, Browne, and Rasbash (2002).

[10] This is simply the sum of the estimated variances from the model in the last note.

finally, by estimating how the total variation in the *economic vote of the chief executive* gets parsed into its three different components, we provided an indication of the type of theoretical variables that might be most powerful in explaining this variation. Recall from Chapter 2 that there are alternative plausible measures of the economic vote. This raises the possibility that the contextual variation we have just described might be dependent on our choice of this particular measure of the economic vote – that is, the *economic vote of the chief executive*. In the next section, we examine whether these descriptions of variation in economic voting are independent of the particular measure of the economic vote employed.

ALTERNATIVE MEASURES OF THE OVERALL ECONOMIC VOTE

In Chapter 2, we discussed two alternative ways of measuring the amount of overall economic voting in an election – the *volatility of the economic vote* and the *economic vote of the government*. As we pointed out in that discussion, there are good theoretical reasons to focus on the *economic vote of the chief executive* as our summary measure of overall economic voting (rather than these other measures). Still, it is certainly worth examining how closely related these different measures are, if only to know whether our results are likely to be dependent on the choice of measure.

The measure of the *volatility of the economic vote* discussed in Chapter 2 tells us how much party support would "change hands" as a result of worsening economic perceptions.[11] Figure 3.5 presents a histogram of the *volatility of the economic vote* for our 163 voting studies. Worsening economic perceptions produce, on average, about seven percentage points of electoral volatility (the median is also seven percentage points). This suggests that in a typical election in our sample of democracies, variations in economic evaluations will generate total shifts in support for political parties that amount to approximately seven percentage points. This is consistent with Blais et al. (2004), who generate a similar estimate of economic-vote volatility, although for a much smaller sample of countries – eleven surveys conducted in Britain, Canada, and the United States. They estimate a mean overall economic vote volatility of 6 percent (a median of 5 percent).

[11] For example, in the 1984 Danish election study, we estimated economic vote effects of 13.4 percent for the Socialists; −6.5 for the Conservatives; −5.8 for the Liberals; −.8 for the Center Party; and −.3 for the Radicals. The sum of the absolute value of these is 26.9. This sum divided by 2 gives a *Volatility* score of 13.5 for the 1984 Danish election study.

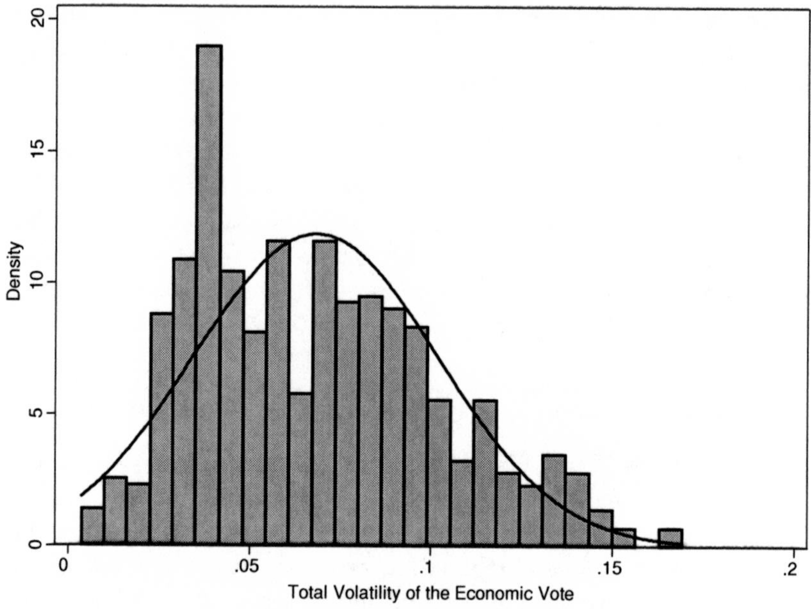

Figure 3.5. Volatility of the economic vote.

In the empirical analyses in subsequent chapters, we use the *economic vote of the chief executive* when we need a measure of the overall level of economic voting in an election, rather than the *volatility of the economic vote*. The main disadvantage of the *volatility* measure, as we pointed out earlier, is that it treats all changes in support caused by changes in economic perceptions as equal evidence *for* economic voting – including changes in support that are "wrong-signed" and would (in our other measures) count *against* economic voting (e.g., improvements in the vote of a chief executive when economic perceptions worsen). Nevertheless, both of these variables could be used as a summary measure of the overall magnitude of the economic vote, and so we would like to know how closely they track one another.

Figure 3.6 summarizes the extent to which our measures of the economic vote track one another. We begin with *volatility* and the *economic vote of the chief executive*. The upper-left panel of Figure 3.6 shows a scatterplot of the *economic vote of the chief executive* against the *volatility of the economic vote*, and it confirms that there is indeed a close relationship between these two measures. By construction, the *economic vote of the chief executive* can never be larger than *volatility*, which accounts for the scatterplot's V-shape. The left boundary of the

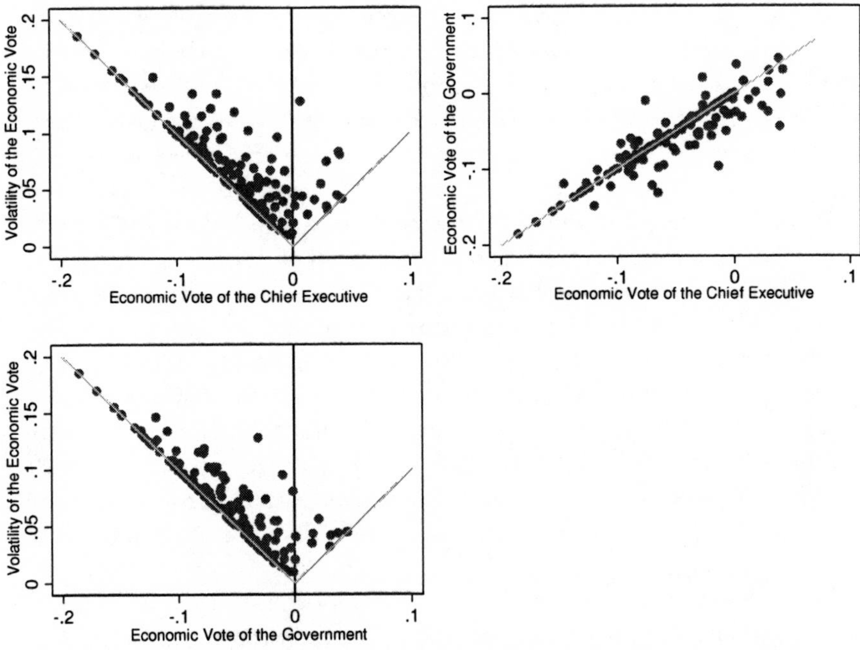

Figure 3.6. Alternative measures of the overall economic vote.

V-shape represents two-party cases in which *economic vote of the chief executive* necessarily equals *volatility*. Although there are relatively few cases, occurrences of positive values of the *economic vote of the chief executive* attenuate the correlation between *volatility* and the *economic vote of the chief executive* because these cases get treated differently in the two measures. In the case of the *economic vote of the chief executive*, they count as evidence of little or no economic voting. However, in the case of the *volatility* measure, positive estimates of the *economic vote of the chief executive* are treated the same (in terms of their weight in the overall measure) as negative estimates of the same size. Consequently, these estimates increase the overall *volatility* score. For the arguments we test in subsequent chapters, it makes more sense to treat positive values of the *economic vote of the chief executive* as evidence against economic voting and, hence, we favor the *economic vote of the chief executive* as our dependent variable.[12]

[12] The R^2 from a simple bivariate regression of *economic vote of the chief executive* against the *volatility of the economic vote* is .5 with a slope coefficient of −.88.

Another alternative measure of overall economic voting is the *economic vote of the government*. Recall from the previous chapter that the most common measure of the *economic vote of the government* that is used in the literature is the sum of the economic votes for each of the cabinet parties.[13] For those countries with single-party governments, this measure will be the same as the *economic vote of the chief executive*. However, differences will occur for those studies in which the incumbent government consists of multiple parties. In these cases, we naturally would expect the sum of the economic vote for each party in the government to be larger (i.e., more negative) than the *economic vote of the chief executive*. However, because the estimates for many cabinet partner parties can be "wrong-signed," this need not be the case. The upper-right panel in Figure 3.6 plots the *economic vote of the government* against the *economic vote of the chief executive*. The graph reveals that (as a result of many "wrong-signed" estimates for cabinet partner parties) variation around the 45 percent line is more symmetric than one might otherwise guess and so there seems to be a fairly good fit between the measures for our estimates. Likewise, the corresponding comparison between the *economic vote of the government* and *volatility* in the bottom-left panel is quite similar to the one directly above it. Furthermore, the similarity between the *economic vote of the chief executive* and the *economic vote of the government* in these data leads to similar maps of economic voting using either concept. For example, the median (and mean) magnitude of the economic vote employing the *economic vote of the government* measure is −5 percent, which is precisely what we obtained using the *chief executive* measure (this only happens because of the surprisingly muted asymmetry in the scatterplot in the upper-right panel of Figure 3.6).

THE DISTRIBUTION OF THE ECONOMIC VOTE OVER INDIVIDUAL PARTIES

Many theoretically motivated hypotheses regarding the economic vote concern the distribution of the economic vote across political parties and, hence, are addressed by none of the three separate measures of the economic vote discussed to this point. The most basic notion of retrospective

[13] Returning to the 1984 Danish election study example, the Conservative, Liberal, and Center parties made up the incumbent coalition government at the time. Recall that we estimated their economic vote as −6.5 for the Conservatives, −5.8 for the Liberals, and −.8 for the Center Party. The sum of these three values gives the measure of the *economic vote of the government*, which is −13.

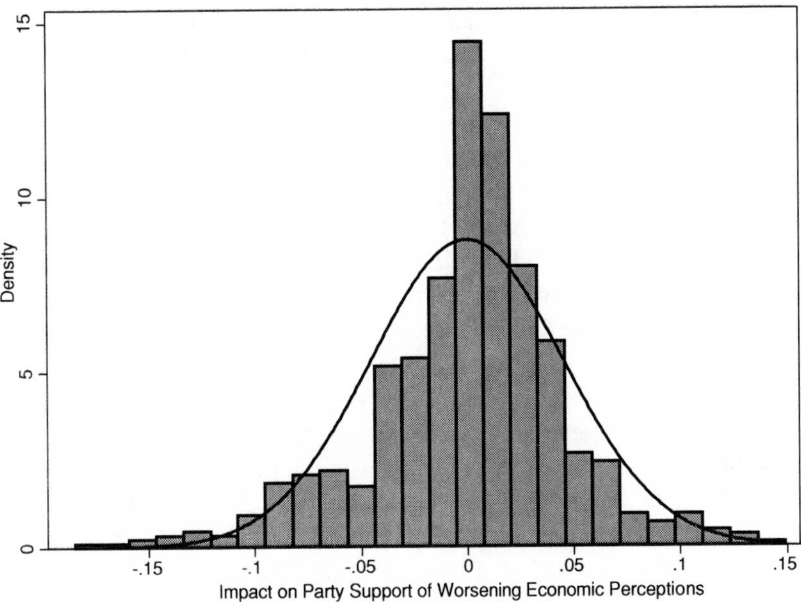

Figure 3.7. Economic vote of political parties.

economic voting suggests that the parties in power will be affected differently by the economy than those parties in opposition. And, as we describe in later chapters, theories of economic voting suggest more refined distinctions regarding the distribution of the economic vote across incumbent political parties or across opposition parties. Arguments, for example, that single out particular parties in a coalition government as being held responsible for economic outcomes (Anderson, 1995) imply that within a specific context, certain governing parties have a larger (or smaller) economic vote than others. An example might be that the prime ministerial party or the party holding the finance portfolio receives a greater economic vote than other parties in a governing coalition. Accordingly, we now describe how the economic vote varies across political parties in our sample. Again, our goal here is not only to establish that these patterns generate results consistent with the current economic voting literature but also to highlight potentially interesting theoretical insights that might result from the analysis of these distributions.

A histogram of the economic vote for each of the 678 cases in our national surveys is presented in Figure 3.7. The parties' economic votes have a normal distribution centered on zero and range from a loss of 15 percent to a gain of 15 percent support. Approximately half of the party economic votes are small, falling between plus or minus 2.5 percent. By contrast, the remaining 50 percent are greater than plus 2.5 percent or less than minus 2.5 percent. And, approximately 25 percent of the estimates are either greater than plus 5 percent or less than minus 5 percent. As we would expect, the tails of this distribution are dominated by cases from countries that tend to have single-party governments. Over half of the cases falling below −10 percent, in fact, are from the United Kingdom and over half of those falling above 10 percent are either in the United Kingdom, Ireland, or the United States.

As we noted earlier and will develop in much more detail in later chapters, arguments regarding the economic vote of political parties draw a basic distinction between the economic vote of incumbent and opposition parties. Our expectations, of course, are that the economic vote of incumbents should be in some sense the mirror image of those of the opposition parties. The box-plots in Figure 3.8 summarize the distribution of economic voting across our sample of 113 parties according to whether each party was an incumbent or in opposition at the time of the survey. Each bar summarizes the impact of a declining economy on a particular party's electoral support. Most important, the overall result is consistent with the literature: incumbents tend to get punished by a deteriorating economy, whereas opposition parties are rewarded when the economy does poorly. This is confirmed by the fact that the median vote for the incumbent parties falls below zero, whereas it falls above zero for the opposition parties. But Figure 3.8 makes quite clear that the economic vote of both types of parties varies considerably. This is evidenced by the fact that the median vote for incumbent parties varies from about −.12 to approximately .02, and for opposition parties from .12 to −.04.

Not only does the economic effect vary across these parties, but there is also considerable variation in the effect for any particular party over the period 1979–2001, and this variation holds up even when we control for incumbent status. We can illustrate this with two extreme cases identified in Figure 3.8. The economic vote of the U.K. Conservatives, when they were the prime ministerial party, ranged between −.17 and .03. And although its economic vote exhibited quite a broad range of values, it was essentially negative (with only one exception) resulting in a median economic vote of −.06. This ranks the party as having one of the strongest incumbent economic votes. The Belgium Christian Democrats, by contrast, have a much lower median incumbent economic vote of −.015, but their vote is more equally spread over both positive and negative values

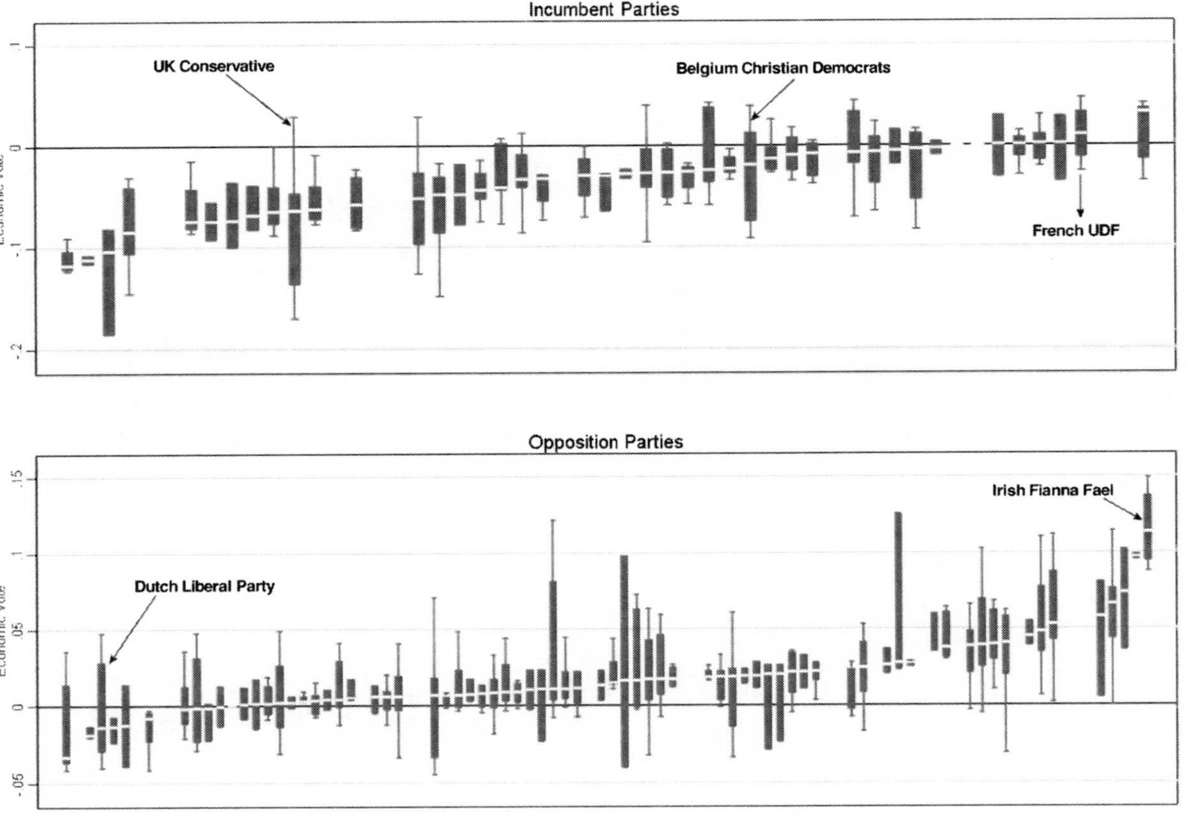

Figure 3.8. Economic vote of incumbent and opposition political parties.

(its largest economic vote is −.09 and its smallest is .04). Despite being an incumbent party, in a number of voter-preference surveys, the Belgium Christian Democrats vote probabilities increase in response to a negative evaluation of economic performance. The French UDF is even more of an anomaly in the sense that when in the governing coalition, three of its four economic votes were positive (its vote probabilities increasing in response to a negative economic evaluation); in fact, the party registered one of the most positive economic votes for an incumbent party (.05).

We see similar variation in parties' economic votes when they are in opposition. The Irish Fianna Fael has the highest economic vote of all opposition parties – its median economic vote is .11 and it ranges between .08 and .15. An example on the other extreme is the Dutch Liberal Party. The Dutch Liberal Party has one of the most negative economic votes of all opposition parties measured either by its median value of −.015 or its extreme positive value of .04. Hence, for some parties, their experiences in opposition produced both electoral rewards and punishments for perceptions of poor economic outcomes.

There are more general patterns in the plots in Figure 3.8 that speak to interesting theoretical issues. A rather significant degree of asymmetry in the incumbent versus opposition economic vote is evident from the slope of the median votes in the two figures: the median economic vote for incumbents is −3 percent, which, in absolute value terms, is almost twice as large as the 1.6 median economic vote for opposition parties. The incumbent vote change is order-of-magnitude consistent with Powell (2000), who reports that the average vote loss for government parties in his sample of 153 elections is approximately 2 percent.[14] Recall from Figure 3.5 that the modal economic vote in our sample of 678 simulated party economic votes is zero. Figure 3.8 gives some insight into which parties have no economic vote. Note that the median economic vote for opposition parties is much more concentrated around the zero line than is the case for incumbents. In a typical election, a much larger number of opposition parties is unaffected by changes in economic evaluations than is the case for incumbent parties. So, for example, when the economy deteriorates and voters abandon the incumbent parties, there are a large number of opposition parties to whom voters are not inclined to switch their vote. Why is this the case? One possible explanation is that

[14] Rose and Mackie (1983) report an average government party vote loss of 1 percent over the entire postwar period; Paldam (1986) reports an average vote loss for governing parties of 1.7 percent.

voters who are responding to bad economic performance are searching for opposition parties that are credible governing parties. There are, in fact, a number of opposition parties that are simply not serious potential governing partners, and these parties may comprise the bulk of those parties that receive no economic votes. We explore these and similar explanations in subsequent chapters.

Although it is true that, in general, incumbent parties tend to be rewarded by an improving economy and the opposition reaps the rewards of a worsening economy, there is considerable variation around this central tendency. The magnitude of this effect appears to be more pronounced among incumbent as opposed to opposition parties. And these effects are more likely to be the case for some parties than others. Moreover, controlling for their incumbent-opposition status, individual parties exhibit considerable variation in their economic vote over our twenty-two–year period – for many parties, it varies over both positive and negative values. Our contextual theory of the economic vote proposes an explanation for this variation in the economic vote of political parties.

We have now examined a number of different measures of economic voting – *the economic vote of the chief executive, the volatility of the economic vote, the economic vote of the government*, and various measures of the economic vote of individual political parties. They all indicate that economic voting is pervasive in Western democracies, although our estimates clearly vary across parties, over time, and cross-nationally. Although economic voting might be pervasive, does its importance compare favorably with other factors that shape the vote decision? We turn to this issue in the next section.

ECONOMIC VERSUS NON-ECONOMIC VOTING

The attention accorded the economy in much of the voting literature is predicated on the widely accepted notion that economic evaluations are one of the more important factors in the vote decision. Thus, whatever the magnitude of the economic vote is in absolute terms, many would argue that it outweighs other factors in the voter's decision (Alvarez, Nagler, and Willette, 2000; Lewis-Beck, 1988; Lewis-Beck and Stegmaier, 2000). In their list of stylized facts about the economic vote, Lewis-Beck and Paldam (2000) suggest that the economy accounts for about one third of the change in the vote. Much of the evidence to this effect comes from U.S. voting studies. Alvarez and Nagler (1995) find that the economy was the dominant issue shaping the 1992 vote, as does Lockerbie (1992). And

Erikson (1989) is quite categorical in arguing that in aggregate-level models, economic factors – specifically income change – outweighed other variables in predicting presidential vote. For the U.K. case, Sanders (2003b) argues, based on the analysis of Conservative Party vote data from 1974 to 1985, that economic evaluations outweigh the impact of partisanship by at least a factor of 3 to 1. Alvarez, Nagler, and Bowler (2000) suggest that in the 1987 UK elections, reprospective economic evaluations were crucial for the incumbent vote while issues played a role in shaping the opposition vote. Similar claims have been made in the comparative voting literature. In his classic treatise on economic voting, Lewis-Beck (1988: 84) concludes that "Changing economic conditions exert a force on Western European voters that approaches and sometimes exceeds the force of more traditional factors." More recent comparative data from Alvarez, Nagler, and Willette (2000) also suggested that the economy tends to weigh more heavily than other factors in the vote decision.

But does it? As we and others have pointed out, the absolute impact of the economy can be small. Indeed, many of the estimates of the economic vote in Figure 3.1 are less than 1 percent, suggesting the economy has a relatively small impact on vote-choice probabilities. For example, we estimate that the economic vote in the 1993 Canadian election was essentially zero, which comports with most accounts of the election. The failed constitutional initiatives of the Mulroney government, the introduction of federal sales tax, and opposition to NAFTA were issues that seemed to have overwhelmed evaluations of the performance of the national economy (not to mention the unpopularity of Mulroney and the disastrous election campaign undertaken by Campbell). Foreign-policy concerns can easily trump the economy, as has been pointed out by Nickelsburg and Norpoth (2000), Mueller (1970), Zaller (2004), and Bueno de Mesquita and Siverson (1995). This may well have been the case with the 2002 German parliamentary elections. Incumbent fatigue (Zaller, 2004) also can overwhelm the importance of economic evaluations – which may have been the case with the 1997 elections in the United Kingdom, in which the incumbent was defeated despite a strong national economy.[15] It also may have contributed to the very small economic vote in the 2000 U.S. presidential elections. Analyzing eleven elections from Canada, the

[15] Our 1997 estimate of the magnitude of the economic vote in the United Kingdom is the second lowest reading over the 1979–2001 sample period, which is consistent with the notion that the economy had relatively little impact on vote choice in this election.

United Kingdom, and the United States, Blais et al. (2004) suggest in fact that issues weight more heavily than the economy in the vote decision.

Clearly, then, issues matter in elections and can sometimes overwhelm economic voting in the vote decision. Still, the examples of this are largely anecdotal or based on small samples. More problematic from the perspective of the economic-voting literature would be evidence that economic evaluations systematically play a minor role in vote choice compared to other factors.

There have been efforts using comparative data to assess the importance of economic voting relative to other factors, but they have been based on small samples of countries. Michael Lewis-Beck's (1988) assessment of the importance of economic evaluations on vote is based on five national surveys, all conducted in 1984. Alvarez, Nagler, and Willette (2000) base their assessments on seven surveys (two each in the United States, the Netherlands, and Canada and one in the United Kingdom). And the Blais et al. (2004) conclusions are founded on eleven election surveys from three countries. We address this particular shortcoming here by basing our comparative assessment on 163 surveys, conducted over a twenty-two–year time period and covering eighteen nations. A variety of factors typically competes for the voter's attention in any particular election campaign. We are simply interested in those competing factors that are most prevalent in the vote calculus and have persisted over time. Accordingly, we explore two factors that meet these criteria: ideology and issues.

Ideology

There is widespread agreement that voters in most developed democracies employ the left-right continuum to organize the political landscape (Fuchs and Klingemann, 1989; Huber and Gabel, 2000; Laver and Budge, 1992). And there is extensive evidence supporting spatial models of vote choice (Enelow and Hinich, 1984; Hinich and Munger, 1997). Hence, movements along the left-right continuum either by voters or by the parties will affect the spatial distance between voters and candidates and, in turn, the voters' support of political parties. In fact, the comparative voting literature offers considerable support for the notion that ideology represents one of the most powerful predictors of vote choice (Dalton, 2002; Franklin et al., 1992).

Accordingly, we compare the impact of left-right self-placement on party support with our estimate of economic voting, employing an estimation strategy similar to the one described in the previous chapter. Most of the studies in our sample employ a ten-unit scale for left-right self-placement that ranges from 1 for most left to 10 for most right. However, in the U.S. national election survey, ideology is typically calibrated with a liberal-conservative self-identification measure. For comparative purposes, we have mapped the U.S. liberal-conservative scale onto a ten-point left-right scale. Fluctuations in the ideological self-placement of the mass public are quite modest. The overall mean left-right score of the 145 studies including this variable is 5.4, with a standard deviation of study means of about 0.4. Within each country, the standard deviation for these series ranges between .11 and .32 and the mean ranges between 4.6 and 5.9. The maximum range of the study mean scores within any country is approximately 1 unit (Belgium, Denmark, United Kingdom, and Spain experience a range of values close to 1), although the typical range is about half a unit.[16] Hence, from one election to the next, the maximum swing in ideological preferences of the electorate typically would not exceed half a unit.

To assess the relative importance of left-right self-identification in shaping voting intention, we estimate a model of the vote for the *chief executive* party that includes both left-right self-placement and retrospective economic evaluations. We estimated a separate model for each of the 145 surveys (from our overall sample of 163) that included a measure of left-right self-identification. The dependent variable in the model is the dichotomous *chief executive* party-vote measure (coded 1 for those supporting the incumbent *chief executive* party), which was described in the previous chapter.[17] *Ideology* is measured employing the de-meaned (employing the survey mean) left-right self-placement of the voter (coded so higher numbers indicate a more right-leaning voter). We employ the same dummy variables measuring retrospective perceptions of the national economy

[16] The other component of spatial models, candidates for political office, also exhibit very stable positioning on the left-right scale. As Poole and Rosenthal (1997) point out, ideological shifts in the Republican and Democratic parties tend to be very gradual. And, as Alvarez and Nagler (1995) suggest in their analysis of the 1992 presidential elections, candidates did not have much of an electoral incentive to shift their ideological positioning. European political parties also exhibit similar stability in their left-right placements (Budge, 1994).

[17] The model estimations are similar to those described in Chapter 2, except that instead of estimating the full MNL model, we simply use a logit estimation and we employ a dichotomous dependent variable for whether or not the party choice is the Chief Executive party. As we show in Chapter 5, this simplification gives results that are virtually identical to the MNL model estimation.

that was utilized for generating economic-voting effects: *Worse*, which equals one if voters thought the economy had gotten worse in the last year; *Better*, which equals one if they thought the economy had gotten better; and *Same*, which equals one if they thought the economy had stayed the same. Two of these, *Better* and *Worse*, were included in the individual-level model. Clearly, we expect these two dummy variables to have opposite signs, with *Worse* being negative and *Better* being positive.

To estimate the impact of ideology on vote choice, we employ the coefficients estimated from each of these 145 individual samples. We begin by estimating a predicted vote for the incumbent with left-right self-placement set to 0 and the *Better* and *Worse* dummies set to 0. We then shift the value of left-right self-placement by 0.5 (the two economic evaluation variables are set to 0 in this simulation, implying a neutral evaluation of the economy) to generate an estimate of the predicted incumbent vote when the sample is made 0.5 unit more conservative.[18] For each sample, we then calculate the difference in the predicted incumbent vote by subtracting the base prediction from that of the more conservative sample. This resulted in 145 simulated effects of a .5 unit shift in the left-right self-identification variable.[19]

Figure 3.9 presents a histogram of the 145 predicted changes in the probability of voting for the chief executive party that results from a change in ideology. This is the absolute value of change in the vote probabilities because, of course, the direction of the predicted change would be a function of the incumbent chief executive party's ideology. The ideology result is very similar to the estimated *economic vote of the chief executive*. In the case of a 0.5 unit change in left-right identification, chief executive party vote shifts, on average, about four percentage points. This compares to our estimate of 5 percent for the *economic vote of the chief executive*.

Ideology is generally considered to be one of the most important factors shaping the voting decisions. As a result, the impact of ideology on party vote probabilities serves as an ideal metric against which to compare our estimate of the economic vote. Our assessments are quite favorable to the notion that economic performance is one of the most important factors shaping voting decisions. The typical shift in voter left-right sentiment

[18] As a benchmark, Lewis-Beck (1988: 84), in comparing the ideology effect to the economic-vote effect, shifts the ideology score 3 units (from 9 to 6), which is six times the magnitude of our simulation and, reassuringly, obtains results approximately seven times the magnitude of ours (an average shift of about 30 percentage points).

[19] The simulated effects and their standard errors were generated using Clarify as described in King, Tomz, and Jason Wittenberg (2000).

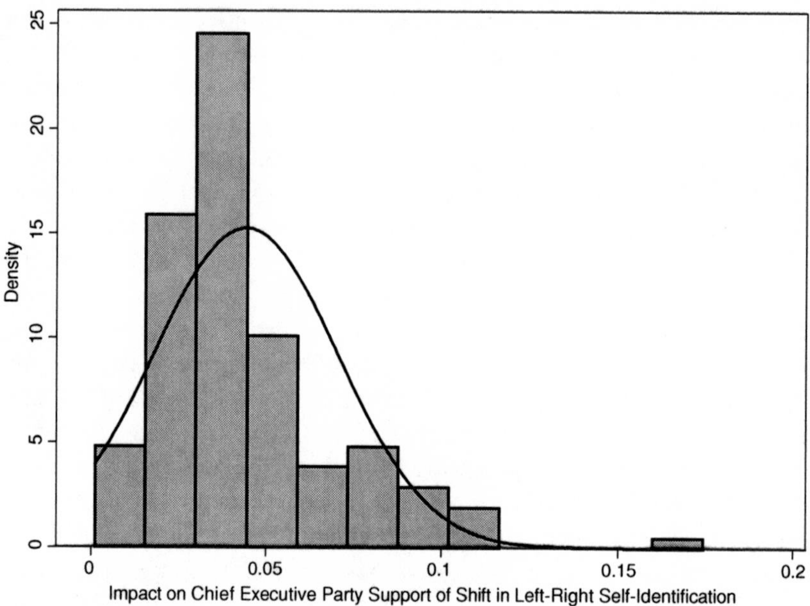

Figure 3.9. Ideological vote for chief executive party.

results in a median change in vote probabilities on the order of 4 percent, which is very similar to the 5 percent effect we estimate for shifts in economic evaluations.

Issues

To test the relative importance of issues, we draw on the postmaterialism items developed by Inglehart (1977). Although hardly a perfect measure (Duch and Taylor, 1993; Duch and Strom, 2004), the concept has the virtue of being included in large numbers of voter surveys. The questionnaire items making up this construct are asked over the entire time period of our study and in 105 of the European studies in our sample.[20] These items are designed to measure the extent to which respondents prioritize different political goals and, in this respect, they are a plausible proxy for the issue preferences of voters. The standard battery of questions asks respondents to indicate which of the following four political goals they would rank as a first and second priority: (1) maintaining order in the

[20] The postmaterialism question was, for the most part, not included in vote-choice studies conducted in non-European countries.

nation, (2) giving the people more say in important political decisions, (3) fighting rising prices, and (4) protecting freedom of speech. Respondents selecting two "postmaterialist" items (items 2 and 4) are coded 3; those selecting two materialist items (items 1 and 3) are coded 1; respondents selecting a mix of materialist and postmaterialist items are coded 2. This construct is widely used in comparative voting studies – particularly in Western Europe – and has been shown to be strongly correlated with vote choice (see Franklin et al., 1992; Kitschelt, 1994). Postmaterialism, like the left-right measure, does not vary significantly over time – the overall standard deviation for country means is about .21 and the maximum variation across studies within any country is on the order of .75 unit. Again, given this relatively modest dynamic variation, we do not expect typical fluctuations in this particular indicator of policy preferences to have a significantly higher impact on vote choice than economic evaluations.

We estimated a model of vote choice that included the same variables as the ideology equations described here, with the addition of the postmaterialism indicator. Following the same strategy that we employed in the case of ideology, we simulated the impact of postmaterialism on vote probabilities by varying the postmaterialism measure in each country from a value of 1.75 to a value of 2.5. Again, this strikes us as a very conservative strategy for assessing the relative impact of postmaterialist issues given the over-time stability of this measure. Figure 3.10 reports the results for these simulations across our sample of European countries. The effect over the 105 samples ranges from 0 to 12 percent, with the distribution clearly skewed toward a very small effect (the simulated effect in about 15 percent of the studies was less than 1 percent). The median-vote probability shift across the surveys we sampled here is slightly less than 4 percent (the mean is 4 percent). It is quite clear that fluctuations in postmaterialism certainly are no more important than the economy in vote choice and likely have somewhat less weight in the voter-choice function.

There are conflicting claims regarding the importance of the economy, relative to other issue concerns, in the typical vote decision. In this section, we provide some insight into the relative importance of the economic vote. Working within the constraints of the common questions included in our 163 voter-preference surveys, we examine the relative impact of two factors that likely compete with the economy for consideration by the voter: ideology and postmaterialism values. Although both of these variables have an important impact on the vote choice, in neither case is

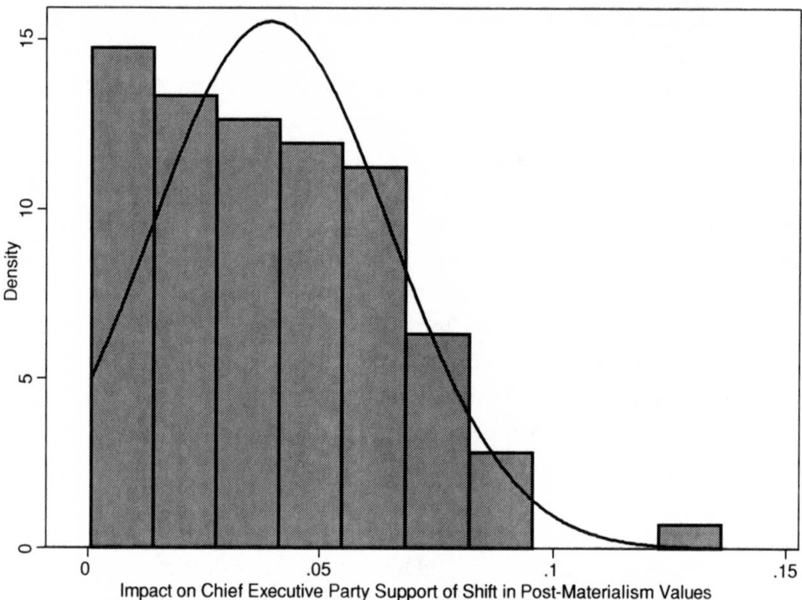

Figure 3.10. Postmaterialism vote for chief executive party.

their impact more important than the economy. At best, these two other considerations have an impact that is similar in magnitude to the economic vote.

SUMMARY

Yes, the conventional wisdom among politicians, political pundits, media personalities, and even academics is that the economy matters when it comes to voting decisions. And even the most casual students of politics would seem to believe that this phenomenon is ubiquitous across the developed democracies. But, surprisingly, the cross-national evidence of the widespread impact of the economy on the party preferences of voters is rather limited. We have assembled a body of evidence that spans a relatively large number of countries (eighteen) and an extensive time period (1979–2001) to provide what we believe is definitive evidence in favor of the conventional wisdom. Yes, there is economic voting in developed democracies. How much economic voting? It varies, of course, but we situate the median impact of economic evaluations on the vote probabilities of parties in an election between 5 and 7 percent, depending on the way we measure it. Moreover, this impact stacks up quite well against other plausible factors that might sway voter preferences for competing political parties. We estimate that a typical change in left-right sentiment (.5 unit) or in postmaterialist values (.75 unit) both shift support for incumbent parties by about 4 percent, slightly less than the mean size of our estimated economic vote.

An equally important goal of this chapter is to demonstrate that there are interesting patterns of variation in this economic vote. The overall picture of contextual variation in the economic vote confirms the general patterns that others have observed – for example, relative rankings of countries (the United Kingdom tends to have more economic voting than the Netherlands) and temporal trends (a recent moderation in the magnitude of the economic vote). This provides face validity for the particular measure of the economic vote that we have adopted in this book.

The extent to which the economic vote varies becomes even more evident once we dig a bit deeper and examine over-time variation within countries. Here, we see examples of a large economic vote in the early 1980s dwindling to virtually no economic voting in 2000 (e.g., Ireland and Germany) or just the opposite (Denmark, for example, where we see economic voting increasing in recent years). We also see examples of economic voting rising and falling over time, or vice versa, such as in the United Kingdom, Spain, and the Netherlands. Unlike most other treatments, we drill down even further and examine the economic vote of each of the political parties. At this level, there are myriad interesting variations: the Dutch Liberal Party, for example, which, when in opposition, frequently gets punished for perceptions of poor economic performance; or the French UDF party that, despite being a member of the governing coalition, rarely is punished for poor economic performance.

Our expectation is that these contextual variations in the overall economic vote and in economic voting for political parties are not just random fluctuations. Rather, we suggest they are the result of instrumentally rational voters responding to features of the political and economic context that also vary over time. The contextual theory we develop in later chapters identifies those contextual features that voters respond to and, hence, that condition the magnitude of their economic vote.

4

Estimation, Measurement, and Specification

The evidence presented in the previous chapter established that economic voting in the world's advanced democracies is both pervasive and variable. The goal of the rest of this book is to identify the political and economic contexts that explain that variation. To do so, we develop a contextual theory of rational retrospective economic voting that points to specific kinds of political and economic institutions as the likely sources of cross-national and temporal variation in economic voting. However, before we make the effort to develop that theory and test its implications, we need first to establish that the variation in our estimates of economic voting described in the last chapter cannot be explained away as an artifact of the empirical methods we have employed to generate them. Three general methodological issues are of concern here: the choice of statistical models, measurement decisions, and model specification. We begin with an explanation of the two main statistical methods we use to conduct the empirical analysis in this and subsequent chapters. We then proceed to analyze our data to determine whether our estimated variation in the economic vote is an artifact of our particular statistical models, measurement choices, or specification decisions.

Two Methods for Exploring the Sources of Contextual Variation in the Economic Vote

In this section, we introduce two general empirical methodologies for testing hypotheses about the impact of contextual variables on individual-level behavioral relationships: The first is a one-stage approach in which the individual-level data from multiple contexts (in our case, voter-preference surveys) are pooled and the impact of context is estimated simultaneously with the individual behavioral relationships of interest.

The other method is a two-stage approach in which the strength of a behavioral relationship is first estimated in each context and then these estimates (in our case, the estimates of economic voting that were presented in the previous chapter) become the dependent variable in second-stage analyses in which the independent variables are measured features of context. The methods have different strengths and weaknesses but, as Bowers and Drake (2005) have argued, they complement one another well and so are best used together.[1] In the empirical chapters that follow, we do just that.

We begin with the observation that our data – multiple individual-level surveys on vote choice and retrospective economic perceptions – can be represented as a hierarchical, multilevel structure with two levels, where level-1 units are individuals (i.e., the respondents in each of the election studies) and level-2 units are the surveys themselves. Since each survey corresponds to a particular country and time point (i.e., the date the survey was administered), this structure allows for variation in the individual behavioral relationship between economic perceptions and vote choice across countries and over time. For illustrative purposes, we focus on how one can model contextual influences on the *economic vote of the chief executive*, but the discussion here applies equally well to all the other concepts of economic voting discussed in Chapter 2, except *general economic voting*.[2] A general representation of the multilevel structure of the data could be written using a logit link function, as follows:

$$v_{ik} \sim Bin(\pi_{1ik})$$
$$logit(\pi_{1ik}) = \beta_{0k} + \beta_{1k}X_{ik} + \phi_1 Z_{ik} \quad (4.1)$$

In this notation, *Bin* is the binomial distribution and v_{ik} indicates a vote for the chief executive by voter i in survey k. X_{ik} are retrospective economic evaluations measured at the individual level and Z_{ik} are other characteristics of individuals that shape vote choice. The vector of coefficients that describes economic voting in any particular survey is β_{1k}, and this (as well as the other coefficients) is allowed to vary from survey to survey. If we

[1] For a more detailed description and comparison of these two approaches, see Duch and Stevenson (2005).

[2] As we noted there, because the *general economic vote* vector has different (and different numbers of) parties for each case, these cannot be combined into a sensible pooled analysis without first defining a different concept of economic voting (e.g., economic vote for the prime minister or government) that makes the different cases conceptually comparable.

think that economic voting is conditioned on known contextual variables that vary over the surveys (i.e., the level-2 units), then we can include measures of these contexts in this general model as interactions.

$$
\begin{aligned}
&v_{ik} \sim Bin(\pi_{1ik}) \\
&logit(\pi_{ik}) = \beta_{0k} + \beta_1 C_k + \beta_{2k} X_{ik} + \beta_3 X_{ik} C_k + \phi_1 Z_{ik} \qquad (4.2)
\end{aligned}
$$

where C_k are contextual variables measured at the survey level. By making different assumptions about the sources and nature of variation in the coefficients in this equation, we produce different specifications that are best estimated using different methods. We use two different strategies for filling out the specification of the model in equation (4.2) and estimating its parameters. Both allow the coefficients describing the economic vote at the individual level to vary systematically as a function of C_k but do not assume this is the only source of variation in the coefficients.[3] One of these produces estimates of the individual-level relationships and the contextual effects in a single step, whereas the other strategy uses two steps to estimate the contextual effects.

One-Stage Strategy

The one-stage strategy pools the data from all the surveys and assumes that, conditional on C_k, variation in the parameters across surveys can be described by a normal distribution. Consequently, estimating variation in the parameters reduces to estimating the parameters of this normal distribution. Specifically, the model assumes that:

$$
\begin{aligned}
&v_{ik} \sim Bin(\pi_{1ik}) \\
&logit(\pi_{ik}) = \beta_{0k} + \beta_{1k} X_{ik} + \phi_1 Z_{ik} \qquad (4.3) \\
&\beta_{0k} = \gamma_{00} + \gamma_{01} C_k + \omega_{0k} \qquad (4.4) \\
&\beta_{1k} = \gamma_{10} + \gamma_{11} C_k + \omega_{1k} \qquad (4.5) \\
&\begin{bmatrix} \omega_{0k} \\ \omega_{1k} \end{bmatrix} \sim N(0, \Omega), \quad \Omega = \begin{bmatrix} \sigma^2_{\omega 0} & \sigma_{\omega 0, \omega 1} \\ \sigma_{\omega 0, \omega 1} & \sigma^2_{\omega 1} \end{bmatrix} \qquad (4.6)
\end{aligned}
$$

[3] An approach that we do not discuss explicitly in this section is the "interactive" model in which the coefficients in equation (4.2) are considered fixed parameters that do not vary randomly over contexts. Essentially, this model assumes that C_k captures all the relevant contextual variation in the parameters. Because interactive models are nested in the alternative multilevel models we discuss, we do not deal with them separately.

This specification only allows for variation in the intercept and the coefficients on economic perceptions, but variation in the coefficients on Z could also be included.[4] Models such as this one are quickly becoming standard in political science (see Snijders and Bosker, 1999, for a good introduction) and are usually estimated using either Bayesian simulation or a quasi-likelihood method developed by Goldstein (1995).[5] The most important feature of the model, for the purposes of this project, is that the estimates of γ_{01} and γ_{11} and their associated standard errors provide direct tests of the impact of measured contextual factors on economic voting. The model does not assume, however, that the measured contextual factors represented by C_k are the only source of variation in the economic vote parameter, β_{1k}. Instead, additional random variation in the parameters is allowed but is assumed to follow a normal distribution.

These distributional assumptions are most helpful in describing individual-level relationships when one has a small number of cases for some of the surveys. In these cases, the estimates of the $\beta_k' s$, for these low-observation surveys "borrow strength" from the other surveys, which (by assumption) arise from the same distribution. Specifically, when information in a survey is sparse, the estimated coefficients for that unit "shrink" toward the estimate one would get from the pooled sample. In the most extreme case, in which some survey had no data at all, this shrinkage would be complete and the estimated coefficient for the case with no data would just be the pooled estimate. In contrast, when there is an abundance of individual-level data in each survey, little information from other surveys may be necessary for precise estimation, and so the individual survey estimates will borrow little from others. Our case resembles the latter one in which there are relatively numerous individual-level data in each survey and, hence, we would not expect much reliance on the pooled sample.

Because the data are pooled in the one-stage strategy, we need to include the same variables (measured in the same way) in the voting model for each survey. With respect to the core variables in the economic-vote equation – vote choice (v_{ik}) and economic perceptions (X_{ik}) – this is not a constraint: we could not estimate the economic voting effect without these two core variables and, as described in Chapter 2, we only included surveys in our study that had comparable vote-choice and perceptions questions.

4 Over- or underdispersion in the individual-level binomial variation can be included at the cost of estimating one additional parameter. The models we estimate include this parameter and test for over- or underdispersion.

5 We use Goldstein's method as implemented in the program Mlwin 2.0.

However, the requirement that the control variables, Z_{ik}, be measured in exactly the same fashion in all the individual-level studies is more constraining.[6] In our case, this means the specification of the individual-level vote-choice model can include only a very limited number of control variables and may necessarily exclude some variables known to be important in specific cases.[7] Later in this chapter, we explore whether our estimates of the influence of contextual variables on economic voting are impacted by estimating a pooled model that excludes possible important confounding variables.

Two-Stage Strategy

An alternative strategy for estimating contextual effects begins with the estimates of the economic vote described in Chapter 3. Recall that these were based on 163 individual-level vote-choice models that took the general form of Equation (4.2).[8] We can use these estimates in a second-stage statistical analysis to test hypotheses about the impact of specific measured contextual variables on economic voting.[9] We do this using "second-stage" regressions of the following general form:

$$EV_k = \alpha_0 + \alpha_1 C_k + \upsilon_k \tag{4.7}$$

where EV_k is, for example, our estimate of the *economic vote of the chief executive* from Chapter 3. Similar equations could be written for

[6] One can imagine pooling data that have different variables in the voting model for each survey by including a large number of interaction terms that activate a particular variable only for the case or cases in which it is appropriate. With five control variables and fifteen countries, this would mean including seventy-five such dummy variables in the model. The practical difficulty of estimating such a model with the thousands of individual cases in the pooled data led us to use alternative methods.

[7] An alternative option is to restrict the pooled data set to those studies that have similarly measured υ_{ik} and X_{ik} and have a full set of similarly measured control variables Z_{ik}. This effectively restricts the estimation of contextual effects to those individual surveys that were designed explicitly to have the same set of variables. An example is Hellwig (2001), who estimates pooled economic vote model employing the CSES studies. This enabled the author to estimate fully specified vote-choice models, although at the cost of including only nine surveys.

[8] For ease of explanation, equation (4.3) is a logit but our estimates generated here were generated from a Multinomial Logit; however, the multilevel structure would be the same.

[9] Jusko and Shively (2005) show that in the case in which the first-stage estimates are coefficients from a linear regression, the coefficients on the contextual variables are consistent.

our estimates of the other concepts of economic voting discussed in Chapter 2.[10]

The "data" that we use for the dependent variable in the second-stage model are the estimates of economic voting obtained in the first stage, so this analysis must account for the uncertainty of these estimates. The common procedure for doing this is to weight the second-stage analysis by the inverse of the standard error of the estimates of the dependent variable. However, as Lewis and Linzer (2005) show, this procedure can produce incorrect estimates of uncertainty because it treats all of the second-stage error as if it came from estimation uncertainty, when, in fact, some of it is inherent to the stochastic process governing the second stage. Lewis provides a weighting procedure that produces appropriate standard errors, but he suggests (and his Monte Carlo results show) that using standard errors that are robust to unspecified forms of heteroskedasticity is almost always as good. Given this (and because we must combine this correction with others discussed later), we adopt the latter procedure.

Another challenge for our second-stage analyses is that our data often include the same party in different surveys. Because we might expect the size of the economic vote for the same party across studies to be correlated (even conditional on a well-specified set of covariates), we need to allow for this in the second-stage estimation. We do so by grouping the data (by party, in this case) and calculating standard errors that allow for an unspecified pattern of correlation within groups, while assuming that there is no correlation across groups. The resulting standard errors, when combined with the correction in the last paragraph, simply allow for unspecified forms of heteroskedasticity across surveys, correlation between surveys when the party included is the same, and no correlation otherwise. These corrections are now commonly used in political science and can be implemented easily with standard statistical packages.[11] Once these corrections are made, we test hypotheses about context by examining the estimates of α_1 from equations of the general form given in (4.7).[12]

We rely primarily on the two-stage estimation method for presenting our empirical results (although, for comparative purposes, each of the

[10] This equation is intended to be general. The actual specification of the second-stage models could take a variety of forms.

[11] We implement this strategy using Stata 9.0's robust and cluster options.

[12] This discussion is intended to be general. The model specifications that we employ are all of this general form but vary according to the hypothesis being tested.

following empirical chapters also includes a one-stage pooled hierarchical model for all of the main results). An obvious question is whether the distribution of contextual variation described in Chapter 3 is sensitive to employing a one- versus a two-stage estimation strategy. Given our relatively large and diverse sample, we can assess whether there are any significant differences associated with employing one or the other of these approaches. We can also examine whether the variation we described in Chapter 3 is sensitive to the measurement and model specification decision we have adopted. We now turn to these empirical analyses.

ESTIMATION EFFECTS

Within the comparative economic-voting literature, the strategies adopted for estimating the economic vote, at the individual level, are quite diverse. The previous section describes one of the more important estimation decisions that need to be made in comparative efforts of this nature. But there are a number of other important estimation choices that we had to make, and these may not necessarily be the choices others would entertain. Accordingly, in this section we review the most important estimation decisions we made and assess whether our choice of specific strategies has implications for the results we described in Chapter 3.

One-Stage versus Two-Stage Strategy

The previous section described two different approaches for measuring the economic vote. The patterns of contextual variation in the economic vote described in Chapter 3 are based on the two-stage approach that involves separate estimations from each of our 163 surveys. One could generate similar descriptions of the economic vote estimating a one-stage hierarchical multilevel model in which the individual-level data from the various surveys are pooled. To compare the two methods, we estimate (1) the economic vote obtained from each survey separately, and (2) the survey-level (or level-2) residuals of a pooled multilevel model. In order to produce the later estimates, we combined individual-level data from our 163 electoral surveys to estimate a single logistic model of the individual-level vote for or against the chief executive party. This self-reported vote was modeled as a function of economic perceptions and a much reduced set of control variables that were available in most of our surveys. However, even with this reduced set of controls, the requirement that we have a set of common control variables eliminated 14 studies so that 146 studies remain in the pooled data set. The hierarchical model we estimate is as follows:

$$logit(\pi_{ik}) = \beta_{0k} + \beta_{1k} Worse_{ik} + \beta_{2k} Better_{ik} + \phi_{1k}\text{Ideology}_{ik} + \phi_{2k}(\text{Ideology}_{ik}{}^{*}\text{CE\_Ideology}_{k}) \quad (4.8)$$

$$\beta_{0k} = \gamma_0 + \omega_{0k} \quad (4.9)$$

$$\beta_{1k} = \gamma_1 + \omega_{1k} \quad (4.10)$$

$$\beta_{2k} = \gamma_2 + \omega_{2k} \quad (4.11)$$

The usual assumption of multivariate normality of the second-level errors is also imposed. The variables included in the model are *Ideology*, which is the de-meaned (employing the survey mean) left-right self-placement of the voter (coded so higher numbers indicate a more right-leaning voter) and its interaction with a dummy variable (*CE_Ideology*) indicating whether the Chief Executive's party is a leftist party.[13] We expect then that the coefficient on left-right self-placement (*Ideology*) will be positive and its interaction with the ideology of the Chief Executive (*Ideology*CE_Ideology*) will be negative. The variable measuring retrospective perceptions of the national economy has been broken into three dummy variables: *Worse*, which equals one if the voters thought the economy had gotten worse in the last year; *Better*, which equals one if they thought the economy had gotten better; and *Same*, which equals one if they thought the economy had stayed the same. Two of these, *Better* and *Worse*, were included in the individual-level model. Clearly, we expect these two dummy variables to have opposite signs, with worse being negative and better being positive. The pooled model is thus limited to one main control variable – the ideology of the voter relative to that of the chief executive. This sparseness in specification is almost always the cost one must pay for pooling data from disparate surveys.

Having pooled the data, we estimated the hierarchical model in equation (4.8), obtaining a single set of coefficients that describe the average relationships across all the studies in the sample. All these estimates were in the expected direction and statistically significant.[14] In equation (4.8) the level-1 units are individuals, whereas the level-2 units are election

[13] In order to include as many studies as possible, we had to combine some left-right self-placement questions that gave the respondents different response options. This was done by normalizing the various scales and then using the normalized scales.

[14] We do not show the coefficients from these models here because they are not needed for this discussion. However, they are provided in Duch and Stevenson (2005).

studies.[15] In this section, we are not really interested in the estimates of the average level of economic voting across surveys (γ_1 or γ_2). Rather, we are interested in the survey-level residuals for each of the k election studies (estimates of ω_{1k} or ω_{2k}) that indicate how the impact of economic evaluations in different surveys deviates from its overall average effect. Specifically, we want to compare these to the economic-vote estimates obtained from the separate, survey by survey estimates.

In order to isolate the effect of the different estimation procedures, we estimate separate logistic regressions for each survey that mirrors the pooled, multilevel specification in equation (4.8) – the interaction term is dropped because *CE_Ideology* does not vary within election studies:

$$logit(\pi_{ik}) = \beta_0 + \beta_{1k} Worse_{ik} + \beta_{2k} Better_{ik} + \phi_{1k} \text{Ideology}_{ik} + \varepsilon_{ik} \quad (4.12)$$

We estimate this logistic model for each of the same 146 election studies included in the pooled model from equation (4.8). This generates 146 estimates of each of the β and ϕ coefficients in the model.[16] In order to compare these estimates to the estimates of the level-2 residuals from the pooled, multilevel model, we generate "survey-level residuals" for the estimated coefficient on the *worse* dummy variable:[17]

$$\psi_{1k} = \hat{\beta}_{1k} - \frac{1}{N}\sum_{k=1}^{K} \hat{\beta}_{1k} n_k \quad (4.13)$$

where n_k is the number of observations in survey k and N is the total number of observations in all the surveys. Figure 4.1 plots these survey-level residuals (on the y-axis) against the level-2 residuals from the pooled multilevel model (ω_{1k} in equation [4.10]. Figure 4.1 reveals a tight fit between the two sets of estimates (the correlation is 0.81). The slight differences in estimates that we do see in Figure 4.1 are in the direction we would expect. In Figure 4.1, we have included both a regression line for the two sets of residuals and a 45-degree line (the expectation if residuals from both models were exactly the same). The manner in which the regression

[15] One could designate a third level for country, but fixed country effects are easier to estimate simply by including country dummies and may make more sense because we probably do not think of these countries as a sample out of a large set of similar units, which is really the motivation for treating the second-level coefficients as random and estimating features of the distribution of these coefficients.

[16] We focus on the coefficient on the worse dummy variable. An examination of the better variable generates the same conclusions.

[17] To be comparable to the multilevel result, this must be the weighted mean (where sample size provides the weight).

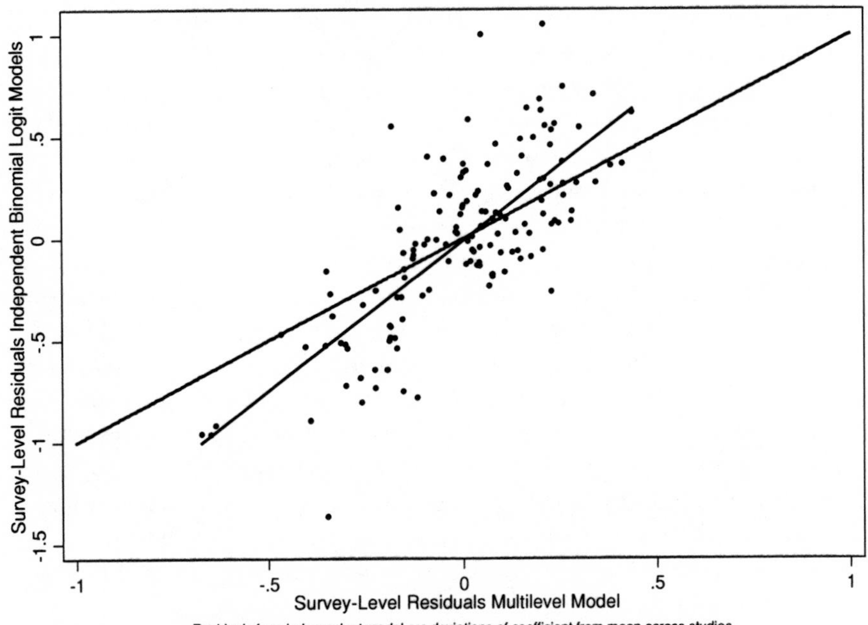

Figure 4.1. Correspondence between estimated coefficients from separate logistic models and pooled multilevel model (with identical control variables in both models).

line cuts the 45-degree line illustrates that when information in a survey is sparse, the multilevel estimated coefficients for that unit "shrink" toward the estimate one would get from the pooled sample. Hence, at the extremes, the residuals are smaller for the multilevel estimates than they are from each of the individual surveys. Overall, though, we can conclude that there is not much systematic difference between the estimates that is due to the estimation method.[18]

Multinomial Estimation

We use multinomial logistic models to estimate the coefficients of the individual-level vote-choice models from which we produce our estimates

[18] One additional difference in the specification results from the fact that in the pooled model, we did not allow random coefficients for ideology and its interaction, whereas in the separate models these coefficients are clearly unconstrained. To be sure this was not critical, we estimated this model as well, but the picture is essentially the same. We keep this presentation because the choice is inconsequential and it requires less notation.

of the economic vote. As we pointed out in Chapter 2, multinomial logistic estimates of well-specified models will give us consistent estimates of the economic-voting effects. Of course, this is not the only strategy available for estimating vote-choice models. And, over the past decade, comparative scholars have become increasingly concerned with identifying which of a number of different available estimation techniques should be employed to properly estimate multiparty vote-choice models (e.g., Alvarez and Nagler, 1998a; Quinn, Martin, and Whitford, 1999). Broadly speaking, there are three approaches that have been employed to estimate discrete vote-choice models: binomial logit models; multinomial logit models, and multinomial probit models. The debate regarding the appropriateness of these different techniques raises the possibility that the variation in our estimates of the economic vote reported in previous chapters is an artifact of the multinomial logistic estimation strategy we have adopted. Because we are in the enviable position of having a very large number of individual-level surveys, we can carefully assess, in fact, whether our estimates of economic voting vary as a function of adopting different estimation strategies.

Until relatively recently, the norm in the economic-voting literature has been to employ dichotomous measures of vote choice, estimated with binomial logit. One strategy (used, for example, by Lewis-Beck, 1988) is to dichotomize the vote choice into a vote for any party in the governing coalition versus a vote for any challenging party. A similar strategy that does not focus only on the governing parties is to estimate separate logistic models for each party, where the dependent variable is coded as a vote for or against each party in turn. Anderson (1995) employs this strategy in his comparative evaluation of economic voting in European democracies, as do Clarke et al. (2004) in their recent analysis of vote choice in the 2001 British elections. Our concern here is to understand whether adopting this binomial logistic estimation strategy results in patterns of economic voting that deviated significantly from the multinomial logit estimates summarized in Chapter 3. Accordingly, in Figure 4.2, we generated estimates from a series of binomial logit estimates for each party's vote (each dependent variable assumes a 1 for votes for the party and a 0 for votes for all other parties) and compare them to the estimates reported in Chapter 3. Clearly, the choice of a binomial or multinomial logistic estimation method is not consequential for our estimates of economic voting. Both estimation methods produce essentially identical results. The only consistent deviation is for the Greek cases: the multinomial estimates for these cases are attenuated toward zero compared to the binomial ones.

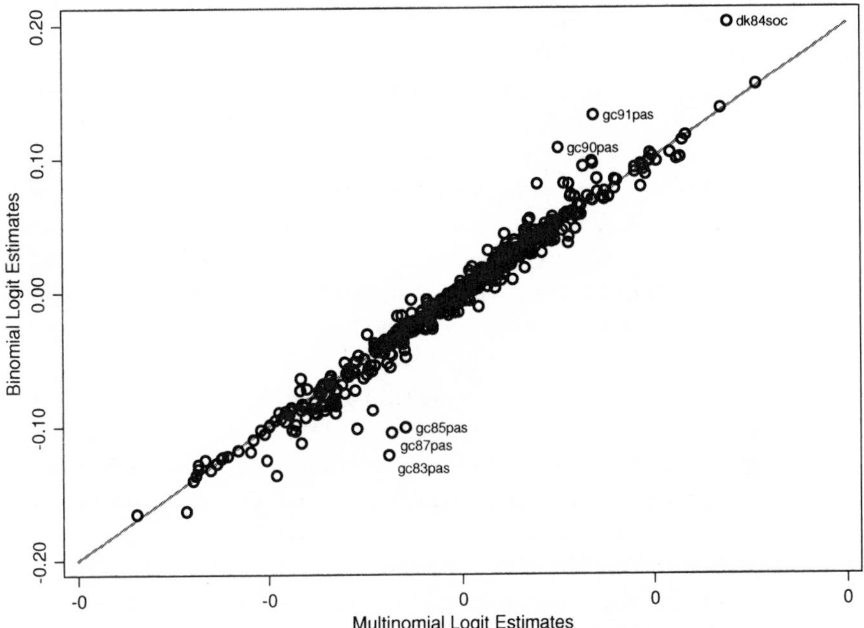

Figure 4.2. Binomial and multinomial logit estimates of economic voting for each party.

The similarity between the two estimation methods likely helps explain why our rank orderings of national average economic vote magnitudes are similar to those of Lewis-Beck (1988) and Anderson (1995), who employ binomial logit for estimating the economic vote.

Multinomial logistic estimations of discrete vote-choice models for political contexts with multiple competing parties have been criticized because the estimator assumes the independence of irrelevant alternatives (IIA). This assumption – that the addition or removal of an alternative will not change the relative selection probabilities of existing choices – seems clearly false for voting models.[19] Multinomial probit allows for a relaxation of the IIA assumption and has, accordingly, been championed by some as a preferred estimation strategy for discrete vote-choice models with multiple parties (Alvarez and Nagler, 1998a; Rudolph, 2003).

[19] The assumption implies that the introduction to the choice set of a new socialist party will not have a disproportionate impact on the votes for the existing socialist and conservative parties; that is, the new socialist party will not take a higher percentage of votes from the older socialist party than from the conservatives.

It is important to note though that the IIA assumption for multinomial logit applies *conditional* on the explanatory variables included in the model. As Train (2003) points out, ultimately a well-specified choice model that accounts for the major factors driving choice will achieve conditional independence of the errors in the value functions, which is equivalent to having IIA hold. To the extent that our multinomial logit models are well specified, we would not expect that their predicted vote probabilities would deviate significantly from those resulting from multinomial probit estimates of the same models.[20] We explore whether this is, in fact, the case by reestimating party vote probabilities for a subset of the surveys in our sample. Specifically, because estimation of the multinomial probit requires a set of alternative specific covariates, we only compare those cases in which we could use the survey data to construct a set of variables measuring the ideological distance between the respondent and each of the parties for whom they could vote.[21] In order to construct this variable, we need a measure of both respondent self-placement on the ideology scale and the placement of parties on the ideology scale. Because these ideological placement questions are infrequently included in election studies, we have a much more restricted sample size here – thirteen surveys.[22] The other variables in the model resembled those described for the fully specified economic-voting models described in Chapter 2.

Figure 4.3 provides two plots. First, we compare estimated vote probabilities from multinomial probit and the multinomial logit models that both contain ideological distance variables. Next, we show these same multinomial probit estimates (again with the ideological distance variable) plotted against estimates from a MNL model that includes left-right self-placement instead of ideological distance variables. It is clear that for these cases, the fit between the predictions is quite close, especially for those generated with the MNL model with left-right self-placement (our usual specification) and those estimated with MNP.[23] These results suggest that in the case of well-specified multinomial vote-choice models – such as the ones

[20] Our concern is only with the robustness of the predicted vote probabilities to differences in specification. We make no claims about the robustness of other quantities that might be of interest for other purposes, such as substitution patterns.

[21] We chose to use ideological distance variables rather than other alternative-specific measures because we had included a similar, nonalternative-specific measure (left-right self-placement) in each of our MNL models.

[22] For a detailed discussion of these analyses and results, see Duch, Stevenson, and May (2007).

[23] A result confirmed by Dow and Endersby (2004) in their comparison of Multinomial Probit and Multinomial Logit.

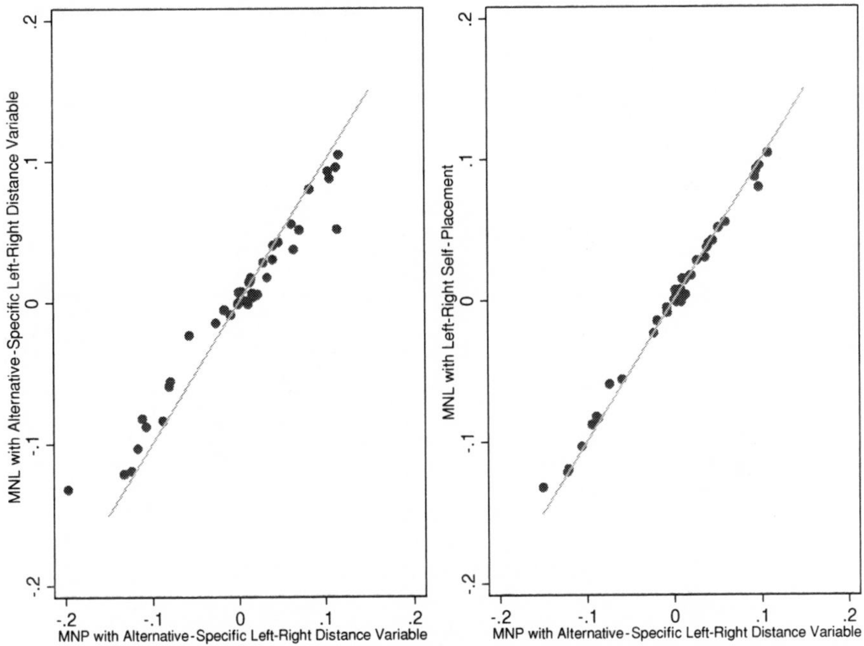

Figure 4.3. MNP and MNL estimates of economic voting for 39 parties in 13 surveys.

we employ to generate the economic votes in Chapter 3 – the predicted vote-choice probabilities generated by MNL and MNP will be very similar.

Asymmetric Economic Vote?

We arrive at our measure of economic voting by taking the coefficients from the multinomial logit estimates and calculating predicted changes in party support for a unit *decrease* in economic perceptions for each individual in the 163 surveys. These predicted changes were then averaged across each sample to generate an economic vote for each party in the country. The decision to estimate economic vote magnitudes based on worsening perceptions rather than improving perceptions was an essentially arbitrary decision on our part. Some have argued that the economic vote is asymmetric in the sense that negative economic outcomes receive more weight in the voter's value function than positive outcomes (Bloom and Price, 1975; Haller and Norpoth, 1994; Nannestad and Paldam, 1997a, 2000; Price and Sanders, 1995). This raises the possibility that our decision to base our estimated economic vote on a negative shift in economic perceptions might inflate our estimates of economic voting. Because we

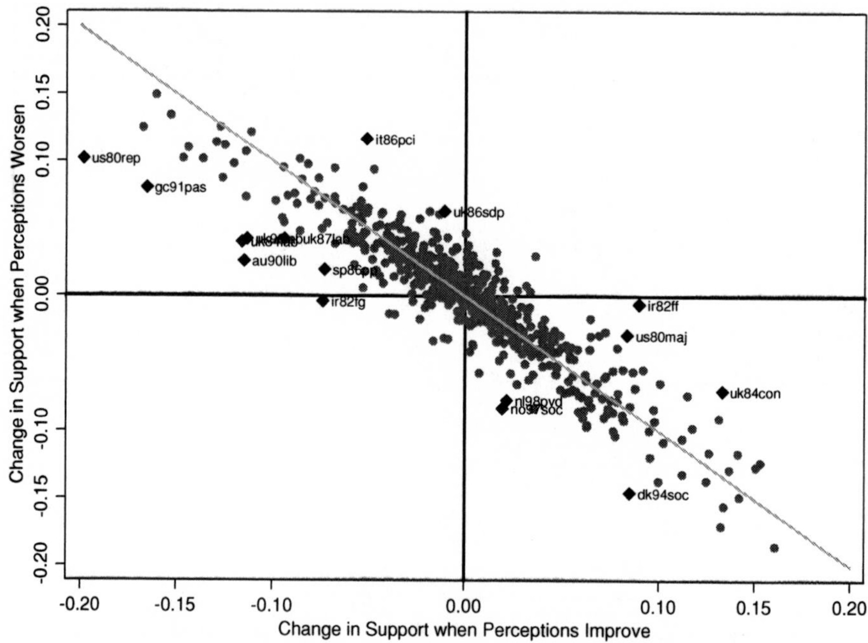

Figure 4.4. Symmetry of economic voting for each party.

used a set of dummy variables to capture perceptions in the individual models, there was nothing in the specification itself that forced our estimates of the economic vote to be the same when economic perceptions worsened or improved by the same amount. Thus, if there is asymmetry, we should see it by comparing the estimated economic vote based on a worsening perception with those based on an improving assessment.

Figure 4.4 compares economic voting for each party when economic perceptions worsen or improve by the same amount. Clearly, there is little evidence for any significant asymmetry in economic voting. This echo's the early U.S. results reported by Kiewiet (1983) and the Western European results of Lewis Beck (1988) that fail to find asymmetry in economic voting. Our results, though, represent the first challenge to this asymmetry argument at the individual level that is based on such a large set of cases.

The estimation issues treated in this section have implications that are much broader than our comparative economic-voting study. Because our project assembles a relatively large sample of individual-level surveys, we can provide a number of unique insights into these debates. First, we provide insights into strategies for estimating contextual effects in multilevel models where there are large numbers of observations for each of the second-level units (i.e., surveys). We compare a two-stage approach with a one-stage pooled strategy and find that there are almost no differences in the results that are due to the estimation approach. This result is likely due to the large number of observations we have for each of our second-level units and so *should not* be taken as evidence that the two methods would produce the same results when the number of observations for some second-level units is limited.

A prominent methodological debate among students of comparative voting behavior concerns the appropriate estimation strategies for vote-choice models in which there are more than two competing parties – hence, a multinomial-dependent variable. Again, given the nature of our sample, we can provide some insight as to whether the adoption of different limited-dependent variable-estimation techniques affects the estimated vote probabilities obtained from these different methods. We estimate party-vote probabilities (based on 146 different voter-preference surveys) employing logit estimation (where each party's vote is estimated in a separate logit equation), multinomial logit, and, for a smaller number of cases, multinomial probit. We then use the resulting coefficients to generate the economic vote of each party. Our comparison of the economic vote of each party, across estimation methods, demonstrates that these three different estimation strategies generate very similar results. At a minimum, this suggests that, at least for the kinds of vote-choice models we employ in this study, the results one can expect from employing any one of these three estimation strategies are likely to be quite similar.

Finally, we address a third estimation issue that is very much particular to the economic-voting literature: the claim that the economic vote is asymmetric and, in particular, that it tends to be stronger in the face of bad as opposed to positive economic evaluations. Again, our large sample size allows us to provide a unique and quite definitive assessment of this claim. Our evidence clearly suggests that there is no asymmetry in the economic vote – we obtain the same results by estimating the economic vote employing the coefficients for both our positive and negative (dummy) evaluation variables.

DIFFERENCES IN THE MEASUREMENT OF THE DEPENDENT VARIABLE

Another potential source of artifactual variation in our measure of the economic vote is differences in the measurement of vote preference. Recall that the 163 voter-preference surveys, from which we estimate the economic vote, asked three types of vote-choice questions. In most of the voter-preference surveys (70 percent), voters were asked a "hypothetical" vote-choice question: Which party they would vote for "if an election were held today." The next most frequent question (25 percent of our surveys) was not hypothetical at all but occurred in postelection surveys usually conducted in the months directly after an election. These questions asked voters to report which party they had voted for in the last election. Finally, 5 percent of our surveys occurred just before an election and asked voters to indicate which party they would vote for in the upcoming election. Survey researchers have certainly established that there are, in general, differences in party support when these different questions are asked (Gelman and King, 1993; Lau, 1994). The best-established result is that postelection vote reports overstate the true support for the winner of the election and that this may come from mostly nonvoters who subsequently report both that they voted and that they voted for the winner. There is also strong evidence of overreporting of voting in postelection surveys (Silver, Anderson, and Abramson, 1986; Wolfinger and Rosenstone, 1980). It is possible that this kind of effect (or others) induces a systematically higher or lower economic vote in our individual-level models.

If there is a systematic effect on our measure of economic-vote magnitudes associated with vote-choice question wording, then it should be apparent in comparisons of the magnitudes we obtain using the different wordings. Figure 4.5 compares the economic vote of the prime minister by question type. In the left-hand graph, we distinguish hypothetical votes from vote intention that refers to an upcoming election and reported vote after the election.[24] The right-hand graph compares the economic vote for cases in which vote intention (whether hypothetical or not) is employed versus those in which reported vote is employed as the dependent variable. It is immediately apparent that if there is overreporting for the winner of the election, it is not reflected in a systematically higher or lower estimate of the economic vote for prime ministers. None of the means of the three types of questions are significantly different from one another.[25]

Question type is not the only measurement issue that might impact the vote-choice question. Another is the proximity of the question to an

[24] There are only six surveys that ask preelectoral vote intention (the middle category in the left-hand graph).

[25] The p-values for significant differences are all greater than 0.5.

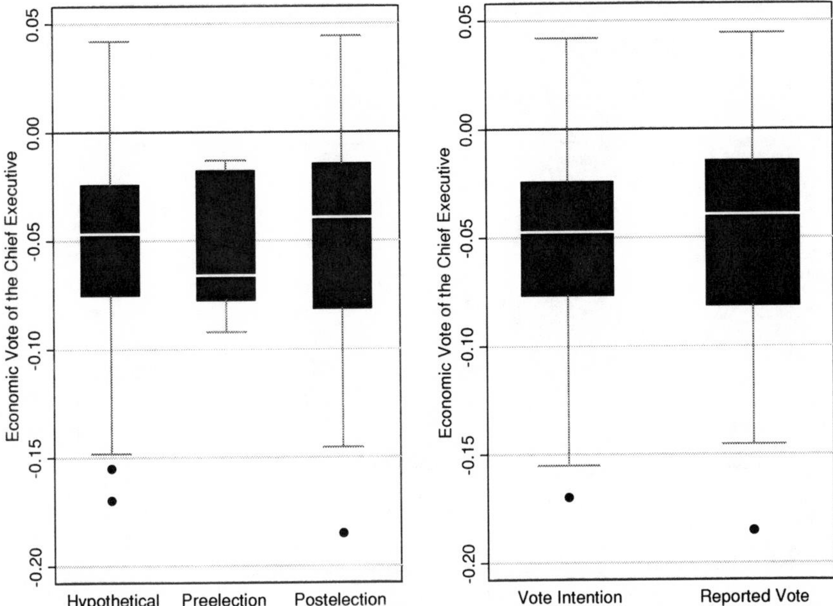

Figure 4.5. Vote choice question and economic vote of the chief executive. Shaded areas of boxplots include the 25–75 percentiles and the "whiskers" extend to 1.5 the interquartile range. The center line is the median.

election (Lau, 1994). For reported vote and preelection vote questions, these generally occur quite close to the election, but for hypothetical vote questions, these can sometimes be asked in surveys that are far from an upcoming election or far from the previous one. Various scholars have suggested that economic voting should decline as a function of the time separating the election and when voters are surveyed (either after or before an election), perhaps because media cues attaching incumbents to economic outcomes are less frequent or because voters are paying less attention. It also could simply be that when the hypothetical vote-choice question is asked closer to an election, it provides a better measure of what the voter would do in an actual election. And there is evidence to suggest that responses to vote-choice questions reflect more information about strategic incentives and issues as the timing of the survey gets closer to the election and, hence, are more strongly correlated to their actual vote choice (Gelman and King, 1993).

We can assess empirically whether the proximity of our sample of surveys to elections had an impact on economic-vote magnitudes. Figure 4.6

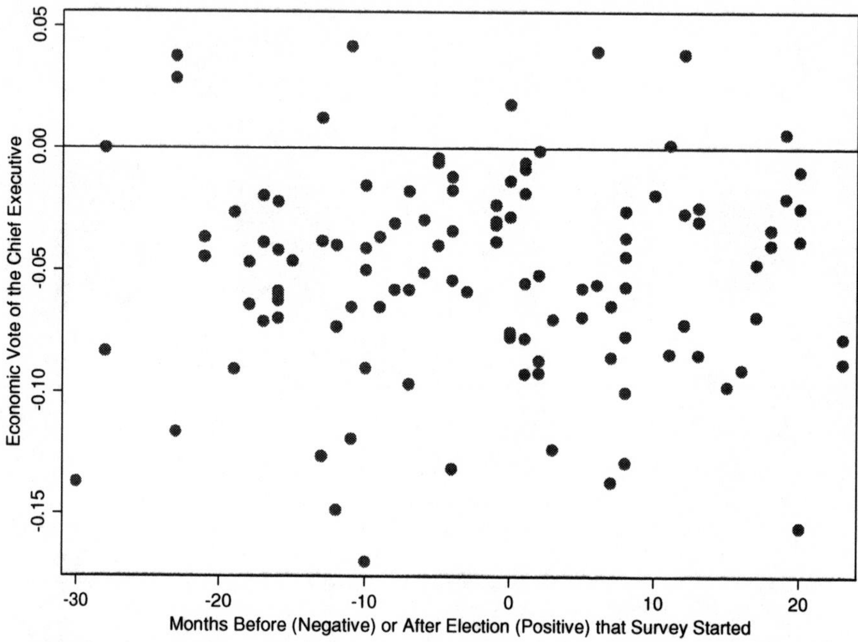

Figure 4.6. Proximity of survey to an election and economic vote of the chief executive.

graphs the economic vote of the prime minister against the time since the previous election or until the next one, whichever is closer. There is no trace in this graph (as well as the corresponding regression) of any systematic relationship between the proximity of the election to the time the survey was conducted and the *economic vote of the chief executive.*[26]

Our dependent variables in the 163 vote-choice models is based on vote-preference questions that varied in terms of whether they referred to a hypothetical as opposed to actual election and whether the questions were asked before or after an election occurred. These variations do not result in any systematic differences in our reported empirical results. These vote-preference questions were asked at different time points relative to actual national elections. Again, we demonstrate that the period in which the surveys were conducted has no systematic effect on the magnitude of the economic vote.

[26] The p-value for a linear regression of proximity to election and economic vote of the chief executive is 0.984.

MODEL SPECIFICATION

Recall from our discussion in Chapter 2 that the specification of the 163 economic-vote models was guided by the prevailing literature on vote-choice models for the sampled country. There are, nonetheless, controversies regarding the appropriate specification of vote-choice models, and economic-voting models in particular. This raises the possibility that model specification may have systematically inflated or deflated our estimates of economic-vote magnitudes. We explore in this section two model-specification issues. First, we examine whether our choice of control variables for these 163 models had any systematic effect on the economic-vote magnitudes summarized in Chapter 3. Second, we assess whether our measure of economic evaluations is sufficiently exogenous of vote preference to provide us with a meaningful estimate of economic voting.

Variation in Control Variables

As we pointed out in Chapter 2, the specification of control variables varies from study to study – the linguistic variable, for example, is, appropriately, included in Canada but excluded from France. This raises the possibility that there is a systematic relationship between the control variables included in our different models and our estimates of the economic vote. So, for example, models that include a measure of social class might generate systematically different estimates of economic-vote magnitudes than those that do not include this variable. If the individual-level models were properly specified so that, for example, those equations that should include social class do include it and those that should not include it do not, we would not expect a systematic relationship between its presence and the impact of economic perceptions on the vote.

Our strategy for exploring the possibility of these kinds of effects was to create measures for each of our 163 studies that indicated which concepts were controlled for in each individual-level vote-choice model and then to use those variables to search for systematic impacts of differences in the sets of control variables on our estimates of economic voting. Importantly, our coding was of the *concepts* controlled for in the models, not the measures used. As we emphasized in Chapter 2, although many surveys include the same concepts, they often measure these concepts differently – so, for example, occupation is often solicited in surveys but the coding into occupation categories can be quite different. For the purpose

Table 4.1. *Control Variables and Economic Voting of the Chief Executive*

Was Some Measure of the Concept Included in Model? (1 = "yes," 0 = "no")	Frequency of Inclusion and Statistical Significance of Impact on Economic Voting
Age	100%
Gender	97%
Education	97%
Left/Right Self-Placement	95%
Religiosity	92%
Occupation or Self-Identified Class	88%
Satisfaction with Democracy	83%
Lives in an Urban Area	78%
Support for EU	65%
Household Income	45%
Union Membership	35%**
Language or Ethnicity	27%
Home Ownership or Lives in Public Housing	24%
Region of Residence	16%
Policy Opinions (various policies)	15%
Party Attachment (U.S. only)	11%*
Feelings or Evaluations about PM Candidates (Australia only)	9%*

* and ** indicate that the means between groups defined by the dummy variable for the *economic vote of the chief executive* is significant at $p < .10$ and $p < .05$, respectively. No test was possible for Age since it was included in all studies.

of this analysis, what matters is whether or not an occupation variable was included in the equation regardless of how it was measured.

Table 4.1 provides the list of concepts that are controlled for in our models and the percentage of our 163 cases that include a measure controlling for the concept. The reported test is simply whether the mean of the *economic vote of the chief executive* differs in models with and without the concept.[27]

For the most part, whether a particular concept was or was not controlled for is unrelated to our estimate of the *economic vote of the chief executive*. For three cases, however, there is a statistically significant relationship. We discuss one of these cases, party attachment, in the next

[27] These tests are from dummy variable regressions that account for correlations between observations of the same party across elections and the fact that the dependent variable is estimated.

section, where we address the issue of the use of party attachment in vote-choice models and defend our decision to include party attachment only in the U.S. case. Another case, candidate evaluations, is also discussed in a later section, in which we show that this variable appears to be necessary to get sensible estimates for the Australian case. However, for the third concept, union membership, a closer examination of the relationship reveals no group of cases that is clearly driving the result, nor does it provide any clear intuition as to why it occurs. We are left then with the possibility that whether or not we control for union membership in different empirical models accounts for some of the systematic variation in our estimates of economic-vote magnitudes. We lack, however, a clear theoretical rationale for understanding why this might be the case. Nevertheless, for the vast majority of the cases, the data seem to support the idea that the list of control variables we include in the model is not driving most of the cross-national and over-time variation in economic voting that we explore in subsequent chapters.

Alternative Specifications

A second issue concerning the set of control variables included in different studies does not concern the presence of systematic differences across studies but instead focuses on our confidence in the specification (and resulting estimates) in a particular study. Specifically, the estimates we provide for each case are not the only ones that could have been obtained. In each case, some alternative set of control variables could be found that would lead to different estimates of economic voting in that case. Our strategy in this book has been to use a set of controls in each case that are well accepted in the literature on economic voting for that case and that will get us as close to the "true" model as possible. Thus, the only alternative sets of control variables that should concern us are those that are as plausible or as well supported in the literature as the ones we choose. If there are alternative specifications that are theoretically credible and that result in very different estimates of economic voting, then we need to qualify our assessment of economic-voting magnitudes with the warning that different reasonable specifications of cases would produce different results.[28]

[28] To be clear, removing control variables from a vote-choice model that are widely recognized as important will very likely have some effect on our estimates of economic voting. Indeed, we should not expect them to be insensitive to these kinds of changes

Of course, our review of the various country-specific literatures on voting behavior did reveal a number of controversies about exactly which variables should be included in vote-choice models. In most cases, however, these were relatively minor controversies and we usually found that the inclusion or exclusion of specific variables did not change our estimates of economic voting significantly. One controversy in the literature on voting behavior, however, is both widespread and consequential for our analysis – whether or not party identification (or attachment) should be included.

The case of the United States is the least controversial. Indeed, our review of the literature on individual-level vote choice in the United States indicates an overwhelming consensus in favor of including party identification as an explanatory variable. The variable has been a pillar of the Michigan School's approach to voting behavior but is also important in the arguments and empirical models of scholars coming from very different theoretical approaches. Fiorina (1981), for example, makes a strong case for including party identification in models of rational retrospective voting.

Kiewiet (1983) questioned the appropriateness of including party identification in models of economic voting on the grounds that party identification might itself be highly correlated with economic evaluations and, hence, bias the estimated effects of these variables. Kiewiet (1983) explored this possibility by estimating two different sets of voting models – one with partisanship included and a second set that substituted a battery of socioeconomic variables for partisanship. The substantive effects of the economic variables in the two different models did not vary significantly, suggesting that, at least in the U.S. context, inclusion of the party-identification variable does not seem to either inflate or underestimate the economic-voting effect. And much of the recent work on economic voting in the United States, such as Erikson, MacKuen, and Stimson (2002), reflects the importance of including this "running tally"

(hence, the need for control variables in the first place). Thus, when we (and the literature) have confidence that a particular variable belongs in the equation, there is no reason to remove it, and the fact that doing so would change our estimates does not create uncertainty about the magnitude of economic voting for the case, as the estimate without the variable is clearly (according to the collected wisdom of the literature) wrong. However, when the literature is uncertain about whether a variable is appropriately included in the vote-choice model and its inclusion or exclusion has an impact on economic voting, then we should be more uncertain that the estimates of the economic voting for the case that are based on an uncertain specification are correct.

as a control variable in economic-voting models. Following this consensus, then, we include party identification in our U.S. equations.

When one goes beyond the United States, one sometimes finds a controversy regarding the appropriateness of including party identification as an explanatory variable in voting models or, more usually, a widespread consensus that it is inappropriate. The principal critique, popularized by Budge, Crewe, and Farlie (1976) but taken up by many other European students of voting behavior, is that outside the United States, the concept of party identification and vote choice cannot really be distinguished empirically (at least, how it is usually measured) because voters simply report their vote choice when asked about party attachment. There has been considerable empirical evidence in support of this contention (Holmberg, 1994; Thomassen, 1976) and so the concept has not often been used in studies of voting behavior in many of the European democracies.[29]

In the Anglo-democracies (including Australia, Canada, New Zealand, and Britain), party identification has been frequently used in voting studies, but its use has often spurred controversy because students of voting behavior have also questioned whether, in fact, it is very distinctive from the vote. The Canadian literature is a case in point. The "Michigan model" has had an important influence on the design of election studies in Canada – hence, considerable attention is given to the inclusion of partisanship questions in Canadian national election studies. Nevertheless, students of Canadian voting behavior seem pretty uniformly convinced that party identification historically has been very low (see the early studies of Meisel, 1975, and Jenson, 1976). And, the evidence seems to suggest that partisanship has been declining in Canada and is becoming increasingly unstable (Bowler, 1990; Clarke, Kornberg, and Wearing, 2000; Stewart and Clarke, 1998).[30] The virtual disappearance of two major Canadian parties in 1993 attests to the relative weakness of party attachments. One of the contributing factors to the weakness or instability of partisanship in Canada is the existence of two distinct party systems at the national and provincial level, which contributes significantly to partisan inconsistency and, hence, instability (Stewart and Clarke, 1998).

[29] Moreover, there has been a widely documented trend of declining partisanship in many advanced democracies that has added to controversies regarding this variable (Dalton and Wattenberg, 2000).

[30] Although, see Schickler and Green (1997), who argue that once measurement error is taken into account, party identification has been relatively stable in Canada and other advanced democracies.

The use of party identification in U.K. voting models evokes similar equivocations as in Canada. In their classic study of the British voter, Butler and Stokes (1976) make the case that party identification is much more unstable than is the case in the United States and that it tends to shift with changes in vote choice. Budge, Crewe, and Farlie (1976) make an even more aggressive case against employing party identification in British vote models on the basis that partisanship is highly correlated with – and likely not causally prior to – vote choice. Subsequent research seems to support this conclusion that conventional measures of party identification in Britain are essentially tapping voting intention (Bartle, 2001; Sanders et al., 2003). In addition, Clarke, Stewart, and Whitely (1997) have documented the extent to which partisanship in Britain is highly sensitive to movements in short-term forces such as economic conditions and issue controversies.

Based on our review of the voting literature, there certainly is some question as to whether party identification ought to be included in the British and Canadian models. And, there clearly are strong grounds for excluding party identification from voting models estimated with European data.[31] Our general rule then was to exclude party identification from our economic-voting models with the exception of the U.S. models, where there is overwhelming consensus that it should be included. But does this decision to include or exclude party identification from economic-voting models have implications for the magnitude of the economic effect? The answer to this question is important in those cases in which the use of the variable is controversial. If the range of estimates of economic voting across reasonable models is large (e.g., models including and excluding party identification), we must qualify the conclusions drawn from any one set of economic voting estimates with the caution that other reasonable but very different estimates are possible. Given this, we explore the impact of including or excluding partisan identification on economic voting in Canada, the United Kingdom, and Australia, the three cases in our sample in which the literature provides little consensus on the issue. Our strategy is simply to estimate models of economic voting with and without partisanship and examine the differences in our estimates of economic voting.

Table 4.2 reports the difference in the *chief executive* vote between the estimates we used in Chapter 3 (that did not include party identification)

[31] In our data from the European cases, the correlation between the party-attachment question and vote choice was so high that they were essentially identical so could not be included in the same model.

Table 4.2. *Change in Chief Executive Vote when Party Identification Dropped from Model*

Survey Year	Britain	Canada	Australia
1979	.006		
1987			.009
1988		.03	
1990			.012
1992	0.00		
1993		−.005	.001
1996			.004
1997	.012	.032	
1998			.01
2000		.046	
2001	.06		.005

The economic vote of the prime minister is larger when it is more negative, so a positive number here indicates that adding party identification to the model decreases the economic vote of the prime minister.

and those we get when we add party identification to these models. With only one exception, all of the models, whether they contained party attachment or not, showed evidence of economic voting in the expected direction – that is, a negative change in support for the prime minister's party when economic perceptions worsened.[32] Furthermore, again with only one exception (the 1993 Canadian election), all the differences between the two estimations suggest that including partisanship tends to attenuate the economic-voting effect. However, only two of the estimates are large enough to really change the substantive picture of the amount of economic voting for the prime minister in the election: the British 2001 and the Canadian 2000 cases.

Sparse versus Rich Specification

Concerns about the sensitivity of variations in the economic vote to model specifications can be addressed in a different way by adopting a uniform specification for all 163 vote-choice models in which all of the explanatory variables were identical. When the explanatory variables in each of the 163 equations are identical, then variations in the magnitude of the

[32] The exception was the Canadian 1997 case, in which party identification was included.

economic vote from one study to the next cannot be attributed to differences in the list of control variables in the models (because it does not vary). We believe our richer specification of each of the 163 vote-choice models provides a better estimate of economic-vote magnitudes in each national context. Nevertheless, if our estimates of the economic-vote deviate significantly from those obtained from a uniform specification, one might reasonably conclude that a significant amount of the contextual variation in the economic vote is driven by model-specification decisions. We can look at the issue of how sensitive the estimates of individual models are to the set of controls included by comparing the estimates from the rich and varied sets of controls that were used to generate the economic-vote distributions in Chapter 3 to corresponding estimates based on a more limited but uniform specification. The sparse but uniform specification includes only the economic perceptions question and left-right self-placement, whereas the rich specifications include the various controls discussed in Chapter 2 (details of the full-specified 163 models can be found at http://www.nuffield.ox.ac.uk/economicvoting).[33]

The comparison in the chart is between sets of controls that are about as different as one could find. The inclusion of left-right self-placement in the sparse model, however, was not only because it could be measured similarly in many models. It also was included because our exploration of different specifications (as we worked with each of the 163 individual-level models) revealed to us an important fact that is reflected in Figure 4.7. If one includes left-right self-placement in a vote-choice model (or we suspect some other variable that "nails down" the voter in a general ideological space), then the estimate of economic voting is fairly stable to even drastic revisions in the list of other controls. The outliers labeled in the figure are exceptions but instructive ones. Outliers below the 45-degree line represent cases in which the magnitude of the estimated economic vote is significantly lower in the sparse specification. Outliers above this line are cases in which the estimated vote is higher in the sparse specification. First, the Irish and British cases comprise the majority of the outliers below the 45-degree line and, in both of these cases, the role of left-right self-placement in vote choice has been frequently questioned in the literature (e.g., Evans 1999a). In the case of our voting models, it appears that in the United Kingdom and Ireland, left-right self-placement is not a sufficient control for generating reasonable estimates of the economic vote – a richer specification seems to be necessary. Indeed, in the British cases, the

[33] Only cases in which we could measure left-right self-placement are included.

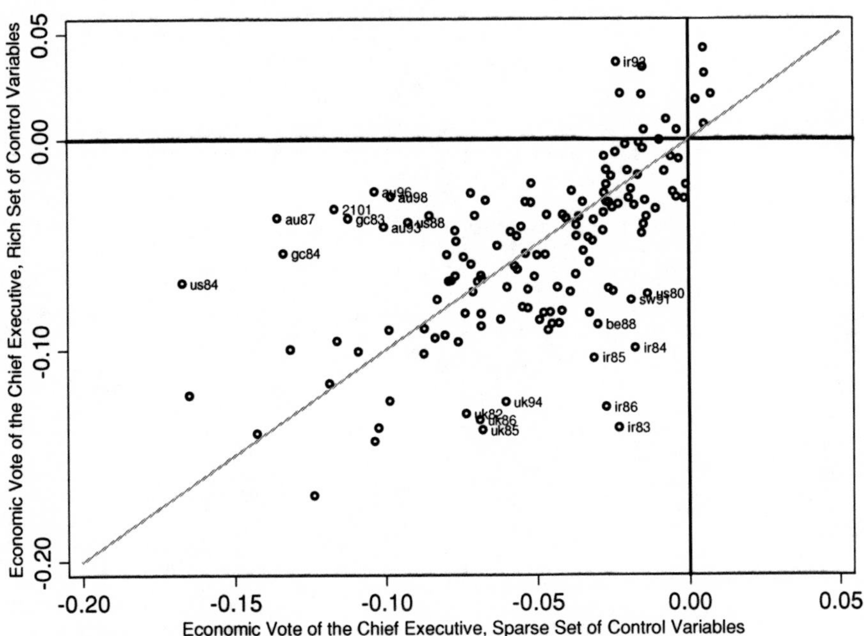

Figure 4.7. Comparison of estimates with rich and sparse sets of control variables.

question is often not even asked in the national elections studies (the cases here come from EuroBarometers). In Ireland, it has long been argued that although a left-right dimension of politics may be emerging, the principal organization of political conflict has traditionally not been the left-right but rather the policies and ideological profiles that surrounded the pro- and antitreaty traditions of the major parties.

Above the 45-degree line, the Australian cases are prominent exceptions. Our investigation of this case suggests that predicted vote is quite sensitive to the inclusion of a prime minister evaluation question.[34] Hence, in this case, adding a control for prime minister evaluation dampens our estimate of the economic vote compared to the sparse model. Finally, we again see that the Greek cases are exceptions – reinforcing a general pattern that is emerging in this chapter: that it is hard to nail down the magnitude of economic voting in Greece, the estimates of which depend more than we would like on various modeling decisions.

[34] On the importance of leadership variables in voting models in the Australian case, see Bean (1996), Bean and Mughan (1989), and Bean (2001).

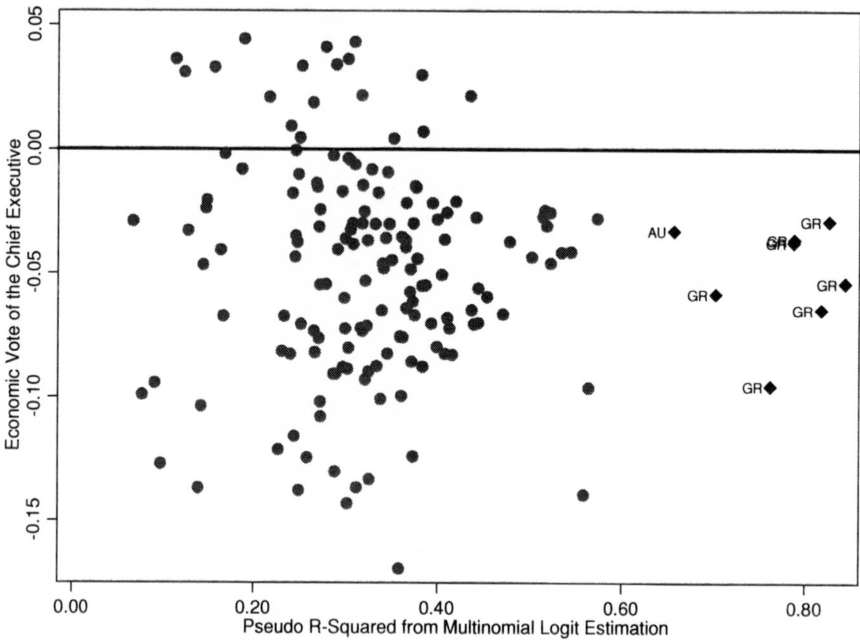

Figure 4.8. Fit of the individual-level model and economic voting for the prime minister.

Fit of the Individual-Level Models

The "fit" of each of the individual-level models varies from one study to the next. At the low end, some of the models have "pseudo-R^2s" in the neighborhood of .07, whereas the outlying Greek cases reach values as high as .8. The typical pseudo-R^2 is about .35. One possibility here is that our estimate of the size of the economic-vote might vary with the fit of each model. It might be the case, for example, that models with a poor fit tend to inflate the economic vote effect because the economic evaluation variable is capturing some of the effect of excluded independent variables. The final question we raise in this chapter is whether the estimates that comprise our map of economic voting vary systematically with the fit of the individual-level models from which they come. To examine this, we graph, in Figure 4.8, the pseudo-R^2 from the multinomial logit estimation of the model against the economic vote of the prime minister.

The graph reveals no clear relationship between this measure of fit and our estimates of the *economic vote of the chief executive*. It does, however, again single out the Greek cases as unusual. The pseudo-R^2s for the Greek cases are much larger than other countries. Our investigation as to why this should be the case suggests that this is a result of a very strong relationship between left-right self-placement and the vote.

Endogenous Economic Perceptions

Typically, economic-voting models – such as the ones generating the economic-vote magnitudes described in Chapter 3 – treat evaluations of the economy as exogenous with the implicit assumption that they reflect some aspect of objective economic performance. But the literature on attitude formation – economic evaluations are attitudes, after all – suggests that voter characteristics will affect the extent to which this "objective" information shapes their economic evaluations as can the survey instrument itself (Palmer and Duch, 2001). One of the pioneers of the economic-voting literature, Gerald Kramer (1983), suggested that individual-level analyses of economic voting are potentially problematic because individual reports of changes in economic outcomes exaggerate net changes that are politically accountable. And he pointed out that when individual-level perceptual errors correlate with partisanship or vote preference, this can inflate the magnitude of the economic vote. More recently, Zaller (2004) echoed this concern, arguing that political sophisticates and partisans resist economic information from the media that is at odds with their partisanship, whereas the economic evaluations of the less partisan are more receptive to media messages regarding economic performance (see also Gomez and Wilson, 2006). This suggests, of course, that certainly for some elements of the population, economic evaluations will be tainted by partisanship. And, depending on the distribution of sophisticates and partisans in the population, this could inflate or dampen the magnitude of economic voting in some contexts.

Evidence from the analysis of individual-level surveys suggests this might be a serious problem for economic-voting studies. Duch et al. (2000) consider the case of economic voting in U.S. presidential elections and conclude that national economic evaluations are strongly shaped by partisan predispositions. Erikson examines individual-level ANES survey data and concludes that "... cross-sectional variation in respondent's reported perceptions of national economic conditions are largely random noise that has no bearing on political evaluations" (Erikson, 2004: 5). And he argues that any observed relationship between economic evaluations and vote choice is an artifact of vote preference shaping individuals' economic perceptions. Based on their analysis of individual-level U.K. panel data, Evans and Anderson (2006) conclude that the causal impact of vote preference on economic evaluations is stronger than the impact of these evaluations on vote choice. Finally, in their study of economic voting in four nations, Wlezien et al. (1997) find that economic evaluations are strongly influenced by vote preference.

If economic perceptions are in fact endogenous, the theoretical implications of endogeneity cannot be denied; however, the practical implications of endogeneity for the quality of the estimates depend on a number of factors that may well vary from study to study. To put it another way, the extent to which endogenous economic perceptions will move estimates of the magnitude of the economic vote away from their true values in a population may well vary from survey to survey depending on the specifics of the empirical model that was estimated. Thus, it is possible that variation in the extent of endogeneity bias across our 163 surveys is driving some of the variation in the map we have drawn. Given this, the only real way to know if this is happening is to reestimate our 163 models using methods that can account for the endogeneity of economic evaluations and then compare these estimates to those in Chapter 3. In this section, then, we report estimates of the *economic vote for the chief executive* that "correct" for endogeneity using a method proposed by Duch and Palmer (2002a) that first purges economic evaluations of the systematic influences of variables like partisanship and political knowledge (as well as others) and then uses these purged evaluations in vote-choice models. The details of the Duch and Palmer (2002a) method are described in Appendix 4.1.

Figure 4.9 compares our estimates of the *economic vote of the chief executive* from models using purged and unpurged measures of economic evaluations, respectively. The result clearly suggests that, despite persistent worries in the literature about the endogeneity of economic perceptions, the practical impact of this problem is relatively small – at least for our goal of making comparative assessments.

Is the contextual variation in the economic vote, such as that which was described in Chapter 3, an artifact of model specification? Again, with the advantage of a relatively large number of individual-level surveys, we are able to provide quite conclusive answers to this question. First, with respect to the control variables included in economic-voting models, as long as left-right self-placement is among the control variables, then the estimate of economic voting is fairly stable to even drastic revisions in the other controls included in the model. Second, although it certainly is the case that subjective evaluations of the economy are influenced by vote preference, this endogeneity has surprisingly little influence

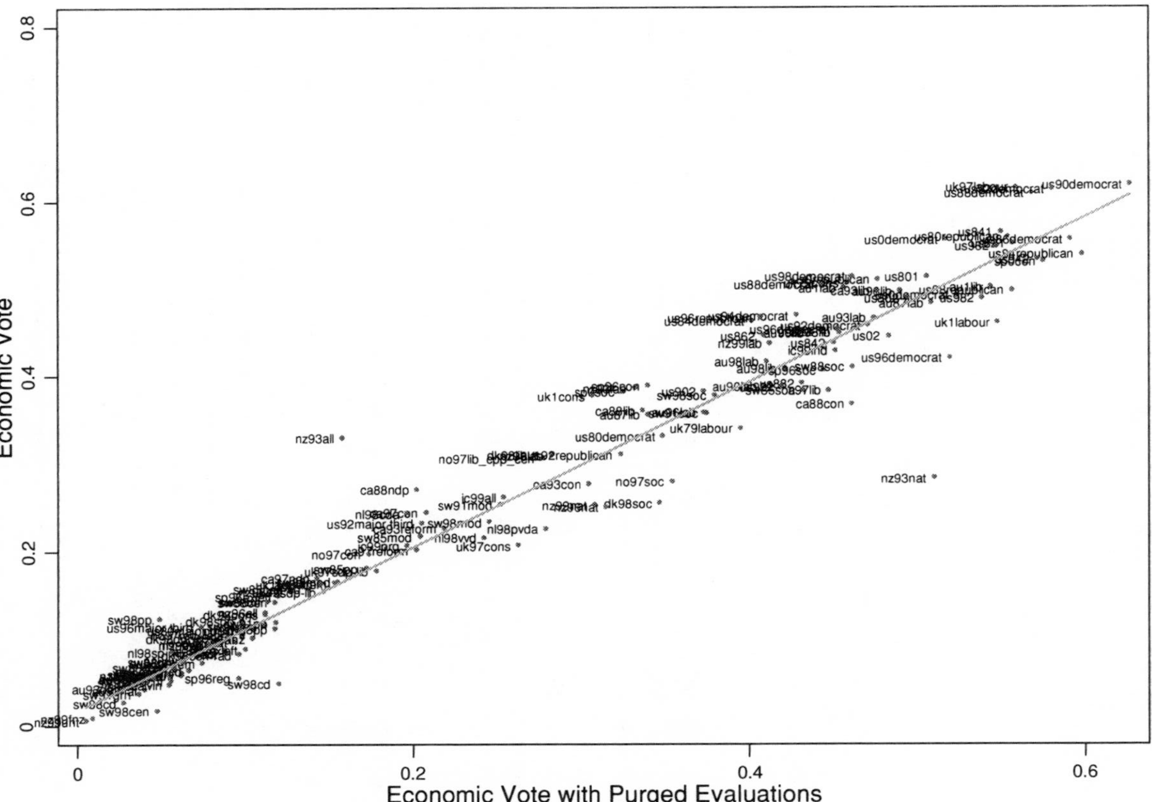

Figure 4.9. Economic vote with and without purged economic evaluations.

on the patterns of contextual variation in the economic vote described in Chapter 3.

SUMMARY

Students of comparative economic voting are primary interested in the contextual variation in the economic vote that we described in Chapter 3. And these estimates are the subject of both the theoretical and empirical efforts we undertake in the rest of the book. But, in order to generate these estimates of the economic vote from our 163 voter preference surveys, we make a number of methodological choices, some of which are the subject of current debates in the literature or some that readers might simply question. There are three broad types of methodological issues associated with estimating contextual variation in the economic vote. This chapter assesses whether our choices in any one of these areas likely affected in any systematic fashion the empirical results we report. We introduce two general empirical methodologies for testing hypotheses about the impact of contextual variables on individual-level behavioral relationships – a one-stage and a two-stage estimation strategy – both of which give very similar estimates of contextual variation in the economic vote. Our comparison of the party-vote probabilities employing logit, multinomial logit, and multinomial probit suggests that these estimation strategies generate very similar results. The measurement of our dependent variable varies somewhat across voter-preference surveys, and we demonstrate, this variation has no significant impact on our results. And with respect to model specification, we demonstrate that our results are very robust to the control variables included in the model, with the provision that left-right self-placement (or some other variable capturing ideology) is among them. We also demonstrate that endogeneity in our measure of economic evaluations has surprisingly little influence on the patterns of contextual variation in the economic vote described in Chapter 3.

This first part of the book has been devoted to measuring the economic vote with the ultimate goal of explaining any cross-national or over-time variation in its magnitude. We provide quite conclusive evidence, based on 163 individual-level surveys, that economic evaluations have a very important impact on vote choice in the developed democracies but that the effect does vary significantly across countries and over time. Part I also outlines the second-stage strategy we employ for modeling contextual variation in the economic vote. We now move on to Part II, in which we propose and empirically test the first part of our contextual theory of economic voting.

APPENDIX 4.1

Following Duch and Palmer (2002a), we can think about economic evaluations (X_i) in the following terms;

$$X_i = \lambda_i X^O + X_i^S + \varepsilon_i$$
$$X_i^S = f(W) \qquad (4.14)$$

where X^O is the objective economic economy, X_i^S captures systematic differences due to information and subjective factors (i.e., W), and ε_i is the stochastic component. In this formal definition, individual-level evaluations contain two forms of "noise": subjective considerations and random fluctuations. Both forms of noise constitute sources of nonattitudes. If we include national economic evaluations in an economic-voting model without controlling for this systematic measurement error (X_i^S), the evaluations will "pick up" the direct effect of partisan predispositions, thereby producing an inflated estimate of the relationship between economic perceptions and vote choice.

Hence, it is important to understand to what extent this endogeneity affects our estimate of the magnitude of the economic vote. By controlling for systematic and random measurement error in economic evaluations, we can estimate whether this error seriously affects estimates of the magnitude of economic voting at the individual level. One approach is to purge X_i, reported economic evaluations, of systematic measurement error (X_i^S), which would result in a measure of economic evaluations that included only factors contributing to meaningful fluctuations in economic evaluations (X^O) and random measurement error (ε_i). This would entail estimating X_i^{Purged}, which is economic evaluations purged of systematic measurement error.

Duch and Palmer (2002a) suggest that the systematic component of the measurement error in economic evaluations consists of three broad factors. First, economic evaluations are shaped by partisanship. Duch and Palmer (2002a) have demonstrated that national economic evaluations are, to a large extent, shaped by partisan predispositions – this is the case in both the American and European contexts. In addition to political partisanship, respondents may rely on personal experiences and regional economic circumstances to formulate an evaluation of the national economy. Citizens who infer national conditions from personal and local experiences are effectively evaluating the economy in a subjective rather than objective manner. Similarly, national economic evaluations may vary across individuals because of differences in levels of information and sophistication about government policy and economic outcomes. Third, social-class differences may systematically shape economic evaluations. Individuals in different socioeconomic circumstances might view the same economy in a very different light (MacKuen and Mouw, 1995). Similarly, citizens of different sexes and races may perceive the economy differently due to biases in their general attitudes toward the economic and political systems (on gender and economic voting, see Welch and Hibbing, 1992).

"Policy-related variation" represents differences in economic evaluations that are grounded in self-interested differences in opinion regarding measures of economic performance and, hence, capture variation in economic evaluations that are grounded in meaningful policy differences, or emphases, across individuals. For example, individuals who value reducing inflation more than maintaining low unemployment (e.g., retired respondents on fixed incomes) might emphasize price stability more than job creation when evaluating the national economy.

Recall, we can identify three factors contributing to systematic measurement error: party identification (PID), information, and socioeconomic status (SES). Accordingly X_i^{Purged} is estimated as follows:

$$\begin{aligned} X_i &= \alpha_1(PID) + \alpha_2(\text{information}) + \alpha_3(\text{SES}) + \alpha_4(\text{policy}) + \varepsilon_i \\ \hat{X}_i^S &= \hat{\alpha}_1(PID) + \hat{\alpha}_2(\text{information}) + \hat{\alpha}_3(\text{SES}) \\ X_i^{\text{Purged}} &= X_i - \hat{X}_i^S \end{aligned} \tag{4.15}$$

The estimate of vote probabilities is, then,

$$\begin{aligned} &v_{ik} \sim Bin(\pi_{ik}) \\ &logit(\pi'_{ik}) = \beta_{0k} + \beta_1 \text{C}_k + \beta_{2k}\text{X}_{ik}^{\text{Purged}} + \beta_3 \text{X}_{ik}^{\text{Purged}}\text{C}_k + \phi_1 Z_{ik} \end{aligned} \tag{4.16}$$

PART II

A Contextual Theory of Rational Retrospective Economic Voting: Competency Signals

Part II begins by developing a rational model of retrospective voting in which voters extract signals about the competency of incumbent politicians from movements in the retrospective economy. Given this model of individual-level economic voting, we can explore how the quality of the competency signal that voters extract from the observed economy may vary across different contexts and, hence, induce different amounts of economic voting. Chapter 5 develops a selection model of the economic vote that first describes the competency signals that voters extract from macroeconomic outcomes. We then explain how the quality of these competency signals condition the economic vote. Contexts in which the quality of these competency signals are high should generate more economic voting.

We argue in this chapter that political contexts can be distinguished in terms of the number of elected versus nonelected decision makers that are shaping political and economic policy making. And our theory suggests that the ratio of these elected to nonelected decision makers can condition the magnitude of these competency signals. As the ratio of decisions by nonelected decision makers to those by elected decision makers rises, the overall competency signal will decline and vice versa.

Chapter 6 provides empirical evidence that voters, indeed, are attentive to fluctuations in the macro-economy and are equipped to undertake the competency-signal-extraction task implied by our theory. The chapter also presents evidence that these competency signals vary over time and cross-nationally in an informative manner and that these signals condition the economic vote consistent with our theory. Chapter 7 presents empirical evidence suggesting that this ratio of nonelected to elected decisions impacts the economic vote consistent with our theory.

5

Competency Signals and Rational Retrospective Economic Voting

INTRODUCTION

In Chapter 3, we highlighted the extent to which economic voting varies from one context to the next. For example, Figure 3.2 from Chapter 3 suggested that in 1985, economic evaluations in the Netherlands had a rather significant impact on vote choice but, ten years later, economic assessments had no effect on the Dutch vote decision. In this chapter, we begin building our explanation for this kind of variation in economic voting. As we discussed in Chapter 2, modeling vote choice is equivalent to properly specifying the voter's value function for each alternative in her choice set (i.e., each party or candidate). The question then becomes: What should these value functions that produce economic voting look like? And how will their parameters vary in different political and economic contexts to produce variation in the economic vote?

THE COMPETENCY MODEL WITH TWO-PARTY COMPETITION FOR A UNIFIED EXECUTIVE

We begin to answer these questions with a theoretical model of economic voting in which the previous economy enters the voter's value function for parties modified by a competency signal. Alesina and Rosenthal (1995) and Persson and Tabellini (1990) have suggested two closely related formal models both with rational, expected utility maximizing voters who maximize their utility by conditioning their electoral choice on the retrospective performance of the economy. The models differ in their assumptions about the information available to voters when they form their expectations about what economic policies politicians will pursue. But these differences only affect implications about the behavior of politicians, not about voters. Specifically, the Persson and Tabellini model implies that politicians will create political business cycles by distorting the preelectoral economy for political purposes, whereas under the (arguably more realistic) information conditions in Alesina and Rosenthal's model, this does not occur. This result is important because it shows that rational retrospective economic voting is not dependent on the existence of preelectoral business cycles or on the existence within the model of an "adverse selection" problem in which politicians have incentives to try to hide their type from voters by manipulating economic policy and outcomes. Retrospective economic voting can occur in such models, but it also occurs in selection models in which politicians have no ability (or incentive) to deceive voters about their competence as economic managers. This result simplifies our analysis of context in these models because it allows us to focus our generalization of the model on the voter's *decision theoretic* problem of choice under uncertainty, rather than on the technically more complicated problem of a strategic interaction between voters and politicians.

We begin, then, by examining Alesina and Rosenthal's model of rational retrospective voting as it was originally conceived and then suggest an extension and reinterpretation of one key component of the model that makes it easier to use the model to generate predictions about the impact of specific changes in political and economic context on the extent of economic voting.[1] The model assumes that two parties compete for unified control of the executive and that this executive can choose an inflation rate directly (their economic policy) that determines growth in the following expectations-augmented Phillips curve:

$$y_{it} = \bar{y} + \pi_{it} - \pi_{it}^{e} + \eta_{it} \tag{5.1}$$

where y_{it} is the rate of economic growth in period t, under incumbent party i; π_{it} is the inflation rate, the level of which is chosen directly by the incumbent party; π_{it}^{e} is the rate of inflation that voters expect the incumbent to choose; $\bar{y}$ is the natural rate of growth; and η_{it} is a random shock to the economy.

The economic shock consists of two parts; as follows:

$$\eta_{it} = \varepsilon_{it} + \xi_t \tag{5.2}$$

[1] We generally follow the notational conventions used in Alesina and Roubini (1997).

One part, ε_{it}, is simply an increment to growth that depends on the identity of the incumbent but not on her economic policy (which is captured in π_{it}). This increment to economic performance is meant to capture the economic impact of the incumbent administration's managerial competence. More specifically, this shock includes any unobserved economic impact of the behavior of the incumbent administration that is not constant over time or administration.[2] We refer to this impact as a "competency shock."

The other part of the total shock to economic growth, ξ_t, although also unobserved and not constant over time, does not depend on the identity of the administration. We refer to it as an "exogenous" shock or sometimes as a "nonpolitical" shock.

Voters cannot observe competence shocks or nonpolitical shocks directly but can glean information about incumbent competence from the fact that the observed economy is partially dependent on it. Of course, to be useful in forecasting the future economy, the level of competence inferred from observed economic performance must provide some guide to the incumbent's future level of competence. Consequently, we assume that competence is persistent over time in the following way:[3]

$$\varepsilon_{it} = \mu_{it} + \mu_{it-1} \tag{5.3}$$

Thus, current competence is just a first-order moving average from a sequence of competency shocks. We assume that each of these competency shocks is drawn from identical distributions, with mean zero and finite variance σ_μ^2. Likewise, we assume that the nonpolitical shocks, ξ_t, are drawn from identical normal distributions, each with zero mean and finite variance σ_ξ^2. We assume that voters know the expected values and variances of these distributions.

All voters in the model are identical and care about achieving the highest possible economic growth and lowest possible inflation in the next period. Specifically, we write the utility of a typical voter in period $t+1$ as a function of which party is elected, what policy that party pursues, and what the resulting level of economic growth will be. Given some

[2] If voters observe the impact of this behavior, it cannot be part of the shock but is part of the observed policy represented by π_{it}. Likewise, any unobserved impact of behavior on growth that is constant is subsumed in the natural rate of economic growth.

[3] One also can discount the impact of past competence, as long as it is at least partially persistent.

governing party, i, that pursues a particular economic policy (a choice of π_{it+1}), the voter's utility in period t + 1 is:[4]

$$u(\pi_{it+1}, y_{it+1}) = -\frac{1}{2}\pi_{it+1}^{2} + by_{it+1},\ b > 0 \qquad (5.4)$$

where b indexes the voter's preference for growth relative to inflation. The particular functional form of utility for inflation and growth is quite flexible: as we will see, any choice that has the voter's utility increasing in growth will produce the same substantive implications for rational economic voting, given the other assumptions in the model. The one provided here is a common formulation in the literature and so was chosen for its familiarity. Because utility is increasing in y and is maximized, for a given y, when inflation equals zero, this expression says that voters prefer more growth and price stability and that they would be willing to trade price increases for growth at a rate governed by the size of b.

Because a voter's future utility will depend on choices made today, he must forecast the likely economic future under different possible incumbents. Our assumption is that these expectations are formed rationally based on all the information available at the time of the election. Politicians in the model all care only about being in office and understand that voters will vote to maximize their expected utility.[5]

Because voters form expectations about inflation and growth rationally, they know that incumbent politicians will pick the level of inflation (and, correspondingly, growth) that will maximize the incumbent's expected utility. Voters are assumed to know current inflation and are never surprised by the government's inflation policy. Consequently, politicians have nothing to gain from doing anything but choosing the voter's optimal inflation rate (zero). Thus, in this simple version of the model, all politicians, no matter how competent, will choose the same economic policy, and differences in growth associated with different politicians can only result from differences in their types (which are exogenous to the model). Clearly, then, the decisions of the politicians play no real role in

[4] It is possible to state the voter's preferences more generally to include the whole sequence of time-discounted future periods; for example, $U = E\{\sum_{t=0}^{\infty} \delta_t u(\pi_{j,t}, y_{j,t})\}; 0 < \delta < 1$. However, the usual assumption restricts the discount factors to make this equivalent to a voter who looks into the future only so far as the next period of incumbency. For our purposes, then, the simpler formulation given in the text is adequate.

[5] We could allow politicians to differ in their policy preferences; for example, leftist politicians might prefer a nonzero inflation rate. As we will see, however, economic voting in the model does not in any way depend on the policy choices of politicians, and so we ignore this complication.

the model and so it is equivalent to a reduced-form, decision-theoretic version of the usual formulation that has been used to explore political business cycles. Because our focus is on the decision of voters given the observed economy and not on the decisions of politicians about policy, this seems an appropriate simplification.

With this, the growth rate from equation (5.1) is just the natural rate plus any shock. Furthermore, voters can actually observe the total shock because they can calculate it via equation (5.1). However, they cannot use that equation to parse out how much of the observed shock is a result of the incumbent's competence because they do not observe the two shock terms separately but only overall growth.

The voters in the model form their expectations about the competence of the incumbent rationally and because of the moving average structure of the competence shock in equation (5.3), growth rates at time t that differ from $\bar{y}$ will provide voters with information regarding the competence of an incumbent reelected for period $t+1$. This follows from taking expectations in equation (5.3) (recall that the unconditional expectation of μ_{it+1} is zero).

$$E\left[\varepsilon_{it+1}\right] = E[\mu_{it+1}] + E[\mu_{it} \mid y_{it}] = E[\mu_{it} \mid y_{it}] \qquad (5.5)$$

Voters form their expectations about the competence of an incumbent reelected in period $t+1$ by evaluating μ_{it} or, more precisely, the noisy signal provided by y_{it}. A key assumption of Alesina and Rosenthal's (1995) model is that voters learn the value of competency with a one-period delay – that is, in period t they know μ_{it-1} but not μ_{it}. Hence, voters base their forecast of the economic competence of the incumbent on both y_{it} and μ_{it-1}. Specifically, in the current period, voters know the competency of the incumbent in the last period, the natural rate of growth, the current realization of growth, and the current economic shock (which is composed of some unknown mix of the current competence of the incumbent and the nonpolitical shock). Growth in the current period is thus:

$$\begin{aligned} y_{it} &= \bar{y} + \eta_{it} \\ &= \bar{y} + \mu_{it} + \mu_{it-1} + \xi_t \end{aligned} \qquad (5.6)$$

Rearranging this gives:

$$\mu_{it} + \xi_t = y_{it} - \bar{y} - \mu_{it-1} \qquad (5.7)$$

where everything on the right-hand side of this equality is observed and so the sum of the terms on the left is also observed, although not the individual components. Denote the sum on the left-hand side as

$k_{it} = \mu_{it} + \xi_t$. Because k_{it} is observed, the voter can compute her expectation about μ_{it} given k_{it} (i.e., her expectation about the incumbent's current level of competence, given the observed level of growth and the incumbent's competence in the last period). To calculate this conditional expectation, we need to know the distribution of both k_{it} and μ_{it}. k_{it} is the sum of two normally distributed random variables, both with zero means and variances σ_μ^2 and σ_ξ^2, respectively. The distribution of k_{it} is thus:

$$k_{it} = (\mu_{it} + \xi_t) \sim N\left(0, \sigma_\mu^2 + \sigma_\xi^2\right) \tag{5.8}$$

Given that both k_{it} and μ_{it} are distributed normally, their joint distribution is bivariate normal and the optimal forecast of μ_{it} given k_{it} is just the conditional expectation, which is computed from the appropriate conditional distribution of the bivariate normal. Using standard results, this conditional expectation is (Greene 2003):[6]

$$\begin{aligned} E\left[\mu_{it} \mid k_{it}\right] &= E[\mu_{it}] + \frac{\sigma_{\mu,k}}{\sigma_k^2}\left(y_{it} - \bar{y} - \mu_{it-1}\right) - E[k_{it}] \\ &= \left(\frac{\sigma_\mu^2}{\sigma_\mu^2 + \sigma_\xi^2}\right)\left(y_{it} - \bar{y} - \mu_{it-1}\right) \end{aligned} \tag{5.9}$$

Because $E\left[\mu_{it} \mid k_{it}\right] = E\left[\mu_{it} \mid y_{it}\right]$, this expression is the rational voter's assessment of the current competence of the incumbent given the observed economy.[7] Furthermore, from equation (5.5), we have $E\left[\mu_{it} \mid y_{it}\right] = E\left[\varepsilon_{it+1}\right]$, so we now have what we need to explore the implications of the model for economic voting by comparing the voter's expected utility for voting for the incumbent in this model to her expected utility for the challenger.

Because there are no incentives to vote strategically in a two-party contest, voters will vote for the party that they expect to deliver the most utility in the next period. So, we can write their expected utility for voting for incumbent party i as equal to the expected utility voters will accrue in the next period if party i is in office.

$$\begin{aligned} E\left[u_{t+1} \mid v_i\right] &= E\left[u\left(\pi_{it+1}, y_{it+1}\right)\right] \\ &= \frac{1}{2}E\left[\pi_{it+1}^2\right] + bE[y_{it+1}] \end{aligned}$$

[6] In general, $E[x \mid y] = \rho_{xy}\frac{y-E[y]}{\sigma_y}\sigma_x + E[x]$, where ρ_{xy} is the correlation between x and y.

[7] $E[\mu_{it} \mid y_{it}] = \frac{\sigma_{\mu,y}}{\sigma_\mu^2+\sigma_\xi^2}(y_{it} - y - \mu_{it-1})$ by applying the same signal-extraction solution as earlier. Furthermore, it is easy to show that $\sigma_{\mu,y} = \sigma_{\mu,k}$, so the claim in the text follows.

$$
\begin{aligned}
&= 0 + b(\bar{y} + E[\eta_{it+1}])_i \\
&= 0 + b(\bar{y} + 0 + E[\varepsilon_{it+1}]) \\
&= b\left(\bar{y} + \frac{\sigma_\mu^2}{\sigma_\mu^2 + \sigma_\xi^2}(y_{it} - \bar{y} - \mu_{it-1})\right) \\
&= b\bar{y} + b\left(\frac{\sigma_\mu^2}{\sigma_\mu^2 + \sigma_\xi^2}\right)(y_{it} - \bar{y} - \mu_{it-1}) \qquad (5.10)
\end{aligned}
$$

Lacking any information about the challenger's level of competence, the voter's expected utility for voting for the challenger, k, is just:[8]

$$
\begin{aligned}
E[u_{t+1}|v_k] &= E[u(\pi_{kt+1}, y_{kt+1})] \\
&= \frac{1}{2}E\left[\pi_{kt+1}^2\right] + bE[y_{kt+1}] \\
&= 0 + b(\bar{y} + E[\eta_{kt+1}]) \\
&= b(\bar{y} + E[\xi_{t+1}] + E[\varepsilon_{kt+1}]) \\
&= b\bar{y} \qquad (5.11)
\end{aligned}
$$

Thus, the voter will vote for the incumbent when the expected utility in equation (5.10) is larger than that in equation (5.11). The difference is:

$$
\begin{aligned}
E[u_{t+1}|v_i] - E[u_{t+1}|v_k] &= b\bar{y} + b\left(\frac{\sigma_\mu^2}{\sigma_\mu^2 + \sigma_\xi^2}\right)(y_{it} - \bar{y} - \mu_{it-1})_i - b\bar{y} \\
&= b\left(\frac{\sigma_\mu^2}{\sigma_\mu^2 + \sigma_\xi^2}\right)(y_{it} - \bar{y} - \mu_{it-1}) \qquad (5.12)
\end{aligned}
$$

This result makes it clear when voters can and cannot extract information from fluctuations in the previous economy in order to access the current competence of an incumbent and cast an economic vote. The term $y_{it} - \bar{y} - \mu_{it-1}$ is simply observed economic performance less the parts of economic growth whose sources are known to the voter. The term captures what the incumbent has "done for the voter lately" (i.e., how the current period differs from the natural level of growth, discounted by the impact of the incumbent's known level of competence in the previous period). We interpret the coefficient on this term, that is, $\frac{\sigma_\mu^2}{\sigma_\mu^2+\sigma_\xi^2}$, as the "competency signal" that controls how much information about the competence of incumbents voters can extract from observed movements in the economy.

[8] Alesina and Rosenthal assume that the expected competence of the challenger is always zero. We discuss what happens when we change this assumption (and why we might need to) in Chapter 8.

This competency signal will always be positive and will approach one as the variance in the random (nonpolitical) shocks to the economy, σ_{ξ}^2, goes to zero. In that case, the voter knows that growth above or below the natural rate is completely caused by competency shocks – consequently, deviations from the natural rate of growth can be completely attributed to the competence of the administration. More generally, if σ_{μ}^2, the variance of the competence term μ_{it}, is large relative to the variance in the nonpolitical component of growth, σ_{ξ}^2, then changes in the economy will provide a strong signal about the competency of the incumbent and the voter will weight the retrospective economy more heavily in her utility function. Alternatively, growth that is above or below the natural rate is a poor signal of the incumbent's competence if observed growth is more likely to result from nonpolitical shocks than from competency shocks – that is, if σ_{ξ}^2 is high relative to σ_{μ}^2.

We can conclude, then, that economic voting in its traditional form obtains in this model – voters will vote against the incumbent when economic performance is sufficiently weak and for the incumbent when it is sufficiently strong. In addition, the economic vote is weighted by a competency signal that captures the extent to which shocks to the economy are a result of the competence of governments.

Competency Shocks, Economic Policy, and Political and Economic Context

Scheve (2004) and others used this formulation of the competency signal to speculate about the way that economic contexts like the extent of trade openness might impact economic voting. For example, Scheve (2004) suggests that increased openness will decrease the size of the variance of exogenous shocks and so increase the extent of economic voting. We could certainly proceed similarly – that is, by speculating about how different political and economic contexts impact the two variance terms in the competency ratio. However, the problem with this strategy is that the theory in its current form provides relatively little guidance about the substantive meaning of these variance terms, and so these sorts of speculations are relatively unconstrained. This is especially true for the concept of the competency shock. What exactly is the distribution of competency shocks and what would account for differences in its variance across contexts? Certainly, we could think of the competency distribution as the pool of political talent available in a country and suppose that this pool differs from country to country in a way that might account for different competency signals (although differences like this seem unlikely across the Western democracies). Alternatively, we could think of the competence distribution as describing the variation within a country of bureaucratic skill, political corruption, or the efficiency of markets that translate policy to outcomes. The point here is that one is relatively free to posit a substantive interpretation for what the competency distribution means and then to suggest what kinds of political and economic contexts would impact the variance of this distribution (and so economic voting).

In addition to ambiguities in the substantive meaning of the variance of the competence distribution, one also must remember that there are two different variance terms in the competency ratio. Thus, it is important that any speculation about the impact of some particular contextual variable on the size of the competency signal addresses how that variable impacts both the variance of competence shocks and the variance of exogenous shocks. In the small literature that has taken this approach, however, it is rare to find discussion of both kinds of shocks.

Given this, in this section we suggest an extension and reinterpretation of Alesina and Rosenthal's model that, we believe, gives the model a clearer substantive interpretation and so allows for more substantively grounded speculations about how different contexts are likely to alter the competence signal and thus economic voting. Furthermore, our extension leads us to identify ways in which variables such as trade dependence and the size of government can impact the competency signal that have not been emphasized in the previous literature. For example, although previous theoretical speculation about the impact of expanded government on economic voting has emphasized the larger number of functions that might well be associated with such an increase, our theoretical formulation makes it plain that other aspects of expanded government – such as the further political insulation of entrenched bureaucracies from electoral control – also may play a role in the ability of voters to extract a clear signal of incumbent competence from observed changes in the economy.

Our modification of the original Alesina and Rosenthal (1995) formulation begins by distinguishing between two types of decision makers, which we call "electorally dependent decision makers" (EDDs) and "nonelectorally dependent decision makers" (NEDDs). The first of these labels (EDD) is just shorthand for referring to the elected officials that comprise the national government and the bureaucracy that is responsible to them. The second label (NEDD) refers to everyone else whose decisions might impact the economy, including individuals, firms, interest groups, nonelectorally dependent (entrenched) bureaucrats, foreign leaders, the WTO, and many more. The reason this distinction is important is that we assume that competency shocks are only associated with the decisions of the EDDs, whereas the exogenous shocks are associated with the decisions of everyone else. Note that included among the NEDDs are government officials from subnational levels of government that contribute to exogenous shocks in the macro-economy. Hence, federalist systems that multiply the number of non-national government entities that contribute to exogenous shocks would have a lower overall competency signal and, hence, less economic voting.[9]

In the model developed here, we assumed a single decision – the setting of interest rates, for example. In fact, EDDs make many economically consequential decisions, as do NEDDs. Just as in the previous model, each of these decisions has some systematic effect on the economy and some random effect, and the competence and exogenous shocks discussed previously are nothing but these many random shocks, summed over the sets of decisions made by elected and nonelected decision makers, respectively.

Formally, let the number of decisions made by EDDs be α and the number made by NEDDs be β and assume, for notational simplicity, that there is a single elected decision maker and a single nonelected decision maker making all of these decisions.[10] With this, we can write the growth equation as:

$$y_{it} = \bar{y} + \sum_{l=1}^{\alpha} \omega_{ilt} + \sum_{l=1}^{\beta} \psi_{lt} \tag{5.13}$$

where ω_{ilt} is the growth shock associated with the lth decision of i, the EDD. Likewise, ψ_{lt} is the growth shock associated with the lth decision

[9] The effect of federalism on the magnitude of the economic vote in national elections is typically explained as the result of an increased level of confusion on the part of voters (Anderson, 2006; Cutler, 2004). In our theory, voters are not confused but rather are fully informed and simply discount the national incumbent's competency signal when there are a larger number of "nonelected" actors affecting shocks to the macro-economy. For similar reasons, we would expect to see relatively low levels of economic voting in state or provincial elections where the importance of "non-elected" actors (i.e., the federal government) on economic outcomes is considerable (Stein, 1990). We are unable to actually test this hypothesized relationship with our sample of countries because they have very little variation on the widely accepted measures of federalism. For example, on the Franzese (2002) measure of federalism, twelve of the seventeen countries for which there is a federalism measure have the lowest score of 1, leaving only five countries that register as federalist (and one, the United States, is a very large outlier compared to the other federalist countries).

[10] This can be extended to represent both the number of decision makers and their volume of decisions although the notation becomes much more complex; the results, nevertheless, are exactly the same.

of the NEDD. Any known or systematic impacts of these decisions on the economy are subsumed in the natural rate of growth or are anticipated by voters and so have no effect on growth.[11]

We assume that for the EDD, the l'th shock is persistent in the same way as in our earlier discussion (i.e., $\omega_{ilt} = \mu_{ilt} + \mu_{ilt-1}$).[12] And we assume that μ_{ilt} and ψ_{lt} are independent normally distributed random variables with zero means and variances σ_μ^2 and σ_ψ^2, respectively.

The growth equation can then be expressed as:

$$y_{it} = \bar{y} + \sum_{l=1}^{\alpha} (\mu_{ilt} + \mu_{ilt-1}) + \sum_{l=1}^{\beta} \psi_{lt} \qquad (5.14)$$

Rearranging this gives:

$$\sum_{l=1}^{\alpha} \mu_{ilt} + \sum_{l=1}^{\beta} \psi_{lt} = \bar{y} - y_{it} + \sum_{l=1}^{\alpha} \mu_{ilt-1} \qquad (5.15)$$

where everything on the right-hand side of this equation is observed and so the sum of the terms on the left is also observed, although not the individual components. Denote the sum on the left-hand side as $k_{it} = \sum_{l=1}^{\alpha} \mu_{ilt} + \sum_{l=1}^{\beta} \psi_{lt}$. Because k_{it} is observed, the voter can compute her expectation about $\sum_{l=1}^{\alpha} \mu_{ilt}$ given k_{it} (i.e., her expectation about the EDD's current overall competence shock, given the observed level of growth and the decision maker's overall competence shock in the last period). To calculate this conditional expectation, we need to know the

[11] Specifically, if $\sum_{l=1}^{\alpha} (\phi_{lit} + \omega_{it})$ is a generic term capturing the total impact of all decisions relevant to the economy that are made by the elected decision maker, rather than simply an inflation choice, we can think of $\pi_{it} = \sum_{l=1}^{\alpha} \phi_{lit}$ as the "policy" part of this impact over which voters have rational expectations. Thus, as before, π_{it} is fully anticipated by the rational electorate (so voters anticipate the many choices the decision maker will make) and can have no real effect on growth (i.e., given rational expectations and the information assumptions from the earlier model, π_{it} will equal π_{it}^e). Consequently, the decision maker will always choose the mix of policies that are most preferred by the voter.

[12] This persistence means we need to think of the lth decision at time t and the lth decision at time $t+1$ as being members of the same "category" of decisions so that the shock to decision l at time $t-1$ tells us something about the shock to decision l at time t. One can simplify matters considerably by assuming that the shocks for all decisions made in a single period by the same decision maker are the same. In that case, we would think of the shock as a sort of characteristic of the decision maker so that all his or her decisions about the economy "worked" a little better or a little worse. An equivalent version of the model would allow for many decision-makers each making many decisions. However, this kind of generalization has no impact on our conclusions, although it does change the substantive interpretation of the persistence assumption, as noted earlier.

distribution of both k_{it} and $\sum_{l=1}^{\alpha} \mu_{ilt}$. $\sum_{l=1}^{\alpha} \mu_{ilt}$ is the sum of α normally distributed random variables each with zero mean and variance σ_μ^2, so $\sum_{l=1}^{\alpha} \mu_{ilt} \sim N(0, \sigma_\mu^2 \alpha)$. Likewise, $\sum_{l=1}^{\beta} \psi_{lt} \sim N(0, \sigma_\psi^2 \beta)$. Thus, k_{it} is the sum of two normally distributed random variables, both with zero means and variances $\sigma_\mu^2 \alpha$ and $\sigma_\psi^2 \beta$, respectively. The distribution of k_{it} is thus:

$$k_{it} = \sum_{l=1}^{\alpha} \mu_{ilt} + \sum_{l=1}^{\beta} \psi_{lt} \sim N\left(0, \sigma_\mu^2 \alpha + \sigma_\psi^2 \beta\right) \tag{5.16}$$

Given that both k_{it} and $\sum_{l=1}^{\alpha} \mu_{ilt}$ are distributed normally, their joint distribution is bivariate normal and the optimal forecast of $\sum_{l=1}^{\alpha} \mu_{ilt}$, given k_{it}, is just the conditional expectation, which is computed from the appropriate conditional distribution of the bivariate normal. Using standard results (Greene, 2003), this conditional expectation is:

$$\begin{aligned} E\left[\sum_{l=1}^{\alpha} \mu_{ilt} | k_{it}\right] &= E\left[\sum_{l=1}^{\alpha} \mu_{ilt}\right] + \frac{\sigma_{\mu,k}}{\sigma_k^2}\left(y_{it} - \bar{y} - \sum_{l=1}^{\alpha} \mu_{ilt-1}\right) - E[k_{it}] \\ &= \left(\frac{\alpha\sigma_\mu^2}{\alpha\sigma_\mu^2 + \beta\sigma_\psi^2}\right)\left(y_{it} - \bar{y} - \sum_{l=1}^{\alpha} \mu_{ilt-1}\right) \end{aligned} \tag{5.17}$$

The numerator of the competence signal is now the variance of the overall competence shock, which is the product of the variance of the distribution of competence shocks associated with a single decision and the number of decisions made by the EDD $(\alpha\sigma_\mu^2)$. This is important because it implies that expanding the number of economically consequential choices that the electorally dependent decision maker makes will increase this product. More substantively, this variance should be larger in countries in which EDDs make more of the economic decisions that determine the country's growth path.

The principal advantage of this formulation of the model is that it alleviates the need to speculate about how differences across cases in particular political and economic institutions lead to differences in the variance of the distribution of individual competence shocks (σ_μ^2) or individual exogenous shocks (σ_ψ^2) across cases. Instead, because these are the variances governing the shocks associated with individual decisions, each of which is likely to have only a very small effect on growth, we can simply assume that these variances are both small (implying that the maximum impacts of any individual decision on growth is small) and constant across cases. So the positive or negative shock associated with any one decision in any one place and time may range in size similarly to any other decision. What differs across context, however, is the number of decisions over which we take the sum. Thus, the task in connecting political and economic institutions to the strength of the competence signal is shifted in our revised model from speculation about the impact of these institutions on the variances of the distributions of competence and exogenous shocks to speculation about how they impact the number of economically consequential decisions subject to electoral control.

Turning back to equation (5.17), because $E[\sum_{l=1}^{\alpha} \mu_{ilt} \mid k_{it}] = E[\sum_{l=1}^{\alpha} \mu_{ilt} \mid y_{it}]$, this expression is the rational voter's assessment of the current competence of the incumbent given the observed economy.[13] Furthermore, from equation (5.5), we have $E[\sum_{l=1}^{\alpha} \mu_{ilt} \mid y_{it}] = E[\sum_{l=1}^{\alpha} \omega_{ilt+1}]$, so we now have what we need to explore the implications of the model for economic voting by comparing the voter's expected utility for voting for the incumbent in this model to her expected utility for the challenger.

The voter's expected utility for voting for incumbent party i is just the expected utility the voter will accrue in the next period if party i is in office.[14]

$$\begin{aligned} E\left[\sum_{l=1}^{\alpha} \mu_{ilt+1} \mid v_i\right] &= E\left[u\left(\pi_{it+1}, y_{it+1}\right)\right] \\ &= \frac{1}{2}E[\pi_{it+1}^2] + bE[y_{it+1}] \\ &= 0 + b\left(\bar{y} + E\left[\eta_{it+1}\right]\right)_i \end{aligned}$$

13 $E\left[\mu_{it} \mid y_{it}\right] = \frac{\sigma_{\mu,y}}{\sigma_\mu^2+\sigma_\xi^2}\left(y_{it} - y - \mu_{it-1}\right)$ by applying the same signal-extraction solution as earlier. Furthermore, it is easy to show that $\sigma_{\mu,y} = \sigma_{\mu,k}$, so the claim in the text follows.

14 All voters in the model are identical and care about achieving the highest possible economic growth and lowest possible inflation in the next period. Specifically, we write the utility of a typical voter in period $t+1$ as a function of which party is elected, what policy that party pursues, and what the resulting level of economic growth will be. Given some governing party, i, that pursues a particular economic policy (a choice of π_{it-1}), the voter's utility in period $t+1$ is, in part:

$$u\left(\pi_{it+1}, y_{it+1}\right) = -\tfrac{1}{2}u(\pi_{it+1}^2) + by_{it+1}, b > 0$$

where in Alesina and Rosenthal's formulation, π is just inflation and b indexes the voter's preference for growth relative to inflation. However, in our formulation, π is a package of policies and b indexes the voter's preference for growth relative to her (nongrowth-related) utility for the overall policy package offered by the government. The particular functional form of the voter's utility is quite flexible: any choice that has the voter's utility increasing in growth will produce the same substantive implications for rational economic voting, given the other assumptions in the model. The one provided here is a common formulation in the literature and so was chosen for its familiarity. In our application, it requires that we normalize the utility of the policy bundle so that the voter's preferred policy is achieved at a level of zero, but this can be done without loss of generality.

$$
\begin{aligned}
&= 0 + b\left(\bar{y} + 0 + E\left[\sum_{l=1}^{\alpha} \omega_{ilt+1}\right]\right) \\
&= b\left(\bar{y} + \left(\frac{\alpha\sigma_{\mu}^{2}}{\alpha\sigma_{\mu}^{2} + \beta\sigma_{\psi}^{2}}\right)\left(y_{it} - \bar{y} - \sum_{l=1}^{\alpha} \mu_{ilt-1}\right)\right) \\
&= b\bar{y} + b\left(\frac{\alpha\sigma_{\mu}^{2}}{\alpha\sigma_{\mu}^{2} + \beta\sigma_{\psi}^{2}}\right)\left(y_{it} - \bar{y} - \sum_{l=1}^{\alpha} \mu_{ilt-1}\right) \qquad (5.18)
\end{aligned}
$$

Lacking any information about the challenger's level of competence, the voter's expected utility for voting for the challenger, k, is just:[15]

$$
\begin{aligned}
E\left[\sum_{l=1}^{\alpha} \mu_{klt+1} \mid v_{k}\right] &= E\left[u\left(\pi_{kt+1}, y_{kt+1}\right)\right] \\
&= \frac{1}{2}E\left[\pi_{kt+1}^{2}\right] + bE[y_{kt+1}] \\
&= 0 + b(\bar{y} + E\left[\eta_{kt+1}\right]) \\
&= b\left(\bar{y} + E\left[\sum_{l=1}^{\beta} \psi_{lt}\right] + E\left[\sum_{l=1}^{\alpha} \omega_{klt+1}\right]\right) \\
&= b\bar{y} \qquad (5.19)
\end{aligned}
$$

Thus, the voter is more likely to vote for the incumbent when the expected utility in equation (5.18) is larger than that in equation (5.19). The difference is:

$$
\begin{aligned}
&E\left[\sum_{l=1}^{\alpha} \mu_{ilt+1} \mid v_{i}\right] - E\left[\sum_{l=1}^{\alpha} \mu_{klt+1} \mid v_{k}\right] \\
&\quad = b\bar{y} + b\left(\bar{y} + E\left[\sum_{l=1}^{\beta} \psi_{lt}\right] + E\left[\sum_{l=1}^{\alpha} \omega_{klt+1}\right]\right) - b\bar{y} \\
&\quad = b\left(\frac{\alpha\sigma_{\mu}^{2}}{\alpha\sigma_{\mu}^{2} + \beta\sigma_{\psi}^{2}}\right)\left(y_{it} - \bar{y} - \sum_{l=1}^{\alpha} \mu_{ilt-1}\right) \qquad (5.20)
\end{aligned}
$$

This result makes it clear when voters can and cannot extract information from fluctuations in the previous economy to access the current competence of an incumbent and cast an economic vote. The term $y_{it} - \bar{y} - \sum_{l=1}^{\alpha} \mu_{ilt-1}$ is simply observed economic performance less the parts of economic growth whose sources are known to the voter. The term

[15] Alesina and Rosenthal (1995) assume that the expected competence of the challenger is always zero. We discuss what happens when we change this assumption (and why we might need to) in Chapter 8.

captures how the current period differs from the natural level of growth, discounted by the impact of the incumbent's known level of competence in the previous period. We can interpret the coefficient on this term, that is, $(\frac{\alpha\sigma_\mu^2}{\alpha\sigma_\mu^2+\beta\sigma_\psi^2})$, as the "competency signal" that controls how much information about the competence of incumbents voters can extract from observed movements in the economy. This competency signal will always be positive and will approach 1 as the variance in the random (nonpolitical) shocks to the economy, $\beta\sigma_\psi^2$, goes to 0. In that case, the voter knows that growth above or below the natural rate is completely caused by competency shocks – consequently, deviations from the natural rate of growth will perfectly identify competent and incompetent administrations. More generally, if $\alpha\sigma_\mu^2$, the variation in the competence term μ_{it}, is large relative to variation in the nonpolitical component of growth, $\beta\sigma_\psi^2$, then changes in the economy will provide a strong signal about the competency of the incumbent and the voter will weight the retrospective economy more heavily in her utility function. Alternatively, growth that is above or below the natural rate is a poor signal of the incumbent's competence if $\beta\sigma_\psi^2$ is high relative to $\alpha\sigma_\mu^2$.

Given our assumption that σ_ψ^2 and σ_μ^2 are constant over all contexts, the impact of political and economic institutions on the strength of the competence signal (and, ultimately, on economic voting) must come through differences in the α and β terms in the previous equations. The numerator of the competence signal is the variance of the overall competence shock $(\alpha\sigma_\mu^2)$, which implies that expanding the number of economically consequential choices that the EDDs make will increase the value of this term. More substantively, the variance in the overall competence shock should be larger in countries in which EDDs make more of the economic decisions that determine the country's growth path.

When comparing the overall competency signal in different contexts, the ratio of nonelectorally dependent to electorally dependent decisions in each context can shape the relative size of their overall competency signals. Consider the case in which the competency signal is larger in one context than another:

$$\frac{\alpha\sigma_\mu^2}{\alpha\sigma_\mu^2+\beta\sigma_\psi^2} > \frac{\alpha'\sigma_\mu^2}{\alpha'\sigma_\mu^2+\beta'\sigma_\psi^2}$$

$$\frac{\beta\sigma_\psi}{\alpha\sigma_\mu^2} < \frac{\beta'\sigma_\psi}{\alpha'\sigma_\mu^2}$$

$$\frac{\beta}{\alpha} < \frac{\beta'}{\alpha'} \qquad (5.21)$$

where α and β are from a large competency signal context and α' and β' are from a small signal context. The resulting inequality in equation (5.21) suggests that the ratio of NEDDs to EDDs in the large signal context must be smaller than this ratio in the smaller signal context. The relative impact of political and economic contexts on the overall competency signal is the magnitudes of these ratios.

Contextual effects that will have the most unambiguous impact on this ratio are ones that simultaneously increase β and decrease α or vice versa. These are cases in which the rising number of NEDDs affecting variations in shocks to the macro-economy is displacing the number of EDDs affecting these shocks. This will generate the inequality in equation (5.21) and an unambiguous predicted effect. Contexts in which the number of NEDDs affecting macro-economic shocks is high will tend to have fewer EDDs impacting macro-economic shocks – hence, an overall signal that is smaller. An example here might be the adoption of monetary unions or common tariff regimes that typically result in a smaller number of EDDs affecting macro-economic shocks (thereby reducing the magnitude of the competency shock term) and a larger number of NEDDs having an impact (thereby increasing the exogenous shock term). The opposite case that results in a strong competency signal is contexts with relatively larger numbers of EDDs and relatively fewer NEDDs. Large states with unitary constitutions and relatively closed economies compared to small states with federal constitutions and that have extensive exposure to international trade might be an example of this case.

There also are contextual differences that only influence the numerator or denominator in these terms. Take the example of holding the numerator constant by setting $\beta = \beta'$ – two such contexts would not differ in terms of the number of NEDDs affecting macro-economic shocks. The inequality in equation (5.21) then simply reduces to $\alpha > \alpha'$; contexts with a higher number of decisions by EDDs affecting economic shocks will have a higher competency signal. An example here might be presidential versus parliamentary constitutions. One might think of presidential regimes as having larger numbers of elected decisions that affect the macro-economy than is the case with parliamentary contexts (on the grounds that there is a fusion of executive and legislative officials in a parliamentary regime, whereas they are elected separately in a presidential regime). Nevertheless, all things being equal, parliamentary and presidential constitutional contexts may have similar numbers of NEDDs impacting a nation's macro-economic shocks. Hence, the result of holding β and β' constant and increasing the number of decisions by EDDs (α) will be a higher competency signal.

Contextual differences will not always generate different competency signals. When the two ratios in equation (5.21) are equal, it is less likely that competency signals will vary across contexts. Obviously, this can happen when $\alpha = \alpha'$ and $\beta = \beta'$. These are simply cases in which context does not matter. A somewhat more problematic case is when the two ratios in equation (5.21) are equal, but $\alpha \neq \alpha'$ and $\beta \neq \beta'$. We expect this to be relatively rare because it presumes that contextual differences reduce or increase both the number of EDDs and of NEDDs in similar ratios to each other.

Our theoretical results in this section provide a foundation for understanding how economic and political context shapes the economic vote. As the ratio of NEDDs to EDD rises, the overall competency signal will decline and vice versa, which, we argue, should impact the economic vote. Our theory does not indicate which specific contexts are associated with particular ratios of NEDDs to EDDs. Hence, in order to generate predictions regarding the impact of economic and political context on economic voting, we need to understand how these contexts impact the ratio of NEDDs to EDDs. Later, we examine a number of such hypotheses by providing arguments about how specific institutional differences across political and economic contexts should impact the ratio of NEDDs to EDDs.

This chapter has developed a selection model of the economic vote that explains contextual variations in economic voting in terms of the quality of the competency signal that voters are able to extract from shocks in macro-economic outcomes. In addition, we have described how the ratio of electorally dependent to nonelectorally dependent decision makers can condition the magnitude of these competency signals. We now turn to examining empirically the nature of economic competency signals, whether voters are attentive to these signals, whether these signals condition economic vote magnitudes, and whether economic and political institutions, through their impact on the competency signal, also affect economic voting in a fashion consistent with our theory.

6

What Do Voters Know about Economic Variation and Its Sources?

Our explanation for contextual variation in economic voting assumes that voters know how much of the variation in random shocks to the economy is due to the competence of the government rather than the influences of nonelectorally dependent exogenous factors.[1] By making this assumption, we were able to derive hypotheses about the way in which variation in the competency signal (and therefore voters' beliefs about this signal) likely impacts economic voting across countries and over time. Furthermore, in elaborating the meaning of the competency signal and thinking about what drives variation in it, we suggest a broad set of political and economic contexts that might systematically condition the magnitude of the signal (e.g., those that impact the relative number or importance of electorally versus nonelectorally dependent decision makers in economic policy making).

This chapter considers whether it is even reasonable to assume that voters have sensible beliefs about the variance in competence shocks to the economy. Or even about the total variation in shocks to the economy. Skepticism abounds in this respect and with good reason. Early efforts by Alesina and Rosenthal (1995) to demonstrate that fluctuations in the U.S. macro-economy might plausibly inform voters about incumbent competency suggested they did not. And even if they did, should we expect the typical voter to pay attention to and have informed beliefs about these signals? Given the often-touted ignorance of voters when it comes to political and economic matters, some skepticism is surely warranted (on levels of political information, see Delli, Carpini, and Keeter, 1996; on levels of information about the economy, see Paldam and Nannestad, 2000). Given this skepticism and given the relatively limited research that has been done

[1] That is, they know $\sigma_\mu^2/(\sigma_\mu^2 + \sigma_\xi^2)$.

on these issues in the existing literature, this chapter explores a variety of original data that we have collected that provides insight into these issues.

How do we do this? Well, our theory is quite precise about the information demands made of the voter. This chapter describes these assumptions, lays out their empirical implications, and provides some initial empirical tests. First, we assume there is a competency signal that is composed of variations in the competence and exogenous shocks described in the previous chapter. Hence, this chapter begins by demonstrating that there is information in economic fluctuations that voters can plausibly use to inform themselves about competency: most important, that there is variation and that the contextual differences (either over time or across countries) can inform voters about the two components of the competency signal. Second, media reporting of economic news is an important – although obviously not the only – source of information regarding fluctuations in the macro-economy. Hence, we expect that the content of economic news will be consistent with our model of how voters extract competency signals from fluctuations in the macro-economy. Third, voters have sensible beliefs about these fluctuations in economic outcomes that are consistent with the signal-extraction efforts we attribute to them. Finally, they use this information to condition the economic vote. We do not pretend to provide the definitive evidence for all four of these claims. Nevertheless, we think the evidence is suggestive enough to invite further inquiry into the sources and nature of voters' information about the economy and its variability.

COMPETENCY SIGNAL EXTRACTION ILLUSTRATED

Our theory of the economic vote assumes that voters observe fluctuations in economic outcomes that inform them about incumbent competency. What are informative macro-economic fluctuations? Take, as an example, the typical voter in the first round of the 2002 French presidential elections. Figure 6.1 (focus on the dots initially) presents the quarterly real GDP growth rates that occurred in the seven years preceding Jacque Chirac's 2002 reelection bid for the French presidency. The annual real GDP growth rate was about 2.4 percent over the course of Chirac's seven-year term (represented by the horizontal line drawn in the figure). But these quarterly readings clearly varied – in the early part of his term, the growth rate almost dropped to zero, rising quite a bit higher than the mean in 1998 and in the year 2000, and then dropping below 1 percent in the first quarter of the election year. Our theory presumes that French voters know

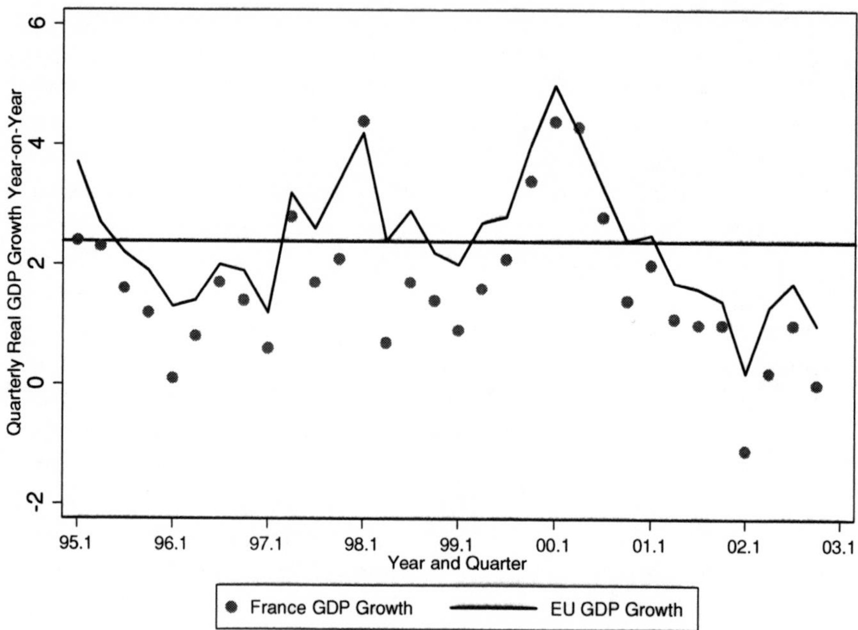

Figure 6.1. French real GDP growth during President Chirac's first term.

$\sigma_{\mu}^{2}+\sigma_{\xi}^{2}$ (i.e., variation in shocks to economic growth); we contend that one source of this knowledge is exactly the kinds of historical variations in economic outcomes that are illustrated in Figure 6.1.

Besides the total variation in macro-economic shocks, our theory assumes voters can separate shocks to the macro-economy that are associated with incumbent competence (σ_{μ}^{2}) as opposed to nonpolitical factors (σ_{ξ}^{2}). So, for example, would the average French voter conclude that elected officials are primarily responsible for the spike in GDP growth to almost 5 percent in the first quarter of 2001 and then its rapid decline to less than 1 percent in the first quarter of 2002? In our theory, they would draw this conclusion, if they believed that σ_{μ}^{2} was large relative to the total variation. In this chapter, we argue that voters who are attentive to global economic outcomes have information that allows them to distinguish the relative sizes of σ_{μ}^{2} and σ_{ξ}^{2}.

It is unlikely that all of the variation in Figure 6.1 is the responsibility of elected French officials. Note, for example, that the spike in GDP growth in the first quarter of 2000 and the steep subsequent decline in GDP growth conformed very closely to overall fluctuations in EU growth – in fact, much of the volatility in French economic growth over the period seems to resemble that of the overall EU economies. Because fluctuations in the two GDP growth rates are so similar, voters are likely to conclude that competency shocks historically have been small relative to exogenous shocks. Consequently, they can infer that the unobserved variance of the competence shocks (σ_{μ}^2) must be smaller than that of the exogenous shocks (σ_{ξ}^2). If these French voters focused exclusively on GDP growth, we would conclude that the overall competency signal is quite small, which, all things being equal, would imply low levels of economic voting. And we believe that voters recognize this is the case; moreover, we hope to demonstrate in this chapter that some voters attribute significant amounts of this variation to global economic influences that are outside of the control of elected officials. The solid-line plot in Figure 6.1 is the quarterly GDP growth figures for the (then) fifteen members of the EU and could assist voters in their signal-extraction task. In this case, our expectation is that French voters will, for the most part, perceive small variation in the competency shock term (σ_{μ}^2) and relatively high variation in the exogenous shock term (σ_{ξ}^2).

Hence, we expect that the typical voter can (a) compare fluctuations in the country's macro-economy with that of the overall global economy; and (b) draw conclusions about the impact of domestic politicians on economic outcomes based on whether variations in the national economy diverge from the global norm? The next section establishes that national economic outcomes, in general, fluctuate in a fashion that likely informs voters of incumbent competency.

CONTEXTUAL VARIATION IN MACRO-ECONOMIC OUTCOMES

We begin by generalizing the French example from Figure 6.1 and demonstrating that, in fact, cross-national variations in macro-economic outcomes can be pronounced compared to within-country variations and so may figure in the voter's efforts to distinguish incumbent competence from random shocks. Figure 6.2 makes a convincing case that cross-national variations in macro-economic outcomes can be large (and persistent) and, hence, they may provide voters with the information necessary to infer the competence of incumbent governments. The first panel in Figure 6.2 presents change in the CPI for the fourteen countries in our sample over the 1979–2002 period – the solid line in the graph represents the mean change in CPI for this sample of countries (weighted for size of the economy). In the early 1980s, we see very significant cross-national variation with countries experiencing changes in their CPI that were as much as 5 percent lower than the mean and as much as 10 percentage points higher. By the end of our sampled period, the range had narrowed radically to between about −2 and +3 percentage points. This is consistent with findings in the political business-cycle literature that the increased credibility of the European Monetary System (EMS) and the reduced number of currency realignments lead to a greater convergence of inflation rates in Europe and a reduction, if not elimination, of a partisan impact on inflation rates in the OECD countries (Alesina and Roubini, 1997: 161).

The second panel in Figure 6.2 presents OECD standardized unemployment rates along with the OECD standardized unemployment rate for the seven major OECD countries that is represented by the bold black line. Unlike inflation, where there was a clear dynamic trend converging on a low rate of inflation among all the countries, average unemployment for the sample has fluctuated significantly around a mean of about 6 percent. There are single countries in the sample that experience radically different rates of unemployment – Ireland registered unemployment rates of 17 percent in the 1980s and early 1990s, but we see these rates drop to less than 5 percent in the early 2000s. Belgium begins the sample period with around 7 percent unemployment but experiences levels exceeding 10 percent in the 1980s and 1990s.

In a fashion similar to unemployment, real GDP per capita growth rates vary considerably over the sampled period. The overall sample mean drops to about 0 percent real growth in the early 1980s, the early 1990s, and the early 2000s, and almost hits 5 percent during the high-growth periods. The equilibrium level is around 3 percent during the period we sampled. It appears that over this sampled period, most countries experienced this full range of fluctuation in real GDP growth (0 to 5 percent) – some even witnessed serious economic contractions in the order of −5 percent, and a couple of countries exceed 10 percent growth for short periods of time. But there is also considerable cross-country variation in the series, although more muted than was the case with unemployment.

These descriptive plots suggest the existence of significant cross-national variations in macro-economic shocks. But we can summarize the plots of Figure 6.2 with a measure of the relative magnitudes of cross-national to within-country variations in macro-economic shocks. We do this in two steps. First, we estimate a ratio, where the numerator is between-country variance and the denominator is the sum of within-country and between-country variance in macro-economic outcomes. To

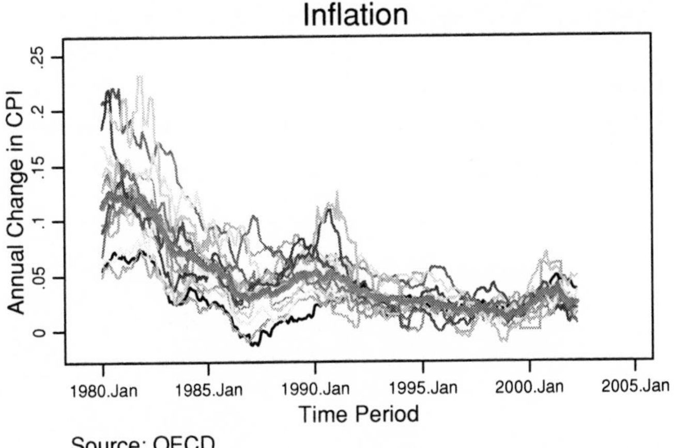

Standardized Unemployment Rate

Unemployment Rate

0
5
10
15
20

1980.Jan
1985.Jan
1990.Jan
1995.Jan
2000.Jan
2005.Jan

Time Period

Source: OECD

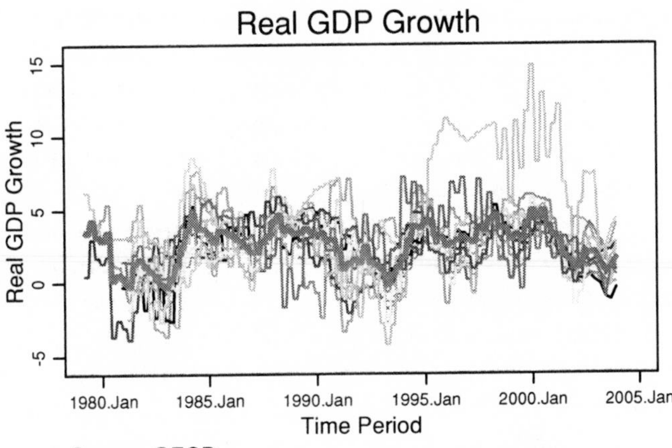

Figure 6.2. Macro-economic outcomes: 1979–2002.

estimate these quantities from data on economic outcomes, we specify a simple random effects model for each of our three macro-economic variables for country j in period t:

$$
\begin{aligned}
Y_{tj} &= \beta_0 + \mu_j + \varepsilon_{tj} \\
\beta_o &= \text{grand mean of } Y_{tj} \text{ all countries and periods} \\
\mu_j &= \text{deviation from grand mean for country } j \\
\varepsilon_{tj} &= \text{deviation from mean for country } j \text{ for period } t
\end{aligned} \qquad (6.1)
$$

The total variance of Y_{tj} is the sum of the variance of μ_j, which we label τ^2, and the variance of ε_{tj}, which we label σ^2. The intraclass correlation coefficient (ρ) captures the extent to which overall variation is a result of differences between countries (Goldstein, 1995). It is defined as

$$
\rho = \frac{\text{variance between countries}}{\text{total variance}} = \frac{\tau^2}{\tau^2 + \sigma^2} \qquad (6.2)
$$

As the proportion of the total variance accounted for at the cross-national levels rises, ρ gets closer to 1. As the intraclass coefficient (ρ) gets larger, cross-national variance in macro-economic outcomes dominates total variation in macro-economic outcomes and voters can infer that national macro-economic shocks are the result of incumbent competence rather than exogenous shocks from the global economy (i.e., $\sigma^2_\mu > \sigma^2_\xi$).

Our expectation is that voters establish the competence of incumbents over macro-economic outcomes based on a sampling of economic outcomes that span a reasonable period of time – this does not result from viewing a single monthly economic outcome. At the same time, we can see from the inflation series in Figure 6.2 that the proportion of total variance in economic shocks accounted for by the competence term may vary over time. Accordingly, we estimate the random effects model over approximately five-year periods (1979–1985, 1986–1990, 1991–1995, 1996–2002). The resulting intraclass coefficients for these periods are summarized in Figure 6.3. Cross-national variations in unemployment clearly dominate total variation in this macro-economic indicator, suggesting that it should play an important role in signaling incumbent competence. Cross-national variations in inflation seem to account for less of the total variation in this series than was the case for unemployment but appear to be relatively significant throughout our sample period. Even though, as we saw in Figure 6.2, total variation in inflation has declined significantly, the portion accounted for by cross-national variations continues

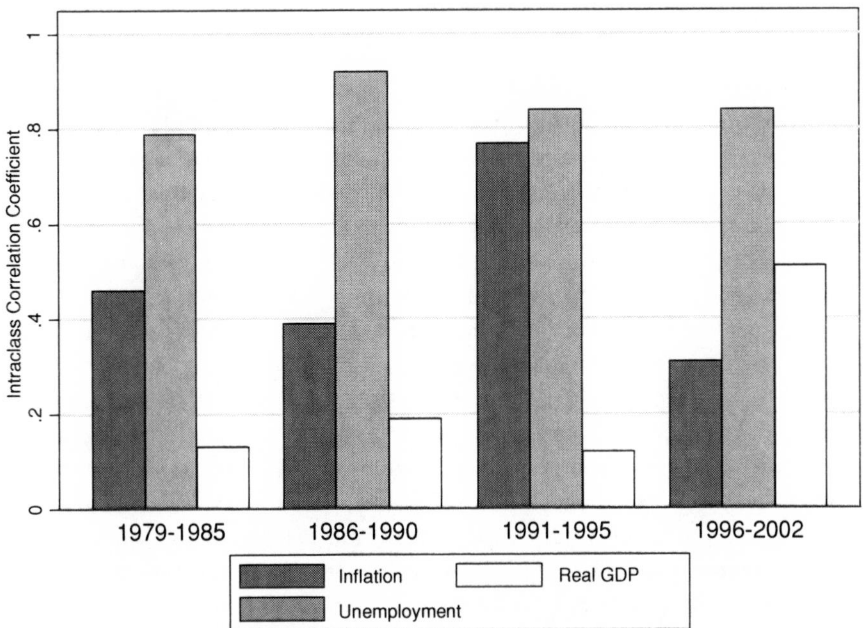

Figure 6.3. Intraclass correlation coefficients for macro-economic indicators.

to be quite significant. Finally, the results for cross-national variations in real GDP confirm the French example in Figure 6.1. For the most part, between-nation variations in real GDP have been small relative to total overall variation in this indicator. Given the magnitude of cross-national variations relative to within-country fluctuations for both unemployment and inflation, we would expect these two series to have a greater impact on economic voting than variations in real GDP growth.

The point of presenting these macro-economic statistics is simply to establish that the real economy fluctuates over time and cross-nationally in a fashion that at least potentially provides voters with the information necessary for undertaking the signal-extraction task described in our theory. The fact that the necessary information is available to voters is obviously no assurance that they pay any attention to it and that voters are ultimately knowledgeable about it. One factor that would certainly contribute to the voter's ability to learn about these economic fluctuations is the reporting of economic news by the media. If the media accords little attention to variations in macro-economic shocks, this would compromise the voter's ability to learn about them. This is an empirical question that we turn to in the next section.

INFORMATION ABOUT VARIANCE IN THE MACRO-ECONOMY

Do the voters get much information about the variance in economic outcomes? There is considerable evidence that the media plays an integral role in shaping economic evaluations, which, of course, are critical to economic-voting models (De Boef and Kellstedt, 2004; Duch and Stevenson, 2007; Erikson, MacKuen, and Stimson, 2002; Nadeau et al., 1999).[2] We believe the media transmits information that helps voters assess overall variance in shocks to the macro-economy. Specifically, media reports of economic performance include extensive references to how the economy has changed. Our analysis of 10,000 front-page newspaper stories reporting on economic outcomes from six countries suggests that about half of these stories include some reference to how the economy changed, either in the current period or over the recent past.[3] Moreover, what typically captures the attention of media outlets are unexpected changes in macro-economic outcomes. Again, a careful analysis of our sample of media reports suggests that these stories tend to focus on the unexpected. Hence, to the extent that the media primes voters to think about the economy at all, it seems to emphasize changes or fluctuations in macro-economic outcomes.

This suggests that fluctuations in the economy trigger media attention. We evaluate the extent to which this is the case by examining media coverage in the United States. For each month over the 1980–2004 period, we conducted a count of *New York Times* and *Washington Post* stories mentioning inflation and a similar count for unemployment. These counts were then averaged over each year in our sample to give us two variables measuring annual average monthly counts of inflation and unemployment stories. We also estimated the standard deviation of inflation and unemployment for each of the years in our sample. Our argument is that greater variation in economic outcomes stimulates greater coverage. This suggests that the count of media stories concerning inflation or unemployment should be higher during periods in which the standard deviations of

[2] The precise manner in which the media affect economic evaluations is the subject of debate – for example, De Boef and Kellsted (2004) suggest the effect is indirect via popular assessments of the president's economic management, whereas Nadeau et al. (1999) argue for a direct effect between the media and economic evaluations.

[3] This project samples newspaper front pages the day of and the day after the release of national economic statistics by the relevant country's statistical agency (from 1980 to 2001). All headlines and stories that mention the economy were coded for content, including the extent to which the information was presented in changes or levels or was compared to previous experiences.

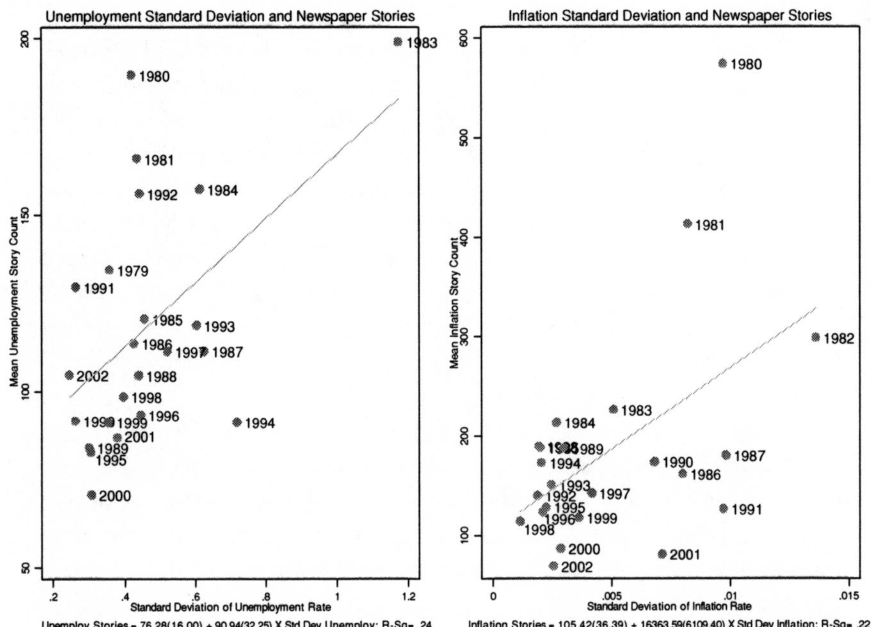

Figure 6.4. Variance in U.S. macro-economy and economic news: 1980–2004. *Note:* Standard deviation in parentheses.

actual inflation or unemployment outcomes are high. Figure 6.4 presents the plots of inflation stories against the standard deviation of inflation rates and unemployment stories against the standard deviation of unemployment rates. The results support the notion that variance in economic outcomes tends to trigger media attention. Note that in both cases, high standard deviations are associated with a high story count. This lends credence to our argument that voters are quite likely to be informed about variance in economic outcomes.

VOTER ATTENTION TO INFORMATION ABOUT VARIANCE IN THE MACRO-ECONOMY

Is there any reason to believe that the average voter in developed democracies pays any attention to information regarding variance in economic outcomes?[4] Some have argued that, in fact, fluctuations in

4 Our focus on the developed democracies excludes, for the most part, countries that have experienced dramatic variances in macro-economic outcomes and where there is no question that citizens have been concerned with variance in addition to growth.

economic outcomes attract considerable attention from the voter. Quinn and Woolley (2001), for example, replicate the Powell and Whitten (1993) aggregate-level analysis of incumbent vote shares and find that, in addition to economic growth, their measure of economic volatility has a significant negative effect on incumbent vote shares (although the conclusions they draw regarding its implication for the economic vote are quite different than ours).[5] Moreover, some scholars have argued that the absence of economic volatility as a public good is widely favored by the voting public, which might be one reason that democracies have lower levels of economic volatility (Rodrik, 1997b). The important point here is that voters – or, at least, the median voter – must be attentive to variance in economic outcomes.

Overall, however, there has been relatively little effort to investigate empirically whether variations in the economy register with the typical voter. As a result, in the spring of 2005, we conducted a six-nation survey that explored voters' beliefs about the variation in their national economies and its sources.[6] One of the questions in this survey asked respondents the following:

> Over the last four years would you say that the economy in [COUNTRY] has experienced very stable growth, somewhat stable growth, somewhat unstable growth, or very unstable growth?

Does this question tap meaningful attitudes about variation in the national economy? One issue here is whether this question is eliciting something other than an overall assessment of economic outcomes, which the typical economic evaluation questions are designed to measure. We can get some indication by correlating responses to this question with responses to the standard retrospective national economic evaluation question.[7] For the combined sample of all six countries, the correlation was 0.56, suggesting that, in fact, these two questions are tapping

[5] Quinn and Woolley (2001: 636) also cite historical Gallup polls from the United States, indicating that respondents consider economic instability to be one of their greatest fears for the country.

[6] The survey was pretested in the United States in the early spring. Details on the six-nation study are available at http://www.nuffield.ox.ac.uk/economicvoting/sixnationsurvey.

[7] This wording of this question for the U.K. survey was as follows: "Now thinking about the economy in the UK as a whole, would you say that over the past year the nation's economy has gotten much better, gotten somewhat better, stayed about the same, gotten somewhat worse, or gotten a lot worse?"

quite distinct attitudes regarding the economy. Also, if responses to this question show systematic variation as opposed to just random fluctuation, we would be inclined to conclude that, yes, it does tap meaningful attitudes. One approach is to examine whether there is a significant degree of agreement among respondents in their answers. Random answers would show no such clustering; rather, randomness suggests answers that are distributed relatively uniformly. Furthermore, we would expect, if voters have well-formed beliefs about variation in the economy, that the proportion of "Don't Know" responses would be similar to their proportion in other surveys that collect other kinds of economic information (e.g., economic retrospections).

Results from each of the six countries clearly suggest that the question is meaningful. Figure 6.5 indicates that in each of the countries, we see a clear modal response and relatively small variances around the modal response.[8] In Denmark, for example, over half the respondents choose the "somewhat stable growth" response. In no case is the modal response less than 40 percent of the sample. Furthermore, the number of "Don't Know" responses compare favorably with levels in other surveys soliciting more standard types of economic beliefs. The highest level of "Don't Know" responses was 6.7 percent of the Danish sample and the lowest was 1.1 percent of the French sample. These compare quite favorably, for example, to the range of "Don't Know" responses to the standard question concerning retrospective evaluations of the national economy that we asked in the same set of surveys: the highest level, again, was 7.5 percent of the Danish sample and the lowest level was 1 percent of the French sample.

The competency elements of our theory suggest that perceptions of economic volatility condition the economic vote. Hence, part of the theory's claim to explain cross-national variations in the economic vote is contingent on significant cross-national variation in average perceptions of economic volatility. The left-hand graph in Figure 6.6 shows that average citizen perceptions of the stability of economic outcomes in their country vary quite significantly across European nations. Danish and British respondents clearly perceive their national economies as turning in very stable growth over the previous four years. By contrast, the Germans and Italians report very high levels of instability in growth outcomes. In short, these individual-level data lend support to the idea that contextual

[8] The response set for this question varies from 1 (Very Stable) to 4 (Very Unstable).

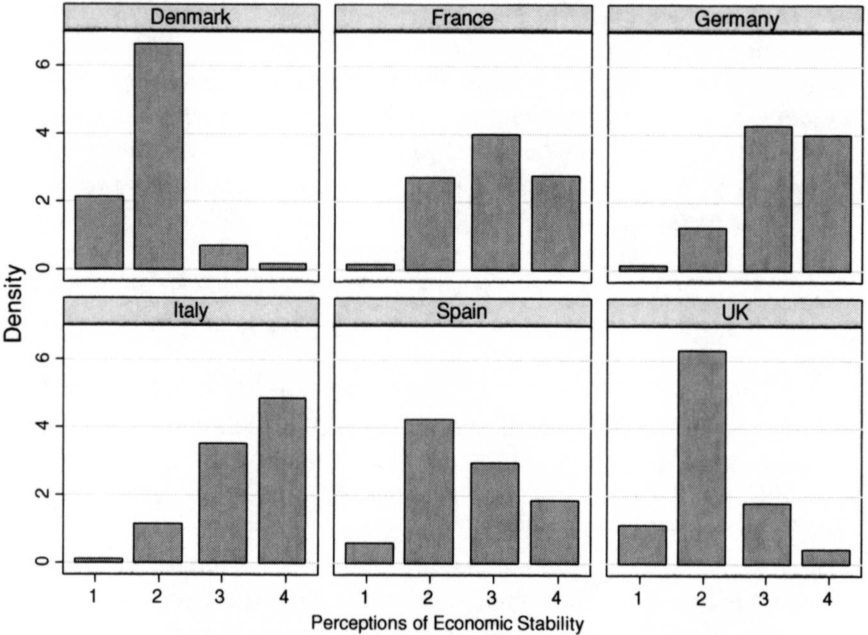

Figure 6.5. Histogram of volatility of economic perceptions, Europe.

variation in the economic vote could come, in part, from differences in the competency signal perceived by the voter.

Of particular concern to our competency argument is whether cross-national variation in perceptions of economic stability is grounded in real variation in the economies of the different countries. We expect citizens in contexts with highly variable economic outcomes to perceive economic outcomes to be highly unstable. The right-hand graph in Figure 6.6 confirms this expectation: Citizens in contexts where the economic outcomes were highly unstable over the 2000–2005 period (measured by the standard deviation of annual growth in real GDP for the period) – Italy, Germany, and France, in particular – have perceptions of economic instability that are much higher than citizens in contexts with more stable economic outcomes – the United Kingdom and Spain. Our evidence, although based only on six countries, is unique in its focus on economic variation and confirms that voters have well-formed beliefs about variation in their national economies and that these beliefs are grounded in economic reality.

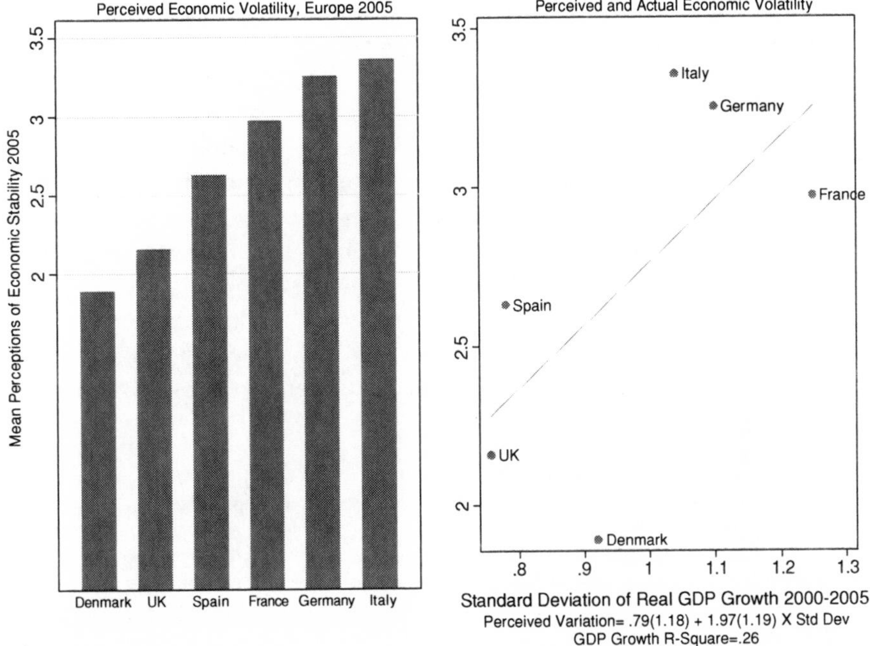

Figure 6.6. Volatility of real GDP and economic perceptions, Europe. *Note:* Standard deviation in parentheses.

THE SOURCES OF VARIATION IN MACRO-ECONOMIC OUTCOMES

Our competency argument assumes that, besides knowing the overall variance in macro-economic shocks, voters also know the relative contributions of σ_μ^2 and σ_ξ^2 to that total. Although models in the political-economy literature often make this assumption (e.g., Cukierman and Meltzer, 1986; Rogoff and Sibert, 1988), there has been little effort to explore empirically whether citizens have perceptions consistent with this characterization. This section addresses the empirical support for this contention.

If voters have a sense of the total variation in economic shocks (i.e., $\sigma_\mu^2 + \sigma_\xi^2$) and, in addition have well-formed beliefs about either one of these variance terms, then they can distinguish between the relative contributions of the two components of this total variation. So, for example, if they have a good sense of how important exogenous shocks are in their national economy (σ_ξ^2) and they have a sense of how much shocks to the economy vary in general ($\sigma_\mu^2 + \sigma_\xi^2$), they should have a sense of how much "room" there is for the competence of the elected government to impact the economy ($\sigma_\mu^2 = (\sigma_\mu^2 + \sigma_\xi^2) - \sigma_\xi^2$). One piece of information that we think helps individuals distinguish exogenous from competency shocks is simply the extent to which the domestic economy depends on global economic outcomes. The greater extent to which citizens believe most domestic economic outcomes are determined by global influences, the less likely they are to conclude that economic outcomes result from the competence of elected officials. Our expectation is that voters have beliefs about the dependency of their national economy on global influences.[9]

To gauge whether citizens have beliefs about the extent the economy is subject to exogenous shocks, we asked respondents in our six countries the following question:

> To what extent is growth in the economy in [COUNTRY] dependent on growth in the other European economies? Would you say extremely dependent, very dependent, moderately dependent, a little dependent, or not at all dependent?

As in the previous question, there was substantial agreement among respondents in each country regarding the extent of global influences on the domestic economy. In each case, more than 45 percent of respondents chose the modal category and no more than 11 percent indicated they could not answer. The fact that the modal response includes such a relatively large number of respondents and that nonresponse is comparatively low suggests that voters are getting consistent information from the media about their countries' position in the global economy.

Furthermore, there is some evidence here that these opinions reflect actual global influences on the domestic economy. Figure 6.7 plots average responses to this question for each country against our measure of trade exposure. Note that three countries with relatively low levels of trade exposure – Italy, France, and Spain – have average responses in the middle category ("moderately dependent"). Denmark, which is the one country in our sample with a very high trade exposure, also is the only country with

[9] Much of the trade-policy literature makes a similar assumption. For example, the preferences that producers and holders of capital have regarding trade liberalization policies are typically portrayed as resulting from (1) self-interested assessments of the relative scarcity of their skills or their capital, and (2) how greater exposure to global competition would affect the returns to their labor or capital. This presumes that individual citizens have basic information regarding the relationship of the nation's economy to global trade. And there is a growing body of literature demonstrating that citizens, in fact, have preferences and beliefs about trade policy (Baker, 2005; Mayda and Rodrik, 2005) that are consistent with these models.

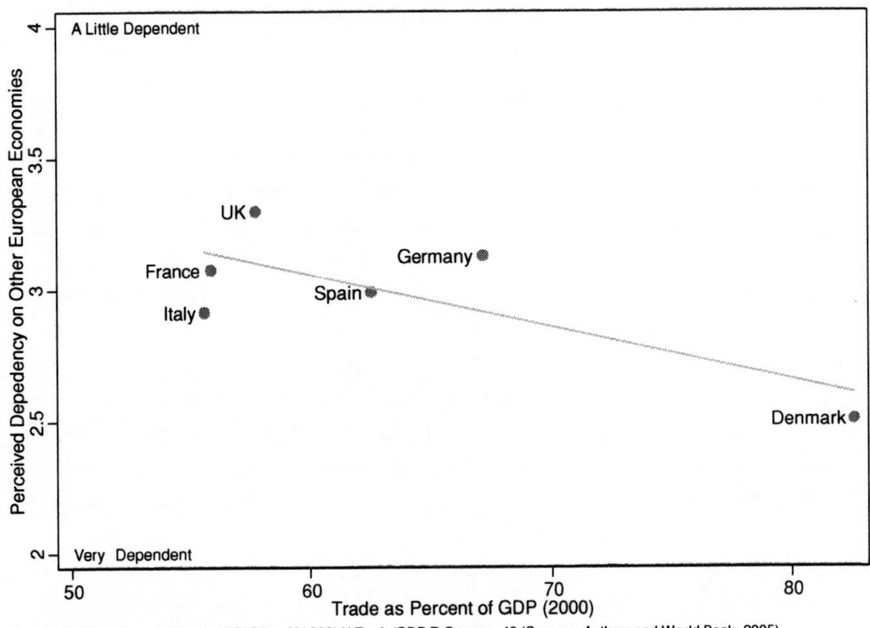

Figure 6.7. Trade and perceptions of dependency on European economies. *Note:* Standard deviation in parentheses.

an average response close to the "very dependent" category. Obviously, this is a very small number of observations. Nonetheless, Figure 6.7 is suggestive of the link between perceptions of dependency and actual trade dependency.

Having reasonably accurate information about the global dependency of their economy is a resource that citizens can employ in distinguishing competency from exogenous shocks to the macro-economy. Figure 6.7 provides some support for the notion that citizens are equipped for the task. We can further explore whether citizens have the information necessary to distinguish exogenous from competence shocks to the macro-economy with a somewhat larger sample of countries from the PEW Global Attitudes Project. PEW asked the following series of questions:

Do you think change in [INSERT EACH ITEM BELOW] is the result of global connectedness?

the availability of good-paying jobs
the working conditions for ordinary workers

the availability of modern medicines and treatments
the availability of food in stores
the gap between rich and poor people

Respondents provided yes or no answers to each question. Although not directly related to the macro-economy, as a whole, these questions provide an indication of the extent to which different national populations perceive that the global economy affects general economic outcomes. We analyzed these items and created a single factor score measuring the extent to which citizens perceived their overall economy to be "globally connected." All of the items loaded quite highly on a single factor with high values indicating global dependency.[10] This is reassuring because it provides some confirmation that there is an underlying attitude anchored on one end by a belief that the national economy is heavily influenced by global forces and, on the other, by a recognition that the national economy is relatively unaffected by global factors.

Again, our argument suggests that populations with heavy exposure to global economic influences should register high levels of "global dependency." We test this hypothesis in Figure 6.8, which plots each country's global dependency score (a high mean score indicates that the population believes the economy is heavily influenced by global forces) against the country's trade exposure (total trade – exports and imports – as a percentage of total GDP). The evidence is quite convincing. Countries with high levels of trade exposure tend to be those in which their population registers a high level of awareness of the extent to which the domestic economy is subject to global economic influences.

One assumption of the competency theory of contextual variation in the economic vote is that voters know the variance in exogenous shocks to the macro-economy (relative to the variance in competency shocks). They can acquire this knowledge by observing the importance of global influences on the domestic economy.[11] The evidence presented here suggests quite clearly that voters are attentive to information regarding the extent to which the domestic economy is subject to exogenous shocks from the

[10] Only developed countries from this sample were included in the analysis – countries with GDP per capita in the year 2000 of more than U.S.$5,000 (1995).

[11] We realize, of course, that not all exogenous shocks to the economy arise from nondomestic sources. Indeed, the theory only distinguishes between governmental and nongovernmental shocks, where the nongovernmental category includes shocks arising from the behavior of any economic actor who voters do not include in the government whose competency they wish to evaluate.

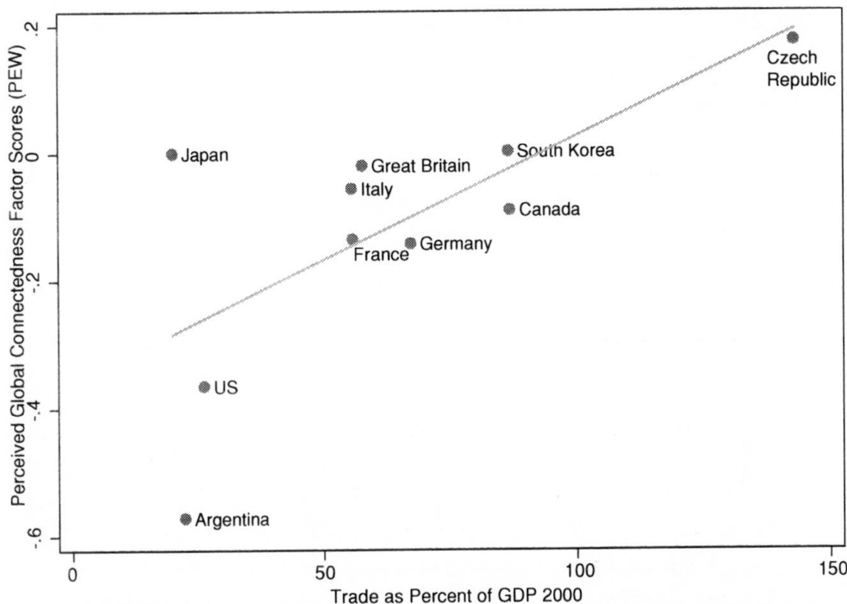

Figure 6.8. Trade and perceptions of global connectedness. *Note:* Standard deviation in parentheses.

global economy. Voters appear to have meaningful attitudes regarding global influences on the economy. More important, cross-national variations in assessments of the magnitude of these exogenous shocks correlate with actual measures of trade dependency, suggesting that these attitudes reflect global influences on the voter's national economy.

INDIVIDUAL PERCEPTIONS OF ECONOMIC VARIATION AND THE ECONOMIC VOTE

We can use our six-nation European survey to explore how perceptions regarding fluctuations in the domestic economy impact the economic vote. Individuals whose perceptions of the domestic economy deviate from their perceptions of the global economy should infer that economic fluctuations are due to the competence of domestic politicians. In contrast, individuals who perceive their national economies to fluctuate in tandem with the global economy would have little reason to conclude that economic outcomes are the result of domestic decision makers. Here, we focus on Europe and treat the overall European economy as the global referent.

Table 6.1. *Perceptions of Stability of National and European Economies*

	European Economy				
National Economy	Very Stable	Somewhat Stable	Somewhat Unstable	Very Unstable	Total
Very Stable	**86**	143	116	27	372
Somewhat Stable	105	**1,114**	596	90	1,905
Somewhat Unstable	35	543	**836**	131	1,545
Very Unstable	27	286	446	**484**	1,243
Total	253	2,086	1,994	732	5,065

Our six-nation study asked respondents to assess the stability of both their national economies and the overall European economy.[12] Table 6.1 presents a cross-tabulation of responses to these two questions. The entries are the numbers of respondents falling in each cell. Respondents falling along the diagonal (in bold) had identical responses for both their domestic economy and the European economy. Off-diagonal respondents represent those who perceived domestic fluctuations as deviating from those of the overall European economy – either being higher or lower. Approximately 50 percent fall on the diagonal with the other 50 percent falling on the off-diagonal cells.

Our theory suggests that those respondents falling in the off-diagonal cells of Table 6.1 (not in bold) – that is, those respondents who perceive their variations in their domestic economic outcomes as deviating from variations in the overall European economy – should conclude that the overall competency signal is stronger than respondents in the diagonal cells. The reasoning here is that fluctuations in the domestic economy that are distinct from those in the overall global economy signal the competency of elected officials. Because the respondents in the off-diagonals perceive a higher overall competency signal, they should, according to our theory, have a higher propensity to cast an economic vote.

We can evaluate this argument empirically by determining whether the respondents in the off-diagonals of Table 6.1, in fact, are more likely to cast an economic vote. Respondents in the six-nation survey were asked to report their likely vote choice if an election were held in the coming

[12] The Europe economy question was worded as follows: "Over the last four years, would you say that the European economies have experienced very stable growth, somewhat stable growth, somewhat unstable growth, or very unstable growth?"

Table 6.2. *Perceived Variations in Economic Variations and the Economic Vote*

	Probit Coefficient (Standard Error)	Probit Coefficient (Standard Error)
Retrospective National Economic Evaluations	0.33 (0.02)	0.29 (0.03)
*Retrospective * Deviation*		0.08 (0.04)
Deviation (Off Diagonal in Table 6.1 = 1)		−0.33 (0.12)
Constant	−1.59 (0.07)	−1.39 (0.10)
Number of Observations	5,834	5,021
Log Likelihood	−3,123	−2,700

Note: Country dummies included in both equations.

days.[13] Responses to this question were used to create a dichotomous incumbent vote variable (respondents indicating a preference for any of the parties in the governing coalition were coded as 1, with the remaining respondents coded as 0). The first column of Table 6.2 reports the probit estimates for this simple economic vote equation (country dummies are included in the regression but their coefficients are not reported). As we would expect, retrospective national economic evaluations are strongly correlated with incumbent vote intention.

Our interest, though, is assessing whether the off-diagonal respondents – those who perceive domestic economic fluctuations as diverging from those in the overall European economy – are more likely to register an economic vote. Accordingly, we created a dummy variable (*Deviation*) that has a value of 1 for all those respondents falling in the off-diagonal cells. This variable, interacted with the economic evaluation variable, indicates whether the off-diagonal respondents have, in fact, higher levels of economic voting as we hypothesized. The second column of Table 6.2 reports these results. In fact, as we hypothesized, respondents who perceive distinct differences in the fluctuations of their national economies, compared to the overall European economy, are more likely to cast an economic vote. This is indicated by the positive and statistically significant value on the *Retrospective*Deviation* interaction term.

[13] The British questioning wording is as follows: "If a general election were held next Sunday, which political party would you vote for?"

These results suggest a rather novel account of how global trends shape economic voting behavior. A frequently made argument is that globalization "homogenizes" national economic outcomes and, as such, could, as our theory even suggests, depress economic voting. But globalization also has two other important effects. First, it raises the awareness voters have of other economies, a conclusion consistent with the results in this section. Second, it also sensitizes voters to the extent to which fluctuations in national economies deviate from global fluctuations. And this, of course, aids voters in the signal-extraction task described in our theory. Voters in this formulation are using information about national and global economic outcomes to condition their economic vote in a fashion that is quite different than traditional accounts. To illustrate, we sketch out an example from the recent history of British economic voting.

COMPETENCY SIGNALS IN THE 1979 AND 1997 BRITISH ELECTIONS

Rarely are *variations* in macro-economic shocks invoked by election scholars as an explanation for the importance of the economy in election outcomes. In fact, economic context in general is rarely considered to be important for conditioning the economic vote. A possible exception is the argument that during particularly bad economic times, the economic vote might rise (Nannestad and Paldam, 1997b). We examine the 1979 and 1997 British elections with the goal of illustrating how economic context likely provides voters with information about incumbent competence and, hence, conditions economic voting.

When Margaret Thatcher defeated the Labour government in 1979, our measure of the economic vote in Britain registered a relatively high value of about 12 percent. Figure 6.9 characterizes the macro-economic context at the time of this election. Inflation, at 14 percent, was clearly a problem, although real GDP growth, at 3.5 percent, was reasonably high, and a level of unemployment hovering around 1.3 million people, although historically high, was low compared to subsequent years when the level ultimately reached 3 million. By contrast, when Tony Blair unseated the Tories in the 1997 election, the economic vote had declined considerably to about 5 percent. Although real GDP growth in 1997 was similar to the 1979 period, unemployment had reached somewhat higher levels than 1979, although inflation was much lower and more stable. Clearly, something about the context of the 1979 election persuaded voters to give priority to their economic evaluations, whereas voters in the

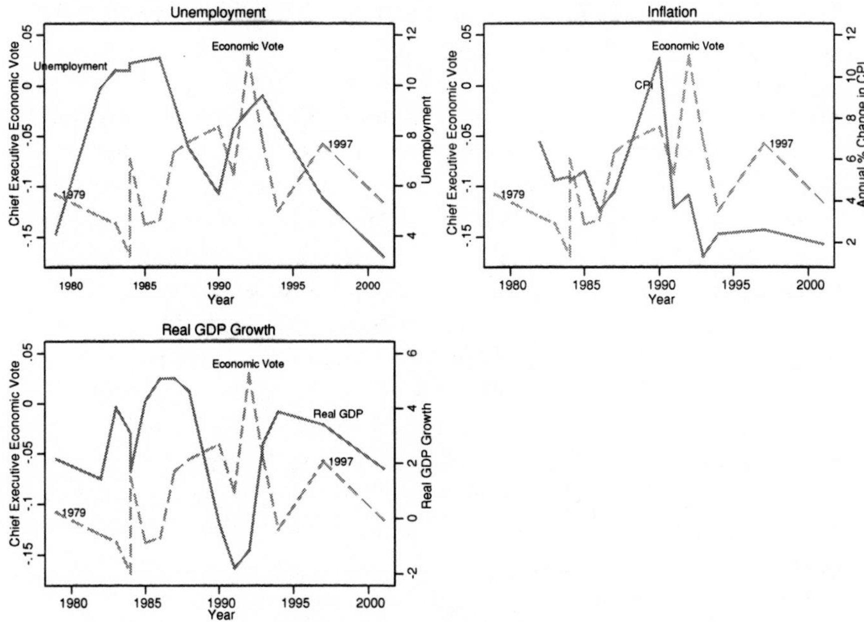

Figure 6.9. U.K. macro-economic outcomes: 1979–2002.

1997 election gave priority to other concerns. We expect this variation results from a much clearer signal regarding the economic competence of the competing candidates in the 1979 as opposed to the 1997 election. But this has not been the explanation favored by the economic-voting literature.[14]

One explanation, frequently invoked in economic-voting studies, is that economic context could be entirely unrelated to these variations in the economic vote – in 1997, noneconomic issues may have simply outweighed economic evaluations in the British voters' utility functions.[15] We entertain this as a perfectly plausible null hypothesis. It may, in fact, be the case that other factors, such as Conservative divisions over the European Union or public dissatisfaction with the government's decision to

[14] See Lewis-Beck, Jerome, and Jerome (2001) for a related account of how relative economic performances (in this case, in Germany and France) can shape the economic vote.

[15] Alt (1991: 241) notes that "the contribution of the economy to the government's overall record depends on the extent to which the economy is perceived to be the most important issue facing the country, something intensively investigated by MacKuen and Combs (1981), who also showed the state of the economy influences the perceived importance of economic problems."

pull Britain out of the ERM, simply overwhelmed economic evaluations (Butler and Kavanagh, 1997).

Particularly negative shocks to the macro-economy ($y_t - \bar{y} - \mu_{i,t-1} < 0$) may trigger a heightened concern with the economy, thereby increasing the relative importance of the economy to other variables in the vote-choice model. The 1979 election occurred in the midst of serious economic decline and extreme popular economic angst, possibly inflating the relative importance of the economy, whereas the 1997 election occurred during a period of comparative prosperity, possibly dampening its importance for vote choice.[16] These significant differences between the macro-economic outcomes in 1979 and 1997 might have exaggerated the importance of economic evaluations in vote decisions in 1979. Figure 6.9 presents the *economic vote of the chief executive* at each of the U.K. elections along with values for three macro-economic outcomes (CPI, Real GDP Growth, and Unemployment, the dashed lines in Figure 6.9). A cursory analysis of the economic outcomes associated with the two elections suggests that only one candidate fits this argument. Real GDP growth is similar during the two elections, so we can eliminate this as a possible contextual effect. Unemployment in this case seems to have either no effect or possibly the opposite effect than one might expect – somewhat higher levels of unemployment are associated with lower degrees of economic voting. Inflation seems to offer the most plausible contextual effect – it is high in the 1979 election, when economic voting was also high, and it was much lower in the 1997 election when we see economic voting at its nadir.

This notion that when the economy is performing particularly poorly people are inclined to factor it into their vote decision is certainly persuasive.[17] And, to the extent that this is the case, fluctuations in inflation appear to be what triggered British voters' economic vote. This certainly was the conclusion that Margaret Thatcher and the Conservatives came to in 1977 as they prepared for the next election (Norpoth, 1992).[18] Their calculations appeared to pay off. Our estimates suggest that the economic vote played an important role in the 1979 vote decision (based

[16] For an excellent assessment of economic voting in the 1979 election, see Norpoth (1992).

[17] Evans (1999a: 151) speculates that this might have contributed to the relative weak impact of economic evaluations on U.K. vote preference during the 1992–1995 period.

[18] In the Conservative Party's economic policy statement issued in 1977, *The Right Approach to the Economy*, controlling inflation was clearly identified as the party's prime economic goal.

on the 1979 British Election Survey, we estimate that a unit deterioration in retrospective economic evaluations reduced the incumbents' vote probability by 11 percent). The implication of this contextual argument is that when the economy is in equilibrium, or possibly even out of equilibrium but in a positive direction, economic evaluations are likely to play a much less important role in the vote decision. In the 1997 election, Conservative strategist Michael Heseltine failed to recognize this possibility, predicting, to the end, a Conservative majority of sixty seats, "... regarding it almost as an iron law that a government which delivered steady improvements in real disposable income over 12 months would win the election..." (Butler and Kavanagh, 1997: 75). As it turns out, Heseltine was wrong – our estimates suggest that the economy played a relatively insignificant role in the 1997 vote decision (the impact for this year is about 5 percent, which is slightly under the overall mean size of the economic vote in our overall sample of elections studies). The Conservatives experienced a resounding defeat in the 1997 election despite a relatively strong economy. The high levels of inflation seemed to have contributed to the importance of the economic vote in 1979, but the particularly low levels registered in 1997, if anything, seemed to have reduced the weight of the economy in the vote decision.

A more systematic review of the data provides virtually no support for this notion that economic voting rises during periods of particularly bad economic performance. Figure 6.10 plots the level of economic voting in Britain against each of the three macro-economic outcome variables. The evidence in the case of real GDP growth is, in fact, exactly the opposite direction; as the economy improves, the economic vote rises. Much of this is driven by the paradoxical cases of 1990 through 1992 when economic growth was either at a standstill or declining. Even though the economy was in particularly bad straits, our economic-vote measures during this period are at their lowest levels for the United Kingdom. Unemployment has an effect in the expected direction – rising unemployment associated with higher economic vote – but the slope coefficients are statistically insignificant in a bivariate regression of the two variables. And there is no relationship in the case of inflation. Hence, we would be hard-pressed to conclude that relatively bad economic conditions trigger higher levels of economic voting.

In our view, a dismal economic performance was not what triggered the importance of the economy in the 1979 vote decision. As Norpoth (1992) points out, by 1979 the British economy had, in fact, improved considerably and was turning in respectable growth and inflation numbers

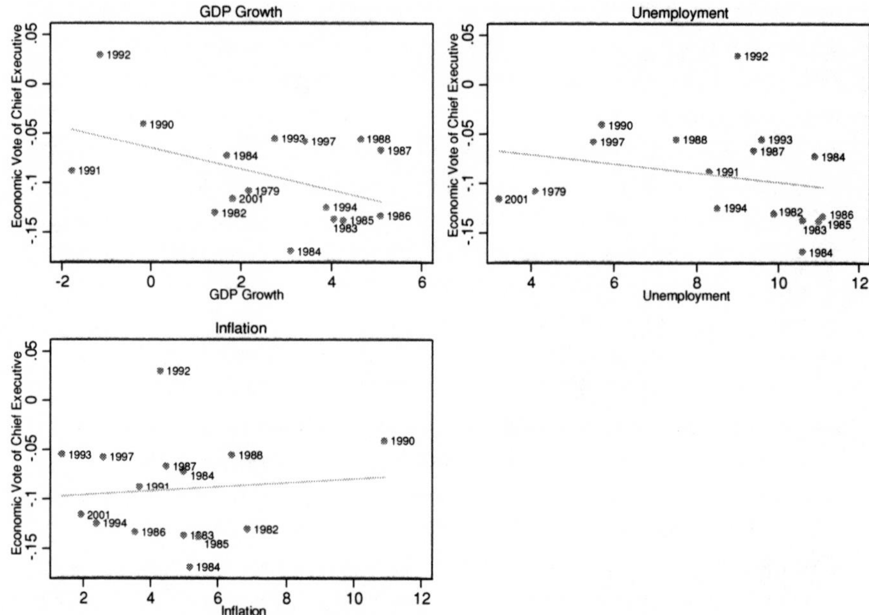

Figure 6.10. U.K. economy and the economic vote: 1979–2002.

(particularly compared to the recent past). Voters clearly had negative views of the government's economic performance, but what led them to incorporate these evaluations into their vote decision were crystal-clear signals that these fluctuations in economic outcomes were the result of the economic management of the incumbent government. The recent history of economic policy making by both parties had been of a "stop-and-go" variety that generated highly volatile economic outcomes. This volatility and the attendant commentary by politicians and the press could leave little doubt regarding the government's responsibility for economic outcomes.[19] But, just in case this was not sufficient, the contrast between fluctuations in the British economy and variations in the international economy provided glaring evidence that British outcomes were not the result of factors exogenous to the incumbent government.

In terms of the signals voters received regarding government competence for macro-economic outcomes, the 1997 election was the exact

[19] The incumbent Prime Minister Callaghan himself, in his 1976 address to the Labour Conference, pointed to these "stop-and-go" policies as having contributed to the country's economic problems (Callaghan 1987: 426).

opposite of the 1979 election. The "stop-and-go" variety of macro-economic management had been abandoned for almost twenty years and fluctuations in the macro-economy had been radically reduced. The British economy was no longer an international pariah as it had been in 1979 – although turning in strong economic performance, the overall economy performed similarly to many other developed democracies. Hence, by 1997, the average voter – and maybe just as important the media coverage of the economy – was more likely to consider fluctuations in the macro-economy as resulting from exogenous factors – such as developments in the global economy or trends in the global business cycles – rather than government policy. It is not that the media did not portray the economy as doing well, it's that there were few credible economic competency signals to which they could respond. The result was not bad media on the economy, as Gavin and Sanders (1997) point out, rather it was that there was very little media coverage of the topic. And, in some sense, this was the uphill, and ultimately unsuccessful, battle that Prime Minister Major fought throughout much of the 1997 campaign.[20]

The relevant contrast between the economic context in 1979 and 1997 is volatility versus stability, not between good and bad economic performance. The competence argument suggests that the decline in economic voting in 1997 results from aspects of the economic context that either decrease variance in the competence signal σ_{μ}^2 or increase variance in the exogenous economic shocks σ_{ξ}^2. We believe that more economic voting occurred in 1979 because economic fluctuations, credibly associated with government policy initiatives, were higher in the period preceding the 1979 election compared to those preceding the 1997 election. This also assumes that exogenous shocks to the macro-economy, unrelated to the incumbent's policies, are relatively similar in the two periods or possibly lower in the 1970s.

One proxy for the overall competency signal in our theory is a measure of the total fluctuations in domestic macro-economic shocks. We do not pretend that this measure is a precise reading on the competency signal during these elections – because it obviously incorporates both exogenous and competency components – but we present it here as a suggestive proxy. Our expectation then is that this measure of variation in macro-economic

[20] This is consistent with the results presented earlier that suggest that the media responds to variations in macro-economic outcomes. Hence, a relatively long period of positive but stable economic performance may, in fact, undermine the strength of the economic vote.

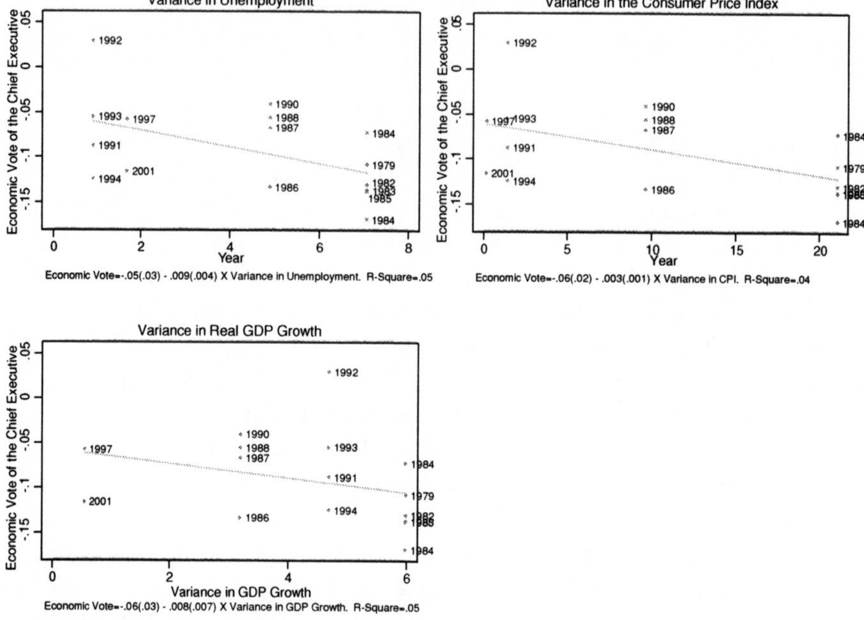

Figure 6.11. U.K. variance in macro-economy and economic vote: 1979–2002. *Note:* Standard deviation in parentheses.

outcomes should be high in the 1979 election and low in the 1997 election. Moreover, economic voting should generally be high when there is considerable variation in macro-economic indicators (in the case of our economic-vote measure, the correlation should be negative because large negative values indicate high levels of economic voting). Figure 6.11 plots the economic vote in the United Kingdom against variations in the three macro-economic indicators. The magnitude of British economic voting is particularly high in the late 1970s and early 1980s – this is also a period of particularly high variance in all three U.K. macro-economic indicators. Economic voting then declines quite precipitously in the later 1980s and 1990s – this is also a period in which variations in the macro-economic measures drop. The implication here is that modest fluctuations in the British macro-economy leading up to the 1997 election, particularly because they tended to be much more in line with global variations, lowered the magnitude of the competency signal. This, in turn, has resulted in less economic voting. By contrast, the late 1970s and the 1980s were clearly periods in which variations in British macro-economic outcomes were quite large and less in step with economic outcomes in the other developed economies. We would argue that this translated into a high competency shock term (σ_μ^2), which in turn implied a larger competency signal. As a result, British voters in the 1979 election were much more likely to attribute economic outcomes to incumbent competence, which resulted in higher levels of economic voting.

The 1979 and 1997 British elections do not, on their own, provide conclusive evidence as to what signals regarding the economic context voters respond to when they weigh the importance of the economy in their vote decision. Nevertheless, they are suggestive and nicely illustrate how economic context affects the economic vote. The economic vote in these two elections diverged considerably as did the overall economic contexts that span the two election periods. We explored the notion that the economy might become more salient in the vote-choice model when economic performance is particularly bad. We found little support for this argument. By contrast, the pattern of fluctuations in British macro-economic outcomes over the past three decades suggests that the signal that seems to matter in the vote choice is variation in shocks to the macro-economy. Consistent with our competency theory, voters seem to use variations in these shocks before an election in order to extract information about the incumbent's responsibility for macro-economic outcomes, which then conditions their economic vote.

SUMMARY

Voters in our competency model of the economic vote are expected to condition their economic vote on a competency signal. And our theory spells out quite explicitly what information about the economy voters are expected to know as part of this signal-extraction exercise. This chapter makes the empirical case that voters, in fact, are informed about the components of this competency signal; that is, the typical variation in competence shocks and in exogenous shocks to the economy.

First, the theory assumes that voters are knowledgeable about the total variance in shocks to the macro-economy. The aggregate time-series of macro-economic outcomes certainly are convincing evidence of considerable fluctuation in macro-economic outcomes in our sample of mature democracies. Our content analysis of media reports of economic outcomes suggests that the typical voter has access to considerable information regarding these fluctuations in macro-economic outcomes. The analysis of major U.S. print media indicates that the count of economic news stories responds positively to variations in macro-economic outcomes. This suggests to us that the media often frame the reporting of economic information in terms of variation (as opposed to levels) in macro-economic outcomes. Furthermore, the attitudes of respondents in our six-nation survey clearly reflect the manner in which the media frames economic news. Respondents to the surveys have meaningful attitudes about the volatility of macro-economy outcomes. Moreover, these attitudes are reasonably well informed in that cross-national perceptions of macro-economic variability correlate quite highly with the magnitudes of actual variations in real GDP.

Second, our theory assumes that voters are able to distinguish variations in competency shocks from variations in exogenous shocks to the macro-economy. Rigorously assessing the voters' capabilities in this regard is challenging. We adopt an indirect strategy here that first assumes that a large part of the exogenous shocks in the economy originate in global fluctuations and that a large part of domestic shocks are attributable to the competence of politicians. Our analysis of dynamic and cross-national variations in aggregate macro-economic time series suggests that the information necessary for this signal-extraction task is certainly available to voters. Being cognizant of the extent to which global factors influence the domestic economy contributes to the voter's ability to extract competency signals from shocks to the macro-economy. The results of both our six-nation study and the PEW GAP suggest that voters do have the information to make such distinctions. Specifically, voters have what appear to be meaningful attitudes regarding global influences on their national economies and cross-national variations in these attitudes indicate that they are reasonably informed.

Hence, given the aggregate and survey-based data analyses presented in this chapter, we conclude that voters do have the information to extract a signal about incumbent competence from movements in the domestic economy (as our theory assumes). But did voters respond to the overall competency signal as our theory predicts? Our six-nation survey allowed us to identify those respondents who exhibited individual-level beliefs that the competency theory predicts will lead to higher levels of economic voting – specifically, individuals who perceive that the variation in the national economy differs from variation in the global economy. The empirical results supported the theory: individuals who believed that the variations in shocks to the domestic economy differed from those in the overall European economy had larger economic votes.

However, our theory can tell us more about how the political and economic context conditions the economic vote. Specifically, in Chapter 5, we provided an interpretation of the competency model that links the strength of the competency signal to the political and economic institutions that regulate the relative influence of electorally accountable versus nonelectorally accountable decision makers on economic outcomes. We examine the empirical evidence for these links in the next chapter.

7

Political Control of the Economy

The previous chapter suggests that voters are attentive to economic fluctuations in a manner consistent with our competency theory. In this chapter, we explore whether there are features of the political-economic context that affect these competency signals in a systematic fashion and, hence, account for the contextual variation in economic voting that we saw in Chapter 3. For example, the evidence presented in the previous chapter suggests that voters understand the extent to which their domestic economy is subject to the influence of global economic factors. Does this help account for the contextual variation in economic voting? Although there has been speculation in the economic-voting literature about the links between these features of the policy-making context and the economic vote (Lewis-Beck, 1988; Powell and Whitten, 1993), the results have been mixed. Improving our understanding of this link requires a more developed theoretical understanding of how individuals use information regarding the political economic context to inform their vote choice.

Our competency theory provides an explanation for why, and how, fluctuations in the magnitude of the economic vote are related to these variations in political and economic contexts. Recall from the theoretical discussion in Chapter 5 that context matters because it influences the number of electorally versus nonelectorally dependent decision makers (or, using our abbreviations, EDDs versus NEDDs) associated with macro-economic policy outcomes, which in turn shapes the size of the incumbent's competency signal. Specifically, the competency signal is a function of the variance in shocks to the economy as well as the variance in the shocks as a result of the managerial competence of elected officials. The variance of competency shocks will be bigger when the number of

EDDs (α) influencing macro-economic outcomes gets bigger. Likewise, the variance of exogenous shocks to the economy (i.e., those not caused by EDDs) rises with the number of economically consequential decisions made by NEDDs (β). The argument is summed up by the ratio $\frac{\beta}{\alpha}$. As the ratio of NEDDs (β) to EDDs (α) rises, the overall competency signal will decline and vice versa. So, for example, in a policy-making context in which, relative to other contexts, responsibility for making economic policies is more shared with NEDDs (this might be the case in a highly corporatist policy-making setting, for example), voters are likely to discount the impact that the incumbent's competency can have on economic growth. Because the importance of the economy in the vote function is determined by the overall competency signal, this ratio of NEDDs to EDDs should be correlated with the economic vote.

This ratio of NEDDs to EDDs effectively defines the policy context that shapes economic outcomes. Although not employing our explicit formulation, many students of comparative political economy over the past four decades have implicitly examined how the mix of NEDDs to EDDs has varied both cross-nationally and over time and have explored its implications for a variety of political and economic outcomes. An early contribution to this debate is Cameron's (1978) classic article exploring the impact of exposure to the global economy on the size of government. Cameron pointed out how economic context – an open economy in particular– can undermine the ability of incumbents to control macro-economic policies. But he argued that the institutional and political responses to the exigencies of an open economy tend to broaden the scope of government, which enhances the ability of government to manage the social and economic disruptions associated with global integration. The conventional view is that these two developments balance each other out in terms of their effect on government's ability to affect economic outcomes: An open economy undermines the ability of government to shape macro-economic policies. On the other hand, expanding the role of the state in the economy is a counterweight because it increases the ability of the government to enact compensating measures.

Recently, we have seen a number of countries adopting liberal economic policies ostensibly in response to the competitive influences of global economic forces. This has led some to suggest a different twist on Cameron's initial argument: in this view, open economies faced with the exigencies of international competition are forced to liberalize (or privatize) their domestic economies. This, in turn, reinforces the constraints on governments, which reduces the role of elected officials in shaping domestic economic outcomes and, consequently, the ability of voters to hold decision makers accountable for economic outcomes (Alvarez, Nagler, and Willette, 2000; Hellwig, 2006). Freeman speculates that "...there is evidence that as privatization and globalization have progressed, democratic citizens have lost faith in their governments' capacities to manage their economies" (Freeman, 2006).

These arguments are very much in the spirit of our competency-signaling theory. They imply that voters are attentive to global economic influences on the domestic economy; voters somehow understand how the policy-making context constrains their economic-policy choices; and they use information about the global and domestic economies to condition their individual-vote choice. These arguments also identify the two features of political economies – an open versus closed economy and extensive versus limited statist institutions – that are critical features of the macro-economic policy-making environment. They help define the balance in economic decision making between electorally accountable decision makers and those who are not. Hence, both features should shape the size of the competency signal. In this chapter, we provide an argument relating changes in the global economy and the scope of government to the magnitude of the competency signal and, given the theory in Chapter 5, to the economic vote. This argument thus provides testable hypotheses about how specific economic and political contexts impact the economic vote.

GLOBALIZATION, COMPETENCE, AND THE ECONOMIC VOTE

We begin by exploring the impact of globalization on the economic vote. The nature of the international economy has changed remarkablely over the past three decades. Global trade as a percent of GDP has increased from 20 percent in the early 1970s to 55 percent in 2003 (IMF, 2005).[1] But this varies rather dramatically by country. For example, the IMF trade intensity score for the European Union (EU) is about .88, for the United States 1.05, and for Canada 2.93 (IMF, 2005).[2] Among the industrialized nations between 1990 and 2003, the magnitude of foreign assets and liabilities has tripled to a remarkable 200 percent (IMF, 2005). Not

[1] Global trade here is defined as the sum of exports and imports of goods and services.

[2] Trade intensity is defined as the ratio of manufacturing trade to total manufacturing GDP (IMF, 2005).

surprisingly, this has created an entire "industry" of scholars devoted to understanding the economic and political implications of these trends.[3] Our interest in rising globalization is twofold. First, it is clear from our theory that this trend should impact the competency signal in some way – although the precise nature of the impact is not obvious. Second, these changes in the competency signal will, in turn, have implications for the magnitude of economic voting.

What are the implications for economic voting? Scholars who previously have addressed the question from various theoretical perspectives disagree. Lewis-Beck (1988) speculated that greater openness might sensitize voters to the importance of economic policies and thereby increase the economic vote. Scheve (2004) argued for the same relationship (higher economic voting in an open economy), although he suggested that it results from lower exogenous shocks (our σ_ξ^2 term) in open economies and, therefore, a higher overall competency signal. Hellwig's (2001) analysis suggested exactly the opposite. Greater openness seems to dampen the positive impact of economic performance on incumbent vote. And this conforms to the earlier speculations of Lewis-Beck and Eulau (1985: 6) and, more recently, Hibbs (2006).

These are essentially disagreements over the relative magnitudes of the competence and exogenous shock terms in the competency signals generated in open- and closed-economy contexts. In Chapter 5, we argued that the variation in these magnitudes across contexts reflects the differences in the number of EDDs to NEDDs. As economies become increasingly integrated into the global economy, the variance in the competency shocks is likely to shrink because the number of electorally dependent decisions affecting the macro-economy decline (i.e., $\alpha_{op} < \alpha_{cl}$, where *op* refers to an open economy and *cl* refers to a closed economy). At the same time, the number of nonelectorally dependent decision makers increases ($\beta_{op} > \beta_{cl}$).

Capital mobility, for example, is one of the defining features of an open economy. And the Mundell-Fleming condition is the classic statement on how increased capital mobility reduces the number of EDDs affecting macro-economic policies and increases the impact of NEDDs.[4]

3 Rodrik (1997a) summarizes many of the arguments that comprise this literature. Fischer (2003) provides a review and careful assessment of the debates regarding the impact of globalization.

4 See the early works of Mundell (1962, 1963, 1964). Our discussion is based on Frieden (1991).

This condition essentially states that a country can have, at most, two of the following three conditions: capital mobility, fixed exchange rates, and monetary policy autonomy (Frieden, 1991). Hence, for example, having opted for capital mobility, if authorities reduce interest rates in order to stimulate the local economy, capital will flow out of the country in search of higher rates abroad and, before this initiative can have its effect, domestic interest rates will have climbed back to world levels (Frieden, 1991: 431). In order to retain autonomy over monetary policy, authorities would need to abandon a fixed exchange rate regime. This condition does not eliminate the ability of governments in an open economy to enact monetary and fiscal policies (Oatley, 1999; Garrett, 1998a, 1998b, 2000) but rather restricts their options given the decision to or not to maintain fixed exchange rates.[5] The Mundell-Fleming condition suggests that the price paid by incumbent governments for participating in the global economy – capital mobility, for example – is a more restricted ability to manage the domestic economy.[6] In terms of our model, the Mundell-Fleming condition suggests that once a country opens up to the global economy by allowing for capital mobility, it essentially cedes a decision option, either the ability to control its exchange rate or the ability to shape monetary policy – and one of these decisions is, in effect, relinquished to nonelectorally dependent decision makers. As Clark et al. (1998) point out, not all countries opt for policies or institutions that increase exposure to these global forces, but once they do, incumbent governments cede considerable control over managing the macro-economy.[7]

Although capital mobility is certainly a defining feature of an open economy, it is not the most visible manifestation to the average voter. The typical voter is much more likely to be cognizant of the increased trade flows that result from an open economy. The macro-economic indicators

[5] And although governments are not obligated to commit to fixed exchange rate regimes under a system of capital mobility, many have taken this option to ward off financial speculation, which in turn has restricted their fiscal policy options (Garrett, 2000).

[6] It is important to point out that we are not drawing any conclusions here regarding the impact of open economies on partisan differences in macro-economic policies (in fact, the evidence of Oatley, 1999, suggesting that partisan differences persist is in our mind quite convincing), nor are we suggesting that open economies necessarily constrain the redistributive and overall taxation policies pursued by governments (Boix, 1998, and Garrett, 1998b, provide convincing challenges to these arguments).

[7] And more recent efforts by proponents of the "new open economy macro-economics" have provided models of the precise impact of these global interdependencies on domestic output and inflation in open economies (Lane, 1997). Good reviews of this literature include Lane (2001) and Sarno (2000).

that typically attract the attention of the national media and politicians are those related to trade flows and trade balances. Trade flows have an impact similar to that of capital mobility on the ability of domestic decision makers to manage aggregate demand and control inflation (Cameron, 1978; Lindbeck, 1975, 1976). Aggregate demand in economies with significant dependence on export markets is subject to external demand and to prices that are determined by global markets beyond the influence of domestic policy makers. High levels of imports subject economies to inflationary (or deflationary) shocks that again are beyond the control of domestic governmental officials (Cameron, 1978). Because trade typically implies specialization resulting from the forces of comparative advantage, the production structure in open economies is often more concentrated than in closed economies (Rodrik, 1998; IMF, 2005). This can exaggerate the extent to which domestic economies are subject to external shocks beyond the control of incumbent policy makers. Rodrik (1998), for example, presents empirical data clearly indicating that more open economies have significantly more volatile GDP growth.[8]

Capital mobility and increased trade flows reduce the control that EDDs have on macro-economic policy outcomes and they subject domestic economic outcomes to greater influence by nonelectorally dependent, and particularly foreign, decision makers. Accordingly, in an open economy the number of NEDDs affecting the macro-economy rises ($\beta_{cl} < \beta_{op}$), whereas the number of EDDs should remain constant or possibly be smaller in an open economy than in a closed one (i.e., $\alpha_{op} \leq \alpha_{cl}$). Hence, we expect the ratio of NEDDs to EDDs will be smaller in a closed economy,

$$\frac{\beta_{op}}{\alpha_{op}} > \frac{\beta_{cl}}{\alpha_{cl}} \qquad (7.1)$$

which suggests a lower overall competency signal in economies that are open to global economic influences.[9] Given this, it follows from the theory in Chapter 5 that open economies will have lower levels of economic voting than closed economies.

To evaluate this hypothesis, we employ a measure of Trade Openness from the World Bank, which is a ratio of total trade to GDP (World Bank, 2004). We think that this is a particularly good measure because it both

[8] See also evidence to this effect for the developing economies in Gavin and Hausmann (1996).

[9] And as Ebeid and Rodden (2006) nicely demonstrate, this effect can differ at the subnational level as a function of the structural features of provincial or state economies.

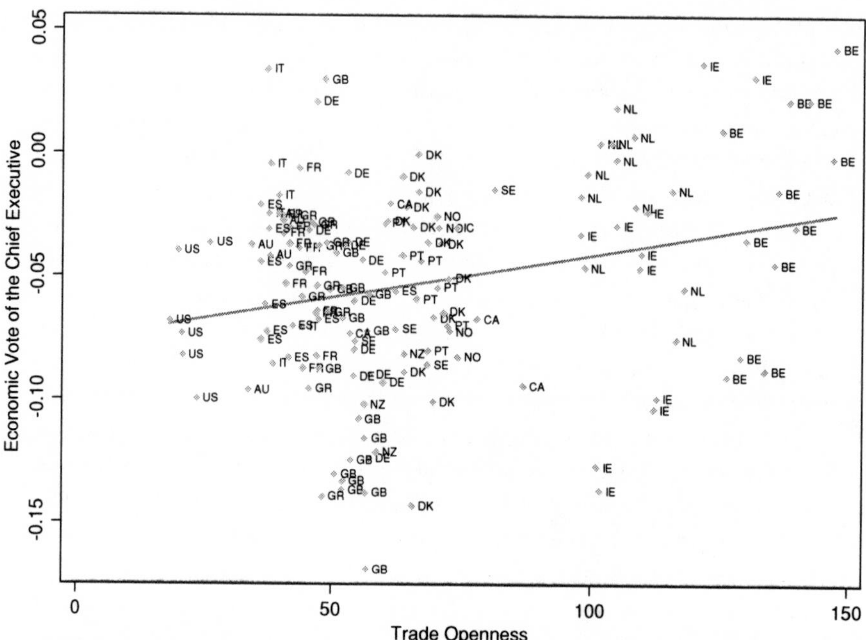

Figure 7.1. Trade openness and the economic vote of the chief executive.
Source: Total trade as a percentage of GDP (World Bank, 2004)
Economic Vote of Chief Executive = -0.08 (7.42) × 0.0004 (2.37) × Trade Openness. $R^2 = 0.04$. Observations = 151.[10]

captures the objective constraints imposed on national economic policy makers and it is also the indicator that typically attracts the most attention of both the media and politicians. Figure 7.1 presents a plot of the *economic vote of the chief executive* against our measure of Trade Openness. First, there clearly is no evidence that the economic vote is higher in open economies, as some have claimed (Scheve, 2004). In fact, openness of the economy is associated with a significantly smaller economic vote. This lends support to our argument that the competency signal in open economies is weaker than in closed economies, which in turn leads to lower levels of economic voting. This is an important result because it suggests that recent rising levels of globalization imply a declining importance for the economy in vote choice.

[10] Estimates are from an OLS regression with standard errors robust to heteroskedacticity and to nonindependence between observations of the same party in different surveys. T-statistics are in parentheses.

THE POLICY-MAKING CONTEXT: LIMITED VERSUS EXTENSIVE STATIST INSTITUTIONS

As our theory predicts, a more open economy seems to suppress the economic vote. The literature identifies two rather broadly different responses to these global trends that potentially have important implications for the economic vote, and democratic accountability more generally. Cameron (1978) and others (Katzenstein, 1985; Rodrik, 1998) argue that economies that are particularly vulnerable to global economic shocks historically have adopted institutions designed to moderate the potential social and economic dislocations resulting from exogenous shocks to the domestic economy. This includes higher levels of government spending on social programs (e.g., unemployment benefits, medical insurance, and pension schemes), greater government-industry-labor coordination on economic policy making, and initiatives designed to maintain international competitiveness (government investment in human capital).[11] Adserà and Boix (2002) demonstrate the empirical relationship between openness and size of the government sector in democracies, although they point out that the expansion of the government sector should be seen as a strategy for building a free-trade coalition. Some see this expansion of the state sector as enhancing democratic governance: a large role for the state increases the ability of citizens to hold decision makers accountable for the economy.

Alternatively, some suggest a liberal convergence in economic policies resulting from the competitive pressures of globalization. Because of global constraints, national governments are forced to liberalize the economy in response to similar initiatives by competing nations, resulting in what some characterize as a race to the bottom phenomenon. These liberal policies typically reduce the scope of government in the economy either through the introduction of more liberal regulatory regimes or privatization of state-owned entities. This "privatization" of domestic economies results in a more limited role of the state in shaping macro-economic outcomes. The conventional wisdom in this case is that a reduced role of

[11] Although it is true that more open economies tend to have an extensive state sector, it is important to point out that this is an historical legacy and that increasing the role of government is not the only policy response to increased exposure to global competition. Garrett (1998b) and Boix (1998), for example, describe the very different policy responses to global competition of the Left and Right in the advanced democracies.

government in managing the macro-economy results in lower democratic accountability.

These arguments raise three interesting puzzles regarding globalization, the government's role in the economy, and the economic vote: What happens to the scope of government in the face of rising globalization? Theoretically, how does the scope of government shape the incumbent's competency signal? What empirical relationship is suggested between the scope of government and the economic vote?

We begin with the theoretical puzzle: the implications of an extensive, as opposed to limited, state sector for the competency signal. A policy context with an extensive state sector increases the number of domestic institutions and other constellations of political actors actively involved in making economic policies – in short, it produces a more "dense" policy-making environment. This results in more "decisions" and more "decision-makers" that contribute to the competency signal that the voters perceive. For example, increasing the scope of government in the economy results in more government entities making decisions that affect the economy. These would include government-owned firms, authorities overseeing infrastructure or energy projects, health services providers, and so on. At the same time, there are more decision makers shaping these policies: executives of government-owned firms, labor unions, competing firms, local mayors, contractors, professional associations, NGOs, consumers, and so on. Most of this expanded group of decision makers is not politically accountable. Accordingly, more of the decisions affecting the economic competency signal perceived by voters are shaped by agents who are not politically accountable. This follows in part because in a context with an extensive state sector, the benefits and costs associated with changing economic priorities are more likely to be borne by greater numbers of interested parties (Becker, 1983; Buchanan and Tullock, 1962).

Short of significant institutional changes designed to reinforce principal-agent oversight, as the scope of government increases, this proliferation of nonelectorally accountable decisions is an inevitable result of the expansion of the government sector. This more dense policy-making environment has an interesting and somewhat counterintuitive implication for the relationship between the breadth of the state sector and the economic vote. If we focus on the ratio of NEDDs to EDDs, $(\frac{\beta}{\alpha})$, as it rises, the competency signal declines, as does the economic vote. We expect this ratio to be large in contexts with extensive as opposed to limited state sectors because an extensive state sector implies that a larger number of interested, and nonelectorally dependent, actors affect economically relevant decisions.[12]

A dense policy-making environment implies a proliferation of actors that affect (or veto) macro-economic policy initiatives, many of whom are not electorally dependent or are not subject to discipline by elected officials – and thus cannot (in the specific sense of our theory) be considered part of the "government" competence of which the voter is trying to determine. It is not simply the proliferation of veto players (Alesina and Drazen, 1991; Henisz, 2004; Olson, 1982; Tsebelis, 2002) that matters here but rather that an extensive state sector attracts the participation of many NEDDs as opposed to EDDs in the policy process. This argument has two important implications for the competency model. First, an extensive state sector will increase the number of the NEDDs. Second, although an extensive state sector also may raise the number of EDDs, it will do so at a more moderate rate than the increase in NEDDs. As a result, we expect the ratio ($\frac{\beta}{\alpha}$) will be higher in extensive state as compared to limited state contexts.

Contexts with a more extensive state sector are hypothesized to have a smaller competency signal and less economic voting. The breadth of the state sector, of course, can be measured in a number of different ways. Accordingly, in order to test this argument, we identify three distinct dimensions of state influence over the macro-economy and explore their impact on the competency signal and the economic vote. First, we explain how a large state role in the economy dampens the magnitude of the overall competency signal and we provide empirical evidence that it reduces the size of the economic vote. Second, we explore how corporatist arrangements – which include an explicit expansion of the set of actors involved in macro-economic management – reduce the overall competency signal and provide empirical evidence that this reduces economic voting. Finally, we explain how increasing government regulatory oversight of the private sector reduces the overall competency signal and demonstrate empirically that it results in lower economic voting.

Size of the State Sector

The size of the state sector refers to the breadth of the state's role in economic transactions and covers such activities as wealth and income

[12] It is important to point out here that our argument has no necessary implications for the quality of economic policy outcomes – our only concern here is unanticipated shocks to the macro-economy.

transfers, consumption of goods and services, and ownership of productive entities. Since World War II, developed democracies have experienced both a rise in the size of the state sector and a more activist role of the government in managing the macro-economy. Franzese (2002a) documents the considerable post–World War II growth in the size of government in the economies of the OECD nations. During this same period, Keynesian notions of macro-economic management became economic orthodoxy for the governments of most developed democracies (Hall, 1989). The size of the government sector has become synonymous with "state capacity" – the ability of the state to manage the political economy (Krasner, 1984). And, as we pointed out earlier, many argue that open economies have embraced a state sector in large measure in order to compensate constituencies negatively affected by global economic shocks (Adserà and Boix, 2002).

A reasonable inference to draw from this literature is that as the state's capacity to manage the economy increases, so should the level of economic voting (Anderson, 1995). As Lewis-Beck and Eulau speculated, "In the nations with more government economic involvement, one could anticipate a stronger association between economics and the vote, since their citizens would be more likely to attribute economic responsibility to government" (Lewis-Beck and Eulau, 1985: 5). Tufte (1978) provided an early catalyst for this notion with his powerful images of Nixon's manipulation of spending on transfer programs just before the 1972 U.S. presidential election. A reasonable generalization is that big government, which implies more redistribution programs, means an expanded opportunity to engage in Nixonian-type manipulations of the macro-economy. The implication here is that big government results in government making more economically consequential decisions and so results in a larger economic vote. Moreover, because the size of the government sector varies significantly cross-nationally (Franzese, 2002a), this raises the possibility that these differences might help explain cross-national variations in the economic vote.

Our argument regarding the impact of an expansive state sector on the overall competency signal, however, suggests exactly the opposite: big government should result in less economic voting.[13] Our case for the

[13] We are not alone in arriving at this prediction. Hibbs (1993) argues that in large welfare states (which, as he points out, are also typically highly exposed to global economic influences), other policies or welfare state spending will dwarf the

notion that big government reduces the competency signal rests on two assumptions proposed in:

$$\beta_s < \beta_l$$
$$\frac{\alpha_l}{\alpha_s} < \frac{\beta_l}{\beta_s} \tag{7.2}$$

where l represents contexts with large government sectors and s represents contexts with small government sectors.

The first assumption simply suggests that there are more NEDDs made in contexts with big government. As government grows and becomes more complex, the number of NEDDs (interest groups, commissions, elected local government officials, for example) affecting macro-economic policies will increase significantly as will the volume of their decisions. We see this as a rather noncontroversial – and easily verifiable – assumption. The second assumption simply recognizes that there are more EDDs in big government contexts but imposes the condition that the ratio of EDDs in large versus small government contexts is smaller than the ratio of NEDDs in large versus small government contexts. This results in the ratio of NEDDs to EDDs in contexts with small government being less than it is in contexts with large government,

$$\frac{\beta_s}{\alpha_s} < \frac{\beta_l}{\alpha_l} \tag{7.3}$$

The ratio in equation (7.3) indicates that the exogenous shock term in large government contexts will be inflated because voters perceive NEDDs as having a disproportionate impact on shocks to the macro-economy. This, of course, depresses the overall competency signal, which we predict will result in a lower economic vote. Accordingly, economic voting should be negatively correlated with the size of the government sector. Figure 7.2 plots the *economic vote of the chief executive* against the magnitude of the government sector. It suggests that economic voting is higher in contexts with more limited government (remember that a large negative value indicates high economic voting). Note that countries with relatively small government sectors such as the United States, the

macro-economic demand management "signals" of the incumbent. As a result, there will be less economic voting in these contexts. Pacek and Radcliff (1995) argue that the size of government moderates economic voting, although their explanation is quite different than ours.

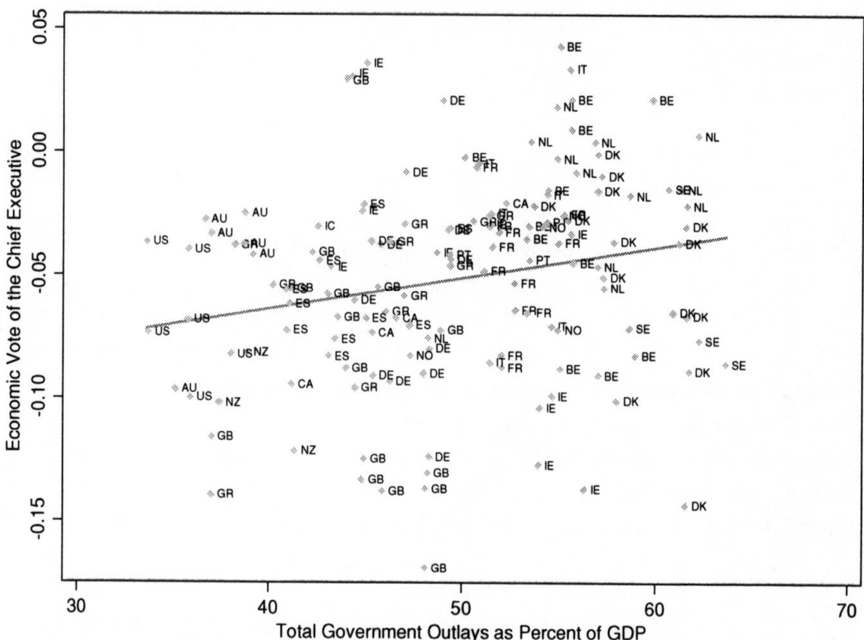

Figure 7.2. Size of government and economic vote of the chief executive.
Source: General government total outlays as percent of nominal GDP (OECD, 2002) Economic Vote of Chief Executive = −0.11 (3.93) × 0.001 (2.06) × (Government Outlays/GDP). $R^2 = 0.04$. Observations=146.[14]

United Kingdom, Greece, Canada, and Spain tend to have much higher levels of economic voting. Conversely, the big government states such as Denmark, the Netherlands, Sweden, and Belgium have lower economic voting.

Big government implies a lower overall competency signal because the ratio of NEDDs to EDDs is greater than in contexts with a smaller government sector. As the competency theory predicts, this results in lower levels of economic voting in contexts with a large government sector. Let's now take a closer look at the notion that this results from a relatively larger number of nonelectorally dependent decision makers affecting macroeconomic policy outcomes.

[14] Estimates are from an OLS regression with standard errors robust to heteroskedacticity and to nonindependence between observations of the same party in different surveys. T-statistics are in parentheses.

Corporatism and Coordinated Wage and Price Bargaining

Falling within our rubric of statist institutions are formal and informal arrangements requiring the participation of key economic actors in major economic policy making – typically referred to in the literature as corporatism or coordinated wage and price bargaining. A number of post–World War II developed economies adopted corporatist policies designed in large part to moderate the magnitude of shocks to the macroeconomy. For the most part, these were open economies that were particularly vulnerable to global economic shocks (Katzenstein, 1985). These initiatives are described by Hall as a "...process of social or economic policy making in which considerable influence over the formulation or implementation of policy is devolved onto the organized representatives of producer groups, often by means of peak-level bargaining about wage settlements" (Hall, 1999: 138).[15] By expanding the role of government to include the negotiation of "social contracts," which typically focused on wages but could include a range of other policies, the expectation was that government could ensure satisfactory levels of real economic growth, restrain inflationary pressures, and avoid excessive levels of unemployment (Franzese, 2002a: Chapter 4).[16]

The institutional actors associated with these efforts to promote coordinated wage and price bargaining (CWB) are a good example of the NEDDs in our competency-signaling model. Corporatist, or CWB, institutions are explicitly designed to increase the number of nonelectorally dependent decision makers influencing macro-economic policy outcomes. In corporatist contexts, key macro-economic policies – price and wage policies – are subject to relatively nonpartisan negotiation among a country's leading interests groups. And corporatist institutions significantly constrain how capital is employed within the country, ranging from investment and disinvestment decisions, wage settlements, and employee benefits. The implications of these institutional features for our competency signal are quite straightforward. They imply that the overall number of economically important decisions in a corporatist setting (cw), compared to a more

[15] Students of European political economy, in particular Schmitter and Lehmbruch (1979) and Lehmbruch and Schmitter (1982), have elaborated a set of measures of neocorporatism and have demonstrated that policy outcomes are correlated with variation in levels of neocorporatism.

[16] There is a general consensus in the literature that levels of CWB have, in fact, declined over the past two decades, although there is some debate as to how quickly and since when (Franzese, 2002b; Golden et al., 1995).

market-oriented setting (m), is shifted from EDDs to NEDDs (even though these decisions might be seen as "governmental" in some sense). This has the effect of increasing the number of NEDDs (β_{cw}) and decreasing the number of EDDs (α_{cw}) in a corporatist context. Accordingly,

$$\beta_m < \beta_{cw}$$
$$\alpha_m > \alpha_{cw} \tag{7.4}$$

This implies that the ratio of NEDDs to EDDs will clearly be higher in a corporatist than a more market-oriented setting,

$$\frac{\beta_m}{\alpha_m} < \frac{\beta_{cw}}{\alpha_{cw}} \tag{7.5}$$

And this, in turn, suggests that the overall competency signal is higher in contexts with more market-oriented institutions as opposed to those with high degrees of corporatism. Because they have a higher overall competency signal, contexts with a low level of corporatism should have a larger economic vote than contexts with high levels of corporatism.

Some readers might find it odd that we suggest that there are more electorally accountable economic decision makers in unregulated versus corporatist labor markets. Any confusion can be resolved by drawing a careful distinction between governmental and electoral accountability. In a free market for labor, the government makes some decisions and is electorally accountable for them (say, investment in education). But in a corporatist system, these decisions, and many others, become party to the overall societal bargain that is as much the responsibility of labor unions and business as it is of the politicians.

Corporatism is measured by an index developed by Golden (2000). The index consists of the factors scores from a principal component factor analysis of four measures that Golden (2000) demonstrates empirically as representing an underlying corporatist dimension: government involvement in private-sector wage bargaining (a 15-point scale, with 1 indicating no government involvement at all and 15 indicating government-imposed wage freezes and prohibition of supplementary bargaining); bargaining level (a 4-point scale, with 1 indicating plant-level bargaining and 4 indicating a centralized bargaining level); confederal involvement (an 11-point scale measuring the extent to which private-sector wage negotiations are determined by bargaining among the confederation of unions – a low score indicating no confederation involvement at all); and adjusted union density (union membership with unemployed, self-employed, and retired members excluded).

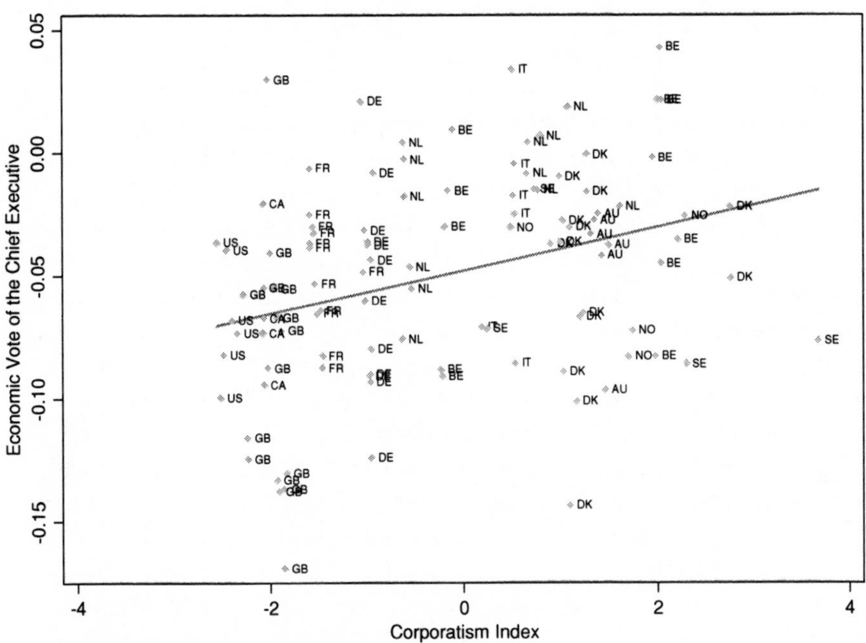

Figure 7.3. Corporatism and economic vote of the chief executive.
Source: Corporatism Index (Miriam Golden, 2000)
Economic Vote of Chief Executive = −0.05 (8.65) × 0.008 (2.64) × (Government Outlays/GDP). $R^2 = 0.04$. Observations = 107.[17]

Figure 7.3 presents a plot of the *economic vote of the chief executive* against an index of corporatism constructed by Golden (2000). Clearly, high levels of corporatism tend to reduce economic voting. This reinforces our contention that the competency signal is higher in contexts with limited statist institutions, which in turn generates higher levels of economic voting.

Regulation Density

The third dimension of an extensive state sector is regulation density. Our reasoning here is similar to our argument regarding size of government. Regulating a complex economy poses a daunting agency problem for elected decision makers (Spiller, 1990). We assume that there are more

[17] Estimates are from an OLS regression with standard errors robust to heteroskedacticity and to nonindependence between observations of the same party in different surveys. T-statistics are in parentheses.

NEDDs in contexts with dense regulations. As regulatory oversight of the private sector grows and becomes more complex, elected officials delegate increasing amounts of authority to nonelected regulatory agents; hence, the number of NEDDs affecting macro-economic policies will increase significantly. Initiating, or increasing, the regulatory oversight of a particular industry, for example, will result in more NEDDs participating in economic policy decisions. This manifests itself in a variety of different forms: industry lobbying efforts, the organization of consultative entities designed to facilitate the government's regulatory oversight tasks, or the formation of independent entities that are given responsibility for regulatory activities. All of these different byproducts of increased regulatory oversight have in common the fact that they diffuse policy-making responsibility to a wider range of NEDDs.

Again, this reasoning can be summarized in our theoretical notation: there are more NEDDs made in contexts with dense regulation. Second, while there are more electorally dependent decisions in dense regulatory contexts, the ratio of electorally dependent decisions in dense (*dr*) versus limited (*lr*) regulatory contexts is smaller than the ratio of nonelectorally dependent decisions in dense versus limited regulatory contexts. This results in the ratio of NEDDs to EDDs in contexts with limited regulation being less than it is in contexts with dense regulation,

$$\begin{aligned} \beta_{lr} &< \beta_{dr} \\ \frac{\alpha_{dr}}{\alpha_{lr}} &< \frac{\beta_{dr}}{\beta_{lr}} \\ \frac{\beta_{lr}}{\alpha_{lr}} &< \frac{\beta_{dr}}{\alpha_{dr}} \end{aligned} \tag{7.6}$$

Figure 7.4 plots the economic vote against regulation density. Regulatory density is measured by a composite index of the extent of government regulation of credit markets, labor markets, and businesses – the index ranges from 0 to 10, with 0 indicating a maximum of government regulatory oversight (Gwartney and Lawson, 2006). Note that a low score on the regulation density variable suggests a highly dense regulatory environment. Accordingly, the plot suggests that the economic vote is suppressed in contexts with high levels of regulation; hence, countries with a relatively low degree of government regulatory oversight tend to have high levels of economic voting. These results reinforce our contention that the competency signal is higher in contexts where the state sector is more limited, which results in more economic voting.

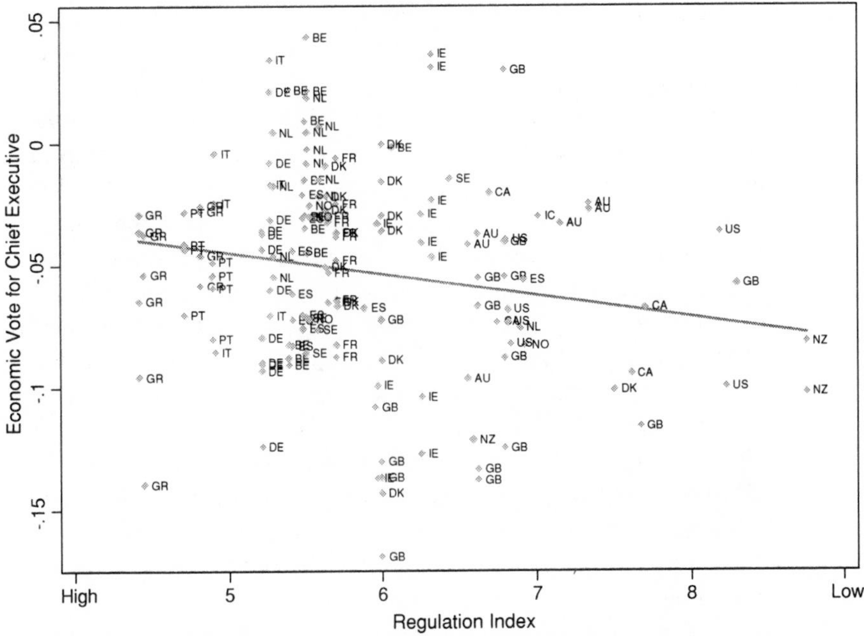

Figure 7.4. Regulatory density and economic vote of the chief executive.
Source: Gwarteny and Lawson (2006)
Economic Vote of Chief Executive = −0.001 (0.03) × −0.009 (2.28) × Regulation Index.
R^2 = 0.03. Observations = 152.[18]

Statist Institutions and the Economic Vote

Our contention is that overall extensive statist institutions increase the impact of nonelectorally dependent decision makers on policy outcomes, which reduces the overall competency signal and lowers the economic vote. We have now explored three dimensions of the statist institutional context. The argument is similar in each case: contexts in which electorally dependent officials have more authority to shape economic outcomes relative to nonelectorally dependent officials (indicated by smaller government, less corporatism, and less state regulation) should increase the size of the competency signal and increase economic voting. The empirical results for simple bivariate models are surprisingly consistent and supportive. We believe these empirical results constitute grounds for the

[18] Estimates are from an OLS regression with standard errors robust to heteroskedacticity and to nonindependence between observations of the same party in different surveys. T-statistics are in parentheses.

general contention that overall competency signals and, hence, economic voting are lower in contexts with an extensive state sector. The hypothesis is worth pursuing further.

We can think of our three measures of the policy context as dimensions of an underlying structural feature of political economies – a limited versus extensive state sector. Factor analysis of these three items indicates that they are tapping this underlying feature of a limited state sector. The factor analysis results in a single dimension, with each item having a reasonably high loading. The factor loadings of the three measures are as follows: Regulation Density is −.67, Corporatism is .59, and Government Size is .80. The alpha reliability statistic for these three items is 0.63, again confirming that it is reasonable to treat these items as measuring a similar underlying concept.

Figure 7.5 examines the relationship between the *economic vote of the chief executive* and the factor scores resulting from our factor analysis of the three statist items. The relationship is quite strong and in the expected direction: contexts with a more extensive state sector have lower levels of economic voting.

A plausible alternative argument here is that our measure of scope of the state sector is actually capturing the extent to which the state has adopted social-transfer policies designed to cushion the impact of economic shocks and that this safety-net effect is actually moderating the magnitude of the economic vote rather than the impact of the ratio of NEDDs to EDDs. This is an argument made by Pacek and Radcliff (1995). We can gain some insight into whether this is the case by identifying what proportion of government expenditures represent social benefits and social transfers. If much of the relationship between our measure of the scope of government and the economic vote is the result of a safety-net effect, then including this as a control variable in the simple regression in Figure 7.5 would significantly attenuate the relationship. In fact, when we include this variable in the equation, the relationship between the extensive state-sector variable and the economic vote is slightly stronger.

$$\begin{aligned}\text{Economic Vote}\\ &= -.11(3.6) + .02(3.3) * \text{Extensive State Sector}\\ &\quad + .16(2.28) * (\text{Social Benefits/Government Expenditures})\\ R^2 &= .12. \quad N = 108 \qquad (7.7)\end{aligned}$$

t-Statistics are in parentheses.

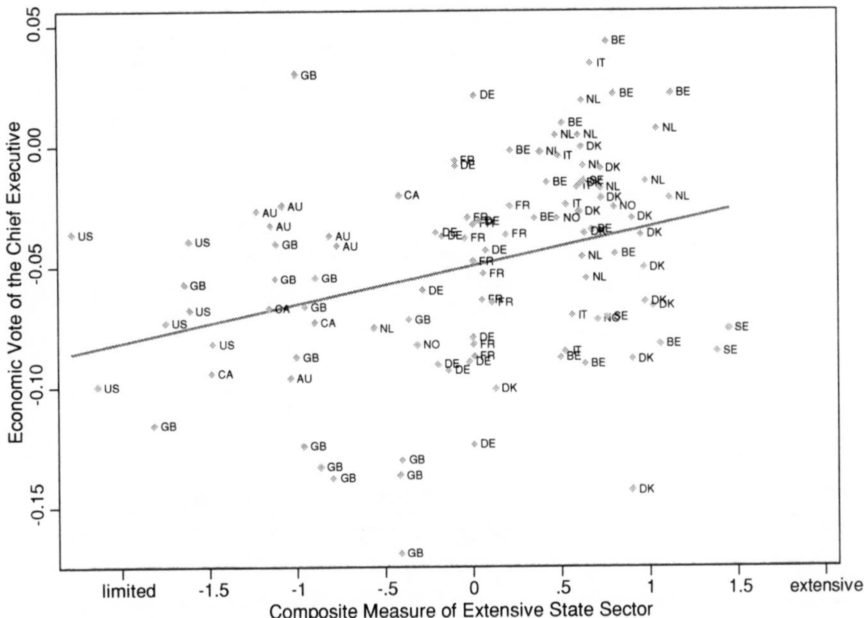

Figure 7.5. Extensive state sector and economic vote of the chief executive.
Source: Limited government factor score from factor analysis of CWB, Regulation Density, and Government Outlays/GDP
Economic Vote of Chief Executive = −0.05 (9.10) + 0.02 (3.08) × Composite Measure of Extensive State Sector. $R^2 = 0.10$. Observations = 107.[19]

Interestingly, though, the percent of government expenditures accounted for by social benefits and social transfers has a positive and significant coefficient confirming the earlier findings of Pacek and Radcliff (1995). Economic voting is somewhat lower in high social-welfare contexts.

Another test of this alternative argument is to substitute the measure of government expenditures as a percent of GDP employed in Figure 7.2 with a measure that includes only expenditures not associated with social benefits or transfers. This results in a weaker relationship with the economic vote but one that is still positive as hypothesized, although slightly below conventional levels of significance – the t-statistic is 1.5.

There is no disputing the fact that the economic vote is lower in contexts with a more extensive state sector. Moreover, this clearly challenges

19 Estimates are from an OLS regression with standard errors robust to heteroskedacticity and to nonindependence between observations of the same party in different surveys. T-statistics are in parentheses.

conventional notions that big government, in itself, signals incumbent responsibility for economic outcomes and, hence, should raise levels of economic voting. Rather, the signal that conditions the economic vote is the relative magnitude of the variance of the competency shock to the variance of exogenous shocks to the macro-economy. As the number of EDDs relative to the number of NEDDs in a national context rises, the overall competency signal gets larger. It turns out that this ratio is larger in contexts with limited statist institutions and, hence, some might say paradoxically, the overall competency signal is stronger in contexts with limited statist institutions, as is the economic vote.

AN OPEN ECONOMY AND AN EXPANSIVE STATE SECTOR DEPRESS THE ECONOMIC VOTE

Globalization and an expansive state sector represent two of the most prominent changes experienced by developed democracies in the post–World War I period. There is a debate as to whether increased globalization has resulted in (1) policy convergence around liberal economic policies, designed to enhance competitiveness; or (2) the expansion of the scope of government, seen as a way to cushion the social dislocation resulting from global competition. Given our empirical results, this controversy has implications for overall levels of economic voting in developed democracies. The notion that openness to the global economy and the size of the government sector are positively correlated implies that these two variables reinforce each other's impact on the economic vote. Alternatively, if these two variables are negatively correlated – resulting from the fact that increased globalization engenders a liberal economic policy response – then their contextual effects on the economic vote would cancel out. With globalization likely to continue increasing, this has interesting implications for economic voting and, by extension, democratic accountability. The former scenario – a positive correlation between globalization and government size – implies declining levels of economic voting, whereas the later scenario – a negative correlation – suggests stable levels of economic voting in the face of rising globalization.

We now explore these two possible empirical scenarios. The first scenario suggests that democracies may fall along a single dimension characterized by open economies with an expansive state sector at one extreme and economies less open to global trade and with a limited state sector at the other. A factor analysis of all four variables described earlier (the open

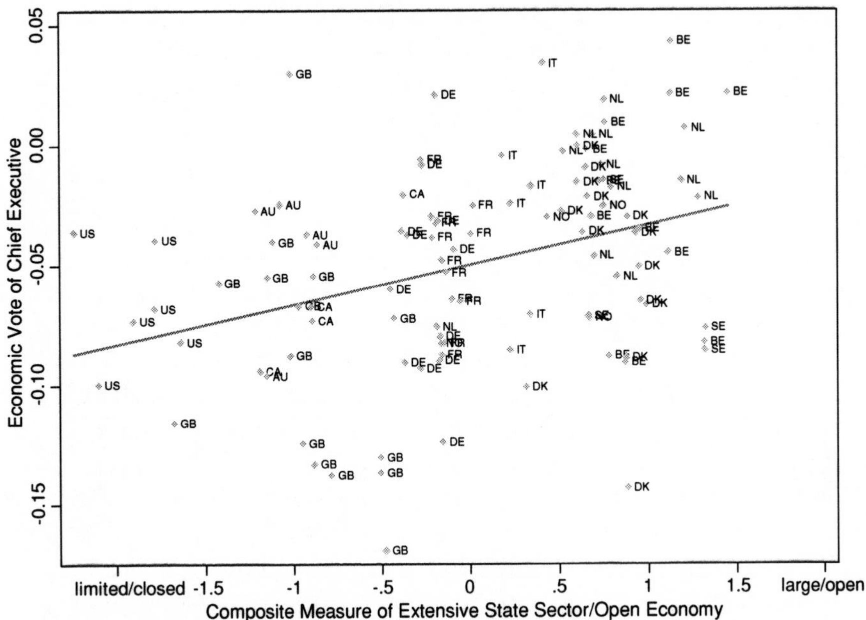

Figure 7.6. Extensive state sector/open economy and economic vote of chief executive.
Source: Composite measure of extensive state sector/open economy factor analysis of Open Economy, CWB, Regulation Density and Government Outlays/GDP
Economic Vote of Chief Executive = −.05 (9.62) + .02 (3.42) × Composite Measure of Extensive State Sector/Open Economy. R^2 = .12. Observations = 106.[20]

economy item and the three limited government items) confirms that this is the case – we obtain a single-factor dimension with each item exhibiting a high loading.[21] Figure 7.6 shows that this composite measure of scope of the state sector and trade openness is significantly correlated with the *economic vote of the chief executive*. Hence, countries with exposure to global trade also will likely have an expansive state sector, and both of these characteristics will have negative effects on the economic vote. It is not unreasonable then to distinguish national contexts in terms of this dimension: contexts with an open economy and an expansive state sector will have relatively low levels of economic voting, whereas contexts with

[20] Estimates are from an OLS regression with standard errors robust to heteroskedacticity and to nonindependence between observations of the same party in different surveys. T-statistics are in parentheses.

[21] The item factor loadings are as follows: trade openness is .60; government outlays is .83; corporatism is .65; and regulation density is −.62.

a closed economy and a limited state sector should have a high economic vote. If globalization continues to increase, and its relationship with size of government persists, this suggests declining levels of economic voting in the future.

MULTILEVEL MODEL RESULTS

This is an important result because it supports the underlying competency model that we described in Chapter 5; it confirms rather counterintuitive predictions derived from the theory in Chapter 5 regarding the impact of globalization and scope of the government sector on the economic vote; and it suggests future trends in economic voting for the developed democracies. Accordingly, we assess the robustness of the finding by estimating a pooled multilevel model. To implement this, we combined individual-level data from our 163 electoral surveys (into a pooled or "stacked" data set) to estimate a single logistic model of the individual-level vote for or against the chief executive party. This vote was modeled as a function of economic perceptions and a much reduced set of control variables that were available in most of our surveys. The requirement that we have a set of common control variables eliminated seventeen studies; therefore, 146 studies remain in the pooled data set. We estimate a sparse individual-level model: it includes an *Ideology* variable that is the de-meaned left-right self-placement of the voter (coded so higher numbers indicate a more right-leaning voter) and its interaction with a dummy variable (*CE˙Ideology*) indicating whether the chief executive's party is a leftist party.[22] We expect then that the coefficient on left-right self-placement will be positive and its interaction with the ideology of the prime minister will be negative. The variable measuring retrospective perceptions of the national economy has been broken into three dummy variables: *worse*, which equals one if voters thought the economy had gotten worse in the last year; *better*, which equals one if they thought the economy had gotten better; and *same*, which equals one if they thought the economy had stayed the same. Two of these, *better* and *worse*, were included in the individual-level model. We expect these two dummy variables to have opposite signs with worse being negative and better being positive. The pooled model is thus limited to one main control variable – the ideology of the voter relative to that

[22] In order to include as many studies as possible, we had to combine some left-right self-placement questions that gave the respondents different response options. This was done by normalizing the various scales and then using the normalized scales.

of the prime minister. This sparseness in specification is the cost one pays for pooling data from disparate surveys.[23]

We also include a variable, *size of chief executive's party*, which is simply the average support for the chief executive's party in the survey. This is constant for each survey and essentially allows the constant-only model (which captures the probability that an ideologically average voter will vote for the chief executive's party) to vary based on the general level of support for the chief executive's party in the population.

More specifically, the basic form of the model, illustrated here with the *extensive state sector* contextual variable, is:

$$v_{ik} \sim Bin(\pi_{1ik})$$

$$logit(\pi_{1ik}) = \beta_{0k} + \beta_{1k} Worse_{ik} + \beta_{2k} Better_{ik} + \phi_1 \text{Ideology}_{ik} + \phi_2(\text{Ideology}_{ik} * \text{CE\_Ideology}_k) \quad (7.8)$$

$$\beta_{0k} = \gamma_{00} + \gamma_{01} Size_k + \gamma_{01} ES_k + \omega_{0k}$$
$$\beta_{1k} = \gamma_{10} + \gamma_{11} ES_k + \omega_{1k}$$
$$\beta_{2k} = \gamma_{20} + \gamma_{21} ES_k + \omega_{2k}$$

where *Bin* just indicates the dependent variable is distributed according to an appropriate binomial distribution with parameter π_{1jk}. *ES* is *extensive state sector* and we assume the errors are distributed according to a multivariate normal distribution, with variances $\sigma^2_{\omega 1}$, $\sigma^2_{\omega 2}$, and $\sigma^2_{\omega 3}$ and covariances $\sigma^2_{\omega 1,\omega 2}$, $\sigma^2_{\omega 1,\omega 3}$, and $\sigma^2_{\omega 2,\omega 3}$. Because we expect support for the chief executive to be negatively related to economic perceptions, we expect $\gamma_{10} < 0$ and $\gamma_{20} > 0$ (recall that the baseline category is voters who think the economy has stayed the same). Furthermore, because a more *extensive state sector* is expected to reduce the size of the economic vote, we expect $\gamma_{11} > 0$ and $\gamma_{21} < 0$ (because this will decrease the difference between the overall impact of better versus worse perceptions).

The multilevel interaction results reported in Table 7.1 strongly confirm the results of the two-stage analyses presented earlier.[24] First, the results in Model 1 are for the core economic voting model and they establish, in fact, that there is a significant economic vote in our sample of 146 voter-preference studies. The coefficient on the *economy got better* dummy

[23] For a detailed comparison of the two-stage estimation strategy and the conventional multilevel interaction method using these data, see Duch and Stevenson (2005).

[24] The estimates were obtained using the PQL second-order linearization method outlined in Goldstein (1995). Diagnostics on estimated residuals at Level 2 suggest that the assumption of normal variance in the level-two coefficients is not violated.

Table 7.1. *Multilevel Logistic Regression Model of Incumbent Vote*

	Model 1	Model 2	Model 3	Model 4
Left-Right Self-Placement (dev. from mean)	0.48 (0.01)	0.48 (0.01)	0.49 (0.01)	0.48 (0.01)
Left-Right Self-Placement × Leftist PM (Leftist PM is an indicator variable)	−0.74 (0.01)	−0.87 (0.01)	−0.75 (0.01)	−0.88 (0.01)
Voter Perceives Economy got Better (indicator variable)	0.43 (0.03)	0.46 (0.03)	0.80 (0.07)	0.45 (0.03)
Voter Perceives Economy got Worse (indicator variable)	−0.55 (0.03)	−0.57 (0.04)	−0.86 (0.07)	−0.56 (0.04)
Limited State Sector Index		−0.02 (0.04)		
Voter Perceives Economy got Better × Limited State Sector Index		−0.23 (0.04)		
Voter Perceives Economy got Worse × Limited State Sector Index		0.22 (0.05)		
Trade Openness Ratio			−0.002 (0.001)	
Voter Perceives Economy got Better × Trade Openness Ratio			−0.005 (0.001)	
Voter Perceives Economy got Worse × Trade Openness Ratio			0.004 (0.001)	
Composite Measure				−0.03 (0.04)
Voter Perceives Economy got Better × Composite Measure				−0.23 (0.04)
Voter Perceives Economy got Worse × Composite Measure				0.20 (0.04)
Size of Chief Executive's Party	5.22 (0.22)	6.15 (0.28)	5.24 (0.23)	6.12 (0.28)
Constant	−2.39 (0.07)	−2.70 (0.08)	−2.28 (0.10)	−2.70 (0.08)
$\sigma^2_{\omega 1}$	0.09	0.06	0.09	0.06
$\sigma^2_{\omega 2}$	0.08	0.06	0.06	0.06
$\sigma^2_{\omega 3}$	0.10	0.08	0.08	0.07
$\sigma_{\omega 1,\omega 2}$	−0.03	−0.02	−0.03	−0.03
$\sigma_{\omega 1,\omega 3}$	0.04	−0.02	−0.03	−0.02
$\sigma_{u\omega 2,\omega 3}$	−0.05	−0.04	−0.03	−0.04
N	201,876	201,876	201,876	201,876

Standard errors are listed below the logit coefficients. All coefficients are statistically significant at $p < 0.05$ except the shaded cells.

variable is positive and statistically significant; and the *economy got worse* variable has a statistically significant negative coefficient.

Model 2 adds two interaction terms to the core equation: the *extensive state sector* variable interacted with each of the *economic perception* variables. The coefficients on these interaction terms are exactly as we would expect. In the case of the *extensive state sector* variable interacted with the *economy got better* variable, the coefficient is negative and significant, suggesting that the impact of this economic perception variable is lower in contexts with more extensive government involvement in the economy (recall that the *extensive state sector index* has a high value for an expansive state sector). The *extensive state sector* variable interacted with the *economy got worse* variable has a positive coefficient, suggesting that the impact of negative perceptions is moderated in contexts with a large government involvement in the economy. There is less economic voting in contexts with an extensive state sector.

Model 3 examines the hypothesized impact of an open economy on economic voting. Again, these results reinforce our earlier conclusions: more open economies have less economic voting. *Trade openness* interacted with the *economy got better* variable has a negative coefficient, suggesting that the impact of positive economic perceptions on vote choice is lower in contexts with higher exposure to global economic influences. And the positive coefficient on the interaction with the *economy got worse* variable suggests that the impact of negative economic perceptions on the vote is lower in open-economy contexts. This confirms that there is more economic voting in contexts less exposed to global influences.

The results for the *trade openness* and *limited state sector* variables in Models 2 and 3 are consistent with each of the individual bivariate analyses presented earlier. Earlier we also provided evidence that countries typically fall along a single continuum characterized by an open economy with an expansive state sector, on one extreme, and a closed economy with limited government on the other. Accordingly, we created a *composite measure* of state-sector expansiveness and trade openness. Model 4 in Table 7.1 confirms that this composite measure has the hypothesized effect on the magnitude of the economic vote clearly suggested by Figure 7.6. The coefficient on this *composite variable* interacted with negative retrospective evaluations is positive and significant, whereas the coefficient on the interaction of this variable and positive evaluations is negative and significant. The *composite variable* interaction term decreases the difference between the overall impact of better versus worse perceptions. This is further strong confirmation that countries with high scores on this *composite measure* – having high exposure to global trade and an expansive state sector – will have less economic voting.

These estimates clearly support the hypothesis because all the coefficients are statistically significant and in the expected direction. Thus, this pooled, multilevel model tells exactly the same story as the second-stage estimates from the two-stage method. Economic voting is depressed in contexts with a more expansive state sector and an open economy.

SUMMARY

Voters in our competency model condition their economic vote on signals regarding the competency of incumbents. One of the results from Chapter 5 indicates that as the ratio of decisions affecting economic outcomes by nonelectorally dependent decision makers (β) to those by electorally dependent decision makers (α) declines, the overall competency signal will rise and vice versa. This theoretical result provides an important explanation for some of the contextual variation in the economic vote that we documented in Chapter 3. The theory does not specify precisely which national contexts have a high versus low ratio of NEDDs to EEDs. This chapter identifies features of the political economic context that correspond to our theoretical notion of EED versus NEDD influences over economic outcomes. We also provide empirical evidence that our measures of political economic context explain variations in the economic vote.

Although not using our explicit theoretical jargon, Cameron's (1978) early essay on open economies essentially makes one of our principal empirical arguments. Open economies reduce the number of electorally dependent decisions over macro-economic outcomes, which implies a weaker competency signal and, hence, should lead to lower levels of economic voting. The empirical results presented in this chapter clearly suggest this is the case.

As Cameron and others also have pointed out, open economies often enact policies that expand the role of the state in the economy. Some see this broadening of the scope of statist institutions as compensating for the erosion of incumbent control over economic outcomes and for the decline in democratic accountability resulting from globalization (Freeman, 2006). To the extent that economic voting can be seen as a measure of democratic accountability, both our theoretical and empirical results are at odds with this perspective. With respect to economic voting, our theory suggests that broadening the scope of the state in fact further weakens the competency signal of incumbent governments – that is, reinforces the weakening effect of the open economy on the competency signal. We arrive at this prediction because we assume that adopting more extensive statist institutions increases the ratio of NEDD versus EDD because it results in a larger number of NEDDs participating in the economic decision-making process.[25] Our theory maintains that this increased ratio of NEDD to EDD lowers the incumbent government's competency signal and should result in lower economic voting, which could be an indicator of less democratic accountability. Again, the empirical results are quite supportive: voters in contexts with extensive statist institutions – measured as the size of the government sector, the extent of corporatism, and the extent of regulatory density – have less economic voting.

This result has important implications for the debate regarding globalization and democratic governance because it provides a rigorous explanation for how globalization affects vote choice. The net implications of globalization for democratic accountability depend on whether greater exposure to the international economy occurs in a context with an extensive as opposed to more limited state sector. A larger government sector may, in fact, moderate the negative social consequences of globalization, but our competency theory suggests that broadening the scope of government's involvement in the economy reinforces the negative consequences of trade openness on democratic accountability. More specifically, increasing the size of the government sector, embracing corporatist institutions, and increasing government regulation reduce the magnitude of the incumbent's competency signal, leading voters to discount the importance of the economy in their voting decision. Paradoxically, countries responding to increased exposure to global economic forces by privatizing their economies and adopting liberal economic policies are more likely to counteract the erosion of democratic accountability associated with globalization.

Accordingly, the debate as to whether increasing globalization will result in policy convergence around liberal economic policies rather than the expansion of the scope of government has important consequences

[25] Of course, this assumption that contexts with an expansive state sector have a high ratio of NEDD to EDD is not empirically evaluated in this book. Nevertheless, as we point out, the assumption is consistent with our understanding of how voters learn about the competency signal and it is, of course, consistent with the empirical data presented in this chapter.

for trends in economic voting in particular and democratic accountability more broadly. We find that openness to the global economy and the size of the government sector are positively correlated. It is not the case that countries with high levels of trade openness have privatized their economies and adopted liberal economic policies.

Our analyses suggest that democracies fall along a single dimension characterized by open economies with an expansive state sector, at one extreme and, at the other, extreme democracies with less exposure to global trade and with a limited state sector. These two trends – a more open economy and an expansive state sector – seem to reinforce each other's negative impact on democratic accountability. This, of course, is a static snapshot of current global realities for advanced democracies of the world. But if this current correlation between the scope of government and exposure to global economic influences persists, then as globalization increases, we can expect declining levels of economic voting and a growing crisis of democratic accountability.

PART III

A Contextual Theory of Rational Retrospective Economic Voting: Strategic Voting

The previous section explored the conditions under which rational voters can extract signals about incumbent competence from movements in the economy. The theory pointed to specific economic contexts that should condition the strength of the competency signal and, consequentially, the importance of the economy in the vote choice. Furthermore, our empirical analysis was largely consistent with those implications. We now propose to explore two aspects of economic voting that were not developed in the model in Chapter 5.

First, in Chapter 8, we generalize the model in Chapter 5 – where only one party was responsible for economic decision making – to multiparty contexts in which policy-making authority may be shared among many – or even all – parties (including opposition parties). We show that in political contexts in which policy-making authority is widely shared, the rational voter's ability to extract an informative signal about the competence of any one party declines. Chapter 9 explores empirically how variations in the distribution of policy-making responsibility among parties currently in government affect the economic vote.

The model developed in Chapter 3 assumed two parties competing for total control of executive authority. Chapter 8 generalizes this model of rational economic voting to contexts in which there are multi-parties (rather than simply two) competing for election and where executive authority is shared (rather than controlled by a single party). This multiparty competition and shared executive authority necessarily introduces incentives for strategic voting. We explore the implications of these incentives by both applying McKelvey and Ordeshook's (1972) model of strategic voting incentives in multiparty contexts to the model in Chapter 5 and by generalizing it to cases in which coalition cabinets can form (or where policy-making responsibility is shared among all parties). We show in

Chapter 10 that the pattern of contention for future executive authority is important for the strength of economic voting. Furthermore, we show that in cases in which the incentives for economic voting created by these two kinds of contexts are opposed, the incentives created by the pattern of competition for future office can trump those associated with the distribution of policy-making responsibility.

8

Responsibility, Contention, and the Economic Vote

MULTIPLE PARTIES WITH A PLURALITY RACE FOR A SINGLE PARTY EXECUTIVE

We begin by considering the case in which multiple parties are competing for a single-party executive – typically the case in the United Kingdom or Canada, for example. Building on the notation introduced in Chapter 5, we now use the letter "*k*" to refer to a generic opposition party (as there can now be more than one) and let **A** be the set of all opposition parties. By the same logic that motivated equation (5.11) in Chapter 5, we can write the voter's expected utility for any of these parties gaining office as:

$$E\left[u_{k,t+1}\right] = b\overline{y}\ \forall k \in \mathbf{A} \tag{8.1}$$

Because voters are rational expected utility maximizers, in a multiparty context we must allow for the possibility of strategic voting. McKelvey and Ordeshook (1972) have addressed how utility maximization is achieved in exactly this kind of decision-theoretic, multiparty plurality situation. Specifically, McKelvey and Ordeshook show that when voters face a decision problem in which they must choose between multiple parties and care only about the winner of the plurality election, the difference in the expected utility from voting for some party *j* versus that of abstaining is:[1]

$$E[u \mid v_j] - E[u \mid v_0] = \sum_{j' \in \mathbf{J}} P_{jj'}(u_j - u_{j'}) \tag{8.2}$$

where **J** is the set of all parties in the legislature and $E[u \mid v_j]$ is the expected utility from voting for party *j*, $E[u \mid v_0]$ is the expected utility

[1] They also assume that the probability of a tie between three or more parties is zero.

from abstaining, and u_j and $u_{j'}$ are the utilities associated with parties j and j' winning the election. $P_{jj'}$ is a "pivot probability" and is defined as the probability that parties j and j' are tied for first place in the plurality race. The subscript on the summation notation is how we indicate that the sum is over all parties in the election.[2]

McKelvey and Ordeshook (1972) show that utility maximization requires a rational voter to vote for the party for which $E[u \mid v_j] - E[u \mid v_0]$ is the largest.[3] The intuition captured in this equation is straightforward: the act of voting for a party can only change a voter's utility by changing the outcome of the election. The likelihood of a voter's vote for a particular party changing the outcome of the election is captured by the probability that this vote is decisive in the contest between this party and each of the other competing parties. Consequently, the voter's expected utility for voting for a particular party is simply the sum of the ways her vote can be decisive multiplied by the utility of the outcome associated with each kind of decisive vote.[4]

2 Any theory in which strategic voting in mass electorates is taken seriously is subject to the criticism that rational voters should never believe their vote is decisive in these kinds of elections. Most scholars who use models of rational voting no longer spend much time defending this assumption, since strategic voting in mass elections is a demonstrated fact (e.g., Cox, 1997; Duch and Palmer, 2002b; Cain, 1978).

3 Palfrey (1989), Myerson and Weber (1993), and Cox (1997) have extended this logic to other voting systems and to a game-theoretic rather than decision-theoretic setting. With respect to different electoral systems in a decision-theoretic setting, the same basic result applies – that is, the pivot probabilities are the key to the voter's calculus. With respect to the decision-theoretic versus game-theoretic treatments, the game-theoretic treatments simply make the pivot probabilities endogenous to the game. The main result of this is to show the existence of equilibria that support different behavior than the decision-theoretic models imply. Fey (1997), however, has shown that when one adds to the game-theoretic models, a realistic account of how voters' beliefs about pivot probabilities might be generated dynamically in an election campaign, the different predictions from the game-theoretic and decision-theoretic models disappear.

4 Here is an example of the calculation that leads to this equation in the three-party case: Let $Prob(a = b)$ mean the probability that party a and party b tie for first place; $Prob(a = b - 1)$ mean the probability that party a trails party b by one vote in the race for first place; $Prob(a = b + 1)$ mean the probability that party a leads party b by one vote in the race for first place; $Prob(a > b + 1)$ mean the probability that party a leads party b by more than one vote in the race for first place (with similar notation for other pairings of parties); and $Prob(a < b - 1)$ mean the probability that party a trails party b by more than one vote in the race for first place. Assuming ties are broken randomly and the chance of a three-way tie is zero, we can write: expected utility of a vote for party a $= E^a = \mathrm{Prob}(a = b)(u_a) + \mathrm{Prob}(a = c)(u_a) + \mathrm{Prob}(a = b - 1)(u_a + u_b)/2 + \mathrm{Prob}(a = c - 1)(u_a + u_c)/2 + \mathrm{Prob}(a = b + 1)(u_a) + \mathrm{Prob}(a = c + 1)(u_a) + \mathrm{Prob}(a < b - 1)(u_b) + \mathrm{Prob}(a < c -$

To combine this analysis of strategic voting with analysis of economic voting from Chapter 5, we simply define u_j in equation (8.2) as $E[u_{i,t+1}]$ from equation (5.10) for the incumbent and as $E[u_{k,t+1}]$ from equation (8.1) for opposition parties. Thus, for the incumbent, we can write:

$$E[u \mid v_i] - E[u \mid v_0] = \sum_{k \in A} P_{ik}(E[u_{it+1}] - E[u_{kt+1}])$$
$$\times \sum_{k \in A} P_{ik}\left(b\overline{y} + b\left(\frac{\sigma_\mu^2}{\sigma_\mu^2 + \sigma_\xi^2}\right)(y_{it} - \overline{y} - \mu_{it-1}) - b\overline{y}\right)$$
$$= b\left(\sum_{k \in A} P_{ik}\right)\left(\frac{\sigma_\mu^2}{\sigma_\mu^2 + \sigma_\xi^2}\right)(y_{it} - \overline{y} - \mu_{it-1}) \qquad (8.3)$$

and for each opposition party, we can write:

$$E[u \mid v_k] - E[u \mid v_0] = P_{ki}(E[u_{kt+1}] - E[u_{it+1}])$$
$$+ \sum_{k' \in A} P_{kk'}(E[u_{kt+1}] - E[u_{k't+1}])$$
$$= P_{ki}\left(b\overline{y} - \left(b\overline{y} + b\left(\frac{\sigma_\mu^2}{\sigma_\mu^2 + \sigma_\xi^2}\right)(y_{it} - \overline{y} - \mu_{it-1})\right)\right)$$
$$+ \sum_{k' \in A} \{P_{kk'}(b\overline{y} - b\overline{y})\}$$
$$= -P_{ki}b\left(\frac{\sigma_\mu^2}{\sigma_\mu^2 + \sigma_\xi^2}\right)(y_{it} - \overline{y} - \mu_{it-1}) \qquad (8.4)$$

There will be as many of these expressions as there are opposition parties and the voter will vote for the opposition party or incumbent for which the relevant expression is the largest. These equations depend on three substantively interesting terms: the competency signal, retrospective economic performance, and the distribution of the pivot probabilities across pairs of parties, which we call the *pattern of electoral contention.*

The first thing to notice about the interaction of these terms is that they imply economic voting of the usual kind. That is, if economic voting is

1)(u_c) + Prob(a > b + 1)(u_a) + Prob(a > c + 1)(u_a); expected utility of abstention = E^0 = Prob(a = b)($u_a + u_b$)/2 + Prob(a = c)($u_a + u_c$)/2 + Prob(a = b − 1)(u_b) + Prob(a = c − 1)(u_c) + Prob(a = b + 1)(u_a) + Prob(a = c + 1)(u_a) + Prob(a > b − 1) (u_b) + Prob(a < c − 1)(u_c) + Prob(a > b + 1)(u_a) + Prob(a > c + 1)(u_a). If we assume, following McKelvey and Ordeshook, that Prob(a = b) > Prob(a = b − 1), then subtracting E^0 from E^a gives: Prob(a = b)($u_a - u_b$) + Prob(a = c)($u_a - u_c$), which is the specific form of the previous equation that is appropriate to this example.

important at all to vote choice (i.e., there is some nonzero P_{ik}), voters will vote for the incumbent party when economic performance is sufficiently good and vote against the incumbent party when it is not.[5] To see this in the simplest case, assume that $P_{ik} > 0$ for only one opposition party. In this case, the voter will cast her vote for the incumbent party if:

$$bP_{ik}\left(\frac{\sigma_{\mu}^{2}}{\sigma_{\mu}^{2}+\sigma_{\xi}^{2}}\right)(y_{it}-\overline{y}-\mu_{it-1}) - \left(b(-P_{ki})\left(\frac{\sigma_{\mu}^{2}}{\sigma_{\mu}^{2}+\sigma_{\xi}^{2}}\right)(y_{it}-\overline{y}-\mu_{it-1})\right) > 0$$

$$2bP_{ik}\left(\frac{\sigma_{\mu}^{2}}{\sigma_{\mu}^{2}+\sigma_{\xi}^{2}}\right)(y_{it}-\overline{y}-\mu_{it-1}) > 0 \tag{8.5}$$

where $P_{ik} = P_{ki}$. Because P_{ik}, b, and $\frac{\sigma_{\mu}^{2}}{\sigma_{\mu}^{2}+\sigma_{\xi}^{2}}$ are all greater than zero by definition, this condition can only be fulfilled if $(y_{it}-\overline{y}-\mu_{it-1})$ is positive. Given a fixed level for the incumbent's competence (i.e., μ_{it-1}), this can only happen if economic performance $(y_{it}-\overline{y})$ is sufficiently positive. If, however, economic performance is sufficiently negative, then this condition will not be fulfilled and the voter will vote for the one opposition party k that has a nonzero probability of being in a tie with the incumbent for an electoral plurality. When P_{ik} is nonzero for more than one opposition party, a similar argument applies.

The second thing to notice about equations (8.3) and (8.4) is that if the incumbent party is either sure to win a plurality or sure to lose it, then there will be no economic voting in this model. Specifically, because the retrospective economy plays no role in conditioning the voters' expectations about the performance of the opposition parties (these expectations are just zero), the voters have no way to choose between different opposition parties. Consequently, even if two such parties were tied for election, this probability is multiplied by a utility difference of zero and so falls out of the model.[6] The obvious empirical implication of this result is that we

[5] Exactly how good or bad economic performance $(y_{it}-\overline{y})$ must be to make $(y_{it}-\overline{y}-\mu_{it-1})$ positive or negative.

[6] We could allow some noneconomic utility that voters attain when a particular party obtains office. This would mean the pivot probabilities for pairs of opposition parties would not fall out of the equation. However, nothing about the economy would be in the retained terms and so we would still conclude that there would be no economic voting if the incumbent is not in competition with some party to win a plurality.

and the inequality in equation (8.5) as:

$$(\gamma_i - \gamma_k) + 2bP_{ik}\left(\frac{\sigma_\mu^2}{\sigma_\mu^2 + \sigma_\xi^2}\right)(y_{it} - \overline{y} - \mu_{it-1}) > 0$$

$$(\gamma_i - \gamma_k)\Bigg/\left(\frac{\sigma_\mu^2}{\sigma_\mu^2 + \sigma_\xi^2}\right) + 2bP_{ik}(y_{it} - \overline{y} - \mu_{it-1}) > 0 \qquad (8.9)$$

This revision of the model, then, makes it plain that the competence signals condition the importance of economic voting relative to other impacts on the vote. When it is large (closer to one), it decreases the weight of $(\gamma_i - \gamma_k)$ relative to $(y_{it} - \overline{y} - \mu_{it-1})$ in the voter's expected utility of voting for a party. Thus, our earlier interpretation of the competence signal as a weight on economic voting stands, as long as we allow some noneconomic sources of utility. We have included these sources in the simplest way, but the interpretation does not depend on that choice. In the models that follow, we retain this revision.

Finally, this modification of the model slightly changes the interpretation of the role P_{ik} discussed earlier. That discussion indicated that if the performance of the economy was sufficiently poor, the economic vote would flow away from incumbents to the opposition party with the largest P_{ik}, even if P_{ik} were very small. All that was required was that $P_{ik} > 0$. If this condition was met, the utility associated with voting for the incumbent would be negative and the utility associated with party k would be positive and so voters would vote for k, even if its chance of tying the incumbent were very small. In the current model, however, $P_{ik} > 0$ is no longer enough for voters to prefer the challenger to the incumbent when $(y_{it} - \overline{y} - \mu_{it-1})$ is negative. Because $(\gamma_i - \gamma_k)$ can now be positive when the economy is performing poorly, a small P_{ik} may make the overall economic term so small (recall that $0 \leq P_{ik} \leq 1$) that a voter who gets some positive utility for voting for the incumbent rather than party k will, nevertheless, vote for the incumbent. Thus, the addition of noneconomic factors simply makes the absolute size of P_{ik} matter to the voter's choice. This is important empirically because it tells us whether economic voting in these systems should require close races for pluralities or only some chance that the incumbent could lose.

Specifically, the earlier model implied that economic voting should be important as long as some challenger had *any* chance of competing for an electoral plurality; however, the new one implies that economic voting should be important when some challenger has a real chance of winning, where the degree of competition required depends on the strength of the typical voter's psychological attachment to the incumbent (or aversion to the challenger). For example, think about how a plurality contest like this might have worked out in postwar Italy. The Christian Democrats dominated the Italian system and many voters had deep ties to the party based on their religious beliefs. In contrast, the closest contender for an electoral plurality was usually the Communists, which remained for many years one of the least reformed in Europe. In this case, it is likely that for the typical voter $(\gamma_i - \gamma_k)$ was quite large, so we would expect economic voting to be important (in a hypothetical plurality race for control of government) only if the race was quite close indeed.

Economic voting in its traditional form continues in this generalization of the model – voters will vote against the incumbent when economic performance is sufficiently weak and for the incumbent when it is sufficiently strong. When economic performance is poor, the voter will vote for the opposition party that is most likely to contend with the incumbent for an electoral plurality. The less the incumbent party contends for an electoral plurality (i.e., it is a sure loser or a sure winner), the smaller the economic vote.

MULTIPLE PARTIES WITH A GENERIC SELECTION PROCESS FOR A SINGLE-PARTY EXECUTIVE

Most executives are not selected directly in a plurality election as assumed in the previous discussion. Usually, there is some selection process following the election in which the electoral result may be but one factor that determines the composition of the government. In order to examine economic voting in these cases, we must generalize the logic of strategic voting. We do that in two steps. Later, we discuss the case of the selection of coalition governments, which is the usual situation in which postelection selection of governments is an issue. However, that discussion will be clearer if we first consider the logically possible (but empirically rare) case in which a single-party government is selected in a postelection process that is only partially based on the electoral result.[10]

[10] Such a system might result when a head of state has discretion in appointing a government and is not constrained to choose the plurality winner.

McKelvey and Ordeshook conceive of the pivot probability, P_{ik}, as the probability that parties i and k are tied in the race for *election* to the executive. Their analysis, however, can be applied to a more general executive selection process in which we define P_{ik} as the probability that parties i and k are tied in the race for *selection* to the executive. This change in language is used to indicate that the selection process may only partly depend on the electoral outcome. For example, it could be that a single-party executive is selected in a bargaining process in which having more votes is helpful but not determinant because other factors such as ideological centrality also impact the selection. One real-world example of this might be systems in which a head of state has some discretion in choosing the new prime minister. In such cases, the head of state may pay close attention to the electoral result but sometimes choose a party that is not the plurality winner for other reasons. Votes can still be decisive in this setting – decisiveness, however, does not correspond to breaking ties for electoral pluralities. Instead, a vote is decisive if it breaks a tie between two parties in their overall chances of being selected as the governing party. For example, selection could depend on two factors, electoral strength and ideological centrality. Suppose that, absent voter *i*'s vote, one party receives 20 percent of the vote and another 30 percent, but the smaller party is closer to the median position than the other to the exact extent necessary to make the selection between the two parties indeterminate. Voter *i*'s vote now becomes decisive in the selection of the executive, even though the two parties' electoral support differs substantially.

With this generalization of the interpretation of the P_{ik}s, the earlier analysis can be directly applied to any process of executive selection that gives executive power to a single party based in part on their electoral support (where, of course, the chance of selection is increasing in that support). Consequently, we can conclude that rational, forward-looking voters in systems that *select* single-party executives will not cast economic votes unless the incumbent party is in a close race with some other party for selection to the executive.

Here, we consider the unusual case in which multiple parties compete for exclusive control of the executive, but the selection of the executive is not based only on which party wins an electoral plurality. We conclude that when economic performance is poor, the voter will vote for the opposition party that is most likely to contend with the incumbent for *selection* to the executive. And, the less the incumbent party contends for selection to the executive (i.e., it is sure not to be selected or it is sure to be selected), the more muted the economic voting.

MULTIPLE PARTIES WITH A COALITIONAL EXECUTIVE

Thus far, we have generalized the notion of pivot probabilities to cover cases in which single-party incumbents are selected rather than simply elected but have not addressed the more usual situation in which post-election executive selection procedures result in a multiparty coalition cabinet. To remedy this, we begin by generalizing the analysis of strategic voting in the last section to cases of coalition government and then use this to generalize Alesina and Rosenthal's (1995) model of retrospective economic voting as well.

In our generalization, we continue to focus on the role that the vote plays in the *selection* rather than the *election* of an executive; however, we further alter the concept of a pivot probability to apply to the situation in which a vote may be decisive in bringing a potential *coalition* (rather than a single party) to power. This requires that we consider the role that the vote for a *party* plays in the selection among potential *cabinets*.[11] The details and formalization of the concept of a pivot probability in this setting are worked out in Appendix A. In that discussion, we define a cabinet as a vector, $\mathbf{g} = \{g_1, g_2, g_j, \ldots, g_J\}$, where g_j is 1 if party j is a member of cabinet $\mathbf{g}$ and zero otherwise. Furthermore, we define a generalized pivot probability, $P_{j,\mathbf{gg}'}$, as the probability that two cabinets, g and g′, are tied for selection *and* that a vote for party *j* will break that tie in favor of cabinet g. More precisely, the formal definition in Appendix A models the cabinet-selection process as having two stages. In the first, each potential cabinet is assigned a selection value based on some selection function that depends on the electoral support of all parties and other nonelectoral factors. Second, the cabinet with the highest selection value is the one that forms. Thus, the idea of being "tied for selection" in this setting means two cabinets have the same selection values and have higher values than any other cabinet. The voter's belief that two cabinets

[11] We concur with Myerson's argument that "Finally, we saw the importance of taking account of how the winners will bargain after the election to control the government. Rational voters should be concerned about their potential effect on this bargaining process, and this concern may be an essential factor to explain the systematic differences between party structures in presidential and parliamentary systems" (Myerson, 1999: 39).

are tied for selection is just $P_{gg'}$. Furthermore, with this generic model of the selection process, we can think of the probability that a vote for party j breaks a tie for selection between g and g′ in favor of cabinet g as the probability that the derivative of the selection function for g, with respect to the vote total of party j, is bigger than the corresponding derivative for g′. In Appendix A, we write this requirement as $P(D_{g,j} > D_{g',j})$, so $P_{j,gg'}$ is just shorthand for $P_{gg'} P(D_{g,j} > D_{g',j})$.[12] In later sections, we examine more closely the form of the derivatives in this definition and use them to define different political contexts in which we expect more or less economic voting. However, at this stage in the argument, all we need to understand is that the generalization of rational economic voting to the coalition context requires that we consider the voter's beliefs about the efficacy of her vote in the process of cabinet selection, as well as her beliefs about which cabinets are likely to tie for selection, given that process. Furthermore, our strategy for generalizing the rational retrospective model to coalition contexts is to incorporate these beliefs into a generalized version of the pivot probability commonly found in models of rational voting.

In what follows, we always indicate the set of incumbent parties as g and generic alternative cabinets as g′ or g″. The set of all such alternative cabinets is **A** (note that this set does not include the incumbent cabinet g). In Appendix A, we show that – analogous to equation (8.6) – we can write:

$$\begin{aligned} E[u \mid v_j] - E[u \mid v_0] = &\sum_{g' \in A} P_{j,gg'}(E[u_{g,t+1}] - E[u_{g',t+1}]) \\ &+ \sum_{g' \in A} P_{j,g'g}(E[u_{g',t+1}] - E[u_{g,t+1}]) \\ &+ \sum_{g' \in A} \sum_{g'' \in A} P_{j,g'g''}(E[u_{g',t+1}] - E[u_{g'',t+1}]) + \gamma_j \end{aligned} \tag{8.10}$$

This expression is just the voter's expected utility gain or loss for voting for party j rather than abstaining. The voter will select the party for which this expression is the highest. It identifies all the ways that a vote for party j can be decisive in bringing one coalition to power rather than another

12 We assume that these probabilities are independent.

and sums the utility change associated with casting a vote for party j rather than abstaining in these situations.[13]

To arrive at an expression for the utility of voting for each party in a coalitional situation, we must derive specific expressions for the expected utilities on the right-hand side of equation (8.10). To do this, we need to generalize Alesina and Rosenthal's model of retrospective economic voting to the case of coalition governments. However, because the voter's expected utility depends, in their model, on economic policy and outcomes, we must first ask what inflation policy a coalition government will choose once in office. Furthermore, because the voter's expected utility for a potential cabinet also depends on its expected competence, we need to ask how the voter can forecast both the competence of the incumbent cabinet as a whole and the competence of other potential cabinets. With answers to these questions, we can then come back to these equations to explore how voters translate the utility they expect to accrue under a potential cabinet into a vote for a given party.

Policy Making in Coalition Cabinets

In this section, our task is to generalize Alesina and Rosenthal's model of retrospective economic voting to provide an expression for the voter's expected utility if the incumbent government were to stay in power, allowing for the possibility that this incumbent government is a coalition among two or more parties. As we pointed out earlier, no government (whether single or multiparty) can gain from choosing a level of inflation higher than zero. Consequently, we can conclude that any assumption about how the parties in a coalition cabinet aggregate their policy preferences should result in the same prediction – the coalition government will choose a zero inflation policy. In contrast to inflation, however, economic growth in the model is not determined only by the policy the government chooses but also by the government's level of administrative competence. If we assume that each party has its own "competence shock," then we will need to specify how the overall competency of the government is determined in order to generalize the model to coalitional cases. Doing so reveals an important dimension of political context that will condition the size of the economic vote in this model.

[13] In Chapter 10, we provide some evidence that individuals have well-formed beliefs about the outcomes of the coalition formation process as well as the process itself.

Assume that each party in the cabinet has its own competency shock that is persistent in the same way as in the single-party incumbent model (i.e., as in equation [5.3]). Thus, if we indicate the set of incumbent parties as **g**, with a typical member *i*, we can write:

$$\varepsilon_{it} = \mu_{it} + \mu_{it-1} \forall i \in \mathbf{g} \tag{8.11}$$

In contrast, there is only one nonpolitical shock and because there cannot be a different level of economic growth for each party, the different party competences must be aggregated in some way to produce an overall level of growth. Suppose that the overall competence of the government in a given period is a weighted average of the competence of the incumbent parties, with weights corresponding to the amount of *administrative responsibility* that the party holds. Call these weights, for each incumbent party at time *t*, $\lambda_{i,t}$. We can thus write:

$$\varepsilon_{\mathbf{g},t} = \sum_{i \in \mathbf{g}} \lambda_{i,t}\mu_{i,t} + \lambda_{i,t-1}\mu_{i,t-1} \tag{8.12}$$

This expression is the overall competence of the government, where we assume $\sum_{i \in g} \lambda_{i,t} = 1$ and that the competence shocks for each incumbent party, $\mu_{i,t}$, are drawn from a normal distribution with mean zero and variance σ_{μ}^{2}.[14] The weights can describe a variety of policy-making processes – from a prime ministerial dominant system (λ_{pm} is close to 1) to a system of equal power sharing ($\lambda_{\mathrm{i}} = 1/\mathrm{n}$ for all n incumbent parties) to a system of proportional responsibility (λ_{i} is proportional to legislative or cabinet seat shares). We have more to say about the influence of the distribution of administrative responsibility on economic voting later, but presently we simply want to use this device to derive the voter's expected utility if the incumbent government retains power the next period (i.e., $E[u_{\mathbf{g},t+1}]$).

If we assume that voters know the distribution of administrative responsibility across incumbents, then what will $E[u_{\mathbf{g},t+1}]$ be? Recall that any cabinet will choose a zero-inflation policy and that voters will correctly anticipate this policy so that growth under any cabinet, **g**, is just the natural rate of growth plus a shock. The shock consists of two parts: the government competency shock, which is just the weighted sum in equation (8.12), and an exogenous random shock that represents the

[14] It is not necessary that the competency shocks for different parties come from the same distribution, but allowing these to be different introduces partisan differences into the model.

politically uncontrollable aspects of growth. Growth in the current period is thus:

$$\begin{aligned} y_{g,t} &= \overline{y} + \eta_{g,t} \\ &= \overline{y} + \varepsilon_{g,t} + \xi_t \\ &= \overline{y} + \sum_{i \in g} \left\{ \lambda_{i,t}\mu_{i,t} + \lambda_{i,t-1}\mu_{i,t-1} \right\} + \xi_t \end{aligned} \tag{8.13}$$

Rearranging this gives:

$$\sum_{i \in g} \left\{ \lambda_{i,t}\mu_{i,t} \right\} + \xi_t = y_{g,t} - \overline{y} - \sum_{i \in g} \left\{ \lambda_{i,t-1}\mu_{i,t-1} \right\} \tag{8.14}$$

where everything on the right-hand side of this equality is observed and so the sum of the terms on the left is also observed, though not the individual components. Denote the sum on the left-hand side as $k_{g,t} = \sum_{i \in g} \{\lambda_{i,t}\mu_{i,t}\} + \xi_t$. Because $k_{g,t}$ is observed (although the split between its two random components is not), the voter's expectation about $\mu_{g,t} = \sum_{i \in g} \{\lambda_{i,t}\mu_{i,t}\}$ given $k_{g,t}$ (i.e., the voter's expectation about the government's total level of competence in the current period, given the observed level of growth and last period's total government competence). To calculate this conditional expectation, we need to know the distribution of both $k_{g,t}$ and $\mu_{g,t}$. $\mu_{g,t}$ is a weighted sum of normally distributed random variables, each with zero mean and variance σ_μ^2. Consequently,

$$\begin{aligned} \mu_{g,t} = \sum_{i \in g} \lambda_{i,t}\mu_{i,t} &\sim \mathrm{N}\left(0, \sigma_\mu^2 \sum_{i \in g} \lambda_{i,t}^2\right) \\ &\sim \mathrm{N}\left(0, \sigma_{\mu_{g,t}}^2\right) \end{aligned} \tag{8.15}$$

Thus, $k_{g,t}$ is the unweighted sum of two normally distributed random variables, both with zero means and variances $\sigma_{\mu_{g,t}}^2$ and σ_ξ^2, respectively. The distribution of $k_{g,t}$ is thus:

$$k_{g,t} = \left(\mu_{g,t} + \xi_t\right) \sim \mathrm{N}\left(0, \sigma_{\mu_{g,t}}^2 + \sigma_\xi^2\right) \tag{8.16}$$

Given that both $k_{g,t}$ and $\mu_{g,t}$ are distributed normally, their joint distribution is bivariate normal and the optimal forecast of $\mu_{g,t}$, given $k_{g,t}$, is just this conditional expectation, which is computed from the appropriate conditional distribution of the bivariate normal. Using standard results on the bivariate normal distribution:

$$E\left[\mu_{g,t} \mid k_{g,t}\right] = E[\mu_{g,t}] + \frac{\sigma_{\mu_{g,t},k_{g,t}}}{\sigma^2_{k_{g,t}}}\left(y_{g,t} - \overline{y} - \sum_{i\in g}\left\{\lambda_{i,t-1}\mu_{i,t-1}\right\}\right) - E[k_{g,t}]$$

$$= \frac{\sigma^2_{\mu_{g,t}}}{\sigma^2_{\mu_{g,t}} + \sigma^2_{\xi}}\left(y_{g,t} - \overline{y} - \mu_{g,t-1}\right) \tag{8.17}$$

where the second line uses the fact that the covariance between $k_{g,t}$ and $\mu_{g,t}$ is equal to $\sigma^2_{\mu_{g,t}}$.[15] Finally, substituting for $\sigma^2_{\mu_{g,t}}$ from equation (8.15) and noting that (in an analogous argument to that in footnote 8 in Chapter 5) $E[\mu_{g,t} \mid k_{g,t}] = E[\mu_{g,t} \mid y_{g,t}]$, we have an intuitive generalization of equation (5.9) to the case of coalition cabinets:

$$E\left[\mu_{g,t} \mid y_{g,t}\right] = \left(\frac{\sigma^2_{\mu}\sum_{i\in g}\lambda^2_{i,t}}{\sigma^2_{\xi} + \sigma^2_{\mu}\sum_{i\in g}\lambda^2_{i,t}}\right)\left(y_{g,t} - \overline{y} - \mu_{g,t-1}\right) \tag{8.18}$$

Thus, allowing parties to have different levels of administrative responsibility makes the voter's overall evaluation of competence of the incumbent government (or the quality of the signal of that competence) a function of the distribution of administrative responsibility in the cabinet. The *responsibility augmented competency signal* varies between zero and one – approaching one as the variance in the nonpolitical shock to the economy approaches zero. Furthermore, the augmented competency signal reduces to the competency signal we derived for the case of unified government only if $\lambda_{i,t} = 1$ for some party (in which case all other parties must have

[15] $\text{Cov}(k_{g,t}, m_{g,t}) = E[(k_{g,t} - E[k_{g,t}])(\mu_{g,t} - E[\mu_{g,t}])] = E[k_{g,t}\mu_{g,t}]$

$$= E\left[\left(\sum_{i\in g}\{\lambda_{i,t}\mu_{i,t}\} + \xi_t\right)\left(\sum_{i\in g}\{\lambda_{i,t}\mu_{i,t}\}\right)\right]$$

$$= E\left[\sum_{i\in g}\{\lambda_{i,t}\mu_{i,t}\}\sum_{i\in g}\{\lambda_{i,t}\mu_{i,t}\}\right]$$

$$= \sum_{i\in g}\lambda^2_{i,t}E\left[\mu^2_{i,t}\right] + \sum_{i\in g}\sum_{i'\neq i\in g}\lambda_{i,t}\lambda_{i',t}E[\mu_{i,t}\mu_{i',t}]$$

$$= \sigma^2_{\mu}\sum_{i\in g}\lambda^2_{i,t} = \sigma^2_{\mu_{g,t}}$$

$\lambda_{i,t} = 0$). Thus, the models are the same when one party has all administrative responsibility.

We can now write the voter's expected utility if the incumbent government stays in power as:

$$\begin{aligned}
E\left[u_{\mathbf{g},t+1}\right] &= \frac{1}{2}E\left[\pi^2_{\mathbf{g},t+1}\right] + bE[y_{\mathbf{g},t+1}] \\
&= b\left(\overline{y} + E\left[\eta_{\mathbf{g},t+1}\right]\right) \\
&= b\left(\overline{y} + E\left[\xi_{t+1}\right] + E\left[\varepsilon_{\mathbf{g},t+1}\right]\right) \\
&= b\left(\overline{y} + E\left[\varepsilon_{\mathbf{g},t+1}\right]\right) \\
&= b\left(\overline{y} + E\left[\mu_{\mathbf{g},t+1} + \mu_{\mathbf{g},t}\right]\right) \\
&= b\left(\overline{y} + E\left[\mu_{\mathbf{g},t}\right]\right) \\
&= b\left(\overline{y} + E\left[\mu_{\mathbf{g},t} \mid y_{\mathbf{g},t}\right]\right) \\
&= b\overline{y} + b\left(\frac{\sigma^2_\mu \sum\limits_{i\in\mathbf{g}} \lambda^2_{i,t}}{\sigma^2_\xi + \sigma^2_\mu \sum\limits_{i\in\mathbf{g}} \lambda^2_{i,t}}\right)\left(y_{\mathbf{g},t} - \overline{y} - \mu_{\mathbf{g},t-1}\right) \quad (8.19)
\end{aligned}$$

Looking back at equation (8.10), the only component we are now missing is an expression for the voter's expected utility in the next period if an alternative government comes to power. This is addressed in the next section.

Evaluating Alternatives to the Previous Government

In comparing the expected utility of a future under the current government with the expected utility of the future under an alternative government, voters will compare $E[u_{\mathbf{g},t+1}]$ with $E[u_{\mathbf{g}',t+1}]$ for all $\mathbf{g}' \in \mathbf{A}$. In the last section, we saw what the first expectation should be, given our generalization of Alesina and Rosenthal's model of retrospective economic voting. In this section, we provide an expression for the second expectation – the expected utility of an alternative government coming to power in the next period. There are different ways that we can think about this term, so we start with a simple assumption that closely matches the treatment of opposition competence in Alesina and Rosenthal's single-party incumbent model. Specifically, we first assume that voters have no information about the competence of nonincumbent cabinets and so assign these cabinets as a whole the unconditional expectation of the known distribution of competence, which is zero by assumption. Thus, because all governments will pursue zero-inflation policies, this results in a correspondingly simple expression for the voter's expected utility if any alternative government comes to power:

$$\begin{aligned} E\left[u_{g',t+1}\right] &= \frac{1}{2}E\left[\pi^2_{g',t+1}\right] + bE[y_{g',t+1}] \\ &= b\left(\overline{y} + E\left[\eta_{g',t+1}\right]\right) \\ &= b\left(\overline{y} + E\left[\xi_{t+1}\right] + E\left[\varepsilon_{g',t+1}\right]\right) \\ &= b\left(\overline{y} + E\left[\varepsilon_{g',t+1}\right]\right) \\ &= b\left(\overline{y} + E\left[\mu_{g',t+1} + \mu_{g',t}\right]\right) \\ &= b\left(\overline{y} + E\left[\mu_{g',t}\right]\right) \\ &= b\left(\overline{y} + E\left[\mu_{g',t} \mid y_{g,t}\right]\right) \\ &= b\overline{y} \end{aligned} \tag{8.20}$$

Using this expression along with the expression for $E\left[u_{g,t+1}\right]$ in equation (8.19), we can express the generalized version of McKelvey and Ordeshook's result as:

$$\begin{aligned} &E[u \mid v_j] - E[u \mid v_0] \\ &\quad = \gamma_j + \sum_{g' \in A} P_{j,gg'}\left(E\left[u_{g,t+1}\right] - E\left[u_{g',t+1}\right]\right) \\ &\qquad + \sum_{g' \in A} P_{j,g'g}\left(E\left[u_{g',t+1}\right] - E\left[u_{g,t+1}\right]\right) \\ &\qquad + \sum_{g' \in A}\sum_{g'' \in A} P_{j,g'g''}\left(E\left[u_{g',t+1}\right] - E\left[u_{g'',t+1}\right]\right) \\ &\quad = \gamma_j + \sum_{g' \in A} P_{j,gg'}\left(E\left[u_{g,t+1}\right] - b\overline{y}\right) + \sum_{g' \in A} P_{j,g'g}\left(b\overline{y} - E\left[u_{g,t+1}\right]\right) \\ &\qquad + \sum_{g' \in A}\sum_{g'' \in A} P_{j,g'g''}(b\overline{y} - b\overline{y}) \\ &\quad = \gamma_j + b\left(\frac{\sigma^2_\mu \sum_{i \in g} \lambda^2_{i,t}}{\sigma^2_\xi + \sigma^2_\mu \sum_{i \in g} \lambda^2_{i,t}}\right)\left(y_{g,t} - \overline{y} - \mu_{g,t-1}\right)\sum_{g' \in A}\left(P_{j,gg'} - P_{j,g'g}\right) \end{aligned} \tag{8.21}$$

There are J of these expressions and the rational voter votes for the party j for which this expression is the largest.

Like equations (8.7) and (8.8) from our discussion of noncoalitional contexts, equation (8.21) has three pieces that interact to produce economic voting and to condition its importance across contexts: the *responsibility augmented competency signal*, retrospective economic performance, and the *pattern of cabinet contention*. In the rest of this section, we explore these pieces, beginning with the *responsibility augmented competency signal*. This signal is:

$$\frac{\sigma_{\mu}^{2}\sum_{i\in \mathbf{g}}\lambda_{i,t}^{2}}{\sigma_{\xi}^{2}+\sigma_{\mu}^{2}\sum_{i\in \mathbf{g}}\lambda_{i,t}^{2}} \tag{8.22}$$

As we discussed at length earlier, the *competency signal* did not vary over parties and so could not affect the voter's choice between them. Incorporating information about the distribution of responsibility within the incumbent administration does nothing to change that conclusion since this distribution (and, therefore, the sums in equation [8.22]) is constant across parties.[16] As before, however, the *responsibility augmented competency signal* does help regulate the relative weight of the retrospective economy compared to other factors in the voter's utility, so can impact the overall importance of economic voting in different contexts.

In the last section, we also discussed the interpretation of the variance parameters in the competency signal and that interpretation remains true in equation (8.22), holding the distribution of responsibility constant. Thus, in the current discussion, we are principally concerned with how the overall weight in equation (8.22) changes when we hold the variance parameters constant and vary the other part of the signal – the distribution of responsibility across parties. This variation is substantively interesting because it represents different power-sharing arrangements within cabinets. Hence, it can help us answer questions about how rational retrospective economic voting may be different in substantively interesting contexts like those in which a prime minister is dominant or those in which cabinet decision making is shared.[17] This question (and others like it) can

[16] Further generalizations of the model, however, eliminate this implication.

[17] Because our discussion is limited at this point to cabinets, we do not address the consequences of more general power-sharing arrangements that extend policy-making responsibility to opposition parties. This generalization, however, is easy to incorporate just by taking the sum in the ratio over all parties instead of just government parties (indeed, we prove the result for the more general case in Appendix A). Because the sum is constant in any case, it does not impact the other parts of the model. We do not do so here, however, because it introduces an awkward disconnect between the rest of the model (which is defined in terms of cabinets) and the responsibility augmented competency signal, which would be defined in terms of the distribution of responsibility generally. Thus, we hold off on this particular generalization until we provide the more complicated generalization of the whole model to focus on competition between alternative distributions of responsibility rather than alternative cabinets.

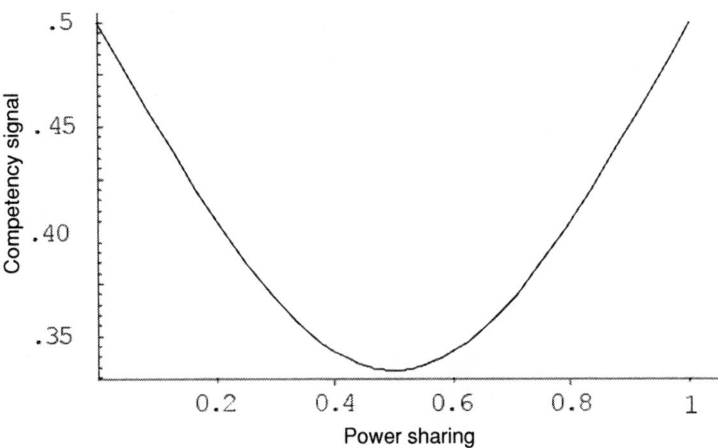

Figure 8.1. The responsibility augmented competency signal for different divisions of responsibility between two parties.

be answered in the context of this model by examining how the *responsibility augmented competency signal* changes when the distribution of the $\lambda_{i,t}$'s change.

Consider first the simple case in which only two parties have any administrative role (e.g., a two-party cabinet). The share of administrative responsibility for the first party is λ_1 and for the second is $\lambda_2 = 1 - \lambda_1$. Figure 8.1 graphs equation (8.22) as a function of λ_1, where we set both the variances in the competency signal to 1. This graph suggests that, at least in the case of a two-party cabinet, the competency signal will be closest to zero when power is shared equally between the two parties. More generally, in Appendix B we show that if we minimize equation (8.22) with respect to the vector of λ_i's in the government, the minimum always occurs when all the λ_i's are equal.[18] Thus, we can conclude that, in general, more power sharing in cabinets decreases the strength of the competency signal.

This result mirrors Powell and Whitten's (1993) clarity of responsibility hypothesis but gives a very different logic for the result. Their argument was based on the traditional accountability model of retrospective

[18] This result is proved for a more general result in which the sum in the ratio is over all parties rather than just cabinet parties. In that case, minimizing with respect to the $J - 1\lambda_j$'s (recall that the λ_j's sum to 1) reveals that the minimum occurs when $\lambda_j = 1/J$ for all J parties. We can restrict attention to just the government parties by holding $\lambda_j = 0$ if party $j \in$ g to get the result reported here. None of these results depend on the variances in the equation.

voting: when voters are faced with a situation in which administrative competence is shared, they find it difficult to attribute responsibility to any party. The intuition for the clarity of responsibility argument is that voters do not have the information they need to assign responsibility for economic outcomes. This in turn reduces the correlation between economic evaluations and vote choice. In contrast, the rational retrospective model of economic voting assumes that voters know the distribution of administrative responsibility perfectly and so it cannot be their uncertainty about this distribution that weakens the economic vote. Instead, power sharing decreases the importance of the economy on vote choice only because it leads voters to attribute more weight to exogenous factors shaping the observed movements in the economy.

The *pattern of cabinet contention* in the model is captured in the last term in the product in equation (8.21), which includes generalized pivot probabilities for all the pairs of potential cabinets that include the incumbent cabinet. All other pairs of pivot probabilities (between two nonincumbent cabinets) fall out of the expression. As in the case of single-party cabinets, this occurs because of our assumption that the retrospective performance of the economy is only informative about the competence of the incumbent cabinet, not alternatives. Thus, the voter assigns the same competence to all nonincumbent alternative cabinets and there is no difference in the voter's expected utility from living under one or the other of these cabinets. The empirical implication of this piece of the model is correspondingly similar to our earlier one for the single-party case: economic voting will disappear if the incumbent cabinet is not in competition to return to power.[19]

The generalized pivot probabilities that remain in equation (8.21) represent the aspects of the *pattern of cabinet contention* that are relevant to this model and so we examine them somewhat more carefully. Recall from the discussion of equation (8.10) that $P_{j.\mathbf{gg}'} = P_{\mathbf{gg}'}P(D_{\mathbf{g},j} > D_{\mathbf{g}',j})$ and $P_{j.\mathbf{g}'\mathbf{g}} = P_{\mathbf{gg}'}P(D_{\mathbf{g},j} < D_{\mathbf{g}',j})$, where $P_{\mathbf{gg}'}$ is the probability that cabinet **g** and **g′** are tied for selection and the D's are derivatives of the selection functions for **g** and **g′** with respect to party *j*'s vote total.[20] In Appendix A, we show that $D_{\mathbf{g},j}$ is equal to $w_{\mathbf{g}}g_j$, where $w_{\mathbf{g}}$ is the derivative of the selection function for cabinet **g** with respect to the electoral

[19] Our assumption ignores the fact that some alternative cabinets may contain cabinet members whose competence in the current cabinet may provide information about the competence of alternatives. We address this limitation in a generalization that follows.

[20] We make assumption #1 from the Appendix A in this discussion.

support for cabinet g and g_j is equal to 1 if party j is a member of cabinet g and zero otherwise. We assume that voters know which parties are in the incumbent cabinet and which parties are in any alternative cabinet they are considering (i.e., they know g_j and g'_j). However, they are uncertain how changes in electoral support for a given potential cabinet impact its selection (i.e., they do not know $w_{\mathbf{g}}$ or $w_{\mathbf{g}'}$ for certain). Their beliefs about these quantities are governed by the probability distributions $f(w_{\mathbf{g}})$ and $f(w_{\mathbf{g}'})$, respectively. We assume that voters believe that more electoral support cannot hurt a party's selection value, so that $f(w_{\mathbf{g}}) = 0$ if $w_{\mathbf{g}} < 0$ and $f(w_{\mathbf{g}'}) = 0$ if $w_{\mathbf{g}'} < 0$. With this, we can rewrite equation (8.14) as:

$$\begin{aligned} E[u \mid v_j] - E[u \mid v_0] &\\ = \gamma_j + Z \sum_{\mathbf{g}' \in \mathbf{A}} P_{\mathbf{gg}'} \left(P\left(w_{\mathbf{g}} g_j - w_{\mathbf{g}'} g'_j > 0\right) - P\left(w_{\mathbf{g}} g_j - w_{\mathbf{g}'} g'_j < 0\right)\right) &\\ = \gamma_j + Z \sum_{\mathbf{g}' \in \mathbf{A}} P_{\mathbf{gg}'} \left(2P\left(w_{\mathbf{g}} g_j - w_{\mathbf{g}'} g'_j > 0\right) - 1\right) & \qquad (8.23) \end{aligned}$$

Z is just the part of the utility difference that does not change over parties. To get the last line, we use the fact that $P(X > 0) = 1 - P(X \leq 0)$.

To facilitate our interpretation of the impact of the *pattern of cabinet contention* on economic voting, we assume the γ's in equation (8.23) are all 0 and assume in all of our examples that $Z > 0$. Furthermore, we initially assume that there are only two cabinets in contention to form the government, the incumbent g and an alternative g′. Given this, the first thing to notice about equation (8.23) is that the direction in which the distribution of cabinet contention impacts utility is determined by $P(w_{\mathbf{g}} g_j - w_{\mathbf{g}'} g'_j > 0)$. If this probability is less than 0.5, the whole equation will be negative; if it is equal to 0.5, it will be zero; and if it is greater than 0.5, it will be positive. Most of our effort in understanding this equation, then, will focus on this probability. We begin by defining the random variables $Y = w_{\mathbf{g}} g_j$ and $Y' = w_{\mathbf{g}'} g'_j$. Thus, we can write $P(Y = y) = f(y) = f(w_{\mathbf{g}})$ if $g_j = 1$ and $P(Y = y) = 0$ if $g_j = 0$.[21] Similar expressions apply for $P(Y' = y')$. Finally, define the random variable $K = Y - Y'$. We want to derive the distribution $P(K = k)$ and use it to find an expression for $P(K > 0)$. Because the distributions of Y and Y′

[21] Recall that we have assumed voters assign zero probability to the event that increased electoral support for a cabinet decreases its selection values. Thus, $f(w_g) = 0$ for $w_g < 0$ and likewise with Y.

have discrete and continuous parts, we must write the distribution of K for each case. This distribution is as follows:

$$P(K = k) = \begin{cases} \begin{array}{cc} 0 & \forall k \neq 0 \\ 1 & k = 0 \end{array} & \text{if } g_j = 0 \ \& \ g'_j = 0 \\ P(Y = k) \quad \forall k & \text{if } g_j = 1 \ \& \ g'_j = 0 \\ P(Y' = -k) \quad \forall k & \text{if } g_j = 0 \ \& \ g'_j = 1 \\ M_k \quad \forall k & \text{if } g_j = 1 \ \& \ g'_j = 1 \end{cases} \tag{8.24}$$

where

$$M_k = \int_{-\infty}^{\infty} \int_{-\infty}^{\infty} f(y) f(y') \delta((y - y') - k) \mathrm{d}y \mathrm{d}y'$$

$\delta(x)$ is the delta function and is equal to 0 for $x \neq 0$. This last expression is a function of k and just sums up the probability of all the events in which Y − Y′ can be equal to k. Now that we have an expression for the density of K, we need P(K > 0). For each of our cases, this is:

$$P(K > 0) = \begin{cases} 0 & \text{if } g_j = 0 \ \& \ g'_j = 0 \\ \int_0^{\infty} P(Y = k) \mathrm{d}k = 1 & \text{if } g_j = 1 \ \& \ g'_j = 0 \\ \int_0^{\infty} P(Y = -k) \mathrm{d}k = 0 & \text{if } g_j = 0 \ \& \ g'_j = 1 \\ \int_0^{\infty} M_k \mathrm{d}k & \text{if } g_j = 1 \ \& \ g'_j = 1 \end{cases} \tag{8.25}$$

With this, we can write:[22]

$$P_{gg'}(2P(w_g g_j - w_{g'} g'_j > 0) - 1)$$
$$= \begin{cases} 0 & \text{if } g_j = 0 \ \& \ g'_j = 0 \\ P_{gg'} & \text{if } g_j = 1 \ \& \ g'_j = 0 \\ -P_{gg'} & \text{if } g_j = 0 \ \& \ g'_j = 1 \\ P_{gg'} \left(2 \left(\int_0^{\infty} M_k \mathrm{d}k\right) - 1\right) & \text{if } g_j = 1 \ \& \ g'_j = 1 \end{cases} \tag{8.26}$$

The integral in the last line will be between zero and one, so the value of the whole term will vary between $-P_{gg'}$ and $P_{gg'}$. An example will help convey the intuitive way in which economic voting occurs in this model. Suppose that there are four parties (a, b, c, and d) and the incumbent cabinet, g, includes a and b. Only one viable alternative government exists, a coalition between c and d (call this g′). Using equation (8.26),

[22] The argument for the first line is somewhat more complicated than the others because it must account for the use of the equality, but this is just a technical issue and has no substantive import.

we can calculate the utility difference in casting a vote for each party and abstaining as follows:

$$E[u \mid v_a] - E[u \mid v_0] = \gamma_a + P_{gg'} Z$$
$$E[u \mid v_b] - E[u \mid v_0] = \gamma_b + P_{gg'} Z$$
$$E[u \mid v_c] - E[u \mid v_0] = \gamma_c - P_{gg'} Z$$
$$E[u \mid v_d] - E[u \mid v_0] = \gamma_d - P_{gg'} Z$$

where Z is just the part of equation (8.21) that is constant over parties.

Because we have assumed that g and g′ are in competition to form the government, $P_{gg'} > 0$ in each of these expressions, so they differ only in their signs. Thus, this example produces economic voting of a familiar kind – when the economic performance has been sufficiently strong (Z is positive), voters will vote for one of the parties in the incumbent cabinet; but when it has been weak (Z is negative), they will vote for some opposition party. More generally, if no members of the incumbent cabinet are in an alternative cabinet that is in contention with the incumbent cabinet for selection, this model implies that the economic part of the voter's expected utility of voting for each party will have different signs for incumbent and opposition parties. This is an important implication since there are many real-world cases in which the membership of the incumbent cabinet and the likely alternatives are distinct. For example, contending cabinets in Irish politics have usually not included the same parties – Fianna Fail ruling alone, Fianna Gael ruling alone, or Fianna Gael and Labour in coalition. Likewise, the Scandinavian party systems often pit socialist coalitions against bourgeoisie coalitions with no overlapping memberships.

Notice, however (ignoring the γs), all we can say about the economic voter's choice is that he will choose an incumbent party or an opposition party – we cannot say which incumbent or opposition party he will choose because the expected utility associated with the economy is the same for all opposition and all incumbent parties, respectively.[23] This is clearly a limitation of the current model because it does not capture important cases in which we think that there is very likely a difference in the way that votes for different parties in a potential cabinet impact the chance

[23] The reason for this is that the voter's utility stemming from economic performance is defined over potential cabinets and the vote for any party in a cabinet has the same effect on the chances of selection as a vote for any other party (i.e., electoral support of the cabinet responds to a change in a vote for each party in the cabinet in the same way – the derivative is 1 for all parties in the cabinet).

of the cabinet's selection. One example is the *formateur* system in which it is the vote of the largest party (in contention for a plurality) that is crucial to the cabinet's formation. In later sections, we partially address this limitation by allowing the role that each party plays in a potential cabinet to differentially impact its electoral support.

More complicated cases than the one in the example can occur when more than one cabinet is in contention for selection. For example, suppose that we have the same situation as the earlier example, except that in addition to the coalition between c and d, a single-party cabinet, $\mathbf{g}''$, consisting only of c, is also an alternative. The relevant utility differences are just:

$$\begin{aligned}
E[u \mid v_a] - E[u \mid v_0] &== \gamma_a + \left(P_{\mathbf{gg}'} + P_{\mathbf{gg}''}\right) Z \\
E[u \mid v_b] - E[u \mid v_0] &== \gamma_b + \left(P_{\mathbf{gg}'} + P_{\mathbf{gg}''}\right) Z \\
E[u \mid v_c] - E[u \mid v_0] &== \gamma_c - \left(P_{\mathbf{g}'\mathbf{g}} + P_{\mathbf{g}''\mathbf{g}}\right) Z \\
E[u \mid v_d] - E[u \mid v_0] &== \gamma_d - P_{\mathbf{g}'\mathbf{g}} Z
\end{aligned}$$

Thus, the voter still has the same utility difference for all incumbent parties, but now if Z is negative (a poor economy), the expected utility of voting for party c will be greater than voting for party d, so (ignoring the γ's) the voter will vote for party c. The reason for this is simply that the voter wants to cast the vote that contributes most to replacing the incumbent. Voters are indifferent as to which of the alternative cabinets comes to power (because they are all judged equally competent) and so party c's membership in more alternatives gives it an advantage. The empirical hypothesis that follows from this is that in the absence of overlapping memberships between the incumbent and alternative cabinets, the greater the number of competitive alternative cabinets to which an opposition party belongs, the more important the economic vote will be (relative to other factors) in the voter's utility for that party. Notice, however, that the voter is still indifferent over which party in the incumbent cabinet he chooses if the economy has been good.

More generally, if the membership of the competitive alternative cabinets is distinct from the incumbent cabinet, the utility of any opposition party is $-Z\sum_{\mathbf{g}'\in\mathbf{A}} P_{\mathbf{g}'\mathbf{g}}$ with all noncompetitive alternatives adding nothing to this sum. Thus, if the economy has performed sufficiently poorly, then the voter will vote for the opposition party that is most competitive overall to be part of an alternative cabinet. Thus, economic voting should be more important to these parties. In contrast, the performance of the retrospective economy will not lead the voter to favor one particular incumbent party or another.

When we turn to the case of a party that is a member of both the incumbent cabinet and a contending alternative cabinet, the voter's utility of casting a vote for the party is more complicated. Consider an example in which there are three parties labeled *a*, *b*, and *c* and the incumbent cabinet consists of parties *a* and *b*. The only contending alternative cabinet is composed of *b* and *c*. In this case, the utility difference for voting for each party versus abstaining is:

$$
\begin{aligned}
E[u \mid v_a] - E[u \mid v_0] &= \gamma_a + P_{gg'} Z \\
E[u \mid v_b] - E[u \mid v_0] &= \gamma_b + \left(P_{gg'} - P_{gg'} + P_{gg'} \left(2 \left(\int_0^{\infty} M_k \mathrm{d}k \right) - 1 \right) \right) Z \\
&= \gamma_b + P_{gg'} \left(2P(K > 0) - 1 \right) Z \\
E[u \mid v_c] - E[u \mid v_0] &= \gamma_c - P_{gg'} Z
\end{aligned}
$$

Notice that $0 \leq (2P(K > 0) - 1) \leq 1$ so that the voter's utility for the party, *b*, that is in both the incumbent coalition and the competitive alternative is always between $P_{gg'}$ and $-P_{gg'}$. This means that however the economy performs, there will always be a party that the voter prefers at least as much as party *b* (party *a* when the economy is good and party *c* when it is not). This result is intuitive because the voter who wants to either keep or remove the incumbent cabinet can do so more efficiently when the whole contribution of the vote is felt in the electoral support of either the incumbent or the alternative but not both.

More generally, the implication of this model is that the economy will be less important to the vote of parties who are members of both the incumbent cabinet and competitive alternative cabinets than it will be for parties whose membership in the incumbent cabinet is distinct from competitive alternatives. This conclusion suggests, for example, that we should expect economic voting to be relatively muted for a party like the Danish Radical Liberals, who have a history of joining coalitions with the Social Democrats on the left as well as participating in right-wing bourgeoisie coalitions.

Finally, if we consider the most general case in which we allow for multiple alternative cabinets and overlapping memberships between the incumbent cabinet and these alternatives, we can break the portion of the voter's utility associated with the economy into four parts that help make the overall message plain. Specifically, we can write this portion of the utility as:

$$Z\left(g_j \sum_{g' \in A} P_{gg'} - \sum_{g' \in A} g'_j P_{gg'} + g_j \sum_{g' \in A} g'_j P_{gg'} \left(2P\left(K > 0\right) - 1\right)\right) \quad (8.27)$$

where the g_j's are defined as usual (i.e., $g_j = 1$ if party j is a member of cabinet g). Thus, when Z is positive, for every pair of cabinets consisting of the incumbent cabinet and an alternative cabinet, the voter's utility for party j goes up if j is in the incumbent cabinet but not in the alternative. The voter's utility goes up by the same amount or less (and may even go down) if j is a member of both the incumbent and the alternative cabinet. This makes it clear that when Z is positive, the voters will vote for the incumbent party with the least "contamination" from membership in viable alternative cabinets. Similarly, if the economy has performed poorly, for every pair of cabinets, the voter's utility for party j goes up if the party is in the alternative cabinet but not the incumbent cabinet; but only goes up by the same amount or less (and may even go down) if the party is a member of both the incumbent and the alternative cabinet. However, because in this case one party may be a member of multiple cabinets that are contesting with the incumbent, it could be that the voter prefers a party that is incumbent but included in a number of alternatives than one that is not incumbent but is in only one alternative. In the most general case, then, we cannot conclude (as we did in the case of only one alternative) that when the economy is poor, the voter will prefer to vote for an opposition party over any incumbent party.[24]

In this section, we extended the model of rational retrospective economic voting to situations in which there are multiple parties competing for positions in potentially multiparty cabinets. We did so under the assumption that voters get no information about the competence of alternative governments from the retrospective economy (even if these

[24] For this to occur, $P(K > 0)$ would need to be < 0.5 for some g and g′. This means that it must be more likely that $wg' > wg$ than the opposite. For example, suppose that the incumbent coalition was a socialist party, center party coalition, but the center announced that it would not rejoin the government but would join one of several possible right-wing coalitions. In this case, the voter may well believe that $wg' > wg$ for each of the possible alternatives coalitions. Suppose they are all competitive for selection. Then, in the face of a poor economy, the voter's utility for the center party will be $Z^* \left(x_1 P_{gg'} + x_1 P_{gg''} + \cdots\right)$ where the x's are all negative and Z is negative, which results in a positive number. This may well be larger than the voter's utility for opposition parties that are in one or more of the coalitions. This scenario, though, seems unlikely.

alternatives contain incumbent parties). If the membership of the incumbent cabinet and contending alternatives is distinct, we predict conventional economic voting. If some parties are members of both the incumbent cabinet and contending alternatives, economic voting in the form described previously is not guaranteed. However, the conditions necessary to cause voters to want to vote for incumbent parties when the economy has been poor are stringent and so unlikely. The interpretation of the competency signal from earlier sections generalizes in this model to the *responsibility augmented competency signal*. This change adds, to our earlier conclusion regarding the competency signal, the additional implication that a more equal division of policy-making responsibility in the incumbent cabinet should depress the economic vote. Our earlier conclusions about the distribution of contention generalize to this model of coalitional executives; specifically, economic voting will be muted if the incumbent government is not in contention to return to office (either because it is sure to be selected or sure not to be). Any opposition party's share of the economic vote will tend to increase in the number of competitive alternatives of which it is a member, as well as in the extent to which these coalitions are likely to tie with the incumbent for selection. The share of the economic vote of parties that are members of both the incumbent coalition and viable alternatives should decrease as the party's memberships in the incumbent and competitive alternative cabinets are less distinct.

MULTIPLE PARTIES WITH A COALITIONAL EXECUTIVE AND OPPOSITION POLICY-MAKING RESPONSIBILITY

In the previous sections, we maintained two assumptions that should be relaxed if we are to apply the model of rational retrospective voting to as wide a set of contexts as we would like. The first of these assumptions restricted policy-making responsibility to parties in cabinets. Clearly, however, other parties influence policy making and, in many contexts (e.g., minority government), this influence is substantial (Strom, 1990; Powell, 2000; Hallerberg, 2000). Thus, the rational voter's beliefs about the distribution of responsibility should reflect this wider notion of responsibility. Second, in the previous sections we maintained Alesina and Rosenthal's (1995) assumption that the retrospective economy provides no information about the competence of nonincumbent parties. Furthermore, in generalizing the model to multiparty cabinets, we adopted the additional assumption that the economy provides no information about the overall competence of nonincumbent cabinets, even when these alternative cabinets include members of the current cabinet. Such an assumption should hardly be maintained in a model in which voters use all the information available to them in forming their beliefs. In what follows, we relax these two assumptions in turn and then discuss whether doing so maintains or changes the various conclusions of previous sections.

We begin by redefining a *distribution of responsibility* to be a vector of shares of policy-making responsibility (with elements λ_j) such that all the parties have shares greater than or equal to zero and the shares sum to 1 across parties. By allowing λ_j to be greater than zero for parties that are not in the cabinet, one can capture more interesting institutional variation than we have so far allowed (i.e., minority governments). Thus, in what follows, we drop our "g" notation for indicating a cabinet and instead use $\boldsymbol{\lambda}$ to refer to a distribution of responsibility across all J parties in the legislature (i.e., $\boldsymbol{\lambda} = \{\lambda_1, \lambda_2, ..\lambda_j, .., \lambda_J\}$). As earlier, a $\boldsymbol{\lambda}$ will be used to refer to the status quo or "incumbent" distribution of responsibility (or for a generic distribution of responsibility when there is no chance of confusion), whereas $\boldsymbol{\lambda}$' and the like refer to nonincumbent, alternative distributions of responsibility.

This generalization can be readily incorporated into the theoretical framework developed in previous sections. Specifically, we can write an expression for the expected utility of living in the next period under the current distribution of responsibility that follows exactly the logic that we developed for the expected utility of continuing the current cabinet. First, we have, mirroring equation (8.19):

$$\begin{aligned} E\left[u_{\lambda,t+1}\right] &= \frac{1}{2}E\left[\pi^2_{\lambda,t+1}\right] + bE[y_{\lambda,t+1}] = b(\overline{y} + E\left[\eta_{\lambda,t+1}\right]) \\ &= b(\overline{y} + E\left[\xi_{t+1}\right] + E\left[\varepsilon_{\lambda,t+1}\right]) \\ &= b(\overline{y} + E\left[\varepsilon_{\lambda,t+1}\right]) = b(\overline{y} + E\left[\mu_{\lambda,t+1} + \mu_{\lambda,t}\right]) \\ &= b(\overline{y} + E\left[\mu_{\lambda,t}\right]) = b(\overline{y} + E\left[\mu_{\lambda,t} \mid y_{\lambda,t}\right]) \end{aligned} \tag{8.28}$$

It can be shown in an argument analogous to the one for cabinets developed earlier that the conditional expectation in the last line is:

$$E\left[\mu_{\lambda,t} \mid y_{\lambda,t}\right] = \left(\frac{\sigma^2_\mu \sum\limits_{j \in J} \lambda^2_{j,t}}{\sigma^2_\xi + \sigma^2_\mu \sum\limits_{j \in J} \lambda^2_{j,t}} \right) (y_{\lambda,t} - \overline{y} - \mu_{\lambda,t-1}) \tag{8.29}$$

This is essentially the same result as in equation (8.18), except that now the summations are over all parties instead of just cabinet parties. Plugging this into equation (8.28), we get a similarly familiar expression for the utility of the status quo distribution of responsibility for another period:

$$E\left[u_{\lambda,t+1}\right] = b\overline{y} + b\left(\frac{\sigma_{\mu}^{2}\sum_{j\in J}\lambda_{j,t}^{2}}{\sigma_{\xi}^{2}+\sigma_{\mu}^{2}\sum_{j\in J}\lambda_{j,t}^{2}}\right)\left(y_{\lambda,t}-\overline{y}-\mu_{\lambda,t-1}\right) \qquad (8.30)$$

Finally, retaining (until the next subsection) the assumption that voters assign zero competence to all alternatives to the status quo distribution of responsibility, the appropriate expression for the utility difference between voting for party j and abstaining (that mirrors equation [8.21] and is proved along with it in Appendix A) is:

$$\begin{aligned}
E[u \mid v_j] - E[u \mid v_0] &= \gamma_j + \sum_{\lambda'\in\Lambda'} P_{j,\lambda\lambda'}\left(E\left[u_{\lambda,t+1}\right]-E\left[u_{\lambda',t+1}\right]\right)\\
&\quad + \sum_{\lambda'\in\Lambda'} P_{j,\lambda'\lambda}\left(E\left[u_{\lambda',t+1}\right]-E\left[u_{\lambda,t+1}\right]\right)\\
&\quad + \sum_{\lambda'\in\Lambda'}\sum_{\lambda''\in\Lambda'} P_{j,\lambda'\lambda''}\left(E\left[u_{\lambda',t+1}\right]-E\left[u_{\lambda'',t+1}\right]\right)\\
&= \gamma_j + \sum_{\lambda'\in\Lambda'} P_{j,\lambda\lambda'}\left(E\left[u_{\lambda,t+1}\right]-0\right)\\
&\quad + \sum_{\lambda'\in\Lambda'} P_{j,\lambda'\lambda}\left(0-E\left[u_{\lambda,t+1}\right]\right) + \sum_{\lambda'\in\Lambda'}\sum_{\lambda''\in\Lambda'} P_{j,\lambda'\lambda''}(0-0)\\
&= \gamma_j + b\left(\frac{\sigma_{\mu}^{2}\sum_{i\in J}\lambda_{i,t}^{2}}{\sigma_{\xi}^{2}+\sigma_{\mu}^{2}\sum_{i\in J}\lambda_{i,t}^{2}}\right)\left(y_t-\overline{y}-\mu_{\lambda,t-1}\right)\sum_{\lambda'\in\Lambda'}\left(P_{j,\lambda\lambda'}-P_{j,\lambda'\lambda}\right)
\end{aligned} \qquad (8.31)$$

where $\boldsymbol{\Lambda}'$ is the set of all non–status quo distributions of responsibility. There will be J of these equations and the voter will vote for the party j for which this expression is the largest. The pivot probabilities, $P_{j,\lambda\lambda'}$ and $P_{j,\lambda'\lambda}$, are interpreted as the chance that $\boldsymbol{\lambda}$ and $\boldsymbol{\lambda}'$ are in a tie for selection and a vote for party j will break the tie in favor of the status quo distribution of responsibility $\boldsymbol{\lambda}$. The formal definition of $P_{j,\lambda\lambda'}$ is in Appendix A. This derivation parallels the one for cabinets but defines the *electoral support* for any distribution of responsibility as the sum of the support for all parties, weighted by their share of responsibility in that distribution. Thus, we have $P_{j,\lambda\lambda'}$ equal to $P_{\lambda\lambda'}P(D_{\lambda,j} > D_{\lambda',j})$, where $P_{\lambda\lambda'}$ is the probability that $\boldsymbol{\lambda}$ and $\boldsymbol{\lambda}'$ are tied for selection and the D's are derivatives of the selection functions for $\boldsymbol{\lambda}$ and $\boldsymbol{\lambda}'$ with respect to party *j*'s vote total.[25] Given our definition of *electoral support* for $\boldsymbol{\lambda}$, each $D_{\lambda,j}$ is equal to $w_\lambda \lambda_j$, where w_λ is the derivative of the selection function for cabinet $\boldsymbol{\lambda}$ with respect to the electoral support for $\boldsymbol{\lambda}$, and λ_j is party *j*'s share of the distribution of responsibility $\boldsymbol{\lambda}$.[26]

This change in focus from cabinets to distributions of responsibility does not change anything substantively interesting in our earlier conclusions about the role of the *responsibility augmented competency signal* in rational retrospective voting.[27] Thus, it is still the case that the *responsibility augmented competency signal* is minimized when parties have equal shares of responsibility. In the current model, however, this equality is across all parties and not just those in the cabinet. Given this, we focus the following discussion of equation (8.31) on the role that the *distribution of contention* plays in conditioning economic voting.[28] Given these definitions and those in Appendix A, we can rewrite equation (8.31) as[29]:

$$
\begin{aligned}
&E[u \mid v_j] - E[u \mid v_0] \\
&\quad = \gamma_j + Z \sum_{\lambda' \in \Lambda'} \left(P_{j,\lambda\lambda'} - P_{j,\lambda'\lambda}\right) \\
&\quad = \gamma_j + Z \sum_{\lambda' \in \Lambda'} \left(P_{\lambda\lambda'} P(D_{\lambda,j} > D_{\lambda',j}) - P_{\lambda'\lambda} P(D_{\lambda',j} > D_{\lambda,j})\right) \\
&\quad = \gamma_j + Z \sum_{\lambda' \in \Lambda'} P_{\lambda\lambda'} \left(P\left(w_\lambda \lambda_j - w_{\lambda'} \lambda'_j > 0\right) - P\left(w_\lambda \lambda_j - w_{\lambda'} \lambda'_j < 0\right)\right) \\
&\quad = \gamma_j + Z \sum_{\lambda' \in \Lambda'} P_{\lambda\lambda'} \left(2P\left(w_\lambda \lambda_j - w_{\lambda'} \lambda'_j > 0\right) - 1\right) \qquad (8.32)
\end{aligned}
$$

where Z represents those parts of the equation that do not differ across parties and we use the fact that $P(x > 0) = 1 - P(x < 0)$.

[25] Recall that the postelection process that distributes responsibility among parties simply implements the distribution of responsibility with the highest selection value.

[26] Again, we make assumption #1 from Appendix A, which just says that w_λ is non-negative for all distributions of responsibility.

[27] Other than the fact, of course, that we now consider the full distribution across all parties rather than cabinet parties.

[28] This distribution is no longer properly called *the pattern of cabinet contention* because it now means the pattern of contention for selection among different distributions of responsibility, not cabinets.

[29] Clearly, the incumbent distribution of responsibility is included in Z so will change when we consider different incumbents, but this does not change the interpretation of how that term impacts economic voting given a distribution of responsibility.

The first point to make about equation (8.32) is that it maintains our earlier conclusion that contention is a critical ingredient in rational retrospective economic voting. The specific form of contention required in this model is contention for selection between the status quo distribution of responsibility and one or more alternatives. That is, if the incumbent distribution of responsibility is sure to be maintained or sure to be changed, then there should be no economic voting in this model.[30]

In order to come to any substantive conclusions about the voter's utility difference for voting for different parties rather than abstaining, we need to evaluate the term inside the sum in equation (8.32) – that is, $P_{\lambda\lambda'}(2P(w_{\lambda}\lambda_j - w_{\lambda'}\lambda'_j > 0) - 1)$. Furthermore, notice that as the probability $P(w_{\lambda}\lambda_j - w_{\lambda'}\lambda'_j > 0)$ approaches 1, this whole term approaches $P_{\lambda\lambda'}$, but as the probability approaches 0, this term approaches $-P_{\lambda\lambda'}$. Consequently, interpreting when the voter's utility difference for voting for party j rather than abstaining will be positive or negative (given Z) reduces to evaluating $P(w_{\lambda}\lambda_j - w_{\lambda'}\lambda'_j > 0)$.

We assume that voters know how much responsibility party j holds in the status quo distribution of authority as well as in any alternative distribution they are considering. Given this, we can write $P(w_{\lambda}\lambda_j - w_{\lambda'}\lambda'_j > 0)$ more conveniently as $P(\frac{w_{\lambda'}}{w_{\lambda}} < \frac{\lambda_j}{\lambda'_j})$, where $\frac{w_{\lambda'}}{w_{\lambda}}$ is a random variable and $\frac{\lambda_j}{\lambda'_j}$ is a known constant.[31] This probability is in the form of a cumulative probability function and, because any such function must integrate to 1 and be nondecreasing, it must be the case that as the ratio on the right-hand side increases, this probability approaches 1. Thus, we can conclude that, given two parties j and i, this probability will be larger for party j if λ_j/λ'_j is larger than λ_i/λ'_i.[32] If we now go back to equation (8.32) and

30 If we imagine that no distribution of responsibility will ever be exactly maintained, this would suggest that we would never see economic voting. This conclusion, however, depends on our assumption that the only distribution of responsibility to which the voter assigns nonzero competence is the incumbent one. In the next subsection, we relax this assumption and so let the voter's information about the competence of different distributions of responsibility change continuously with the similarity of the alternative to the status quo. This is sufficient to soften our conclusion to one in which economic voting should be greater when distributions of responsibility "close" to the status quo are competitive (with alternatives that are not close to the status quo distribution).

31 We assume $\lambda'_j > 0$. It is not difficult to account for the case in which $\lambda'_j = 0$, but doing so does not change the substantive message or add any additional insight, so we do not present the additional qualifications that would be required to include this case in the current discussion.

32 Notice that this does not require that we assume that the voter's beliefs about the ratio of derivatives on the left-hand side of the inequality are the same across

focus on the case in which there is only one alternative distribution of responsibility, we can conclude that as λ_j/λ'_j gets larger (i.e., party *j*'s share of responsibility in $\boldsymbol{\lambda}$ increases relative to its share in $\boldsymbol{\lambda}'$), the change in utility associated with voting for party *j* rather than abstaining will move away from $-P_{\lambda\lambda'}Z$ and toward $P_{\lambda\lambda'}Z$.

This is a natural generalization of our earlier result for cabinets. In that case, if a party was a member of the incumbent cabinet but not the alternative, the voter's utility for voting for that party was $P_{\lambda\lambda'}Z$. In contrast, if the party were a member of the alternative and not the incumbent cabinet, the utility was $-P_{\lambda\lambda'}Z$. In the current case, "incumbency" is not a discrete category so we get an appropriately continuous result in which having relatively more responsibility in the incumbent distribution of responsibility than in the alternative pushes the voter's utility toward $P_{\lambda\lambda'}Z$ and away from $-P_{\lambda\lambda'}Z$.

Notice that this change overturns our earlier result that the voter's utility of voting for different members of the incumbent cabinet was the same, as long as these parties were not members of a viable alternative cabinet. In this generalization, this result does not hold because the distribution of responsibility distinguishes between shares of responsibility among different cabinet members and so voters distinguish between the contributions that votes for different cabinet members will have on the selection of the incumbent distribution of responsibility.[33] More specifically, they believe these contributions are proportional to the parties' shares of responsibility. In this way, the generalized model produces an implication that is close to Anderson's (1995) suggestion that increased cabinet responsibility should enhance a party's economic vote. This implication, however, comes from a completely different logic than Anderson suggests.[34] Indeed, it does not even stem from the voter's attempt to extract a signal about the

the parties being compared, since this is true by definition. Specifically, $w_{\boldsymbol{\lambda}}$ is the derivative of the selection function for λ with respect to the total electoral support for λ and so will be the same across all parties. It would be strange to assume voters' beliefs about this quantity would vary across parties, given the quantity itself does not vary.

33 If we assume that opposition members have no responsibility, then we can properly call this the *distribution of responsibility within the cabinet* and say that the voter believes the impact of her vote on the reselection of the cabinet (meaning the exact replication of the shares of responsibility of the incumbent parties in the cabinet) to be proportional to the party's share of responsibility.

34 In fact, Anderson (1995) reviews three different reasons that one might expect economic voting to differ among coalition partners, none of which have much in common with the explanation proposed here.

competence of different parties from the previous economy (as did our earlier conclusion about the impact of power sharing on the economic vote of the *whole* cabinet or distribution of responsibility). Instead, this implication stems directly from our assumption that voters believe the impact of a vote for party j on the selection of a distribution of responsibility $\boldsymbol{\lambda}$ is proportional to party j's share of responsibility in $\boldsymbol{\lambda}$ and that they want to vote rationally to maximize that impact.[35]

To stimulate better intuition for the implications of this generalization, we can examine an example that parallels the first one we provided following equation (8.26). In that equation, we had four parties, two of which were in the incumbent cabinet and two of which were in the only viable alternative cabinet. To parallel this but make it relevant to the analysis of more widely shared responsibility, suppose that responsibility, $\boldsymbol{\lambda}$, assigns 60 percent the responsibility to party a, 20 percent to party b, and 10 percent to parties c and d, respectively (i.e., $\lambda = \{.6, .2, .1, .1\}$). There is only one viable alternative distribution of authority: $\lambda' = \{.1, .1, .2, .6\}$. Given equation (8.32), the difference in the voter's expected utility of voting for each party rather than abstaining is[36]:

$$E[u \mid v_a] - E[u \mid v_0] = \gamma_a + \left(P_{\lambda\lambda'}\left(2P\left(\frac{w'_{\boldsymbol{\lambda}}}{w_{\boldsymbol{\lambda}}} < 6\right) - 1\right)\right) Z$$

$$E[u \mid v_b] - E[u \mid v_0] = \gamma_b + \left(P_{\lambda\lambda'}\left(2P\left(\frac{w'_{\boldsymbol{\lambda}}}{w_{\boldsymbol{\lambda}}} < 2\right) - 1\right)\right) Z$$

$$E[u \mid v_c] - E[u \mid v_0] = \gamma_c + \left(P_{\lambda\lambda'}\left(2P\left(\frac{w'_{\boldsymbol{\lambda}}}{w_{\boldsymbol{\lambda}}} < \frac{1}{2}\right) - 1\right)\right) Z$$

$$E[u \mid v_d] - E[u \mid v_0] = \gamma_d + \left(P_{\lambda\lambda'}\left(2P\left(\frac{w'_{\boldsymbol{\lambda}}}{w_{\boldsymbol{\lambda}}} < \frac{1}{6}\right) - 1\right)\right) Z$$

If $f(\frac{w_{\lambda'}}{w_\lambda})$, the probability distribution governing voters' beliefs about the ratio $\frac{w_{\lambda'}}{w_\lambda}$ is the same over parties, then (again, ignoring γ) the voter will vote for party a when Z is positive and party d when Z is negative.

More generally, if there is only one alternative to the status quo distribution of responsibility and the economy has performed well, the voter will vote for the party with the highest ratio of shares of responsibility

[35] This implication differs from Anderson (1995) to some degree since it applies to all parties and not just cabinet parties. Empirically, then, we expect the strength of economic voting for a party to be proportional to the party's overall policy influence, not just its share of influence in cabinet.

[36] Recall that in equation (8.32), $P(w_{\boldsymbol{\lambda}}\lambda_j - w_{\boldsymbol{\lambda}'}\lambda'_j > 0)$ can be expressed as $P(\frac{w_{\boldsymbol{\lambda}'}}{w_{\boldsymbol{\lambda}}} < \frac{\lambda_j}{\lambda'_j})$.

in the two competing distributions of responsibility. Likewise, when the economy has performed poorly, the voter will vote for the party with the lowest ratio. As in the case of cabinets, the message is clear: a party will benefit more from rational economic voting when a vote for the party unambiguously helps or hurts the selection value of the incumbent distribution of responsibility; that is, the party that offers the voter a *distinctive* choice.

Allowing more than one competitive alternative distribution of responsibility complicates the calculation of utilities in the model. However, it does not change the message that a party's share of the economic vote will be greater when the party's role in the incumbent distribution of responsibility is more distinct from its role in competitive alternatives.

In this section, we extended the model of rational retrospective economic voting to situations in which there are multiple parties competing for shares of policy-making responsibility. We continue to do so under the assumption that voters get no information about the competence of alternative distributions of responsibility from the retrospective economy (even if these alternative distributions assign responsibility to some parties that held responsibility under the status quo distribution). This model generalizes our previous finding that if the membership of the incumbent cabinet and contending alternatives is distinct, we get economic voting in a traditional form. In the current case, however, "incumbency" is not a discrete category so we get an appropriately continuous result in which having relatively more responsibility in the incumbent distribution of responsibility than in the alternative pushes the voter's utility toward $P_{\lambda\lambda'}Z$ and away from $-P_{\lambda\lambda'}Z$. Thus, for a negative Z (a poor economy), the voter will turn away from parties that hold more responsibility in the incumbent distribution of power than in contending alternatives.

MULTIPLE PARTIES WITH A COALITIONAL EXECUTIVE, OPPOSITION POLICY-MAKING RESPONSIBILITY, AND RATIONAL BELIEFS ABOUT THE COMPETENCE OF ALTERNATIVE GOVERNMENTS

The assumption that voters have no information about the competence of alternative cabinets or distributions of responsibility seems unjustified in a model in which voters use information rationally. Specifically, some alternatives to the status quo will necessarily include parties that were in the previous cabinet or for which λ_j was positive in the previous period. Consequently, the voter may have information about the competence of these parties that should bear on the evaluation of possible governing alternatives.

In order to allow for this possibility in the model, we begin by writing an expression for the expected utility of living under some alternative distribution of responsibility in the next period that does not assume expected competence is zero:

$$\begin{aligned} E\left[u_{\lambda',t+1}\right] &= \frac{1}{2}E\left[\pi^2_{\lambda',t+1}\right] + bE[y_{\lambda',t+1}] = b(\overline{y} + E\left[\eta_{\lambda',t+1}\right]) \\ &= b(\overline{y} + E\left[\xi_{t+1}\right] + E\left[\varepsilon_{\lambda',t+1}\right]) \\ &= b(\overline{y} + E\left[\varepsilon_{\lambda',t+1}\right]) = b(\overline{y} + E\left[\mu_{\lambda',t+1} + \mu_{\lambda',t}\right]) \\ &= b(\overline{y} + E\left[\mu_{\lambda',t}\right]) = b(\overline{y} + E\left[\mu_{\lambda',t} \mid y_{\lambda,t}\right]) \end{aligned} \tag{8.33}$$

Notice that we write $\boldsymbol{\lambda}'$ everywhere except in the conditional on the last line. This is important. This conditional expectation is the expected value of the current competence of the alternative distribution of administrative responsibility ($\boldsymbol{\lambda}'$) given the observed economy under the status quo distribution ($\boldsymbol{\lambda}$). In order to calculate this expectation, we have to unpack the voter's overall assessment of the current competence of the government and get an expression for expectations about the competence of each individual party. With this in hand, we can construct the voter's expectations for the competence of various alternative governments. In doing this, we should expect the current economy to provide no information about the competence of parties that have no administrative responsibility under the status quo distribution of responsibility. Thus, the voter's belief about the competency of such parties should just be the mean of the competency distribution (i.e., zero). However, if a party does have a share of the incumbent distribution of responsibility, the voter should use information about the economy in producing expectations about that party's competence. If we write the voter's expectation about the competence of party i, given the economy under incumbent distribution of responsibility $\boldsymbol{\lambda}$ as $E\left[\mu_{i,t} \mid y_{\lambda,t}\right]$, then we expect that, in general, $E\left[\mu_{i,t} \mid y_{\lambda,t}\right] \neq 0$ for parties in which $\lambda_i \neq 0$. What is $E\left[\mu_{i,t} \mid y_{\lambda,t}\right]$? In Appendix C, we solve the signal extraction problem that leads to the following intuitive result:

$$E\left[\mu_{i,t} \mid y_{\lambda,t}\right] = \left(\frac{\sigma^2_\mu \lambda_{i,t}}{\sigma^2_\xi + \sigma^2_\mu \sum\limits_{j\in J} \lambda^2_{j,t}}\right)(y_{\lambda,t} - \overline{y} - \mu_{\lambda,t-1}) \tag{8.34}$$

Thus, the voter's expectation about the competence of party i is just the competency signal associated with the incumbent distribution of responsibility $\boldsymbol{\lambda}$, weighted by party i's role in that distribution. This expression is in line with our intuition that if λ_i is zero, then the conditional expectation of party i's competence will also be zero. Furthermore, the expression implies that:

$$E\left[\mu_{\lambda,t} \mid y_{\lambda,t}\right] = \sum_{i \in J} \lambda_i E\left[\mu_{i,t} \mid y_{\lambda,t}\right] \tag{8.35}$$

With these two expressions, we are now in a position to propose how the voter can estimate the current competence of any alternative government. Specifically, we suggest that:

$$\begin{aligned} E\left[\mu_{\lambda',t} \mid y_{\lambda,t}\right] &= \sum_{i \in J} \left\{\lambda'_{i,t} E\left[\mu_{i,t} \mid y_{\lambda,t}\right]\right\} \\ &= \sum_{i \in J} \left(\frac{\sigma_\mu^2 \lambda_{i,t} \lambda'_{i,t}}{\sigma_\xi^2 + \sigma_\mu^2 \sum_{j \in J} \lambda_{j,t}^2} \right) \left(y_{\lambda,t} - \overline{y} - \mu_{\lambda,t-1}\right) \end{aligned} \tag{8.36}$$

Thus, the voter assessment of an alternative government's current competence is formed by weighting the current competence of each party by the role the party will play in the alternative government and summing over all parties. If the alternative distribution of executive responsibility is the same as the status quo distribution (i.e., $\boldsymbol{\lambda} = \boldsymbol{\lambda}'$) this expression reduces to the expression in equation (8.29), as it should. In contrast, if no party with a share of responsibility in the status quo distribution of responsibility also has a share of responsibility in the new distribution, this expectation is zero.

With this, we can write the utility the voter expects if some alternative distribution of executive authority should obtain as:

$$\begin{aligned} E\left[u_{\lambda',t+1}\right] &= b\left(\overline{y} + E\left[\mu_{\lambda',t} \mid y_{\lambda,t}\right]\right) \\ &= b\overline{y} + b\left(\frac{\sigma_\mu^2 \sum_{i \in J} \lambda_{i,t} \lambda'_{i,t}}{\sigma_\xi^2 + \sigma_\mu^2 \sum_{j \in J} \lambda_{j,t}^2} \right) \left(y_{\lambda,t} - \overline{y} - \mu_{\lambda,t-1}\right) \end{aligned} \tag{8.37}$$

To finish the derivation and get an expression equivalent to the last line of equation (8.32) but allowing nonzero competence for alternatives, we just substitute the last line of equation (8.37) into the first line of equation (8.31):

$$
\begin{aligned}
E[u \mid v_j] - E[u \mid v_0] &= Z \sum_{\lambda' \in \Lambda'} P_{j,\lambda\lambda'} \left(\sum_{i \in J} \lambda_{i,t} \left(\lambda_{i,t} - \lambda'_{i,t}\right) \right) \\
&\quad + Z \sum_{\lambda' \in \Lambda'} P_{j,\lambda'\lambda} \left(\sum_{i \in J} \lambda_{i,t} \left(\lambda'_{i,t} - \lambda_{i,t}\right) \right) \\
&\quad + Z \sum_{\lambda' \in \Lambda'} \sum_{\lambda'' \in \Lambda'} P_{j,\lambda'\lambda''} \left(\sum_{i \in J} \lambda_{i,t} \left(\lambda'_{i,t} - \lambda''_{i,t}\right) \right) \qquad (8.38)
\end{aligned}
$$

where

$$
Z = b \left(\frac{\sigma_\mu^2}{\sigma_\xi^2 + \sigma_\mu^2 \sum_{j \in J} \lambda_{j,t}^2} \right) \left(y_{\lambda,t} - \overline{y} - \mu_{\lambda,t-1} \right)
$$

Again, there will be J of these expressions and voters will vote for the party for which this expression is largest. Z differs from our earlier definitions but is still constant over parties. Unlike our previous generalizations, in which our conclusions about the responsibility augmented competency signal stayed the same from model to model, so that we focused on the implications for the distribution of contention, this generalization changes both our previous conclusions about contention and our conclusions about the competency signal. To make our discussion of these changes more transparent, we begin with a discussion of the case in which each pair of distributions of responsibility that are in contention include the status quo distribution. This case focuses attention on the responsibility augmented competency signal because where there are no pairs of competitive alternative distributions, our conclusions regarding the distribution of contention are exactly the same as those in the earlier section. Specifically, under this assumption, we can write equation (8.38) as:

$$
\begin{aligned}
&E[u \mid v_j] - E[u \mid v_0] \\
&\quad = Z \sum_{\lambda' \in \Lambda'} P_{\lambda\lambda'} \left(2P\left(w_\lambda \lambda_j - w_{\lambda'} \lambda'_j > 0\right) - 1\right) \left(\sum_{i \in J} \left(\lambda_{i,t}^2 - \lambda_i \lambda'_i\right) \right) \qquad (8.39)
\end{aligned}
$$

The first two terms in the product impact economic voting in exactly the same way as in the last section. However, with the addition of nonzero competence for alternative distributions of responsibility, we

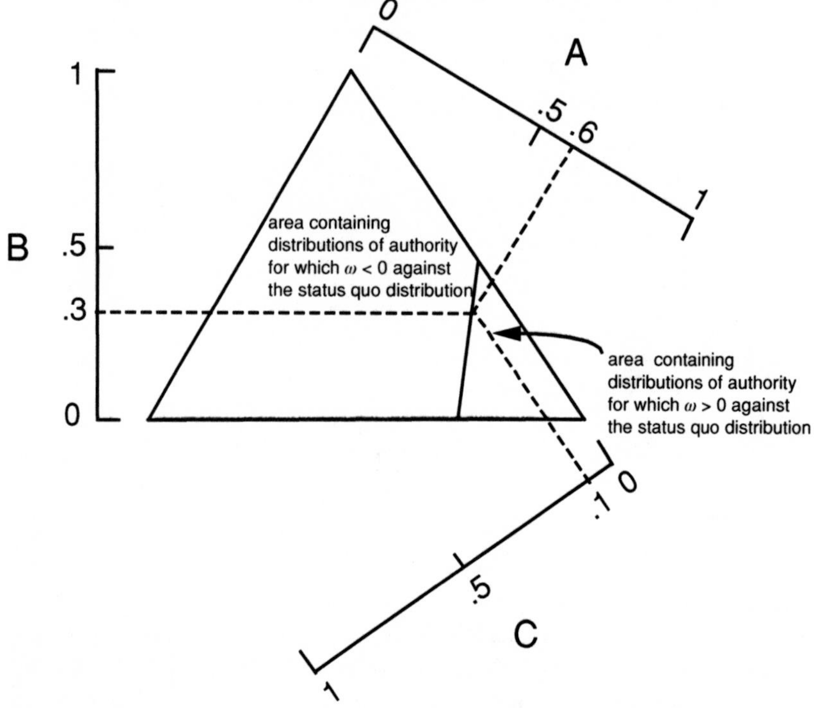

Figure 8.2. The sign of the competence signal for all possible distributions of responsibility in a three-party example. *Note:* $\omega = \sum_{i \in j}(\lambda_{i,t}^2 - \lambda_{i,i})$ and labeled axes are sharing of party responsibility.

have altered the competence signal that voters use to weight economic voting. Specifically, although the signal is still constant over all parties, it is now not always positive. In equation (8.39), the sign of the last term depends on which alternative distributions of authority are in contention. If the competitive alternatives are very different from the status quo distribution (giving parties with large shares of responsibility under the status quo small shares under the alternative and visa versa), then $\sum_{i \in J} (\lambda_{i,t}^2 - \lambda_i \lambda_i')$ will be positive. Indeed, it reaches its maximum, given a fixed $\boldsymbol{\lambda}$, for distributions in which $\lambda_i \lambda_i' = 0$ for all parties, meaning that no parties hold responsibility in both the status quo and alternative distributions. In contrast, it is equal to zero when there is no difference between the alternative and status quo distributions of responsibility.

The easiest way to understand what this means for economic voting is to examine the example provided in Figure 8.2. In this example, there are three parties and the status quo distribution of responsibility assigns 60 percent of the responsibility to party A, 30 percent to party B, and 10 percent to party C. This ternary diagram maps this point in the lower right-side portion of the triangle and shows all the other possible distributions of responsibility (the area of the triangle). $\sum_{i \in J} (\lambda_{i,t}^2 - \lambda_i \lambda_i')$ is positive for any distribution of responsibility, $\boldsymbol{\lambda}'$, in the large area to the left of the solid line bisecting the triangle. In contrast, $\sum_{i \in J} (\lambda_{i,t}^2 - \lambda_i \lambda_i')$ is negative for the distributions of responsibility to the right of the solid bisecting line. Note: $\omega = \sum_{i \in J} (\lambda_{i,t}^2 - \lambda_i \lambda_i')$ in Figure 8.2 and labeled axes are shares of party responsibility.

If there are only two distributions of responsibility in contention (the status quo and some alternative), this means that if the other term in equation (8.39) is positive for some party and, for example, the economy is improving, the utility associated with voting for this party will be positive if the competitive alternative is to the right of the bisecting line and negative if it is to the left. The "preferred" alternatives to the right are those that, in general, concentrate even more responsibility on the parties that had the most responsibility in the status quo distribution. Focusing only on the area to the right of the bisecting line, almost all of these preferred alternatives increase the responsibility of party A, which was most responsible for the good economic performance. It is interesting, however, that, in this example, there is a relatively small area in which preferred alternatives increase the responsibility of the second most responsible party, B. Instead, the improvement in A's position is more often at the expense of B, if only because B has more responsibility to lose than does C. Substantively, this is intriguing. It suggests that when we allow voters to use information about the current competence of incumbents to infer the competence of alternative distributions of responsibility, then economic success may lead to a concentration of the vote on the party with the most responsibility as a way to produce a new cabinet that "rewards" this party at the expense of the others. If we were to make the reasonable assumption that, in this example, party A held the prime ministry and party B was a cabinet partner, then the implication is that the good economy would cause votes to flow to the prime minister and away from both the opposition party C and the smaller cabinet partner B. The implication, more generally, is that economic voting in its traditional form (i.e., electoral rewards for incumbents and punishments for opposition) should apply most strongly to the leading parties in the cabinet and least strongly to partners, who may (in this model) have the opposite result. In the empirical chapters that follow, we are interested in whether the economic vote (in its traditional form) is more consistent for parties with a greater share of responsibility.

Of course, it is also clear from the diagram that $\sum_{i \in J} (\lambda_{i,t}^2 - \lambda_i \lambda_i')$ can be positive for some alternatives that give less responsibility to the leading party. This small area is the triangle to the right of the bisecting line that is above the dashed line leading to A's axis. In this area, the alternatives award greater responsibility to B at the expense of A. However, it is also the case that in this area, the ratio λ_A / λ_A' (i.e., party A's share in the status quo over its share in the alternative) is greater than 1, while B's share is less than 1. But, recall that in the last section we saw that $P_{\lambda\lambda'}(2P(w_\lambda \lambda_j - w_{\lambda'} \lambda_j' > 0) - 1)$ would be bigger for party j than for party i if $\lambda_j / \lambda_j' > \lambda_i / \lambda_i'$. Thus, in this area, parts of equation (8.32) other than $\sum_{i \in J} (\lambda_{i,t}^2 - \lambda_i \lambda_i')$, which is positive, will likely be bigger (and more likely to be positive) for A than for B, so that the overall utility of voting for party A in this region may well be bigger than B even in this region. Finally, we can consider the third term in equation (8.38), which allows the possibility of economic voting when the status quo distribution of responsibility is not in contention with any cabinet but rather two alternatives are in contention with each other. The interpretation of this term is essentially the same as the previous one. Specifically, if the status quo distribution of responsibility is not in contention, then we can write:

$$E[u \mid v_j] - E[u \mid v_0]$$
$$= Z \sum_{\lambda' \in \Lambda'} \sum_{\lambda'' \in \Lambda'} P_{\lambda'\lambda''} \left(2P\left(w_{\lambda'} \lambda_j - w_{\lambda''} \lambda_j' > 0\right) - 1\right) \left(\sum_{i \in J} \left(\lambda_i \lambda_i' - \lambda_i \lambda_i''\right) \right) \tag{8.40}$$

Notice that it still contains the elements of the status quo distribution of authority because it is only through their responsibility for current economic outcomes that voters have any information at all about the competence of the parties in these contending alternatives. Clearly, if no party in either alternative held responsibility in the status quo distribution, these terms will be zero and there will be no economic voting. Furthermore, if λ_j' and λ_j'' are very similar to one another for most parties, this term will be small and economic voting will be muted. So again, we find that distinct alternatives enhance economic voting.

Also, notice that if those parties in the two alternatives that had some experience in the previous distribution of authority have equal shares of power in the new distribution, this sum will be zero. For example, suppose that the incumbent distribution of responsibility was a "grand coalition" in which two large parties shared power equally and all other parties had no responsibility at all. Furthermore, suppose that this coalition breaks up and cannot reform, and that the only contending alternatives are two one-party governments in which one or the other former partners rules alone.[37] Under these circumstances, the sum in the equation (8.40) is $(.5^{*}1 - .5^{*}0) + (.5^{*}0 - .5^{*}1) = 0$. The intuition of this result is clear: because the only information the voter has about the competence of the parties comes from economic outcomes under the status quo distribution of responsibility, and voters apportion responsibility for those outcomes to the two large parties equally, they must conclude that the two alternatives they must decide between have the same level of competence. Because of this, they cannot distinguish between them and so there will be no economic voting in this case (since in our example these are the only contending distributions).

The most prominent cases of "grand coalitions" in the Western democracies are those in Austria and Germany and these look a lot like the example that we gave. The theory would thus suggest that economic voting during the reign of such coalitions should be muted. In this section, we extended the model of rational retrospective economic voting to situations in which there are multiple parties competing for shares of policy-making responsibility, but the voter can use information about the participation of parties in the incumbent distribution of responsibility to infer the competence of new alternative distributions that involve those parties.

The model leads to two main conclusions that finish our generalization of the rational retrospective model of economic voting. Economic voting in a general form is apparent in this model. First, if all the contending distributions of authority include the status quo distribution, the expected utility of voting for a party, when the economy has been good, is greater for parties that have a relatively greater share of the incumbent distribution of responsibility and is larger overall when the differences between the contending alternatives and the status quo distribution are large. When the incumbent distribution of responsibility is not competitive, the previous point still holds but economic voting overall is larger as there are greater differences between non–status quo distributions of authority that are in contention. Again, then, economic voting depends both on sufficient

[37] The same result applies to any coalitions of parties that include only one of the two large parties but give some responsibility to other parties that did not serve in the previous distribution of responsibility. This follows from the fact that these other parties can contribute nothing to the sum in equation (5.2) because they had no responsibility in the status quo distribution.

representation of the incumbent distribution of responsibility in the new distribution and on distinctiveness among alternatives.

SUMMARY

Most economic voting takes place in contexts with multiple parties. This chapter extends the competency results from Chapter 5 to accommodate economic voting in multiparty contexts. Our assumption that voters are fully informed about the political and economic context implies that voters will condition their economic vote on the distribution of policy-making responsibility and on the pattern of cabinet contention.

Multiple parties also introduce the possibility of shared responsibility in governing. And voters in our model are assumed to be fully informed about how power is shared by parties in governing coalitions but also more broadly in the legislative process. The results presented in this chapter make it clear that the distribution of administrative responsibility should condition the extent of economic voting as well as its distribution across parties. Specifically, as responsibility is more equally shared, economic voting in an election should generally decrease. Furthermore, as a given party's share of responsibility decreases, the economy should be down-weighted in the voter's utility for that party. In general (where there are more than two parties), this should lead to less of an economic vote for that party. In Chapter 9, we explore how economic voting varies with these beliefs about the distribution of administrative responsibility.

Multiple parties introduce the likelihood of strategic voting. Our generalization of the rational retrospective economic voting model to the case of multiparty competition allows our rational voters to condition their votes on the likely results of the election – specifically, the distribution of policy-making responsibility that will likely result from the election outcome. We showed that the economy would only be important to the utility comparisons between parties that were "in competition" to receive a share of responsibility after the election. In simple plurality systems, this meant competing to win the most votes but in other systems, this meant being a part of competitive alternative cabinets or, more generally, competitive distributions of responsibility. Furthermore, if the incumbent (party, cabinet, or distribution of responsibility) was not in contention, either because it was sure to win or sure to lose, economic voting would be muted. Finally, in the models of contexts that allowed coalition cabinets and shared responsibility, the distinctiveness of the alternatives mattered to both the overall magnitude of the economic vote and its distribution across parties. In general, those parties whose role in the incumbent cabinet (or in the incumbent distribution of responsibility) was distinct enough from its role in contending alternative cabinets received a greater share of the economic vote than those whose roles were not distinct. In Chapter 10, we explore the implications of these arguments by evaluating the extent to which the economic vote is important to parties that are (or are not) in contention for different roles in the cabinet.

9

The Distribution of Responsibility and the Economic Vote

Two theoretical propositions come out of the discussion of administrative responsibility in the last chapter, each of which produces a straightforward hypothesis. The first concerns the distribution of the economic vote across parties. Parties with a greater share of the status quo distribution of administrative responsibility will receive a greater share of the economic vote than parties with a smaller share. The second concerns the overall size of the economic vote across all parties in an election. As the status quo distribution of administrative responsibility over parties becomes more equal, the overall economic vote declines.

The main task in testing these empirical hypotheses is the measurement of voters' beliefs about the share of administrative responsibility that each party holds. A variety of indicators of the status quo distribution of policy-making responsibility has been discussed in the literature: the current distribution of cabinet membership, the current distribution of cabinet portfolios, the coalition status of the government, the majority status of the government, the influence of the opposition on the government, the extent of collective cabinet responsibility, the distribution of legislative seats, the distribution of ministries specifically dealing with economic matters, and the role of the president. Furthermore, the values of these variables are so widely reported and so well known that we can assume voters' beliefs about them closely mirror the empirical reality, at least on average. Thus, in this chapter, we examine how these different indicators of the distribution of responsibility are related to both the overall economic vote and its distribution across parties.

Of course, we are not the first to examine the empirical relationship between administrative responsibility and economic voting. As we emphasized in Chapter 1, Powell and Whitten (1993) used aggregate electoral data to explore whether various measures of power sharing, such as coalition and minority status, depress economic voting. Palmer and Whitten (2000) used a composite measure of shared responsibility in their aggregate analysis of individual-level data. Anderson (1995) examined how a party's share of cabinet portfolios conditions the relationship between the macro-economy and aggregate party popularity in five countries. At the individual level, Andersen (2000) examined the effect of the incumbent party's share of cabinet portfolios in an interactive model using survey data for thirteen European surveys. Hellwig (2001) estimated the impact of the effective number of parliamentary parties on individual-level economic voting using nine surveys from the Comparative Study of Electoral Systems project. Lewis-Beck offered an explanation for cross-country differences in individual-level economic voting in his five-country study that was based on variation in the number of parties in the cabinet. The results of each of these previous studies provide support for one or both of the hypotheses given herein. Taken together with these previous analyses, the results in this chapter leave little room to doubt that the distribution of administrative responsibility is an important factor conditioning both the magnitude of the economic vote across elections as well as its distribution across parties. The rest of this chapter is divided into two main sections corresponding to the two empirical hypotheses described earlier.

ADMINISTRATIVE RESPONSIBILITY AND THE DISTRIBUTION OF THE ECONOMIC VOTE ACROSS PARTIES

Our first hypothesis suggests that parties with a greater share of the status quo distribution of administrative responsibility will receive a greater share of the economic vote than parties with a smaller share. In testing this hypothesis, we adopt a number of different approaches to measuring each party's administrative responsibility.[1] First, there are institutional factors that affect the distribution of administrative responsibility between the executive and the legislature. In presidential systems, administrative responsibility will be shaped by whether or not the presidential party commands a legislative majority and whether it competes for executive

[1] More precisely, the theory is about the voter's beliefs about the distribution of administrative responsibility across parties. In using measures of the actual distribution of administrative responsibility in place of these beliefs, we assume that these beliefs reflect the real distribution.

power with other executive parties. Because of the fusion of legislative and executive powers in parliamentary systems and their institutional separation in presidential systems, the level of administrative responsibility of the typical prime minister is likely to be greater than that of the typical president (in a presidential system), even when the later controls a majority in the legislature. Second, in parliamentary systems, the distribution of administrative responsibility should reflect characteristics of the incumbent cabinet: the administrative responsibility of a prime ministerial party that controls all the cabinet seats and/or commands a legislative majority will typically be greater than the administrative responsibility of prime ministerial parties that do not. Third, a typical party's share of administrative responsibility should be closely connected, in parliamentary systems, to its position within or outside of the cabinet. Whether the party is the prime ministerial party, a coalition partner, or an opposition party will affect its distribution of administrative responsibility and, hence, its economic vote. One useful gauge of a parliamentary party's level of administrative responsibility is its share of cabinet portfolios, which according to our theory should be strongly correlated with its share of the economic vote. In the sections that follow, we present empirical tests of these propositions using the size or the share of the economic vote for individual parties as the dependent variable in our analyses.

PRESIDENTIAL PARTIES AND THE DISTRIBUTION OF THE ECONOMIC VOTE

There are only two countries in our sample that have directly elected presidents who have significant administrative responsibility: the United States and France. We begin, then, with an analysis of economic voting for presidential parties in these cases. For the United States, the available data include both surveys that ask voters about their presidential vote and those that ask them about their legislative vote. We can explore economic voting for the party of the president in either case. Likewise, surveys exist that ask French voters which parties they support in the legislature as well as for president. However, because the surveys that include the presidential vote question have not also included an appropriate economic perceptions question, our analysis of French economic voting for the party of the president only includes cases in which voters were asked about their legislative vote.

Economic Voting for Presidential versus Nonpresidential Parties

If we assume that voters think administrative responsibility is disproportionately in the hands of presidents, our first hypotheses translates directly into the expectation that presidential parties will have a greater share of the economic vote than nonpresidential parties. Because in two-party systems the economic vote of one party is just the opposite of the economic vote for the other, in the two-party U.S. system, we simply expect that changes in party support because of worsening economic perceptions will be negative for presidential parties but positive (and the same size) for nonpresidential parties. This has certainly been the prevailing wisdom in the U.S. case, in which estimates of economic voting have typically found that the president's party is hurt by poor economic performance (Erikson, 1989, 1990; Kramer, 1971; Norpoth, 2001). Similarly, our own estimates of the *economic vote of the chief executive* in the United States (reported in Figure 3.2 in Chapter 3) were consistently negative. Figure 9.1 reports our estimates of the magnitude of the economic vote for French parties in legislative elections. This chart allows us to compare the size (or, with some work, the share) of the economic vote of French presidential parties to the size of the economic vote for all other parties. The estimated economic votes for presidential parties are listed first and have gray-colored bars.

This figure makes it clear that, like the U.S. case, the size of the economic vote for French presidential parties is typically larger than the economic vote of other parties.[2] The economic vote of the president's party is negative in nine of eleven cases and is the largest negative economic vote in six of those cases. Of course, there are exceptions to this trend. Most prominently, in 1986, 1987, 1993, and 1994, the Rassemblement pour la République (RPR), as well as other parties in 1993, experienced more negative economic voting than did President Mitterrand's Socialist Party. Interestingly, these are exactly the periods in which Mitterrand was forced to cohabitate with a prime minister from the RPR. We will come back to this fact later, when we ask how the economic vote of prime ministerial parties compares to that of presidential parties. However, for now, the main message from Figure 9.1 is that the economic vote of the French presidential party is typically greater than the economic vote of

[2] We also have examined the *share* of the economic vote more directly by inspecting percentages of the economic vote rather than its size. However, we save the presentation of this analysis for a later section in which we present the French results along with those of other systems.

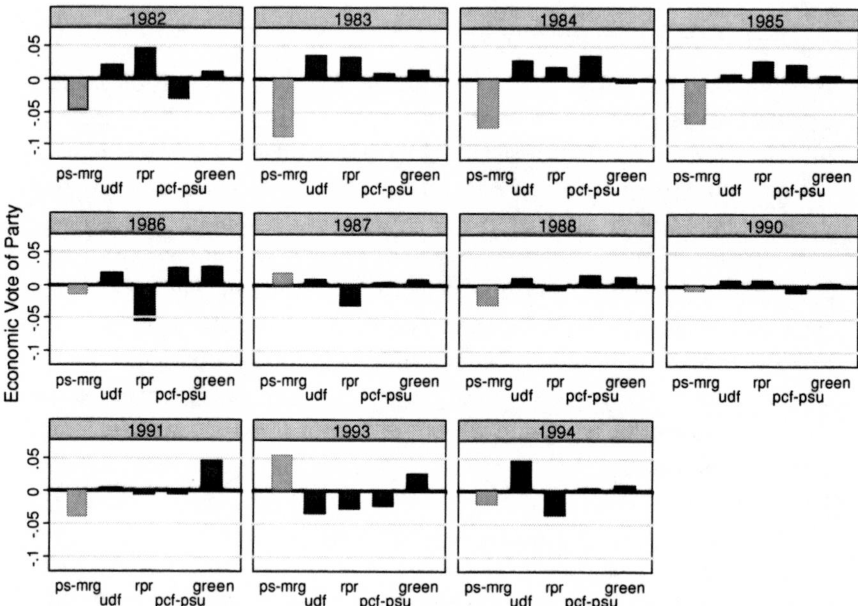

Figure 9.1. The economic vote of french presidential parties versus nonpresidential parties. Gray bars in this graph are for presidential parties.

other parties in the same elections, with the possible exception of prime-ministerial parties during periods of cohabitation.

ECONOMIC VOTING FOR PRESIDENTIAL PARTIES UNDER DIVIDED VERSUS UNIFIED GOVERNMENT

The sharing of administrative responsibilities in presidential systems is usually referred to as "divided government." This occurs when different parties control the executive and legislative branches of government (Elgie, 1999; Shugart and Carey, 1992). There is evidence that divided government weakens the economic vote for presidential parties – much of it based on aggregate-level analyses. For example, Lewis-Beck and Nadeau (2000) produce such evidence for French presidential voting. Employing a sample of elections from both mature and new democracies, Hellwig and Samuels (2007) confirm that the economic vote for the president becomes insignificant, whereas the PM party's economic vote becomes much larger, in periods of cohabitation (or divided government). There is convincing evidence from the United States that divided government either at the national or state level results in a smaller economic vote for the executive (president or governor). Leyden and Borrelli (1995) find that state unemployment impacts vote choice more strongly in states with unified as opposed to divided government. Lowry, Alt, and Ferree (1988) demonstrate that the impact of a state's fiscal condition on vote choice (for both gubernatorial and state legislative candidates) is more pronounced after periods of unified party control of the state government. By contrast, Norpoth's analysis of individual-level data from the 1992 and 1996 U.S. national elections suggests that divided government does not "divert" the economic vote from the presidential party to the majority party in Congress (Norpoth, 2001). Our estimates of the size of the economic vote in different electoral contexts in both the United States and France allow us to assess the impact of divided government on economic vote magnitudes.

Divided government has been the norm in the United States during the period under study here (only the short period of unified Democratic government in the early 1990s is an exception) and has occasionally occurred in France.[3] In France, these periods also produce shared control of the executive in a situation referred to as "cohabitation." Unlike in the United States, divided government in France also means that an opposition prime minister and cabinet will be installed, and this locus of executive authority will compete with the president for control. Indeed, with no legislative majority and the government ministries controlled by the opposition, French presidents during periods of cohabitation may be especially powerless.[4] This contrasts sharply with the experience of divided government in the United States, in which the president's party retains control of the executive apparatus even when faced with a majority opposition in the legislature. Our expectation is that voters will attribute less administrative responsibility to presidents under periods of divided government than during periods of unified government and that this difference should be more severe for French presidents who also must "cohabitate" with the opposition within the executive.

To test these expectations, it was necessary not only to compare the average economic vote of presidential parties under unified and divided

[3] The current era of divided government in the United States began in 1956 when the Republicans won the presidency but failed to carry Congress (Fiorina, 1992). See also Brady (1993) for a discussion of divided government in the United States.

[4] During the time period covered in our analysis, there were two periods of cohabitation: 1986–1988 when Mitterrand (Socialist) was president and Chirac (RPR) was his prime minister; and 1993–1995 when Mitterrand was president and Edouard Balladur (RPR) was prime minister.

Table 9.1. *Average Economic Vote for Presidential Parties in Different Contexts*

	Divided Government or Cohabitation (C1)	Unified Government (C2)	p-value for rejecting the hypothesis that C1 = C2
U.S. Presidential Election	−0.06 (0.02) n = 5	−0.10 – n = 1	0.29
French Legislative Election	0.01 (0.03) n = 4	−0.05 (0.03) n = 8	0.004
U.S. Legislative Election	0.012 (0.038) n = 9	−0.016 (0.03) n = 2	0.19

Tests are F-tests for equality of the coefficients in a dummy variable regression in which each cell represents a separate indicator variable in the regression (with appropriate handling of the constant and robust standard errors). In cases in which difference of means tests (with unequal variances) could be calculated (i.e., with more than one observation in a cell) the results from these tests are essentially identical to the F-tests.[29]

government but also to control for whether the election study asked voters about their presidential or legislative vote. The results of these tests are in Table 9.1. The table reports the average economic vote for presidential parties in each indicated context and the accompanying tests are from an appropriately specified dummy variable regression (see the footnote to the table).

Although we have limited data on presidential parties, the data that we do have all support the proposition that economic voting for presidential parties will be muted under periods of divided government. Consistent with our hypotheses, in each type of election considered, the average economic vote for presidential parties under divided government is smaller (less negative) than under unified control. Furthermore, the biggest

[5] The differences between the averages in the first and third rows of the table are statistically significant (as are those between the first and second). This supports the often-noted idea that economic voting is more important in presidential elections than in legislative elections (Kiewiet, 1983; Erikson, 1989; 1990 for the United States; and Lewis-Beck and Nadeau, 2000, 2004 for France). This was clear in the description of U.S. economic voting provided in Chapter 3. However, because we lack data on economic voting in French presidential elections, the evidence provided here does not contribute much strength to what is already the common wisdom. It is worth noting, however, that if voters think administrative responsibility is disproportionately in the hands of presidents and thus question the utility of casting economic votes in legislative races, this result supports our argument.

difference in the average economic vote between unified and divided control is, as we expected, in the French case (in which divided government also implies executive cohabitation). Of course, the small number of cases forces us to be cautious in our interpretation. Although the difference between periods of divided and unified government for the French case is both large and statistically different from zero, the two results for the U.S. case are not as large and are not statistically significant. Taken together, however, the strong French results and the directionally consistent U.S. results suggests that divided government suppresses the economic vote.

Economic Voting for Presidential versus Prime Ministerial Parties

The principal institutional difference between presidential and parliamentary systems is the formal sharing of administrative responsibility between the executive and the legislature in the former case and the fusion of these responsibilities in the latter case. We expect that the combining of legislative and executive functions in the parliamentary case will result in higher levels of economic voting for prime ministerial parties compared to presidential parties, even in the case when the president's party commands a majority in the legislature. First, a number of scholars who compare the institutional powers of prime ministers to those of presidents have noted that single-party prime ministers controlling a majority of seats in the legislature tend to be more powerful than presidents (e.g., Linz, 1990, 1994; Sartori, 1994). In these situations, prime ministers can not only dictate the administration of public policy but also, because of the strong party discipline in most parliamentary systems, can dominate the legislative agenda to an extent that is unobtainable by most presidents (Ogg, 1936).[6]

Second, even when single-party prime ministers do not control a majority in the legislature, they retain considerable agenda-setting powers in most parliamentary systems – most important, the more or less exclusive right to initiate legislative proposals. In contrast, the presidents in our sample are largely dependent on legislative parties to pursue their legislative agenda and so, without a parliamentary majority, the president's agenda is unlikely to move easily through the legislature.

[6] A clear exception here is the presidential regime in Russia, where the rules regarding presidential vetoes and decrees give him almost unchallengeable power (Parrish, 1998).

Table 9.2. *Average Economic Vote for Presidential and Prime Ministerial Parties*

	Economic Vote for Single-Party Prime Ministers	Economic Vote for Presidents	
	All Are Legislative Election Studies	French Legislative Election Studies	U.S. Legislative Election Studies
Divided Government/ Cohabitation	−.052 (0.03) 19	.01 (0.03) 4	0.012 (0.038) 9
p-value for difference in means test between column 1 and each other column	–	p < 0.015	p < 0.001
Unified Government	−.068 (0.04) 49	−.053 (0.03) 8	−.016 (0.03) 2
p-value for difference in means test between column 1 and each other column	–	p < 0.11	p < 0.10

Numbers in cells are mean *economic vote of the chief executive*, the standard deviation of this variable (in parentheses), and the number of observations for the case, respectively. Only cases of presidential parties or parties of single-party majority prime ministers are included. For France, which has a PM and president, only the economic vote of the presidential party is included.

"Unified Government" for parliamentary systems means the party of the prime minister controls a majority in the legislature. "Divided Government" for parliamentary systems means that the party of the prime minister does not control a majority in the legislature.

The p-value is from a difference in means test allowing for unequal variances. Specifically, it is a test that the value in the first column is smaller (more negative) than the corresponding row value in each of the other columns.

The evidence comparing the economic vote of single-party prime ministerial parties to that of presidential parties is presented in Table 9.2 and favors the hypotheses that the economic vote of prime ministerial parties is larger than that of presidential parties. Specifically, when we compare the economic vote of presidential parties and prime ministerial parties in elections in which voters were asked about their legislative vote choice, all the evidence (from either the United States or France and for both unified and divided government) indicates that the economic vote

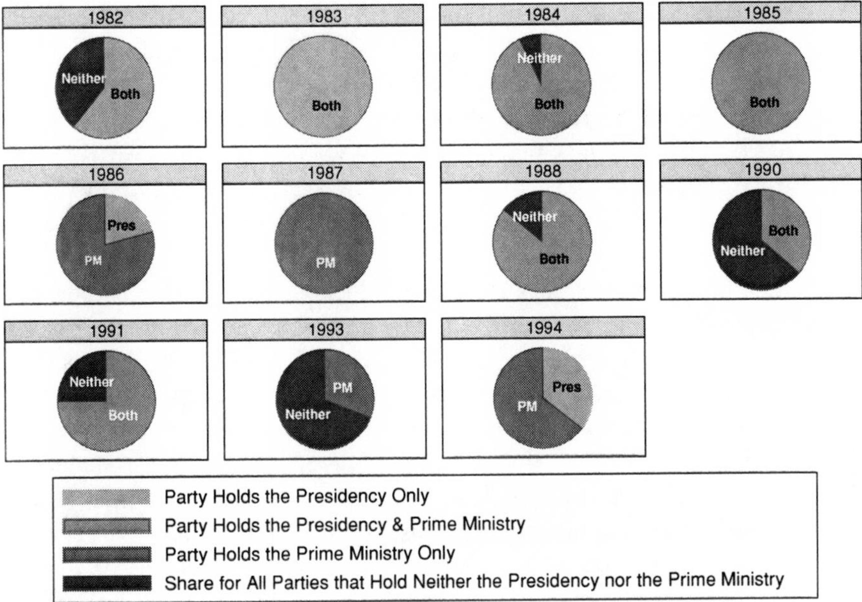

Figure 9.2. The Share of the Economic Vote of French Presidential and Prime Ministerial Parties. The area of each slice represents the share of the "negative economic vote" that accrued to the party (or parties) indicated by the label on the slice.

of single-party prime ministerial parties is larger than that of presidential parties.[7]

Another way to examine the question of whether presidential or prime ministerial parties have a larger economic vote is by looking more closely at the one case in which these kinds of parties can exist in the same system at the same time. If our hypothesis is true, then we would expect the party holding the prime ministry to capture a larger share of the economic vote in a given election than the party of the president, when these two offices are controlled by different parties. The relevant data are provided in Figure 9.2. This figure shows the total share of the negative economic vote that was captured by prime ministerial, presidential, and

[7] We chose only to examine evidence from a comparison of election studies of the same type (i.e., all legislative elections in both the presidential and prime ministerial systems). Thus, the U.S. case is the economic vote for the president's party when voters are asked about their choices in the legislative election. This focus allows us to avoid conflating differences in office (presidential or prime ministerial parties) with differences in the type of vote-choice question.

nonexecutive parties for each of the election studies we have for France. The "negative economic vote" is just the sum of the economic vote for all parties that experienced a decline in their support when the economy worsened (i.e., all the parties with negative projecting bars in Figure 9.1). If a party type does not appear in one of the pie graphs, no party of that type experienced a negative economic vote (and following the discussion in Chapter 2, we can think of the economic vote in these cases as zero).

There are four cases in our data in which there was an incumbent French president who was from a different party than the incumbent prime minister (at the time of the survey). These were in 1986, 1987, 1993, and 1994. Notice first that in each of these four cases (and, indeed, in all eleven cases), the prime ministerial party experienced a negative economic vote, as expected. In contrast, during two of the cases of cohabitation (1987 and 1993), the presidential party did not experience a negative economic vote at all. Furthermore, in the other two cases (in which the prime ministerial and the presidential parties were the only two to have a negative economic vote), the prime ministerial party's share of the economic vote was almost three times larger than that for the presidential party. Thus, in the head-to-head competition for economic votes that the French cases highlight, we find evidence consistent with the idea that French voters see the prime minister as more responsible for economic policy and concentrate their economic votes accordingly.[8]

In sum, if we make the plausible assumption that single-party prime ministers have more administrative responsibility than presidents, our evidence about the relative level of economic voting for prime ministerial parties and presidential parties tends to support our first hypothesis – that

[8] In a related finding, Lewis-Beck and Nadeau (2000) find that in two French presidential elections under cohabitation (1988 and 1995), the economic vote on the second ballot is much higher when an incumbent prime minister (whose party controlled the cabinet) was running – this was the case in 1988 but not in 1995. This suggests that under cohabitation, voters recognize the prime ministerial party as responsible for economic management and are more likely to include the economy in their vote-choice decision if the prime ministerial candidate is actually one of the presidential candidates. In general, Lewis-Beck and Nadeau (2000) conclude that economic voting is moderated under cohabitation. Likewise, in a poll of four hundred French voters aimed at accessing the distribution of responsibility for economic outcomes to the president or prime minister, Lewis-Beck (1997b) finds the economy to have a greater influence on approval for the prime minister than for the president.

a greater share of administrative responsibility should lead to a greater share of the economic vote.[9]

THE ECONOMIC VOTE OF PRIME MINISTERIAL PARTIES LEADING DIFFERENT TYPES OF CABINETS

We have seen that the magnitude of the economic vote responds, as expected, to differences in the distribution of responsibility in different kinds of presidential systems and between presidential parties and single-party prime ministers. Following the same logic, we can look within parliamentary systems and examine whether the economic vote for prime ministerial parties varies with the degree to which administrative responsibility is concentrated in their hands or distributed to other parties as well. Our assumption is that single-party prime ministers hold a greater share of administrative responsibility than prime ministers who head coalition cabinets. Furthermore, prime ministers who do not control a majority in the legislature hold less administrative responsibility than those who do. If these assumptions are correct (and voters beliefs actually reflect the distribution of administrative responsibility), our theory implies that the economic vote for prime ministers should be highest for single-party prime ministers who command a legislative majority and lowest for coalition prime ministers who do not command a legislative majority. The order of the intermediate cases (i.e., single-party minority prime ministers and majority coalition prime ministers) will depend on which effect (coalition government or majority status of the government) impacts the distribution of administrative responsibility more.

We begin by examining how the size of the economic vote for prime ministers varies by majority and coalition status separately. The data are provided in Figure 9.3 and, as expected, they show that the economic vote for prime ministerial parties in coalition cabinets is muted relative to the economic vote for prime ministerial parties that govern alone (the right-hand panel). Likewise, majority cabinets tend to have a bigger economic vote than minority cabinets, although this difference is not large (the left-hand panel).

In order to better understand how the coalition and the majority status of the cabinet affects the prime minister's retrospective economic vote, we

9 A cautionary note here, though, is the finding in Hellwig and Samuels (2007) suggesting that the economic vote under presidential regimes is similar, if not higher, than in parliamentary regimes.

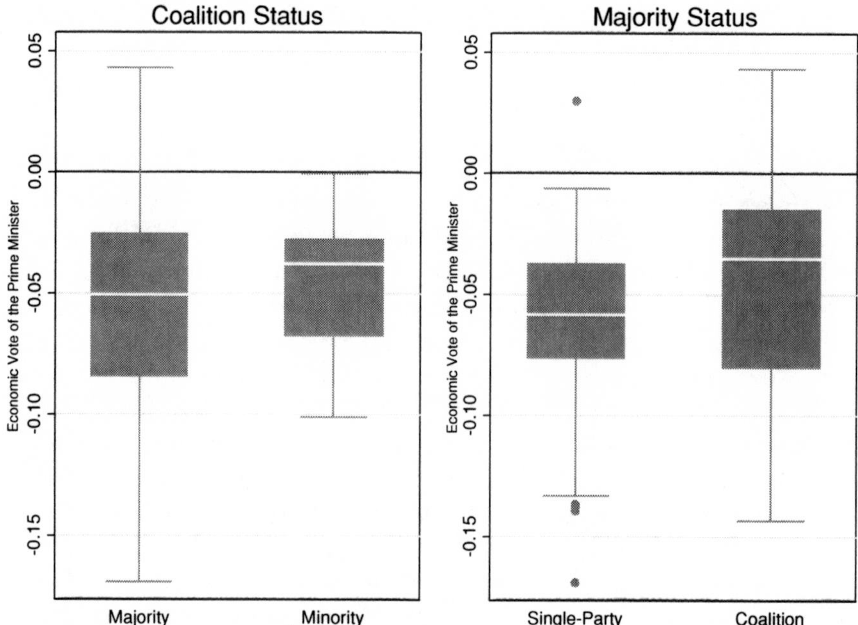

Figure 9.3. Economic voting for prime minister parties by majority and coalition status. Shaded areas of box-plots include the 25–75 percentiles and the "whiskers" extend to 1.5 in the interquartile range. The centerline is the median.

regressed the economic vote of prime ministers on dummy variables for the coalition and majority status of the cabinet. Furthermore, we examined if the relationship changed when we allowed these variables to interact. This produced the coefficients and standard errors in Table 9.3 and the predicted values and p-values for significant differences in Table 9.4.

These results make at least one conclusion unequivocally clear: the support of single-party majority cabinets depends more heavily on the economy than any other cabinet type. Not only are the coefficients on coalition and minority status negative and highly significant in both equations, but the corresponding predicted values for the economic vote of single-party majority prime ministerial parties are also statistically different from (and larger than) the economic votes of all the other kinds of prime ministerial parties (Table 9.4).

Beyond this, the estimates can also tell us something about differences in the magnitude of the economic vote between other types of parties, though these contrasts are not nearly as clear as the difference between single-party majority prime ministers and all of the other kinds

Table 9.3. *Economic Voting for Prime Ministerial Parties: The Impact of Coalition and Majority Status*

Dependent Variable: Negative of the Economic Vote	OLS Coefficient (t-ratio)	OLS Coefficient (t-ratio)
Coalition Government	−0.023	−0.026
(1 = "yes", 0 = "no")	(−2.38)	(−2.31)
Minority Government	−0.014	−0.021
(1 = "yes", 0 = "no")	(−2.11)	(−2.32)
*Coalition Government * Minority*	--	0.017
Government	--	(1.19)
Constant	0.067	0.069
	(9.93)	(7.85)
Number of Observations	146	146
Adjusted R-Squared	0.08	0.09

OLS regression with standard errors robust to heteroskedacticity and to nonindependence between observations of the same party in different surveys.

of parties. Specifically, although the estimates of the magnitude of the economic vote for the four different cabinet types are in the same order in both model specifications, the statistical significance of these differences depends on the specification. If one is willing to make the restriction that the insignificant interaction term in Table 9.3 is really zero, then we find

Table 9.4. *Predicted Size of the Economic Vote: Different Types of Parliamentary Cabinets*

	P = 0.043, p = 0.028		
	Single Party, Majority	**Single Party, Minority**	
	0.067	0.053	
	0.069	0.048	
	50	19	
p = 0.024 *p = 0.028*			*P = 0.02* *p = 0.31*
	Coalition, Majority	**Coalition, Minority**	
	0.044	0.030	
	0.042	0.038	
	66	11	
	p = 0.04, p = 0.73		

The first and second numbers in each cell are the predicted sizes of the economic vote for the type of party based on the coefficients in columns 1 and 2, respectively, of Table 9.3. The last number is the number of cases in the category. Italicized numbers are p-values for rejecting the hypothesis that the predicted values in the adjacent columns or rows are equal. The p-values for the difference in the northwest and southeast cells are 0.005 and 0.008, respectively, and for the northeast and southwest cells are 0.41 and 0.57, respectively.

that leading a coalition cabinet dampens the economic vote of the prime ministerial party more than leading a minority cabinet. This is reflected both in the differences in the size of the coefficient estimates for minority and coalition status in Table 9.3, as well as the larger differences in the predicted values between the rows of Table 9.4 (going from majority to minority) versus differences between the columns (going from single party to coalition).

The fact that in both specifications prime ministerial parties, leading single-party minority cabinets, have the second largest economic vote is perhaps surprising given the much discussed difficulty that minority cabinets have in policy making, relative to majority cabinets. However, an examination of the specific cases of single-party minority government on which these estimates are based may suggest an explanation. Specifically, these cases are all large parties that hold a dominant position on at least one side of the political spectrum in each country. Some are "almost majority" governments, whereas others (e.g., the Scandinavian Socialists) tend to rule when they face a badly divided opposition. Laver and Shepsle (1990) provide one explanation for the existence of such governments, which suggests that parties that hold a very strong bargaining position with respect to postelection policy making will sometimes be able to rule alone even when they only hold a minority of seats. Thus, our sample of single-party minority governments may be "self-selected" so that they are exactly those parties that are well positioned vis-à-vis other parties to dominate policy making. Some evidence for this comes from the fact that all of our single-party minority cabinets except one hold a plurality of seats in the legislature as well as the median position on at least one of the two policy dimensions described in Mueller and Strom (2000). More convincing evidence, however, comes from our use of Laver and Benoit's *Winset* program to calculate whether these cabinets tend to be the kind of "strong" cabinets that Laver and Shepsle's theory identifies as capable of ruling alone despite holding a minority of seats. When we make this calculation for each case, we find that twelve of the nineteen single-party minority cabinets in our sample are formally "strong" parties by Laver and Shepsle's criteria.[10]

[10] Specifically, in a two-dimensional space defined by economic policy on one hand and social policy on the other, no party preferred any possible alternative cabinet to the one in which the ruling party controlled all the portfolios (we used positioning data from the manifestos project but, in some cases, substituted it for Laver and Benoit [2006] or Laver and Hunt's [1990] data when the case was close to the period to which that data applied).

Thus, when we look closely at these single-party minority cabinets, it is less surprising that they should mimic their majority counterparts. What is perhaps more surprising is that voters seem to be aware of this strength and so treat these parties almost as if they were majority governments.

THE DISTRIBUTION OF THE ECONOMIC VOTE AMONG PARTIES PLAYING DIFFERENT ROLES IN (AND OUT OF) GOVERNMENT

In the analyses so far, we have only compared the economic vote of different kinds of prime ministerial parties. However, our hypothesis that a party's share of administrative responsibility should impact its share of the economic vote applies to parties playing various roles in government and opposition. In this section, we examine whether these differences in roles are, indeed, associated with differences in the importance of economic voting among the parties.

The Distribution of the Economic Vote among Prime Minister, Partner, and Opposition Parties

Our theory implies that economic voting should be more important for prime ministerial parties than it is for their partners and more important for these partners than it is for opposition parties. In order to assess these hypotheses empirically, we need to explore differences in economic voting among different kinds of parties that compete with each other in the *same* election.[11] When we look at the economic vote for parties within the same election, however, we face a practical problem in examining the data: the economic vote must sum to zero across parties in an election. Clearly, if there are only two parties in the system, the size of the economic vote for the prime ministerial party and the opposition party must necessarily be equal (in absolute value) and so there is little point to examining the share of the economic vote that each party received (they will always have equal shares).[12] In contrast, in the multiparty case, there is room for the total economic vote to be distributed among different parties

[11] As in the other parts of this book, whenever we refer to "cabinet partners" or a "cabinet partner," we mean non–prime ministerial parties who hold seats in the cabinet. When we need to refer generically to any party in the cabinet (including the prime minister), we use the term "cabinet party" or "government party."

[12] These shares will either both be equal to zero (if change in the support for the prime minister because of a worsening economy is in the "wrong" direction or is really

in various patterns. Our hypothesis is that the lion's share of the negative economic vote should go to the prime ministerial party, followed by other cabinet parties, with the least economic voting going to opposition parties.[13] When examining distributional hypotheses of this sort, we want to rely on techniques that focus our attention on the *shares* of the overall economic vote that different parties receive and that are sensitive to the compositional nature of economic voting (i.e., that shares sum to 1).

Thus, to examine these data, we first divide the parties in each election into two groups: those that experienced a negative economic vote and those that experienced a positive economic vote.[14] As shown earlier, the prime ministerial party will usually be included in the group of parties that has a negative economic vote, as will the cabinet partners, although not as reliably. In the data examined here (which excludes two-party cases and multiparty cases in which only one party had a negative economic vote), the economic vote was negative for 80 percent of the prime ministers and 65 percent of the cabinet partners. Of course, opposition parties also experience negative economic voting in some of our cases, but this is much less common (41 percent of opposition parties). We compare the extent of negative economic voting for prime ministers, cabinet partners, and opposition parties in two different ways. First, we simply examine the average size of the negative economic vote for parties of each type that are in comparable electoral situations. Specifically, we can only make this kind of comparison if we control for the number of parties in a given election that have a negative economic vote (e.g., if four parties are splitting −10 percent of the vote, then they will tend to have smaller shares than if two parties split this same change). Figure 9.4 provides the relevant data for elections in which the negative economic vote was split among two, three, and four parties, respectively.

zero) or both equal to 1 (when changes in support for the prime minister are nonzero and in the expected direction).

[13] Recall that as we developed the theory in Chapter 8, we successively relaxed the definition of "incumbency" until it was possible for the theory to predict negative economic voting for opposition parties that had some role in policy making. Nevertheless, if this responsibility is less than that of cabinet partners, the hypothesis here follows.

[14] As discussed earlier, a "negative economic vote" is just a negative change in support due to a worsening in economic perceptions. By definition, the negative economic vote in a given electoral situation will equal the positive economic vote and so we examine only the negative half here. Furthermore, as we have shown, the economic vote for prime ministers is overwhelmingly negative, so this is the most relevant comparison.

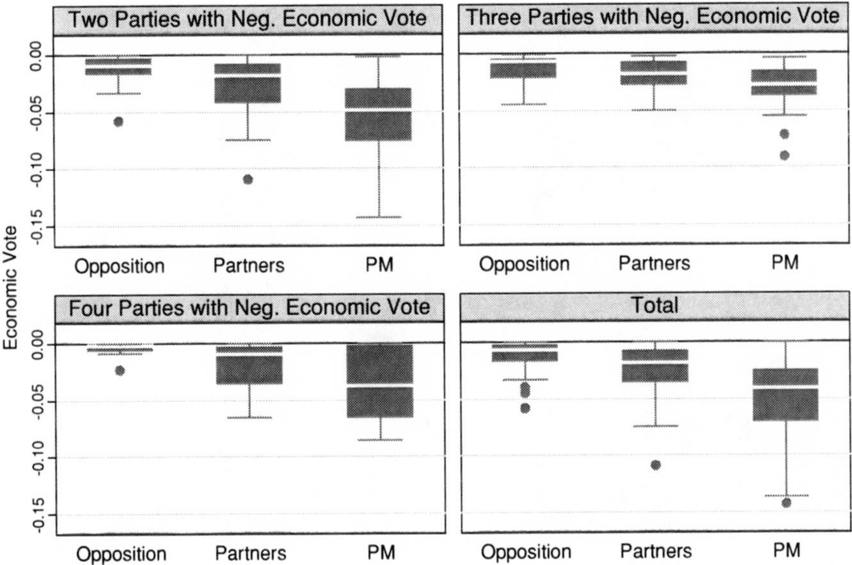

One case with five parties that had negative economic votes is not graphed.

Figure 9.4. Share of the negative economic vote: Prime ministers versus cabinet partners and opposition parties. Shaded areas of box-plots include the 25–75 percentiles and the "whiskers" extend to 1.5 in the interquartile range. The centerline is the median.

The results convincingly confirm our expectation that prime ministerial parties will have a larger economic vote than other parties and that cabinet partners have a larger negative economic vote than opposition parties.

We also can examine the data in a different way that separates information on the overall size of the economic vote from the distributional information about the share of the economic vote held by each party. To do this, we calculated the sum of the negative economic vote in each election study and then calculated the share of that total that accrued to each party (assigning zero to parties whose votes were positive). Figure 9.5 shows the average of these shares for parties playing different roles in (or out of) the cabinet. Because only cases with the same number of parties receiving a negative economic vote can be so compared, we provide a separate graph for each set of cases.

This graph reveals that whatever the overall size of the negative economic vote in an election, most of it goes to the prime ministerial party – no matter whether the opposition, other cabinet partners, or both also get a negative economic vote. Furthermore, this evidence also shows that cabinet partners get a bigger share of the economic vote than opposition

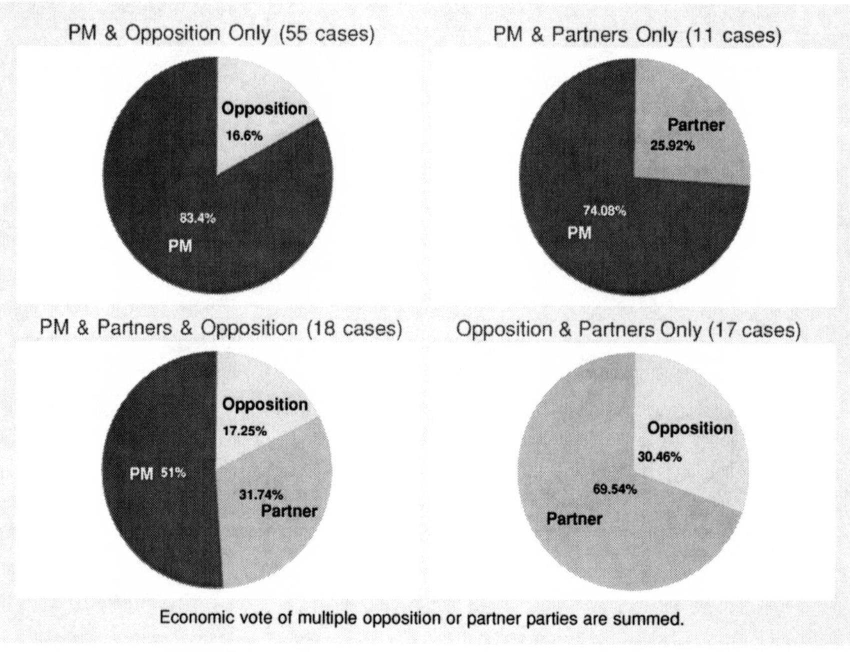

Figure 9.5. Average distribution of the negative economic vote: Prime ministerial, partner, and opposition parties.

parties. Assuming that voters attribute more administrative responsibility to cabinet partners than to opposition parties, this clearly supports the hypothesis that the distribution of the economic vote is a function of the distribution of administrative responsibility across parties.

We can also examine a statistical model of the relationship in Figure 9.5 that takes account of the compositional nature of the vote choice in the statistical model (King and Katz, 1999). Specifically, for each of the four situations in Figure 9.5, we create a dependent variable that corresponds to the percent of the negative economic vote that each party received (each dependent variable is a vector with elements that are the percentage of the vote that each party type received in a given electoral situation). Each of these dependent variable vectors will necessarily sum to 1 across party types and, consequently, they will not even approximate the assumptions necessary to use regression reliably. Hence, we transform the elements of these vectors by forming ratios of the shares for different party types (just choosing an arbitrary type as the denominator of the ratio) and then taking logs of these ratios. We then regress these log-ratios on a set of constants.[15] This exercise provides a reliable test of whether the apparent differences in the proportions in Figure 9.5 are statistically different from zero. The result of these tests confirm, with high levels of confidence, that the differences are indeed different from zero (even the apparently small difference between the shares for opposition and partner parties in the lower left graph can be statistically distinguished from zero, with a p-value of .056).

Parties with Control of the Economic Affairs and Finance Ministries

Our theory suggests that the importance of retrospective economic voting to a party support depends on the ability of voters to discern that party's competence based on movements in the economy. This only follows, however, because in our theory, competence in economic management is ultimately consequential for *economic* outcomes. Thus, it is really not the distribution of administrative responsibility *in general* (which, of course, concerns a variety of policy outcomes unrelated to the economy) that should condition retrospective economic voting but rather the distribution of administrative responsibility for economic management specifically. The recognition that our use of the term "administrative responsibility" is really just a shorthand for "administrative responsibility for economically consequential decisions" allows us to propose that the voter should attribute more administrative responsibility to parties that hold key positions in economic management than to those holding other positions. Concretely, we expect that parties controlling ministries such as finance, economic affairs, and the treasury will have a larger economic vote than other parties, even if these others have parties have significant administrative responsibility in other areas.

In this section, we explore whether parties that hold these positions have a systematically different economic vote than similar parties that do not. Clearly, this will not be an interesting question for single-party governments in which the same party holds all the cabinet ministries, including the prime ministry. Likewise, it would not be an interesting question if prime ministerial parties in coalition cabinets also consistently controlled the finance portfolios. In fact, the prime minister's party frequently does not control the finance ministry: if we look at all coalition cabinets from

[15] For the case in which there are three party types, there are two log-ratios, so we need to estimate a system of two equations. We use seemingly unrelated regression to do so.

Table 9.5. *Predicted Size of the Economic Vote: Parties Holding the Finance Ministry, the Prime Ministry, or Both*

	$p = 0.08$		
	Not PM, **Not Finance Ministry** 0.005 (0.0001, 0.011)	**PM,** **Not Finance Ministry** 0.028 (0.002, 0.053)	
$p = 0.004$			$p = 0.30$
	Not PM, **Finance Ministry** 0.020 (0.012, 0.03)	**PM,** **Finance Ministry** 0.043 (0.024, 0.061)	
	$p = 0.02$		

Numbers in the cells are predicted amounts of economic voting for the type of party based on the coefficients from the regression model from footnote 18. Italicized numbers are p-values for rejecting the hypothesis that the predicted values in the adjacent columns or rows are equal. The p-value for the difference in the northwest and southeast cells is 0.0001 and for the northeast and southwest cells is 0.51.

1960 to 2002 (for the countries in our sample), the prime minister's party controlled the finance ministry 59 percent of the time.[16] When, in addition to the finance ministry, there was also an economic affairs ministry, it was controlled by the prime minister's party 34 percent of the time.[17] Figure 9.6 shows (for coalitional governments) the extent of economic voting for finance ministers compared to other cabinet partners, controlling for whether the party also held the prime ministry. The economic vote of parties that hold the finance ministry is greater (more negative) than other parties, which clearly supports our hypothesis and suggests that voters make rather subtle distinctions in the distribution of administrative responsibility.[18]

The predicted values and significance tests provided in Table 9.5 show that there is always a larger economic vote for parties holding the finance ministry compared to those who do not, regardless of whether the party also holds the prime ministry. However, this difference is only statistically

[16] This is calculated over months, thereby allowing for changes in the composition of cabinets.

[17] Cabinets almost always include a finance ministry but have a separate economic affairs ministry only about half the time.

[18] The regression results for Figure 9.6 are as follows: *Economic Vote for Parties Holding Finance Ministry in a Coalition Government* $= 0.005(1.96) + 0.023(1.74) \times$ Dummy Variable Indicating Party Holds Prime Ministry $+0.015(2.84) \times$ Dummy Variable Indicating Party Holds Finance Ministry $- 0.0004(-0.03)$ Prime Ministry*Finance Ministry. $R^2 = 0.19$. Observations = 156.

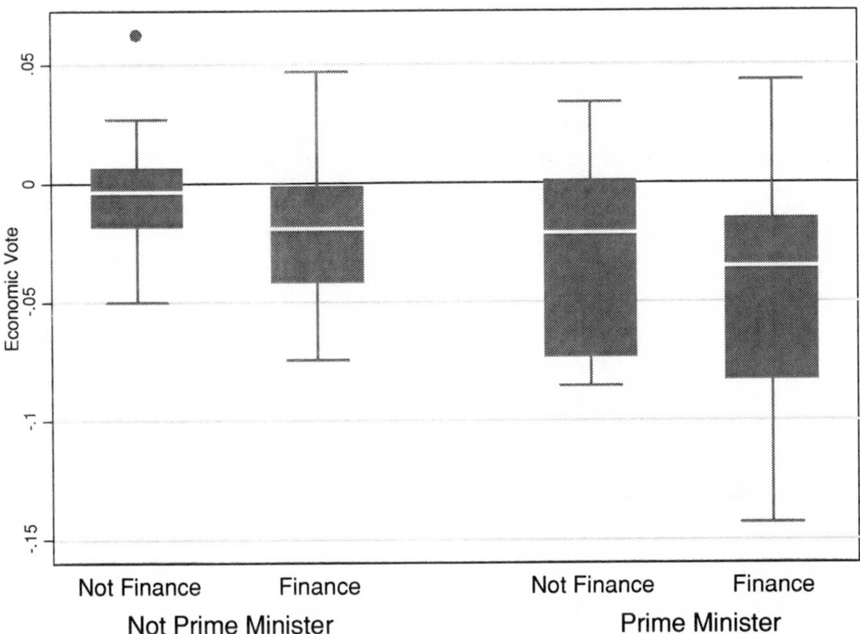

Figure 9.6. Economic vote for parties holding the finance ministry, coalition governments. Shaded areas of box-plots include the 25–75 percentiles and the "whiskers" extend to 1.5 in the interquartile range. The centerline is the median.

significant for cabinet partners. These results suggest an interesting modification to our earlier conclusions about the impact of holding the prime ministry on a party's economic vote. Specifically, although in the last section we saw that prime ministers have a substantially larger economic vote than their cabinet partners (a conclusion widely shared by students of comparative economic voting), the analysis in this section suggests that this difference may be in part because most prime ministerial parties also control the finance ministry. In contrast, when different parties hold these two positions, the electoral fate of the finance minister is almost as dependent on the economy (an economic vote of .02) as is the electoral fortunes of the prime minister (an economic vote of .028).[19]

Given the strength of our results for the importance of the position of finance minister in the distribution of the economic vote, one may wonder

[19] An interesting implication for future research is that if prime ministers recognize this, they should use it when negotiating the distribution of cabinet portfolios. They should offer the finance ministry to other parties when they expect the economy to decline and keep it for themselves when the economy is likely to be strong.

whether there is any evidence that voters actually appreciate the different roles that different parties play in economic policy making. Although the best evidence would ask voters directly about these beliefs, some indirect evidence can be gleaned from a new data set on newspaper reporting of economic news that we are currently developing for the larger research project of which this study is a part. That dataset codes newspaper stories about the economy for a variety of variables, including references and attributions of responsibility to different political actors. With these data, we can examine how often newspaper stories in different countries mention the prime minister or the finance minister in connection with economic news. This provides direct evidence about the availability of the kinds of information that inform voters of the relative influence of parties holding the prime ministry and finance ministry on policy making.

Thus far in the project, we have collected data from twenty-eight newspapers (four papers each in Canada, Belgium, Norway, the United States, the United Kingdom, France, and Ireland) from 1980 to 2002. We distinguished two types of newspaper stories: (1) all stories concerning the economy, and (2) other kinds of stories that mentioned the incumbent government. Our measure of the extent to which voters receive information about the finance minister's connection to the economy is the relative frequency that the finance minister is mentioned in economic stories compared to all stories (including noneconomic ones).[20] Table 9.6 summarizes the results and shows that newspapers are four times more likely to mention the finance minister in a story about the economy than they are to mention the prime minister. Furthermore, this is in contrast to other kinds of stories in which the incumbent government is mentioned, where the prime minister is slightly more likely than the finance minister to be mentioned.

This evidence suggests that the finance minister tends to be highlighted in media discussions of the government (about half the economic stories that mention anyone in the government mention the finance minister) and is the dominant government figure associated with reporting about the economy. In our view, this gives some credence to the notion that the

[20] Because this analysis is only meant to be illustrative, we forego a detailed discussion of the methodology for this extensive project. In short, however, we sampled newspaper stories from the front page of the four leading newspapers in each country. We coded all the stories that appeared either the day of or the business day after the official release of either monthly or quarterly economic statistics on unemployment, inflation, or GDP/GNP.

Table 9.6. *Mentions of Prime Minister and Finance Minister in Newspaper Stories about the Economy*

	Prime Minister Mentioned	Finance Minister Mentioned	Neither Mentioned	Newspaper Stories
All stories in which a member of cabinet is mentioned	2,012 (49%)	1,836 (45%)	608 (6%)	4,068 (100%)
All economic stories	50 (3%)	113 (16%)	1,685 (91%)	1,848 (100%)

The 4,456 mentions in the first row come from 4,068 stories (in some stories, both are mentioned).

finance ministry is not just an important institutional player in the making of economic policy, but that the media provides the kind of information that would allow voters to understand this as well.

Overall, this section provides convincing evidence that voters attribute more responsibility for economic policy making to parties holding economic ministries than to others and that these parties have correspondingly larger economic votes.

The Distribution of Cabinet Seats

Voters appear to establish their assessment of party competence – which, in turn, conditions their economic vote – based on reasonably sophisticated assessments of the administrative roles of parties within the governing coalition. Each party's share of cabinet seats strikes us as an indicator of a party's administrative responsibility that is even more accessible to voters. We have already established that prime ministerial parties register a greater economic vote than other parties. Hence, what is of particular interest here is whether the economic vote of cabinet partners is positively related to their share of cabinet seats. Figure 9.7 plots the relationship between the economic vote for cabinet partners (excluding prime minister parties) and their share of cabinet seats. The relationship is in the predicted direction with a statistically significant slope coefficient and so is consistent with our hypothesis.[21]

[21] As readers might expect, if we include the prime ministerial parties in the plot and regression, the relationship is much stronger.

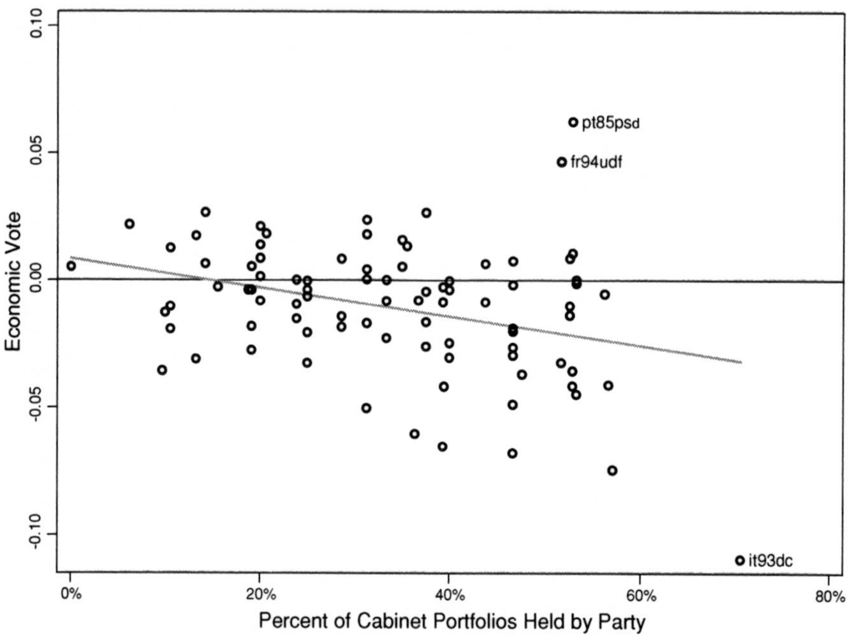

Figure 9.7. Economic vote and share of cabinet seats, cabinet partner parties only. Economic Vote for Cabinet Partners = 0.007 (1.25) − 0.057 (2.42) ×% of Cabinet Seats Held. R^2 = 0.10. Observations = 84.[22]

Thus far, we have examined how four different dimensions of administrative responsibility impact the distribution of the economic vote across parties. For presidential systems, we found that presidential parties that command a legislative majority have a greater economic vote than presidential parties that do not. Similarly, we found that the economic vote of prime ministerial parties is largest when the prime minister leads a majority single-party cabinet, smaller when the prime minister leads a majority coalition or minority single-party cabinet, and smallest when the prime ministerial party leads a minority coalition cabinet. Likewise, we showed that a party's share of the economic vote is tied closely to its role in government: prime ministerial parties experience the most economic voting, coalition partners less, and opposition parties the least.[23]

[22] OLS regression is with standard errors robust to heteroskedacticity and to non-independence between observations of the same party in different surveys. Numbers in parentheses are t-ratios.

[23] Of course, here we mean only those opposition parties that experience a "negative economic vote" when economic perceptions worsen. Other opposition parties may (and usually do) have large "positive economic votes."

Furthermore, control of the finance ministry increases a party's economic vote. Finally, we found that each party's share of cabinet portfolios, a summary gauge of a party's level of administrative responsibility, impacts its economic vote.

THE DISTRIBUTION OF ADMINISTRATIVE RESPONSIBILITY AND OVERALL ECONOMIC VOTING

The previous section was concerned with how the distribution of the economic vote across parties depends on the distribution of administrative responsibility. In this section, we change our focus: instead of focusing on parties, we ask how aggregate features of the distribution of administrative responsibility (i.e., whether it is concentrated or diffuse) impact the overall level of economic voting in an election. Specifically, the second general hypothesis that we proposed at the beginning of this chapter was that as the status quo distribution of administrative responsibility over parties becomes more equal, the smaller was the overall economic vote.

To test this hypothesis, we construct a measure of the concentration of administrative responsibility, where we initially use each party's share of cabinet ministries to indicate its share of administrative responsibility and later construct a more general measure that accounts for opposition influence on policy making. Specifically, given n parties in an election, we can define an associated hypothetical distribution of responsibility in which all parties get equal shares of responsibility. Formally, this is just a vector – call it δ – in which each party's share of responsibility is $1/n$. Our theory suggests that this vector of equal shares is the distribution of responsibility that will lead to the *least* amount of economic voting in an election. We can then define a corresponding vector consisting of the real shares of administrative responsibility for each party in a given case. If we call this vector λ, then the vector distance between λ and δ is an intuitive measure of the degree to which responsibility is concentrated in the system.[24] If administrative responsibility is equally shared across parties, then the elements of λ will be equal to the elements of δ and the vector distance will be zero no matter how many parties are in the election. Likewise, the distance between the two vectors will be greatest when administrative responsibility is concentrated on one party. One potential drawback of the measure is that while its lower bound is always zero, its upper bound – which, again,

[24] The vector distance is just the square root of the summed squared differences in the elements of the two vectors.

occurs when one party has all the administrative responsibility – will differ depending on the number of parties. Specifically, the more parties in the system, the bigger this upper bound will be. If one thinks that voters see power as more concentrated as the number of parties excluded from power is bigger, then this differing upper bound is appropriate. However, if (for example) voters perceive power as equally concentrated when one party holds all the power in a two-party system and when one party holds all the power in a five-party system, then we need to normalize this distance by dividing by the upper bound. We report results using the second strategy, though the choice is not empirically consequential. We call this measure *concentration of responsibility* and it can take values between zero (equality) and 1 (complete concentration of responsibility in one party).

The results of our analysis of the impact the concentration of responsibility on the economic vote of the prime minister is provided graphically, along with the corresponding bivariate regression results, in Figure 9.8. The results of the analysis support the hypothesized negative relationship – more concentrated responsibility results in higher levels of economic voting. The flatter of the two regression lines includes all the cases and the steeper one excludes the cases on the right-hand side of the figure in which power is completely concentrated in a single party.

This evidence thus supports our second hypothesis. However, it is based on a measure of the concentration of responsibility that is built from the distribution of cabinet portfolios exclusively. Consequently, it does not capture dispersion in the distribution of administrative responsibility that is due to an institutionally strong opposition or the majority/minority status of the government.[26] With respect to the first of these factors, we would expect administrative responsibility to be more widely shared when legislative institutions give the opposition significant power over policy making and an institutional ability to review and alter the decisions of the executive. With respect to the second factor, we have already discussed

[25] Estimates are from OLS regression with standard errors robust to heteroskedacticity and to nonindependence between observations of the same party in different surveys. Numbers in parentheses are t-ratios. For the U.S. case, the presidential party is coded as holding all administrative responsibility and only presidential election studies are used.

[26] In contrast, the coalition status of the government is captured in the distribution of cabinet portfolios because single-party cabinets will necessarily have all portfolios held by a single party.

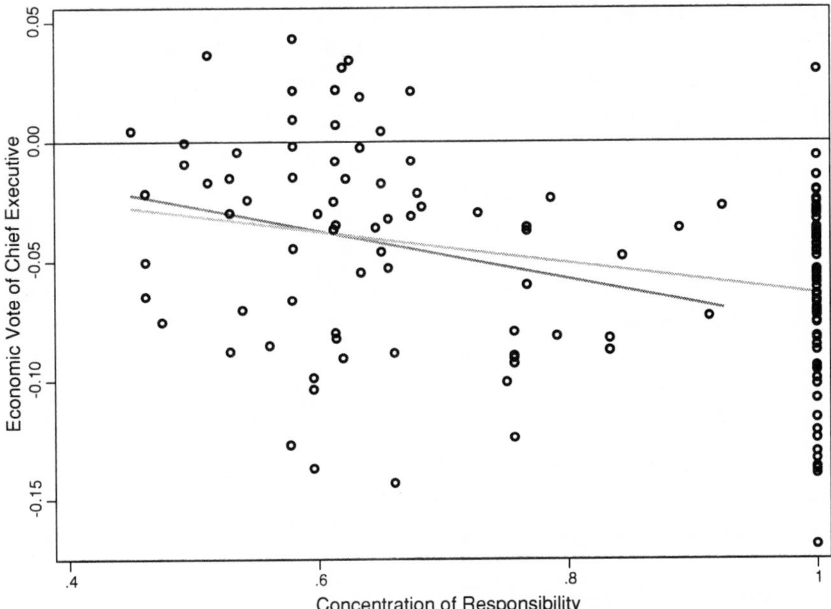

Figure 9.8. Concentration of the distribution of responsibility and economic voting for the chief executive. The flatter regression line corresponds to the following regression: Economic Vote of Chief Executive = −0.002 (0.08) −0.066 (2.81)* Concentration of Responsibility. $R^2 = 0.10$. Observations = 152.[25] The steeper line excludes the cases in which concentration of responsibility equals 1.

the idea that oppositions may be empowered relative to the executive when the cabinet does not control a majority of seats in the legislature. This general expectation, as per our previous discussion, may be different for single-party minority governments versus coalition minority governments because the former may obtain sole control of the government exactly because they occupy an unassailable bargaining position in the legislature.

With these ideas in mind, we seek to develop a measure akin to the concentration of authority measure used previously but one that weights opposition parties more heavily in situations of single-party minority or coalition minority government and institutionally powerful oppositions. We do so in two steps. First, we construct an index of opposition influence that combines information on the institutional strength of the opposition in each of our countries with the majority status of the government. Next, we normalize this measure to vary between zero and 1 and use it to build a linear combination of the cabinet seat share and legislative seat share of each party. The justification for the second step is simply that the distribution of policy-making power in a system in which the executive was powerless relative to the legislature would be well approximated by the distribution of legislative seats. In contrast, in a system in which the cabinet had all the power, legislative seats would be meaningless and only the distribution of cabinet seats would be relevant. Thus, for intermediate cases in which opposition influence is between these extremes, we combine these two distributions, mixed by an appropriate weight for the extent of opposition influence.

We develop an appropriate weight for mixing the cabinet seat and legislative-seat distributions by focusing on two institutional distinctions. First, we distinguish three kinds of cabinets and give them decreasing scores for susceptibility to opposition influence: coalition minority governments (the most susceptible to opposition influence), single-party minority governments (the next most susceptible to opposition influence), and all majority governments (the least susceptible to opposition influence). Second, we measure the institutional strength of the opposition using information from Powell (2000). Powell uses four institutional features of legislatures to assign countries to high, medium, and low categories of institutional strength of the opposition. The four features are (1) whether the legislature has a large number of standing committees that mirror the government ministries, (2) whether committee chairs are controlled by the government or shared by the opposition, (3) whether the government controls the legislative agenda, and (4) whether the government limits the ability of the committees to amend proposed legislation. The resulting classification of countries is provided in Table 9.7.[27] It is identical to Powell's classifications except for Italy, since our coding of Powell's four variables for our cases gave Italy a score that put it in the "high" category as opposed to "medium" (where Powell has classified it).[28]

With these data and the data on the majority status of the government, we created a weight for each case in the data that took a value of 1 when the strength of the opposition was high and the cabinet was a minority coalition and zero when the strength of the opposition was low and the cabinet was a majority (either coalition or single party). Intermediate

[27] These institutional features vary little over our period and so we classify each country for the whole period.

[28] Giving the four factors equal weight gives Italy the same score as most of the other countries in the "high" category and a greater score than the others in the "medium" categories.

Table 9.7. *Classification of Institutional Strength of the Opposition*

High	Medium	Low
Belgium, Denmark, Germany, Italy, Netherlands, Norway, Spain, Sweden	Canada, United States	Australia, France, Greece, Ireland, New Zealand, United Kingdom

From Powell (2000), with one exception.

cases fell between these extremes.[29] The distribution of this weight for the countries included in the analyses is in the Appendix to this chapter. To create our new measure of the concentration of administrative responsibility, we used this weight, as described previously, to form a linear combination of the vector of cabinet-seat shares and legislative-seat shares for the parties. Specifically, if c_i is party *i*'s cabinet-seat share, s_i is its legislative seat share, and φ is the opposition influence weight for the case, then the party's share of administrative responsibility is $(1 - \varphi)c_i + \varphi\, s_i$. This measure will sum to 1 across all the parties and can be used in the procedure described in the last section to create a measure of the extent to which the real distribution of responsibility differs from an equal distribution. This new measure of concentration of responsibility is graphed against the economic vote of the prime minister in Figure 9.9.

This graph looks similar to Figure 9.8, as it should, because the variable on the x-axis is constructed, in part, from the one used in that figure. The result of accounting for opposition influence in our measure of the concentration of responsibility is reflected in the differences between the figures. Specifically, the current graph includes cases with considerably more dispersed responsibility than the previous one. For example, all of the Norwegian cases in our sample had single-party minority governments and a strong legislative committee system but score a 1 on our previous measure of concentration of responsibility because one party holds all the cabinet portfolios. However, the current measure scores the four Norwegian cases around 0.5.

Despite these (and other) differences in the data, the impact of using this index on the relationship is not large and the implied substantive effect of

[29] Institutional strength of opposition was coded 0 for low, 1 for medium, and 2 for high. Majority status of the government was coded 0 for majority, 1 for single-party minority, and 2 for coalition minority. The opposition influence weight was calculated as follows: (institutional strength of opposition score + majority status score)/4.

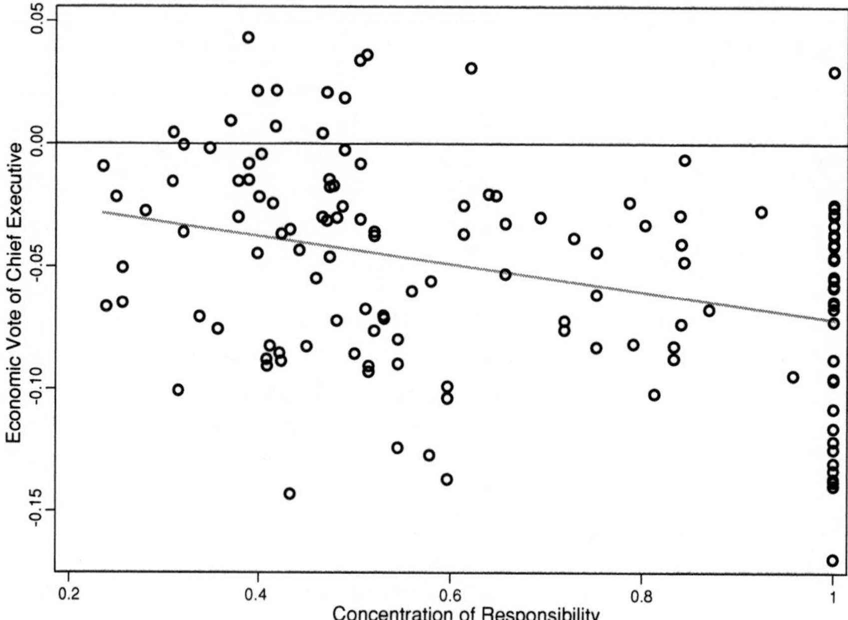

Figure 9.9. Concentration of the distribution of administrative responsibility and economic voting for the chief executive, opposition influence included. Economic Vote of Chief Executive = −0.015 (1.18) −0.057 (3.40) × Concentration of Responsibility with Opposition Influence. $R^2 = 0.10$. Observations = 137.[30]

concentration of responsibility on the economic vote is not significantly different in the two cases. However, the new measure is directionally consistent with our expectations – that is, the impact of an empowered opposition on the distribution of administrative responsibility is to make it more equal and that depresses the magnitude of economic voting in the system. Overall, however, this impact is quite small compared to the impact of the distribution of responsibility that stems from the role that parties play in the cabinet.

THE CONCENTRATION OF RESPONSIBILITY IN AN INTERACTIVE MODEL

As we discussed in Chapter 4, the two-stage analysis reported herein can be replicated employing a one-step approach in which we combine our

30 We measure *concentration of responsibility* using the first of the two measures that were described in the last section because we wanted to maximize the number of cases in this analysis.

individual-level datasets and estimate a random-coefficients, multilevel model with a more limited, uniform specification of the individual-level vote-choice models. By including interactions between economic perceptions and *concentration of responsibility*, we can capture how differences in this contextual variable impact the individual decision to vote for the chief executive's party. We estimate the same core model described for the random coefficient model in Chapter 7.[31] The basic form of the model, with the size variable, is:

$$v_{ik} \sim Bin(\pi_{ik})$$

$$logit(\pi_{ik}) = \beta_{ok} + \beta_{1k}Worse_{ik} + \beta_{2k}Better_{ik} + \phi_1 \text{Ideology}_{ik} + \phi_2(\text{Ideology}_{ik} * \text{CR\_Ideology}_k) \quad (9.1)$$

$$\beta_{0k} = \gamma_{00} + \gamma_{01}Size_k + \gamma_{01}CR_k + \omega_{0k} \quad (9.2)$$

$$\beta_{1k} = \gamma_{10} + \gamma_{11}CR_k + \omega_{1k} \quad (9.3)$$

$$\beta_{2k} = \gamma_{20} + \gamma_{21}CR_k + \omega_{2k} \quad (9.4)$$

where *Bin* just indicates that the dependent variable is distributed according to an appropriate binomial distribution with parameter π_{jk}. *CR* is *concentration of responsibility* and we assume the errors are distributed according to a multivariate normal distribution, with variances $\sigma^2_{\omega 1}$, $\sigma^2_{\omega 2}$, and $\sigma^2_{\omega 3}$ and covariances $\sigma^2_{\omega 2,\omega 2}$, $\sigma^2_{\omega 1,\omega 3}$, and $\sigma^2_{\omega 2,\omega 3}$. Because we expect support for the chief executive to be negatively related to economic perceptions, we expect $\lambda_{10} < 0$ and $\lambda_{20} > 0$ (recall that the baseline category is voters who think the economy has stayed the same). Furthermore, since greater *concentration of responsibility* is expected to increase the size of the economic vote, we expect $\lambda_{11} < 0$ and $\lambda_{21} > 0$ (because this will increase the difference between the overall impact of better versus worse perceptions).

Table 9.8 provides the estimates for the unknown parameters in equations (9.1) – (9.4). These estimates clearly support the hypothesis because all the coefficients are statistically significant and in the expected direction. In particular, *concentration of responsibility* interacted with positive economic evaluations is positive and significant and its interaction with negative evaluations is negative and significant. Thus, this pooled, multilevel model tells exactly the same story as the second-stage estimates from

[31] The estimates were obtained using the PQL second-order linearization method outlined in Goldstein (1995). Diagnostics on estimated residuals at Level 2 suggest that the assumption of normal variance in the Level 2 coefficients is not violated.

Table 9.8. *Multilevel Model of Effective Number of Concentration of Executive Responsibility and Economic Voting*

Left-Right Self-Placement (deviation from mean)	0.49
	(0.01)
Left-Right Self-Placement × Leftist PM (Leftist PM is an indicator variable)	−0.75
	(0.01)
Voter Perceives Economy Got Better (indicator variable)	0.46
	(0.03)
Voter Perceives Economy Got Worse (indicator variable)	−0.58
	(0.03)
Concentration of Responsibility (deviation from mean)	0.84
	(0.15)
Voter Perceives Economy Got Better *Concentration of Responsibility	0.58
	(0.15)
Voter Perceives Economy Got Worse *Concentration of Responsibility	−0.97
	(0.15)
Size of Chief Executive's Party	4.61
	(0.25)
Constant	−2.21
	(0.07)
$\sigma^2_{\omega 1}$	0.07
$\sigma^2_{\omega 2}$	0.08
$\sigma^2_{\omega 3}$	0.07
$\sigma_{\omega 1,\omega 2}$	−0.04
$\sigma_{\omega 1,\omega 3}$	−0.02
$\sigma_{u\omega 2,\omega 3}$	−0.03
N	201,876

Standard errors listed below logit coefficients. All coefficients are statistically significant at $p < 0.1$. In the case of the United States, the dependent variable is vote for the party of the president. Congressional election studies are excluded.

the two-stage method – shared power decreases the *economic vote of the chief executive.*

SUMMARY

This purpose of this chapter was to explore the influence of the distribution of administrative responsibility on both the extent of economic voting and its distribution across parties. Our contextual theory of rational retrospective economic voting suggests that voters know the distribution of administrative responsibility and that, along with other information in the responsibility augmented competency signal, this information alters the weight that voters assign to movements in the previous economy in their vote calculus. These theoretical expectations were expressed in two general empirical hypotheses relating the distribution of the economic vote across parties to each party's share of the economic vote, as well as to the overall size of the economic vote.

The empirical results in this chapter are uniformly consistent with these hypotheses. Specifically, we find that in presidential systems, economic voting is higher under unified as opposed to divided government; single-party prime ministers tend to experience more economic voting than presidents; prime ministers leading single-party majority cabinets have a larger share of the economic vote than prime ministers leading coalition or minority cabinets; in coalition cabinets, prime ministerial parties receive the lion's share of the overall economic vote and their cabinet partners most of the rest; parties that control the finance ministry have a larger economic vote than parties who do not, and the size of this effect is almost as large as the impact of holding the prime ministry; and a governing party's economic vote is closely tied to its share of cabinet seats. Finally, consistent with our second hypothesis about the distribution of responsibility and the overall level of the economic vote, we find that there will be more economic voting in an election in which the distribution of administrative responsibility is more concentrated around a small number of parties.

All these empirical results support what has become an impressive body of empirical evidence (at both the aggregate and individual level) linking administrative responsibility to economic voting (e.g., Anderson, 2000; Powell and Whitten, 1993). Given the strength of our results and its consistency with previous work, we think it is safe to conclude that the distribution of responsibility is an important factor conditioning the economic vote in Western democracies.

Our results are also consistent with the theoretical model described in Chapter 8 and so may lend some support to the view of economic voting described there. However, we recognize that the empirical work in this chapter does nothing to distinguish our explanation from other theoretical possibilities. Most of these possibilities build informally on the clarity of responsibility argument, which assumes that the main factor that prevents economic voting in situations of diffuse responsibility is the voter's inability to determine who is responsible for policy making. Our theoretical story differs in that we assume voters are fully informed about the distribution of responsibility across parties and they use this information in a rational fashion to condition the magnitude of their economic vote. Thus, the economic vote is depressed when responsibility is diffuse, not because of the voter's ignorance about the roles that parties play in government but because they must use the same amount of information (observed movements in the economy) to make more complicated inferences about party competence. Of course, the existence of these different theoretical possibilities does nothing to detract from the strength and importance of the empirical result itself, but simply argues for future work that seeks different kinds of empirical leverage that would allow us to distinguish between them.

Appendix 9.1. *Influence of the Opposition Weight Used to Construct Concentration of Responsibility Measure that Was Used in Table 9.12 and Figure 9.10*

	Opposition Influence Weight				
	0	0.25	0.50	0.75	1
Australia	6	0	0	0	0
Belgium	0	0	12	0	0
Canada	0	4	0	0	0
Denmark	0	0	3	1	10
France	9	2	1	0	0
Germany	0	0	12	0	0
Greece	11	0	0	0	0
Ireland	8	3	0	0	0
Italy	0	0	6	0	0
Netherlands	0	0	12	0	0
New Zealand	2	1	0	0	0
Norway	0	0	0	4	0
Spain	0	0	6	4	0
Sweden	0	0	0	4	0
United Kingdom	16	0	0	0	0
Total	52	10	52	13	10

10

The Pattern of Contention and the Economic Vote

The previous chapter established that voters condition their economic vote on the current distribution of policy-making responsibility among parties competing for election. In this chapter, we examine whether the data also support our theoretical proposition that voters condition their economic vote on the extent to which parties are "in contention" for policy-making responsibility in the future. Our theory assumes that voters know the extent to which different parties and coalitions of parties contend for significant shares of policy-making responsibility. We support this assumption with survey evidence from three countries that shows that voters are surprisingly well informed about the pattern of cabinet contention, even in very complex coalitional systems. With this assurance that, in the few cases for which we have direct evidence, our information assumptions are plausible, we next propose two different methods for measuring beliefs about cabinet contention in the larger number of cases in our sample (for which direct survey data about beliefs are not available). Finally, in the rest of the chapter, we use these measures to test three general hypotheses (all implied by the theory in Chapter 8) about how the pattern of contention for policy-making responsibility conditions economic voting.

VOTER BELIEFS ABOUT THE PATTERN OF CONTENTION

Our model of economic voting assumes that voters have knowledge about which parties or coalitions of parties are likely to form the government or otherwise participate in policy making. Only with such knowledge can they assess whether their vote can make a difference in shaping the future distribution of administrative responsibility. We do not, however, have direct measures of the voters' assessment of these patterns of contention for most of the studies in our sample.[1] Consequently, in this chapter, we pursue an alternative strategy: we measure voters' beliefs about that pattern of contention by identifying and measuring the sources of these beliefs. If we can do so successfully, we can test our theoretical hypotheses by examining whether variation in the sources of beliefs leads to the expected variation in retrospective economic voting.

We begin by providing evidence that voters are actually capable of forming sensible expectations about the outcome of the process by which governments are forming and the distribution of policy-making authority. This evidence comes from a set of surveys that were conducted in the week before the Danish elections of 2001, the Norwegian elections of 2001, and the Dutch elections of 2002 – three elections in which the coalition possibilities were unusually varied and unsettled in the weeks before the elections. The surveys asked respondents which party was most likely to obtain the prime ministry following the election and which parties where most likely to join a given prime minister in the cabinet. Our brief summary of the survey results suggests that even in these very complex cabinet-formation situations, voters had little trouble understanding and forecasting the likely outcome of the coalition-formation process.[2]

The 2001 Norwegian election was, by all accounts, particularly unpredictable. Eight major parties stood for election (and were included in the survey) and, in the months leading up to the election, the incumbent Labour government steadily lost support until it was running even with the Conservatives as the election approached.[3] For the first time, it was possible that Labour would not win the most votes. This fact and the failure of any group of parties to commit to rule together after the election made the situation particularly uncertain.

In Denmark, the election held on November 20, 2001, was also unusual.[4] Leading up to the election, the Social Democratic incumbent government was losing ground to the Liberal Party and, for the first time

[1] There are, though, some survey-based studies demonstrating that voters perceive these patterns of contention and condition their voting behavior in a fashion that is consistent with strategic voting theories (Duch and Palmer, 2002b; Johnston et al., 1992: 197–211).

[2] Complete details of the survey are available at http://www.nuffield.ox.ac.uk/economicvoting.

[3] The parties were the Labour Party, the Conservatives, the Christian People's Party (KrF), the Center Party, the Liberals, the Socialist Left, and the Red Alliance.

[4] The main parties in the election were the Social Democrats, the Liberals, the Conservatives, the Socialist People's Party, the Radical Liberals, the Center Democrats, the Christian People's Party, the Danish People's Party, and the Progress Party.

since 1920, it looked like the Liberals would replace the Social Democrats as the largest party in Denmark. At the same time, far right parties such as the Danish People's Party (DPP) were doing very well in the polls and made the issue of reforming Denmark's liberal immigration laws (and the ability of these immigrants to access a generous welfare system) the main issue of the campaign. The electoral weakness of the Social Democrats and the popularity of relatively extreme parties opened up the postelection coalition possibilities because it made the formation of a nonextremist rightist majority or a leftist majority more difficult.

Finally, the Dutch election of May 2002 was perhaps even more uncertain (and certainly more dramatic) than the Danish and Norwegian elections. Support of the incumbent "purple" coalition of the PvdA, D66, and the Liberals (VVD) had been declining and it seemed unlikely the incumbent government would reform, although certainly some of the partners might be in the next government. Indeed, the incumbent government itself had been a novel coalition that would have been unheard of in the many years of dominance by the Christian center parties. However, what really introduced uncertainty into the coalition possibilities was the rise of two right-wing populist parties, Livable Netherlands and Ljist Pim Fortuyn.[5]

The first evidence about voter beliefs in these elections that we examine comes from a question asking voters which party would most likely provide the prime minister following the election. The distribution of responses in each of the three cases is provided in Table 10.1. It is clear that in each case, responses were concentrated on only two or three parties, with essentially no responses identifying other parties (Pim Fortuyn providing the only possible exception).

We can get an even better sense of how well voters do at identifying the likely prime ministers by comparing the aggregate distribution of responses to predictions from a statistical model of prime ministerial selection that mirrors those that have been used successfully in the literature to predict the identity of the prime minister in large samples of elections (Warwick, 1996).[6]

Clearly, voter's beliefs about which party will become prime minister are quite close to the predictions that political scientists make. In Norway

[5] Of course, the assassination of Pim Fortuyn just days before the election also complicated the situation, but the survey, which was in the field at the time, was suspended as a result of this event and so all the respondents (over half the target of one thousand) were interviewed before this.

[6] The variables usually used include functions of each party's size, change in size, ideological position, and history of incumbency.

Table 10.1. *Voters Beliefs about Prime-Ministerial Contention*

	Number of Respondents Who Chose Party	% of Respondents Who Chose Party	Probability of Becoming PM for Various Plausible Values of Predictors
Norway 2001			
Labour	319	33%	8–82%
KrF	306	32%	6–45%
Conservative	139	14%	2–55%
Total for Top 3	764	79%	96–99%
Progress	7	.7%	< 2%
Center	2	.2%	< 2%
Socialist Left	1	.1%	< 2%
Liberal	1	.1%	< 2%
Red Alliance	0	0%	< 2%
Another Party	0	0%	–
Don't Know	191	20%	–
Total	775	100%	100%
Denmark 2001			
Social Democrats	174	17%	36%
Liberals	760	73%	56%
Conservatives	2	.2%	1%
Total for Top 3	936	89%	93%
Socialist PP	0	0%	< 1%
Radical Liberals	0	0%	< 1%
Center Democrats	0	0%	< 2%
Christian PP	0	0%	< 1%
Unity List	0	0%	< 1%
Danish PP	0	0%	< 3%
Progress	0	0%	< 1%
Another Party	0	0%	–
Don't Know	110	11%	–
	936	100%	100–100%
Netherlands 2002			
PvdA	115	20%	12%
Liberals	88	15%	6%
CDA	190	32%	52%
Total for Top 3	393	67%	70%
D66	3	.5%	1%
Green Left	8	1.5%	4%
United Christians	0	0%	2%
SGP	0	0%	2%
Pim Fortuyn	29	5%	16%

	Number of Respondents Who Chose Party	% of Respondents Who Chose Party	Probability of Becoming PM for Various Plausible Values of Predictors
Live. Netherlands	0	0%	2%
VSP	0	0%	3%
Another Party	0	0%	–
Don't Know	156	26%	–
	589	100%	100%

The predictors were largest party, seat shares, change in shares, median party, and previous PM (Stevenson, 2003). For Norway, predictors were set at plausible values given the preelectoral polls (for vote shares and who would be the largest party). Also, the identity of the previous PM was varied between the Labour Party and the KrF to reflect the fact that both had been incumbent PMs since the last election. Predictors were set at plausible values given the preelectoral polls (for vote shares and who would be the largest party). For other cases, the variation in predictions from different plausible values of the predictors was not large; so only one value is given.

and Denmark, both the statistical models and the surveys concentrate almost all the probability on the same parties, whereas in the Netherlands, both our models and the voters are more uncertain. It seems then that, at least with respect to beliefs about which parties are in contention for the post of prime minister, voters are very well informed. Indeed, the distribution of beliefs seems to pick out the same parties as our statistical models and evidence about as much overall uncertainty as the statistical models.

Respondents in the study were also asked to indicate which parties they thought would most likely join a given prime minister in the cabinet. Table 10.2 only summarizes these results for Denmark because the results for Norway and the Netherlands suggest the same substantive message.

This table reveals a correspondence between the respondents' beliefs and the predictions of the statistical model. There are no large disagreements for Social Democratic cabinets, and for the Liberals the discrepancies are only for the Progress Party and the Conservatives. In the case of the Conservatives, voters were fairly certain the Liberals would ask the Conservatives to join them in a coalition government if they obtained the prime ministry, and this was widely discussed as a viable partnership (which, in fact, occurred). However, because of the fairly substantial ideological distance between the parties (at least in the data on which

Table 10.2. *Beliefs about Cabinet Partnership, Given Beliefs about Which Party Will Become PM, Denmark, 2001*

	If Social Democrats Obtain the Prime Ministry		If Liberals Obtain the Prime Ministry	
Party	% of Respondents Indicating Party Was a Likely Partner	Predicted Probability of Becoming a Cabinet Partner[1]	% of Respondents Indicating Party Was a Likely Partner	Predicted Probability of Becoming a Cabinet Partner
Social Democrat	–	–	0.021	0.025
Liberal	0.063	0.022	–	–
Conservatives	0.040	0.098	0.762	0.319
SPP	0.454	0.451	0.009	0.011
Rad. Liberals	0.563	0.642	0.084	0.024
Center Dem	0.149	0.153	0.289	0.218
Christian PP	0.023	0.123	0.270	0.277
Unity List	0.098	0.107	0	0.004
Danish PP	0.028	0.012	0.233	0.347
Progress	0	0.010	0.005	0.310

The predictors of cabinet-partner selection were the party's seat share, changes in seat shares, median party, being in the previous cabinet with the designated PM, and ideological distance from the designated PM.

the predictions rely), the statistical models find this outcome less likely. With respect to a Liberal/Progress Party partnership, voters disagreed with the predictions of the empirical model, believing strongly that Progress would not join a Liberal cabinet. This outcome results from the empirical model's inability to distinguish between the Danish People's Party and the Progress Party (while voters seem quite able to make the distinction). Both parties are on the extreme right, but the Danish People's Party had recently supplanted Progress as the principal alternative in this region of the political space. Voters seem to have been aware of this changing of the guard whereas the empirical model missed it.

It seems then that even these differences underscore the main message from this example: voters have a good sense of which parties are likely to join a given prime minister in the cabinet. Indeed, if they put these beliefs together with their beliefs about who is in contention to become prime minister, they should have little trouble distinguishing likely cabinet combinations from unlikely ones. Overall, the evidence suggests that voters, even in complex coalitional systems, do have well-formed beliefs about the likely outcomes of coalition formation.[7]

Because we do not have survey measures of the voters' beliefs about government formation for the large number of cases in our sample, we instead use a more indirect approach. Specifically, we try to identify the sources of voter beliefs about the pattern of cabinet contention and then use measures of these sources as proxies for the beliefs themselves. We develop two sets of measures. The first measurement strategy adopts an "historical approach." It assumes that voters' expectations about the current pattern of governmental contention among the parties will reflect historical patterns of cabinet participation. We develop a number of specific "historical" measures; each is built from information on the history of office holding between January 1960 and the date of the survey corresponding to the data point. Thus, the average voter's "memory" in our surveys extends from twenty to forty years into the past and always includes most of her adult political life (the average respondent is about forty years old at the time of the surveys).

The second general measurement strategy we use assumes that voters form their beliefs about the future distribution of executive authority rationally using some "model" of the process of government formation and all the available information relevant to that process. Thus, we can build plausible measures of the rational voter's beliefs about the likely outcomes of government formation from estimates of well-specified statistical models that predict which parties will govern based on observable variables available to the voter at the time of the election (we call this the "rational approach"). The specifics of the statistical models will vary depending on the systems under consideration (i.e., the voter's "model" of government formation – and, hence, the best statistical model – will likely be different in systems in which the executive is usually composed of a coalition versus a single party) and are explained in the relevant sections here.

Patterns of Contention among Opposition Parties

The first hypothesis that we examine concerns how the pattern of contention impacts the distribution of economic voting among opposition

[7] Kedar (2005a, 2005b) incorporates a similar view of the voter's knowledge of coalition-formation outcomes and presents data suggesting that their voting decisions compensate for expected policy outcomes that result from the composition of these coalitions.

parties. Specifically, for multiparty oppositions, all the versions of our contextual theory of rational economic voting that made a distinction between opposition and incumbent parties implied that *economic voting will be more important to the support of opposition parties that are members of more, and more competitive, alternative governments than it will be for other opposition parties that are not* (see, for example, equation [8.27]).[8]

To examine this hypothesis empirically, we begin with the historical approach to measuring voter beliefs about the governmental contention of opposition parties. Our hypothesis says that for opposition parties, as $g'_j \sum_{\mathbf{g}' \in \mathbf{A}} P_{\mathbf{gg}'}$ gets bigger, opposition party j's economic vote will get bigger; where g'_j is an indicator variable equal to 1 if party j is a member of alternative cabinet **g'** and 0 otherwise. In other words, as j is a member of more alternatives with larger values of $P_{\mathbf{gg}'}$, then it will have a larger economic vote. To build a measure of this quantity for some party j, we need an estimate of $P_{\mathbf{gg}'}$ for each possible alternative cabinet and then we can simply sum these estimates over all the alternatives cabinets of which party j is a member. In the historical method, our strategy is to estimate $P_{\mathbf{gg}'}$ as the historical frequency with which the cabinet alternative $\mathbf{g}'$ was actually in office (going back to January 1960).[9] Clearly, this will be zero for any alternative that has never been in office and will move toward one as the coalition has spent more time in office. We calculate the measure monthly from 1960 and use the data point for each party for the month in which the election survey was conducted. For example, if the election survey under consideration was conducted in January 1980 and a specific alternative coalition had been in power for eighteen months in the 1970s, then we assign its chances of forming as 18/240 (where the denominator is the number of months between January 1960 and January 1980).

Figure 10.1 gives an example of the measure for Germany and illustrates how well it captures our intuition about which parties in Germany

[8] We use the term "government" generically to mean a single-party executive, a coalition cabinet, or a distribution of responsibility. When a hypothesis does not refer to all these types of governments, we use the more specific designations. We also call the extent to which a party is a member of more, and more competitive, alternative governments its level of governmental contention, or cabinet contention as appropriate, or sometimes (when there is no confusion) just its level of contention.

[9] Because $P_{\mathbf{gg}'}$ is the probability that cabinet $\mathbf{g}'$ ties with the incumbent cabinet **g**, this measurement strategy assumes that a cabinet's historical frequency of ruling is not just positively related to its chances of forming in the current period but also to its chances of tying with the current incumbent. Thus, the measure assumes the current incumbent is itself competitive.

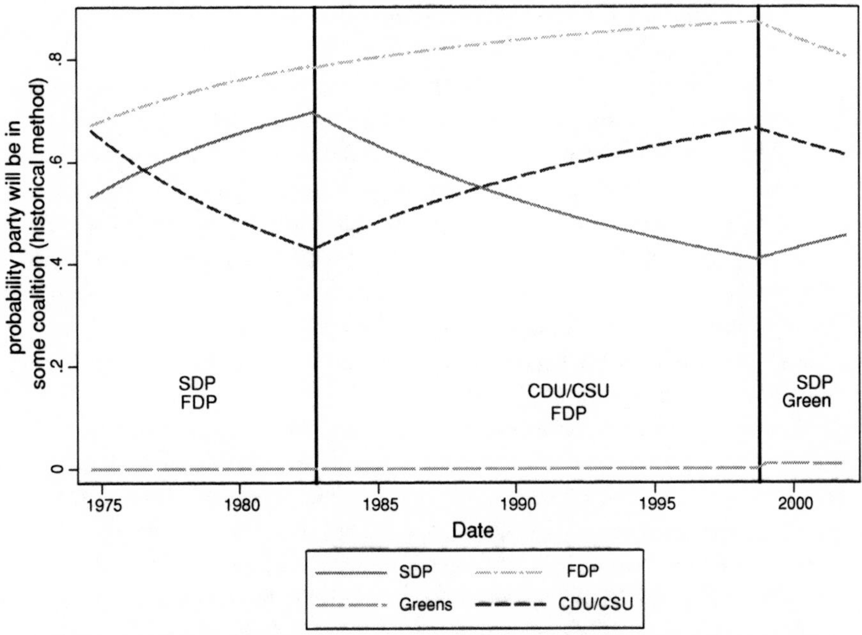

Figure 10.1. Historical measure of cabinet contention by party for Germany. Each time point in the line is calculated by first calculating the historical frequency between the time point and January 1960 that each possible alternative cabinet has served and then summing these over all alternative coalitions of which the party was a member. The vertical lines are periods with different incumbents and the incumbent cabinet is listed in the bottom half of the graph.

are (and are not) members of the competitive alternative cabinets. Notice, for example, that the score for the FDP is high throughout the period. This is because the FDP is a member of both of the coalition alternatives that have historically ruled in Germany (the CDU/CSU – FDP coalition and the SDP-FDP coalition).[10] Likewise, for both the SDP and the CDU/CSU, the measure suggests about a 50 percent chance of entering government. The measure also moves over time in an intuitive way – as a party spends more time as the incumbent, the measure increases and as it is out of government (thus, by definition, not a member of one of the competitive alternatives), its score decreases.

Notice that the historical frequency of rule for each possible alternative cabinet sums to 1 across all cabinets in any given month (but not over

[10] The only reason this number is not 1, is because of the short-lived SDP-CDU/CSU coalition in the 1960s and the CDU/CSU-DP coalition that was in office when our measurement period started in January 1960.

parties – so the lines in the graph will not sum to 1). Furthermore, when we sum these frequencies across the coalitions of which a given party is a member (at one particular time point), the sum of this number will, by definition, be equal to the percentage of months since 1960 that the party has been in the cabinet. Thus, it is possible to calculate our measure without actually writing out all the possible coalitions and their historical frequencies – instead, we can simply calculate how often each party has been in a cabinet.[11] This also has the advantage that when we calculate the measure in this way, it is easier to modify it to include discounting, to deal with other special cases in the data, and to account not just for a party's record of cabinet participation but also how it participated (i.e., whether it was a PM or a partner).[12]

Figure 10.2 graphs, for multiparty systems (and surveys for which there are more than two opposition parties), the economic vote for each opposition party against its previous record of office-holding. The hypothesis (and measurement assumptions) suggests that voters will not consider opposition parties with short histories of cabinet participation likely members of competitive alternatives and so will have relatively muted economic votes.[13] This expectation is confirmed in Figure 10.2 (a large positive value here indicates that the opposition party is rewarded by perceptions of poor economic performance). Indeed, considering that the impact on economic voting of any one context interacts with other contexts in a multiple conjunctural relationship, we should expect to see, if our hypothesis is true, exactly the kind of wedge shape to the data that is apparent in Figure 10.2. That is, when parties have little experience as incumbents, the impact of the economy on their support will be low, but when they have a lot of experience, the impact of the economy on

[11] This works for opposition parties but not for incumbent parties, because for these parties we need to subtract the reformation probability of the incumbent cabinet from the sum (it is not included in the sum for opposition parties by definition).

[12] We have calculated both the measure described here and the simpler measures that we use in the text and they correlate at .99 for our sample. The only reason this correlation is not perfect is that some of the "parties" in our data set are actually party groups that were combined in the estimation of the economic vote. Such combinations are relatively rare, never cross the opposition/incumbency divide, and make sense ideologically. However, they do mean that the different parties in the group will have different histories of government service, and so to use them together, we have to average them at any given month. Consequently, there are slight deviations between the measures in some cases (the two measures are identical in 96 percent of the cases).

[13] We use the term "members of alternative governments" to generically include alternatives with only one party.

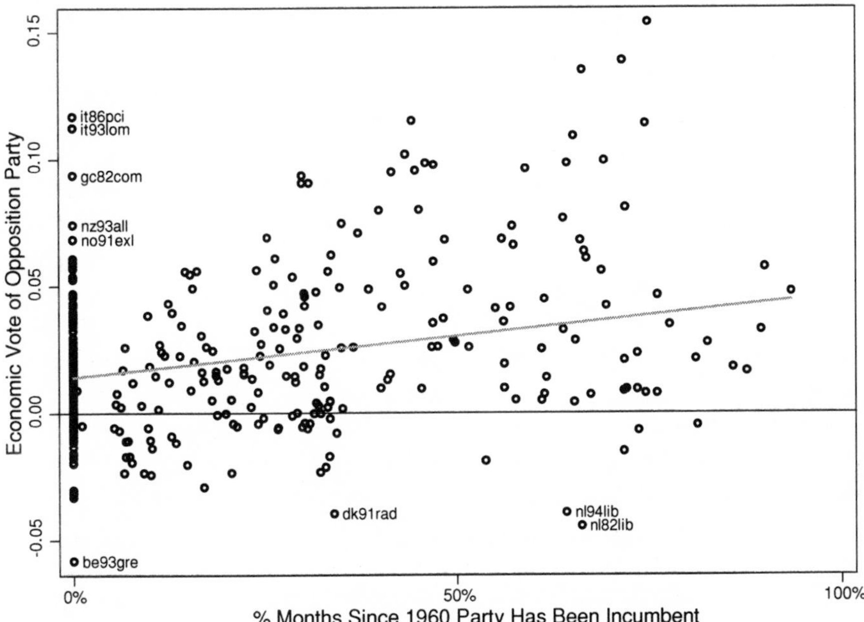

Figure 10.2. History of incumbency and the economic vote of opposition parties in multiparty systems. Only cases in which there were at least two opposition parties are included. The variable on the x-axis is equivalent to a measure (described in the text) that uses the historical method to calculate the probability that each opposition party will enter the cabinet as a member of some alternative.

their electoral support *may* be high, but may not be depending on other factors.

The main exceptions to the wedge-shaped pattern in this graph are the three cases in the upper-left corner of the graph that had sizeable economic votes but no previous experience in government (the Italian Lombard League in 1993, the Italian PCI in 1986, and the Greek Communists in 1982).[14] The exception of the Italian Lombard league likely reflects the inability of the historical record to capture voter beliefs at the

[14] The other two notable but less exceptional cases are the New Zealand Alliance in 1993 and the extreme left in Norway in 1991, which combines the Left Socialists and the Communists. In the first case, it is likely that the result for the Alliance (which was the alternative to the large Labour party in the opposition) reflects the impact of the voter's overwhelming concern with the 1993 referendum on electoral reform, which the Alliance supported and both large parties did not (Labour in opposition and the National Party in government). Although we controlled for voters' preferences on this referendum in the individual-level analysis of this case, it could be that the division between the Alliance on one side and Labour and the

time of this survey because it occurred just as the historical Italian party system was breaking down and a whole set of new alternatives to the previous political parties was emerging. As Verzichelli and Cotta (2000) put it, between 1992 and 1994, "new or previously excluded parties captured a significant part of the political space that the center parties had controlled.... Suddenly, all the parties gained a reasonable expectation to win access to the government."[15] Thus, at least with respect to the voters' beliefs about governmental contention, the Lombard League may have been seen as more of a contender than history would otherwise have suggested.

For the other two exceptions, we have no obvious explanations. In the case of the Italian PCI outlier in 1986, the five-party government (the DC, PSI, PRI, PSDI, and PLI) at the time included all the parties that had ever served in government after 1946, which may have left economic voters that wanted to vote against the government with little alternative other than to vote for the Communists. However, this plausible explanation for the *distribution* of the economic vote among the Italian parties can not explain why the *size* of the economic vote in this case was so large. Our theory says that rational economic voters faced with no competitive alternative to the incumbent (or alternative governments comprised of only incumbents) would simply not use the economy in their vote choice. Indeed, in the other three surveys in which the same situation occurred (1987, 1988, and 1990), the overall level of economic voting is quite low, as the theory predicts.

The Greek 1982 case presents even more of a mystery because it is only the most extreme case in a more general pattern of unexpected results for Greece. Specifically, in almost all of the surveys we have for Greece, our estimates reveal that when the Socialist PASOK is in power, the opposition party that is the primary recipient of the economic vote is not its principal rival, New Democracy, but rather the Communists.[16] In contrast, when New Democracy is in power, the economic vote shifts support between

National Party on the other reinforced in the mind of voters the role of the Alliance as the chief alternative to the current administration rather than Labour.

[15] In addition, the Lombard League had been around for some time at this point whereas the later restabilization of the new political system around two broad coalitions – that would leave Forza Italia and not the Lombard League as the leader of the right – had not yet emerged.

[16] In the individual-level estimates, we combine the Communist Party of the Interior with the Communist Party of the Exterior and add the EDA in 1982 and 1983 and the NAP in 1990 and 1993.

New Democracy and PASOK, as the theory predicts. We have no explanation for this result; however, as we noted earlier, the Greek case was the case in which our estimates of economic voting were the most uncertain and in which the individual models seemed most sensitive to specifications issues. The problem may lie in the estimation of the economic vote itself.

Despite these three exceptions, the evidence in Figure 10.2 supports the usefulness of the pattern of governmental contention in explaining the distribution of the economic vote across opposition parties. Before providing the statistical model corresponding to Figure 10.2 (and that accounts for the various dependencies in the data), we explore some alternative ways to conceptualize the relationship between a party's history of cabinet participation and economic voting and then examine all the corresponding statistical models in the same table.

In some countries, voters have come to expect a single party to control the cabinet and in others, voters may understand that the primary competition that shapes the membership of a coalition cabinet is the race for the prime ministry rather than for cabinet partnership (i.e., the *formateur* systems mentioned in Chapter 8). Indeed, no matter what kinds of cabinets usually form, the question of which party will provide the prime minister is a focus of speculation and media attention in every parliamentary system. This suggests that voters may pay more attention to and have better developed beliefs about the pattern of contention for the prime ministry rather than for cabinet membership in general (a contention supported to some extent by the survey data presented at the beginning of this chapter). Thus, we might expect the relationship between the governmental contention of opposition parties and economic voting to be even stronger when we measure beliefs about governmental contention using each party's history of holding the prime ministry rather than is history of incumbency in general.[17] Figure 10.3 provides this graph and confirms our expectation that an opposition party's history of service as the prime minister is strongly related to its economic vote.

In comparing Figure 10.3 to Figure 10.2, three additional exceptions to the expected wedge-shaped pattern emerge – all from Belgium. However,

[17] Like the previous measure, there are two equivalent ways of calculating this. First, one could estimate the probability with which each coalition alternative forms (counting coalitions with the same membership and different prime ministers as different alternatives) and then sum all these probabilities for cases in which a given party is prime minister. When the probability of the coalition forming is equal to its historical frequency, however, the resulting measure for each party will be equivalent to the historical frequency with which the party was prime minister.

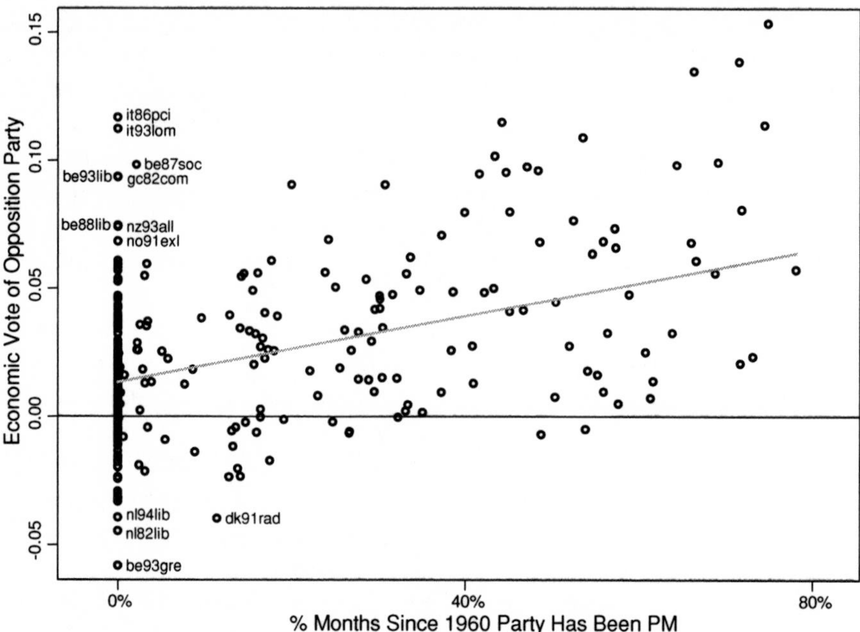

Figure 10.3. History of holding the prime ministry and the economic vote of opposition parties in multiparty systems. Only cases in which there were at least two opposition parties are included. The variable on the x-axis is equivalent to a measure that uses the historical method to calculate the probability that each opposition party will enter the cabinet as the prime minister in some alternative.

as we will see later, when we examine the other hypotheses implied by our theory, we find that these exceptions are really quite consistent with the more general logic of the theory that accounts for the various separate hypotheses in this chapter. Specifically, in systems (e.g., in Belgium) in which there is a perennial prime ministerial party that tends to form coalitions with different sets of smaller coalition partners (e.g., the Belgian Christians), the theory suggests that the economic vote should be concentrated on these contenders for cabinet partnership rather than on the dominant prime minister. Accordingly, in these contexts, there will be a number of contenders for cabinet partnership that should have relatively large economic votes even though they have had very little, if any, history of holding the prime ministry.

There are a number of additional ways that we can examine the relationships in Figure 10.2 and Figure 10.3. Specifically, we may first want to alter our measures of cabinet participation to account for the fact that most scholars who invoke adaptive or "historical" belief formation usually assume that people who form their beliefs in this way discount older information relative to more recent information. We accommodate this in our models by substituting the history of government service in the graphs with a measure that discounts this history so that service in the past is weighted less in voter beliefs than more recent service.

A second modification to these analyses is to focus on shares of the economic vote for opposition parties rather than absolute levels of the economic vote for these parties. This removes any influence of the magnitude of the economic vote from the measure and focuses instead on the distribution of the economic vote (whatever its overall size) across parties.[18] This distributional focus is useful, given that our theory implies that differences in the distribution of contention across parties should impact both the absolute size and the share of a party's economic vote.

Table 10.3 provides estimates of regression models for different combinations of these alternative specifications (in addition to estimates for the relationships graphed in Figure 10.2 and Figure 10.3). All of the models follow the procedures for specifying empirical models of contextual effects outlined in Chapter 4. Again, however, we should remember that these estimates are only approximate because they assume that the impact of the independent variables are additive, when we know that the appropriate functional relationship should account for multiple conjectural causation. In our graphs, this was apparent in the triangular patterns in the data, which also showed clearly that the linear approximation tends to understate support for multiple conjectural hypotheses because the additive model incorrectly counts many of the cases that occur at the wide end of the triangular data pattern as evidence against the hypothesis.

The estimates in Table 10.3 are all statistically significant, in the expected direction, and tell the same substantive story about the relationship between the pattern of governmental contention of opposition parties and the distribution of the economic vote among them. Thus, we can safely conclude that when voters' beliefs about the pattern of governmental contention are shaped only by the parties' records of office-holding, the importance of the economy will be weakest for the opposition parties least likely to contend for office.

The history of previous service in government is only one kind of information that voters can use to form their beliefs about which opposition

[18] To calculate shares of the opposition economic vote, we have to first set opposition economic votes that are in the "wrong direction" to zero. We then simply sum over opposition parties and divide each (modified) share by that sum.

Table 10.3. *History of Governmental Contention and the Economic Vote of Opposition Parties*

Ind. Vars. \ Dep. Var.	Econ Vote	Econ Vote Share	Econ Vote Share*	Econ Vote	Econ Vote	Econ Vote Share	Econ Vote Share*	Econ Vote
% months party has been incumbent	.03	.40	1.69	–	–	–	–	–
	(2.53)	(2.89)	(2.90)	–	–	–	–	–
% months party has been incumbent, discounted	–	–	–	.04	–	–	–	–
	–	–	–	(2.95)	–	–	–	–
% months party has been PM	–	–	–	–	.06	.67	2.88	–
	–	–	–	–	(4.20)	(4.19)	(3.92)	–
% months party has been PM, discounted	–	–	–	–	–	–	–	.04
	–	–	–	–	–	–	–	(2.95)
Constant	.01	.28	−.95	.01	.01	.28	−.94	.01
	(6.65)	(9.78)	(−6.93)	(5.97)	(7.33)	(11.67)	(−8.02)	(5.97)
N	401	398	398	401	401	398	398	401
R^2	0.08	0.09	–	0.07	0.17	0.15	–	0.07

Numbers in cells are coefficients and t-ratios. All models except those indicated by the * were estimated using OLS regression with standard errors robust to heteroskedacticity and nonindependence between observations of the same party in different surveys. Those marked with an * use GLM to account for the fact that the share of the economic vote is a proportion (as recommended in Papke and Wooldridge, 1996).

parties are or are not in governmental contention. Our alternative measurement approach assumes that voters form their beliefs about the likelihood of different government alternatives (and the resulting chances that a given party will enter government) rationally. This measure mimics the rational voter's likely "model" of government formation. It is derived by estimating a statistical model that predicts which governments will form as a function of the observable characteristics of parties that are generally recognized as affecting government formation.[19] We do this differently depending on whether the system under consideration is one in which coalition cabinets usually form (the "coalitional" cases) or one in which single-party cabinets are the norm (the "noncoalitional" cases).[20] In noncoalition countries, the "model" that rational voters likely use to forecast the outcome of the government formation process (and the role of the vote in that process) is a simple one: the plurality party will form the government and rule alone. Assuming that voters' beliefs about which parties contend for a plurality are an increasing function of the parties' shares of electoral support, we should expect each opposition party's electoral support at the time of the survey to be positively related to its economic vote.

Our best available measure of electoral support is simply the survey marginals for the vote-choice questions that were used in the surveys from which we estimated the economic vote.[21] In Figure 10.4, we graph this measure against the economic vote for opposition parties in noncoalitional systems in which there were multiple opposition parties (and at least two of these were included in our individual analysis of the case).

This graph (and the corresponding statistical models in Table 10.4) clearly supports the expectation that in multiparty noncoalitional systems, the economic vote of opposition parties will be higher the more likely the party is to compete with the incumbent for a plurality. The

[19] As with the historical measure, we are trying to measure $g'_j \sum_{g' \in A} P_{gg'}$ and so require an estimate of $P_{gg'}$. In the historical approach, we estimate this quantity with the historical frequency with which cabinet g' formed. In the current method, we estimate this quantity from a statistical model of cabinet formation that incorporates most of the information about party ideologies and the electoral/bargaining situation that might be available to voters to inform their choice.

[20] The noncoalitional countries in our sample are the United States, United Kingdom, Spain, Greece, Canada, Australia, and New Zealand before 1995.

[21] For cases in which a survey asked about reported vote instead of vote intention, the survey marginals are likely to be biased in favor of the incumbent. However, in this case, we get the same result if we substitute actual electoral support instead.

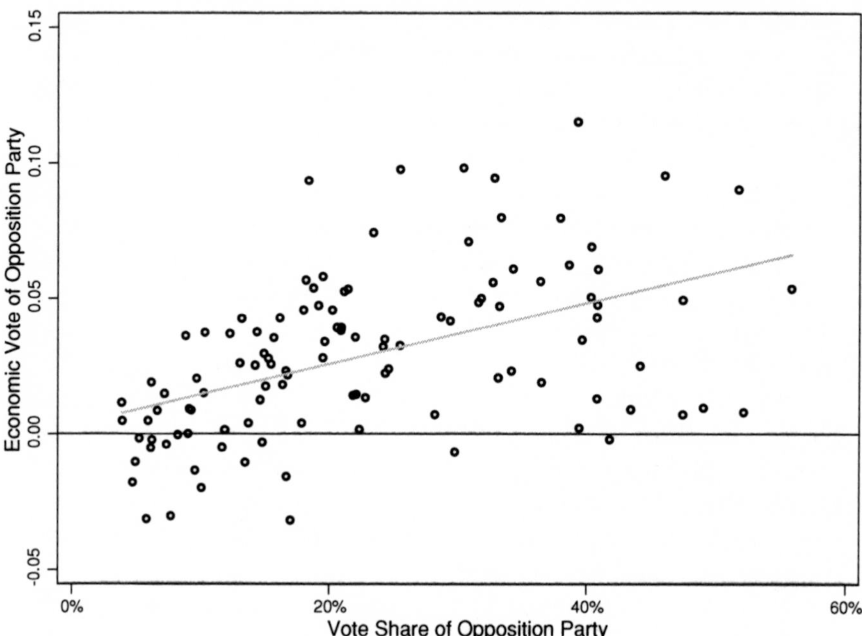

Figure 10.4. Party vote share and the economic vote of opposition parties in noncoalitional systems in multiparty systems. Only cases in which there were at least two opposition parties are included. The variable on the x-axis is the percentage of respondents indicating support of a given party (among those indicating they supported some party) at the time the survey was conducted.

relationship is statistically significant and positive despite the fact that, again, the graph shows the telltale signs of multiple conjectural causation that were discussed earlier.[22]

When we turn from noncoalitional systems to those in which coalition governments often form, the rational voters cannot use the simple plurality winner model to forecast the outcome of cabinet formation. Instead, they must consider which characteristics of parties and coalitions other than their size might impact cabinet formation. We try to measure the voters' rational beliefs about which coalitions will form in coalitional systems by building an empirical model of coalition formation that is based on much of the observable information that voters might use to form their

[22] In this graph, the two main exceptions from noncoalitional systems that appeared in Figure 10.2 – the Greek Communists in 1982 and the New Zealand Alliance in 1993 – are no longer exceptions.

Table 10.4. *Predicted Governmental Contention and the Economic Vote of Opposition Parties*

Dep. Var. / Ind. Vars.	Noncoalitional Systems			Coalitional Systems		
	Econ Vote	Share of Econ Vote	Share of Econ Vote*	Econ Vote	Share of Econ Vote	Share of Econ Vote*
Share of Vote	.11	1.32	5.82	–	–	–
	(4.16)	(5.17)	(4.38)	–	–	–
Predicted	–	–	–	.03	.61	2.74
Probability of Entering Government	–	–	–	(2.14)	(2.79)	(2.94)
Constant	.003	.12	−1.67	.009	.20	−1.34
	(0.71)	(1.89)	(−4.97)	(3.55)	(5.58)	(−7.28)
N	111	111	111	290	287	287
R^2	0.23	0.30	–	0.05	0.11	–

Numbers in cells are coefficients and t-ratios. All models except those indicated by the * were estimated using OLS regression with standard errors robust to heteroskedacticity and nonindependence between observations of the same party in different surveys. Those marked with an * use GLM to account for the fact that the share of the economic vote is a proportion.

beliefs. We then use this model to predict which coalitions will form in our cases and construct measures of voters' beliefs from these predictions. We use the models and data from Martin and Stevenson (2001) to estimate a slightly modified version of their empirical model of coalition formation in coalitional systems.[23]

After obtaining the coefficients from this model, we used them along with appropriate data from each of our 163 cases to produce "out-of-sample" forecasts of the probability that each possible coalition that could have formed (had a cabinet formation taken place at the time of the survey)

[23] Our version of their model forecasts the probability that any potential coalition forms as a function of the minimal winning status of the potential coalition, its majority status, the number of parties in the potential coalition, whether it contained the largest party, the extent of ideological division in the potential coalition, the extent of ideological division in the potential majority opposition (for minority potential coalitions only), the extent of antisystem presence in the potential coalition, whether it contained the median party on a left-right dimension, whether the system had an investiture vote (interacted with majority status of the potential coalition), whether the potential coalition contained the incumbent prime minister, and whether the potential coalition was the incumbent coalition.

would have, in fact, formed.[24,25] In cases in which our cases overlap with Martin and Stevenson's, our predicted probabilities of formation correspond quite closely to theirs.[26] In this section, we use these estimates of the probability that each potential coalition might form to construct a measure of the voter's belief that each opposition party will get into the new cabinet. To do this, we simply sum up the formation probabilities of all the coalitions for which a given opposition party was a member. The result is an estimate of the probability that the party will join some cabinet.

Figure 10.5 graphs this measure against the economic vote for opposition parties. The graph shows the expected triangular pattern of data and the linear approximation also makes the positive relationship between

[24] All of the variables except one were constructed as described in Martin and Stevenson, 2001. We had to estimate the seat shares that parties would likely obtain if an election were held at the time of the survey. We did this by forecasting seats from the survey marginals for vote choice in the survey. To produce this forecast, we first estimated the functional relationship between votes and seats in each country using Mackie and Rose's electoral data and applied the best fitting function to our survey marginals to generate our predictions. For cases in which a break in the party system occurred (e.g., Italy and New Zealand), we used the actual seat shares from the most proximate election to the survey. Because we are only concerned with coalitional systems, which tend to be highly proportional, the forecast was usually close to linear. For ideology, we used the same manifestos scores as in Martin and Stevenson but again used those from the most proximate election. One difference with their model is that in our simplification, we dichotomized their continuous antisystem variable and so, in creating our predictions, also created a dichotomous variable for whether a party was an antisystem party (and whether a coalition contained such a party).

[25] An important issue in using the survey marginals to measure the support of parties at the time of the survey (and then to calculate seat shares) is raised by the difference between surveys that ask the voters for their vote intention and those that ask the voters to report their vote in an election that has just happened (although often up to three months previously). It is well known that the survey marginals for such reported votes are generally biased in favor of the parties that "won" the election and (quite likely) for the parties that formed the government. Thus, if we use survey marginals to help produce the predicted probability that different cabinet forms, we are likely to get results that over predict the coalition that did form (as well as other coalitions involving the incumbents). Thus, the results in this chapter that rely on predicted probabilities of cabinet formation where run both including and excluding the few surveys that asked the vote-recall question. The differences in results, however, were minor.

[26] They reported a success rate of about 50 percent within sample prediction of the coalition that forms. Although this is the best success rate of any empirical model in the literature, it still alerts us to the fact that this measure is not even a perfect measure of the probability each cabinet will form, let alone a perfect measure of voter beliefs about these probabilities. The predicted probabilities (in addition to the program for producing them) are available from http://www.nuffield.ox.ac.uk/economicvoting.

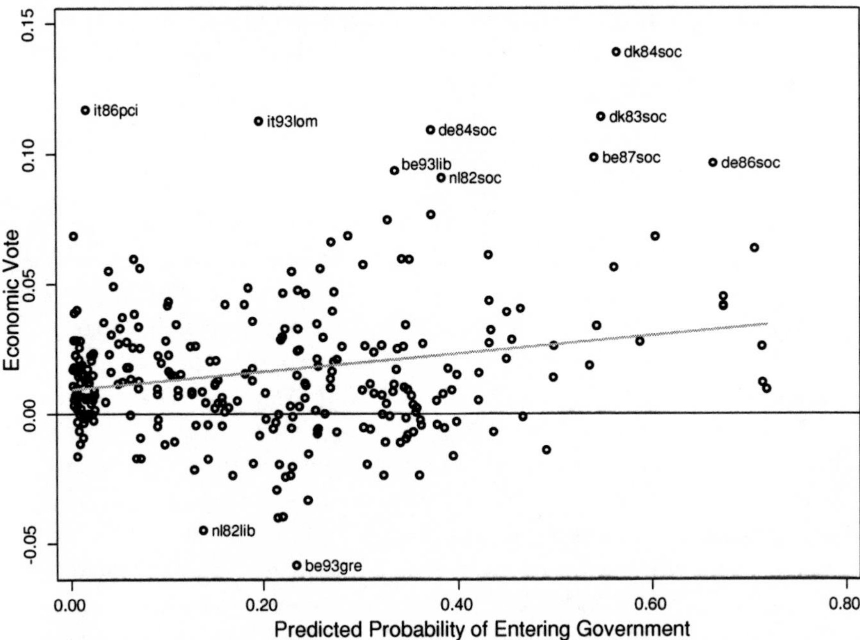

Figure 10.5. The predicted probability of entering government and the economic vote of opposition parties in coalitional systems. Only cases in which there were at least two opposition parties are included. We calculated the variable on the x-axis by first estimating the probability that each alternative cabinet forms (using our implementation of Martin and Stevenson's, 2001, empirical model of cabinet formation); and, second, summing these probabilities over cabinets in which a given opposition party is a member.

the variables plain. However, the main exceptions to the relationship that appeared when we assumed voters formed their beliefs about formation adaptively persist when we assume they form them rationally. That is, the Italian PCI in 1986 and the Lombard League in 1993 both have a relatively high economic vote despite a low estimated probability of entering the cabinet. On the whole, however, the evidence in Figure 10.5 supports the hypothesis that opposition parties that do not contend for cabinet membership will have low levels of economic voting, whereas those with higher levels of contention may have higher levels of economic voting.

Table 10.4 presents the statistical models corresponding to Figure 10.4 and Figure 10.5 and the two versions of those models that use shares as the dependent variables. As with the historical measures, when we use measures that try to capture rational belief formation about the pattern of governmental contention, the impact of all of our various measures are statistically significant and in the expected direction. Thus, we are confident that, as our theory predicts, the pattern of governmental contention is an important contextual influence on the distribution of the economic vote among opposition parties.

The Pattern of Contention among Incumbent Parties

The hypotheses explored in this section and the next both concern the relative importance of economic voting among incumbent parties. Specifically, our theory suggests that there are two aspects of the pattern of contention in coalitional systems that are important to incumbent parties. First, *economic voting should be smaller for parties that are members of incumbent cabinets that are not in contention with other alternatives – either because the cabinet is unlikely or it is certain to reform.* In either case, pivot probabilities between the incumbent cabinet and alternatives will be near zero, so we should see little economic voting. In addition to this implication, however, the theory also implies that *economic voting should be smaller for incumbent parties that are members of competitive alternative cabinets than it is for incumbents who are not.* Thus, even if the incumbent cabinet is in contention to reform, the economic vote of cabinet members that are also members of competitive alternatives should be muted. For example, some frequent incumbent parties, such as the Belgian and Dutch Christian parties or the German FDP, owe their longevity as cabinet members not only to the frequent reformation of the same cabinet but also to the fact that they are members of all the competitive alternatives. Thus, whatever cabinet reforms, they will be part of it. Our theory tells us that the economic vote of such parties should be depressed relative to their cabinet partners.

Of particular theoretical interest are those cases in which these perennial cabinet parties also take a large share of cabinet seats or provide the prime minister (e.g., in the Italian, Dutch, and Belgian cases, but not the German case). For these cases, the implication of our theory for the pattern of contention works *against* the widely studied clarity of responsibility argument, which predicts that parties with a greater share of cabinet responsibility will experience a relatively greater economic vote than their partners.[27] Thus, this implication will help us to determine empirically

[27] It also works against the effects of the concentration of responsibility that are predicted by our theory and were tested in the last chapter. However, the implications are not *contradictory* – because the theory simply says both influences are in operation simultaneously. This is not the case with the clarity argument, which has

whether the pattern of contention adds something to the political context conditioning economic voting that is distinct from the impact of the distribution of responsibility. Specifically, in the clarity of responsibility argument, it is exactly those perennial parties that are always in cabinet, usually dominantly so, that should leave the voter most clear about whom is responsible for policy. In contrast, in our theory, even though these parties have high responsibility (and so the responsibility augmented competency signal may be large), that fact will not matter to rational voters because the party is sure to be in whatever government that forms.

In what follows, we examine evidence about the relationship between voter beliefs about the competitiveness of incumbent parties and the size of their economic votes. We begin, in this section, by examining the second hypothesis noted earlier: that is, incumbent parties that are members of competitive alternative cabinets will have muted economic votes relative to their cabinet partners who are members of fewer, or less competitive, alternatives. Before turning to the data, however, there are two points we should clarify about how we have chosen to present the results.

First, as we have already pointed out, our theory implies (1) a quadratic relationship between the vote for any particular incumbent party and the overall level of contention of the incumbent cabinet; and (2) given this overall level of competitiveness, a linear relationship between the extent to which the party is a member of competitive alternatives and its economic vote.[28] This implies that we should examine the later relationship while controlling for the former, which is what we do in the next section. However, in this section, our graphs and statistical models of the linear relationship between incumbent-party participation in competitive alternatives and the economic vote ignore this control. This is a useful separation pedagogically (because it allows us to delay our rather extended discussion of how we measure the control variable) and does little harm, as the linear relationship that we explore in this section turns out to be very strongly apparent in the data and (as we show in the next section) robust to the control for the overall competitiveness of the cabinet.

Second, in the various analyses that follow, we examine both the size of the economic vote for incumbents and shares of the economic vote among incumbents. This is useful because although the hypothesis applies most

no mechanism that would explain a depressed economic vote for perennial prime ministers, to which voters should easily attribute policy-making responsibility.

[28] Of course, given the multiple conjunctural nature of all our hypotheses, we should more properly say that the theory implies a set of relationships that should be *approximated* by quadratic and linear functions, respectively.

clearly to *shares* of the economic vote among the incumbent parties, it also applies to the *size* of the economic vote, *ceteris paribus*. If we consider two parties, one that is in many alternative cabinets and another that is not, and they are in essentially the same position with respect to all other variables, the former should have a smaller economic vote than the latter – even though the overall amount of economic voting in the two systems should be the same. Given this, we present statistical results for both shares and size of the economic vote, though our graphs concentrate on the more visually helpful size measures.

As in the previous section, we begin our empirical analysis with the measurement assumption that the voter uses the historical frequency with which a cabinet formed as an estimate of the probability that it will form in the current period. Thus, the sum of these estimates over all alternative cabinets of which the incumbent party is a member is our estimate of the extent to which the party is a member of competitive alternatives (note that the probability the incumbent cabinet will reform is not included in this sum). Furthermore, because the hypothesis is about the extent to which a given cabinet member is a member of competitive alternatives *relative* to its cabinet partners, we normalize the measure by the overall probability that some alternative to the cabinet will form. Thus, our final measure is the probability that the incumbent party will enter the new cabinet in some alternative to the incumbent cabinet, given that the incumbent does not reform.[29] We expect the economic vote to decline as the value of this variable is bigger.

Figure 10.6 graphs this measure against the economic vote of incumbent parties. Clearly, parties that are members of almost all the competitive alternative cabinets (i.e., near 100 percent on our measure) have depressed economic votes relative to other parties, and we once again can see the expected triangular shape to the spread of data (i.e., the small end of the triangle on the right side of the graph expanding downward toward the left). The two largest exceptions to this pattern are the Italian Christian Democrats in 1993, which had a large economic vote despite the fact that

[29] For example, suppose a party is a member of three-cabinet competitive cabinets A, B, and C, where A is the incumbent cabinet and the probabilities of formation are .3, .2, and .1, respectively. In addition, there is one alternative cabinet, D, of which the party is not a member. If D has a formation probability of .4, the party's score on our measure would be $(.2 + .1)/(.2 + .1 + .4) = .3/.7 = .43$. The probability that some alternative to the incumbent will form is .7, while the probability that the chosen alternative includes the party is .3, so the probability that the party gets into cabinet, given some nonincumbent alternative forms, is .43.

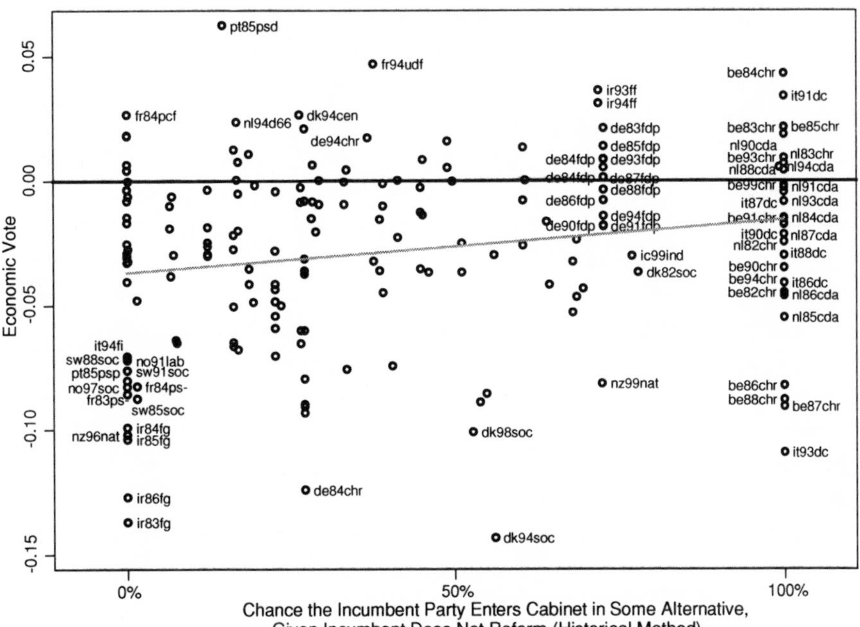

Figure 10.6. Extent to which incumbent parties are members of competitive alternative coalitions and the economic vote in coalitional systems. Larger negative numbers indicate a larger economic vote for the incumbent party. We calculated the variable on the x-axis by first estimating the probability that each alternative cabinet forms (using the historical method described in the text); then summing these probabilities over cabinets, other than the incumbent cabinet, in which a given incumbent party is a member; and, finally, normalizing this number by the total probability that some cabinet other than the incumbent would form.

they were a member of all the coalitions that had historically formed in Italy, and (to some extent) the Danish Socialists in 1994. As we pointed out in our earlier discussion of the success of the Lombard League in 1993, it is not really surprising that history is not a clear guide to the beliefs of Italian voters in this period. Just as these voters may have perceived the untried Lombard League as a viable alternative governing party, by 1993 they very likely saw the Christian Democrats' lock on the cabinet as slipping. Thus, although just a few years before (i.e., 1987, 1988, and 1991) the Christian Democrats had the expected depressed economic vote of a perennial cabinet member, by 1993 their dominance was already in question.

The evidence from Figure 10.6 applies to all incumbents. However, there are two reasons to think that the relationships we expect to see for incumbent parties should be more apparent among a sample of parties with greater responsibility in cabinet than they are for the sample of all incumbents. First, our theory implies (and the data analysis in Chapter 9 confirms) that the economic votes of parties holding less responsibility in the cabinet are depressed relative to others; the principal distinction is between prime ministerial parties and their partners. Because of this, the economic votes of partner parties will be closer to zero than that of prime ministers and, as a result, other relationships will necessarily be harder to detect over the background noise.

Second, recall that in its most general version (see the discussion following equation [8.37] in Chapter 8), our theory implied that voters wishing to use their vote most efficiently to change (or retain) the status quo distribution of responsibility should move their votes between those parties with the largest shares of responsibility in the current distribution of responsibility to (or from) those parties with the smallest shares (as long as these parties also have a large share of responsibility in some competitive alternative). This means that voters have an incentive to concentrate economic voting on the coalition members with the most responsibility (e.g., the prime ministerial party) – not only because the responsibility augmented competency signal is larger for these parties but also because the pattern of contention makes this strategy the most efficient way to achieve their goals.

Given these theoretical arguments, as well as the empirical results in the last section, we expect that the predicted linear relationship between incumbent party membership in competitive alternative coalitions and economic voting to be more apparent in our sample of prime ministerial parties than in the whole sample of incumbents. This is exactly what we find when we examine the two groups of incumbents separately. Indeed, this should not only be true for the hypotheses we are examining in this section but also for the other hypotheses we explore in the next sections; and the data do, in fact, bear this out. Given this, in the rest of this chapter, we focus our discussion on the sample of cases that the theory tells us should most clearly reflect the expected relationships.

To be clear, these hypotheses *do* apply to all cabinet members – it is just that the theory tells us that it should be harder to see the relationships in a sample of cabinet partners than in a sample of prime ministers. And, as we said, we do generally find weaker results (in terms of statistical significance) for cabinet partners compared to prime ministers. It is important to emphasize, however, that the evidence in our sample of cabinet partners never actually contradicts our theoretical expectations. Indeed, the directional evidence is always the same for the partners and prime ministers;

it is just that in the former case, we often cannot statistically distinguish effects from zero. For example, cabinet partners who are members of competitive alternative cabinets do tend to have smaller economic votes than those who are not, but this difference is less apparent for partners than prime ministers. Furthermore, looking at Figure 10.6, there is really only one case in our data in which a frequent partner party is also a member of most of the competitive alternative cabinets (the German FDP).[30] And, as the theory predicts, the average economic vote of this party is rather sharply smaller than other, less perennial partners. Specifically, the mean economic vote for the German FDP is −0.00017 compared to an average economic vote of −0.0136 for the other partners in Figure 10.6 – a difference that is significant at $p < 0.005$.[31]

Thus, although in general the results for cabinet partners mirror the results for prime ministers, the expected relationships are less statistically detectable than for prime ministerial parties (with the exception of the contrast between the FDP and other partners). The extent of this difference is illustrated in Figure 10.7, which graphs the same relationship as in Figure 10.6, but only for prime ministerial parties. Clearly, the expected relationship is much clearer in the second graph, and the empirical models bear this out as well.

Examining Figure 10.7, there are three different groups of cases to consider. The first is those at the far right of the graph. These cases are ones in which the prime ministerial party is part of every alternative coalition with any significant probability of forming (which, given the historical method used to calculate this probability, means the party is a member of all alternative coalitions that have been in office for any significant length of time since 1960). These are the Dutch and Belgian Christian parties and the Italian Christian Democrats before 1994. On the other side of the graph are cases of incumbent prime ministers who are a part

[30] Looking at the right side of Figure 10.6, all of the parties except the FDP are either prime ministers (e.g., the Belgian and Dutch Christian Parties) or are one-time partners that normally hold the prime-ministry (e.g., the Italian Christian Democrats in 1993). Thus, the FDP is the only usual partner party that compares with the perennial prime ministers in terms of the number and competitiveness of the alternative coalitions to which it belongs.

[31] Notice that just as the perennial prime ministers in Belgium and the Netherlands contribute many of the "wrong-signed" economic votes for prime ministers, the FDP provides a disproportionate number of these "wrong-signed" economic votes of cabinet partners. Furthermore, this is despite the fact that the party held the finance ministry during this period (recall that we saw in the last chapter that holding the finance ministry enhanced a party's economic vote, all else being equal).

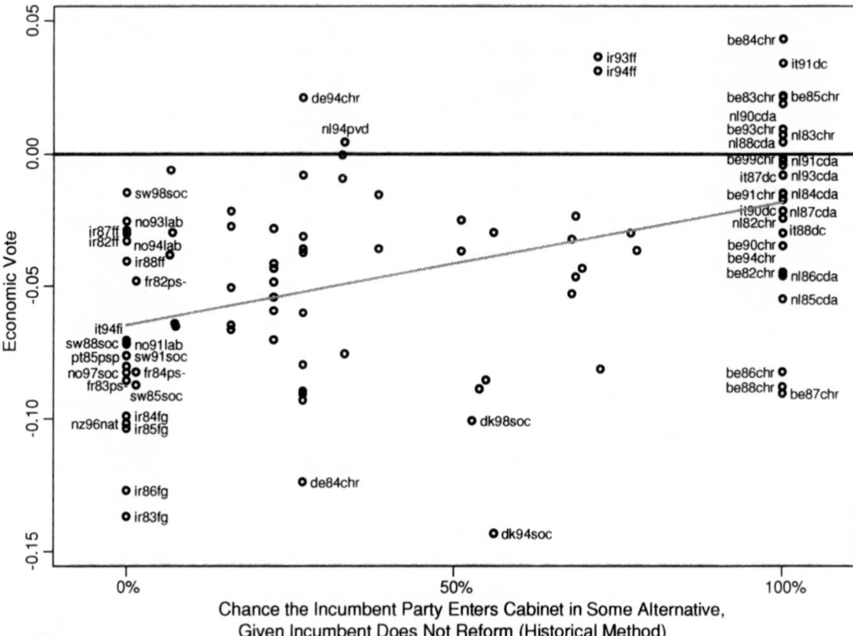

Figure 10.7. Extent to which incumbent prime ministers are members of competitive alternative coalitions and the economic vote in coalitional systems. Larger negative numbers indicate a larger economic vote for the incumbent party. We calculated the variable on the x-axis by first estimating the probability that each alternative cabinet forms (using the historical method described in the text); then summing these probabilities over cabinets, other than the incumbent cabinet, in which a given incumbent party is a member; and, finally, normalizing this number by the total probability that some cabinet other than the incumbent would form.

of few of the historically frequent coalition alternatives. Here, it is important to remember that the measure does not include the current incumbent cabinet and so it is *not* a measure of the chance that the party will return to government in *any* coalition. For example, in the mid-1980s, Fine Gael was in government with the Irish Labour Party, and because it had not coalesced with any other party (or ruled alone) since 1957, it would be unlikely to return to government other than in a coalition with Labour (at least from the point of view of a voter forming his beliefs about likely cabinets based on history). Thus, our theory suggests that the economic voter who wanted, for example, to retain the Fine Gael–Labour government could use his vote most efficiently by voting for Fine Gael because none of this vote would contribute to some other coalition forming. Finally, parties in the middle of the graph are members of some contending alternatives and not others. For example, in 1998 the Danish Social Democrats were in government with the Radical Liberals; however, they also had been a member of five other governments between 1960 and 1998. Furthermore, several bourgeoisie coalitions had formed during the period that excluded the party all together. Thus, although a vote for the Social Democrats would certainly contribute to keeping the SD-RL coalition in power, it also would contribute to the chances that some other historically plausible cabinet (like the recent SD-Liberal-Center Democratic coalition) would come to power (which is not what an economic voter trying to retain the incumbent coalition would like to see happen).

Table 10.5 provides the statistical model to accompany Figure 10.7 as well as a number of alternative specifications and measures. In each of these specifications, we provide one model that controls for the percentage of cabinet seats held by the prime minister. As mentioned earlier, a number of results in the theory suggest that a greater share of cabinet responsibility should lead to greater economic voting. Although focusing only on prime ministers probably captures most of this impact, there is some variance in the share of the cabinet seats that different prime ministers hold, and so it is worth controlling for any additional impact. Looking at the results, the dampening effect of membership in competitive alternatives remains strong when controlling for the prime minister's share of cabinet seats. Furthermore, estimates for the effect of this control variable are either consistent with the results reported in the previous chapter (e.g., in the share equations) or insignificant (in the size equations).[32] The relative size of the effects suggests that strategic considerations about cabinet contention are at least as important (if not more so) to the economic votes of prime ministers as is their share of cabinet responsibility.[33]

Another particularly revealing implication of this hypothesis turns the story around. Specifically, if the economic vote for perennial prime

[32] We should not make too much of this one null result because in all the other equations reported in subsequent tables, the variable is significant and in the expected direction.

[33] We really do not want to emphasize this sort of "Which variable is more important?" question because it is really only appropriate for additive models (if that); and, of course, we only use the additive model as an approximation to the more complex multiple conjunctural causal structure that is implied by our theory. Nevertheless, we can conclude from these results that there is evidence that it cannot just be something like clarity of responsibility driving differences in economic voting, because this evidence clearly indicates an important role for strategic considerations about the pattern of cabinet contention that have nothing to do with the current distribution of responsibility.

Table 10.5. *Historical Measures of Contention and the Economic Vote of PM Parties*[34]

Ind. Vars. \ Dep. Var.	Econ Vote		Econ Vote Share		Econ Vote Share*	
Probability of entering government in some alternative other than incumbent coalition, given incumbent does not reform (historical method)	.05 (5.36)	.05 (3.42)	−.46 (−5.05)	−.25 (−2.95)	−2.51 (−3.30)	−1.51 (−2.31)
Percent of cabinet ministries held by party	– –	.002 (0.08)	– –	.60 (2.95)	– –	4.64 (3.63)
Constant	−.06 (−9.92)	−.06 (−2.69)	.94 (14.18)	.44 (2.18)	2.39 (3.41)	−1.02 (−0.97)
N	98	98	96	96	96	96
R^2	.21	.21	.25	.34	–	–

Numbers in cells are coefficients and t-ratios. All models except those indicated by the * were estimated using OLS regression with standard errors robust to heteroskedacticity and nonindependence between observations of the same party in different surveys. Those marked with an * use GLM to account for the fact that the share of the economic vote is a proportion (as recommended in Papke and Wooldridge, 1996).

ministers is depressed relative to their partners, and cabinet partners have small economic votes in general, then when we find cabinet partners with large economic votes, we would expect them to be from systems with perennial prime ministers. That is, in systems with perennial prime ministers that also tend to switch partners regularly, we should expect the locus of competition over the economy to center on partner parties – because this is the only way the rational voters can use their vote to impact the composition of the cabinet. Thus, we would expect parties with relatively little cabinet responsibility in these systems to have larger economic votes than otherwise expected. Figure 10.8 provides the data necessary for examining this expectation.

[34] Models that control for party size give almost identical results for the history variables.

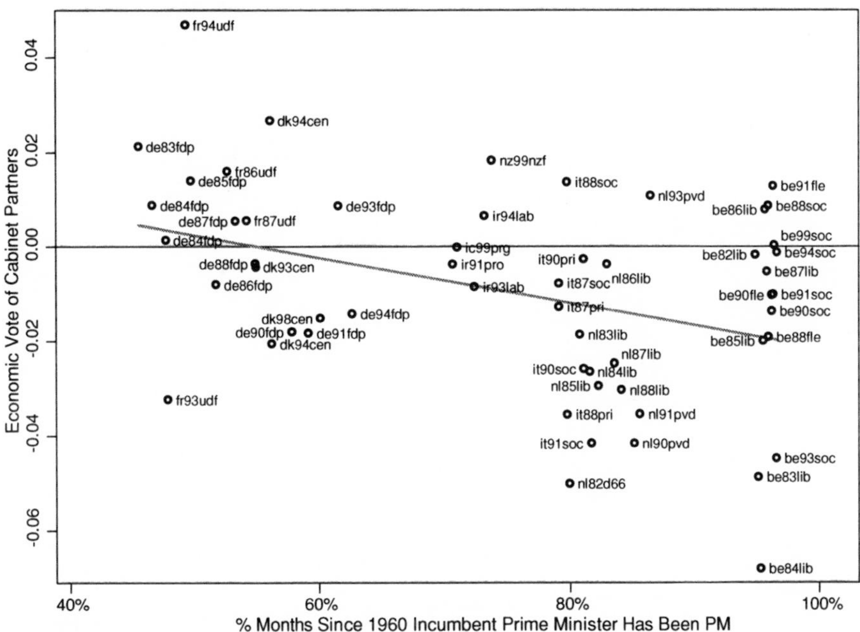

Figure 10.8. The economic vote of cabinet partners and the historical competitiveness of their prime ministers. Larger negative numbers indicate a larger economic vote for the incumbent party. The variable on the x-axis applies to the incumbent prime ministerial party that is in office with the graphed partner party.

The graph plots the economic vote of *partner* parties as a function of their *prime minister's* history of office-holding. Thus, partner parties on the right-hand side of the graph come from systems with perennial prime ministers and they do tend to have larger economic votes than cases in which the prime minister's party is more competitive.[35] This graph (and the corresponding regressions) supports the idea that parties such as the Dutch and Belgian liberal and socialist parties, which have regularly competed with one another to be the partner of the dominant Christian party, have larger economic votes than one should expect for their status as partners – a fact strikingly consistent with the logic of strategic economic voting (and not with any sort of clarity of responsibility argument).

As we did for opposition parties, we can also explore this hypothesis when voters form their beliefs rationally. Likewise, as in that analysis, we

[35] Because our hypothesis is about the comparison of partners of perennial PMs to partners of competitive PMs, we exclude partners of PMs that had no significant history of office-holding (our theory is unclear what we should expect the economic votes of these parties to be relative to other kinds of partners).

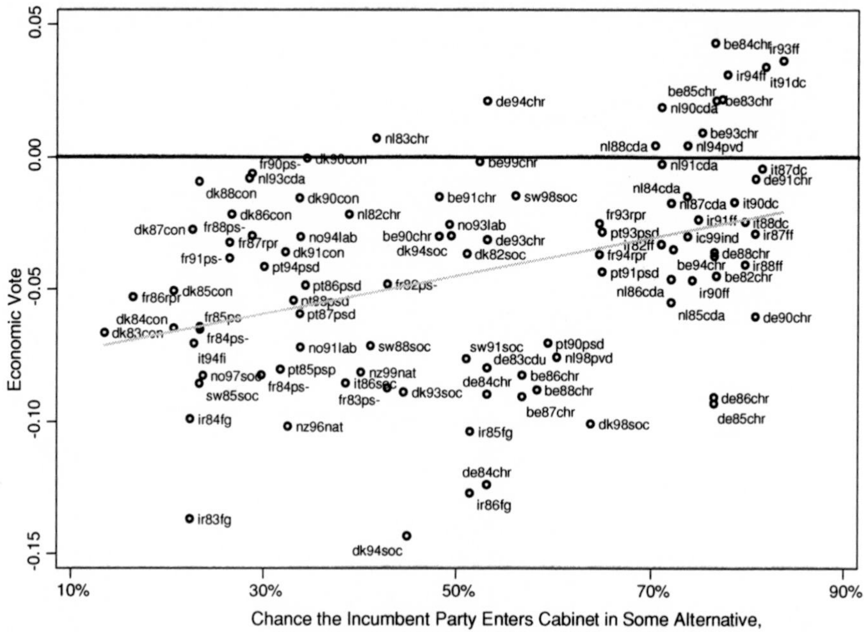

Figure 10.9. Extent to which incumbent prime ministers are members of competitive alternative coalitions and the economic vote in coalitional systems (rational method). Larger negative numbers indicate a larger economic vote for the incumbent party. We calculated the variable on the x-axis by first estimating the probability that each alternative cabinet forms (using the rational method described in the text); then summing these probabilities over all nonincumbent cabinets in which a given incumbent party is a member; and, finally, normalizing this number by the total probability that some cabinet other than the incumbent would form.

build our measure of the voter's rational beliefs by first using an empirical model to estimate the probability that each potential cabinet forms (as a function of its observable characteristics). Next, for each incumbent party, we sum these estimates over all the cabinets in which the party participates. Finally, we normalize this probability by the total probability that a cabinet other than the incumbent will form. As before, the result is a measure of the probability that any particular incumbent party will continue in some alternative cabinet, given that the incumbent cabinet does not form (only this time, the probabilities are from our empirical model instead of historical frequencies).

Figure 10.9 graphs the relationship between this measure of the chance of entering the new government and the economic vote of prime ministerial parties in coalitional systems. Clearly, the relationship is in

Table 10.6. *Predicted Cabinet Contention and the Economic Vote of Prime Ministers*

Dep. Var. / Ind. Vars.	Econ Vote		Econ Vote Share		Econ Vote Share *	
Probability of entering government in some alternative other than incumbent coalition, given incumbent does not reform (rational method)	.07 (2.83)	.07 (2.99)	−.50 (−1.54)	−.42 (−2.57)	−2.72 (−1.33)	−3.27 (−3.09)
Percent of cabinet ministries held by party	– –	−.04 (−2.00)	– –	.82 (4.98)	– –	6.33 (5.66)
Constant	−.08 (−5.22)	−.05 (−2.45)	.93 (5.56)	.38 (1.99)	2.49 (1.85)	1.12 (−0.96)
N	97	97	95	95	95	95
R^2	.14	.18	.08	.35	–	–

Numbers in cells are coefficients and t-ratios. All models except those indicated by the * were estimated using OLS regression with standard errors robust to heteroscedacticity and nonindependence between observations of the same party in different surveys. Those marked with an * use GLM to account for the fact that the share of the economic vote is a proportion (as recommended in Papke and Wooldridge, 1996).

the expected direction and, as Table 10.6 shows, is also statistically significant.

As with our historical measure, the cases dominating the right side of the graph are the perennial prime ministers in Belgium, Italy, and the Netherlands. It is encouraging that the rational measure, which is built quite differently from the historical measure and, indeed, uses no information about historical office-holding, agrees with the historical measure that these parties are very likely to be in whatever new cabinet forms.[36] Even more encouraging is the fact that the message of the graph, as well as the estimates in Table 10.6, mirrors that of our earlier analysis: the more

[36] The rational and historical measures are correlated at .42 for coalitional prime ministers. The un-normalized measures are correlated at .53 for these same cases.

that the incumbent prime minister is a member of competitive alternative cabinets, the smaller the size (and share) of its economic vote.

As in the earlier analyses, Table 10.6 provides a number of different statistical models of the general relationship graphed in Figure 10.9. Again, these analyses provide support for our hypothesis that, in coalitional systems, economic voting should be smaller for incumbent parties that are almost certain to be a member of any new cabinet that forms. Furthermore, the relationship persists when we control for the different shares of cabinet responsibility that different prime ministers hold, reassuring us that both effects are important.

The Reselection of the Incumbent Government and the Overall Economic Vote

One of the implications of our theory was that overall economic voting should be muted when the incumbent government is not in contention to be reselected to govern. Contention has two sides – an incumbent could fail to be in contention either because it is not likely to be reselected or because it is sure to be reselected. We expect, then, that the relationship between voter beliefs about the reselection chances of the incumbent and economic voting will be quadratic – reaching a minimum when the voter is either sure the incumbent government will be reselected or sure it will not be.

There are two caveats to this hypothesis that are important to account for in our empirical analysis. First, we should recall that for any given incumbent party, the competitiveness of the government as a whole is only one influence on its economic vote. In the last section, we also saw that the extent to which the party is a member of alternative coalitions is also important. Thus, in the analysis in this section, which concentrates on the relationship between the competitiveness of the incumbent cabinet as a whole and the economic vote of the prime minister (our preferred measure of overall economic voting), we need to control for the extent to which the prime ministerial party is a member of competitive alternative cabinets (by including measures from the last section as control variables in our regressions).

The second caveat that we need to consider is that although several versions of the theory presented in Chapter 8 implied that there should be no economic voting if the incumbent cabinet was not in contention to reform, this exclusive focus on the incumbent cabinet was relaxed when we (1) generalized the theory to allow for opposition parties to have some policy-making responsibility (so that we had to think in terms of a "status quo distribution of responsibility" rather than an "incumbent cabinet"); and (2) allowed voters in our theory to infer nonzero levels of competence for distributions of responsibility other than the status quo distribution. Thus, in our most general model, we replaced the implication that the incumbent (or status quo) distribution of responsibility must be in contention for economic voting to occur with a continuous version of that hypothesis. That is, economic voting will be depressed if the competitive distributions of responsibility are either very dissimilar to the status quo distribution or very similar to it.[37] Substantively, this generalization is important because it allows us to think about, for example, cases in which the exact incumbent cabinet is not competitive but similar cabinets are (e.g., a small party that was an incumbent is sure not to return but all the other parties are likely to). From the economic voter's point of view, it may well make sense to cast an economic vote that helps this "almost incumbent" cabinet either remain in office or be removed. Furthermore, because the theory says that these similar cabinets need to be competitive (i.e., it can neither be sure that a cabinet similar to the incumbent will form or that none will), we expect a quadratic relationship between the competitiveness of cabinets similar to the incumbent and the overall economic vote.

In what follows, we develop a measure of the overall competitiveness of cabinets similar to (or exactly the same as) the incumbent cabinet. One can think of this measure as the "familiarity" of the incumbent cabinet in that it attempts to account not just for how often the exact previous cabinet has been in power in the past, but also how often similar cabinets have been in office. As with our other historically based measures, this measure begins with the assumption that voters believe those governments that have tended to be selected in the past also will be selected in the future. Clearly, such voters must give all incumbent governments some chance of reselection, as by virtue of being incumbent, the government

[37] Recall that the logic for the first part of this hypothesis (i.e., the economic vote should be depressed if the alternatives similar to the status quo distribution are not at all competitive) comes from the fact that if no parties in an alternative distribution of responsibility held any responsibility in the status quo distribution, then the voter has no information about the competence of any party that matters to the new distribution. Likewise, the logic for the second part of the hypothesis (i.e., if all the alternative distributions of responsibility that are in contention are very similar to the status quo, then the economic vote will be depressed) comes from the fact that if an alternative just reproduces the status quo distribution of responsibility, the voter has no real choice and so has no incentive to cast an economic vote.

has been selected previously. However, there are clearly differences across different incumbent governments in the extent to which they have a history of selection and reselection. Our measurement assumption is that voters consider it more likely that familiar cabinets will reform than is the case with unfamiliar cabinets. Thus, the expectation from our theory is that economic voting will be depressed when the cabinet is either very familiar or very unfamiliar.

Our measure of familiarity not only accounts for the history of the specific incumbent cabinet but also how different it is from other familiar combinations (perhaps the only difference is the addition of a small and inconsequential party to an otherwise familiar governing combination). For example, we want to be able to distinguish the familiarity of a government like the Dutch incumbent cabinet in 1981 (the CDA, PvdA, and D66), in which the smallish D66 joined the familiar Christian-Socialist coalition, from that of the PvdA, D66, Liberal coalition of 1994, which was, most observers would agree, much less familiar to voters. Indeed, the latter coalition represented a combination of major political forces (the liberals and socialists) that had never previously coalesced. Our measure of the incumbent government's "familiarity" consists of scoring each government according to how often its members have previously governed and then taking the average of these experiences.[38] We then weight the average by the share of legislative seats each party brings to the government. This down-weights the impact of adding small parties to coalitions in which the larger parties are familiar incumbents. The measure thus corrects the problem of counting all unique governing formulas as equally unfamiliar (a score of 0 would indicate the most unfamiliar coalition – one in which none of the members had ever served in cabinet). However, the measure is still lacking in at least one important respect. The problem is illustrated by the second example we gave earlier. Adopting this measurement strategy would assign the Dutch incumbent coalition in 1994 (between the Pvda, Liberals, and D66) a familiarity score of .58, which, compared to similar scores for other alternatives, seems rather high. This relatively high score results because the Liberals and the Socialists had served, by that time, quite often in government – although always as junior members of a Christian-led coalition. This change in status is not

[38] We could calculate how often each government had served rather than its members. However, by building up our measure from the experience of the members rather than the government as a whole, we can more easily discount the "uniqueness" of coalitions that simply add small parties to familiar alternatives.

well reflected in our measure, so the government comes out as more familiar than, we think, most voters were likely to find it.

We adjust our measure to address this problem by calculating not just the experience each incumbent party has in government but also the experience they have in the specific *role* they are playing in the government, where we distinguish only between being the prime minister and being a non-prime ministerial cabinet partner. With this, instead of counting the PvdA in 1996 as having served in government 34 percent of the months since 1960, it is scored as having served 0 percent of the months since 1960 as prime minister. This changes the overall familiarity score to .08 (we continue to weight by the percent of seats the party contributes to the cabinet). Finally, we discount service in governments so that more recent stints in government are weighted more in voter's beliefs about reformation than government participation that occurred farther in the past.[39]

We find that this measure captures most of the variation in familiarity that observers would expect. Figure 10.10 maps the variation in familiarity of the incumbent government for all the countries in our sample in which multiple parties usually compete. The big changes in the graphs correspond nicely to what we would expect and across the graphs the differences in familiarity scores also reflect, in our view, a reasonable understanding of the differences across countries in how familiar various incumbent cabinets were likely to have been to voters.

The least familiar cases are what we would expect: the Dutch case discussed previously, the first PASOK government in Greece, and the first Italian cabinet to emerge from the new party system. Likewise, the most familiar cases are found after long periods of rule by the same cabinet – that is, the German Christian–Liberal coalition, the decade of rule by the Spanish PSOE, and the British run of Conservative governments. The big changes in the graphs also identify the important transitions in the pattern of office-holding, during which voters who form their beliefs adaptively would have had considerable uncertainty about the future. For example, in Denmark, the large drop in the familiarity of the incumbent cabinet in the early 1980s reflects the emergence of the rightist bourgeoisie coalitions as a viable alternative to the Social Democrats.

[39] We use an exponential weighting function, δ^{m}, where m is the number of months between the current month (for which a score is being calculated) and the month in the past that is under consideration (ultimately, we sum over all months since 1960). We choose $\delta = .99$, which means that service five years in the past is discounted by about a half and ten years in the past by about a third. The specific details of this calculation are available at http://www.nuffield.ox.ac.uk/economicvoting.

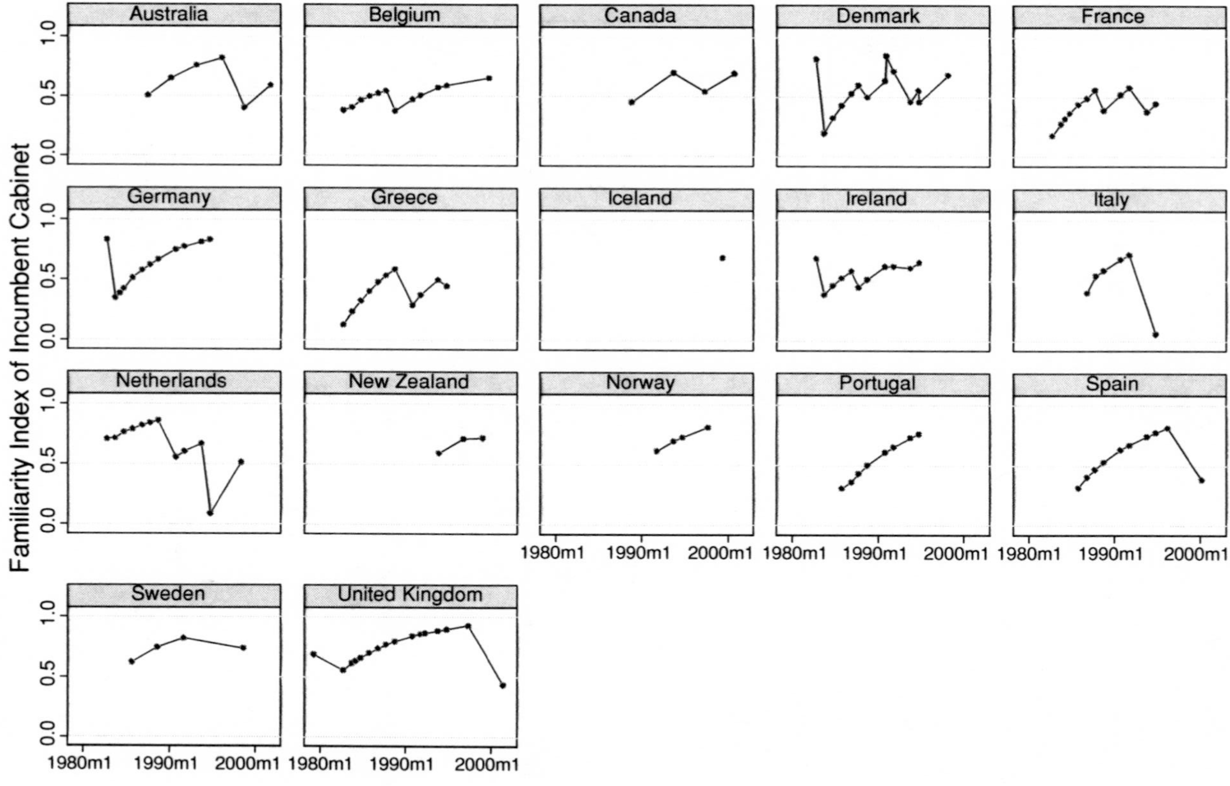

Figure 10.10. A familiarity index for incumbent cabinets.

With this measure in hand, we can now graph the familiarity score against our measures of economic voting in each of our cases.[40] We use the economic vote of the prime minister as our measure of the economic vote.[41] Because the interpretation of the familiarity score may be qualitatively different in coalitional and noncoalitional systems, we graph these two cases separately. Specifically, in coalitional systems, changes in the familiarity of the incumbent are often induced by a new coalitional formula coming to power, but this is not the case in noncoalitional systems in which the same pairs of parties compete election after election for office. Thus, in the later case, our measure of familiarity reflects the extent to which in recent years the control of government has or has not been volatile.

Figure 10.11 presents the graph of economic vote against familiarity for noncoalition cases. On the left of the graph are incumbents that follow a long period in which another party, now in opposition, was in power; the middle of the graph are cases in which power is switching more regularly between parties; and the right side of the graph are cases in which the incumbent has dominated the government for some time. Clearly, measuring familiarity in this way, we get a strong quadratic relationship between familiarity and the economic vote as we expect (with the now familiar exception of the Greek 1982 case). Furthermore, the multiple conjectural nature of our hypotheses implies, in this case, that economic voting will be low at high and low values of our familiarity score and *may* be large in the middle. Thus, the fact that the bowl shape in the figure is "filled in" is completely consistent with the theory, although it tends to depress the significance of the quadratic approximation.

In coalitional cases, we can interpret our familiarity score in roughly the same way as we did in the case of noncoalitional cases, but now some of the differences in scores reflect changes in coalition partners rather than how long the incumbent has been in office. On the far left of Figure 10.12 are some of the more unique governments in the data – the Dutch Pvda-Lib-D66 coalition discussed earlier, the bourgeoisie coalition that emerged in the early 1980s in Denmark, the first Italian cabinet lead by Forza Italia,

[40] Of course, these graphs are illustrative because we have emphasized that it is important in examining the competitiveness of the incumbent cabinet to control for the extent to which the prime ministerial party is a member of contending alternative cabinets. We include this control in the empirical models corresponding to the graphs, but because these models tell, more or less, the same story as the graphs, it is worthwhile (we think) to present the pictures.

[41] Other measures of the overall size of economic voting in the election (e.g., the mean economic vote of the government parties – with wrong-signed economic vote set to zero) produce similar results.

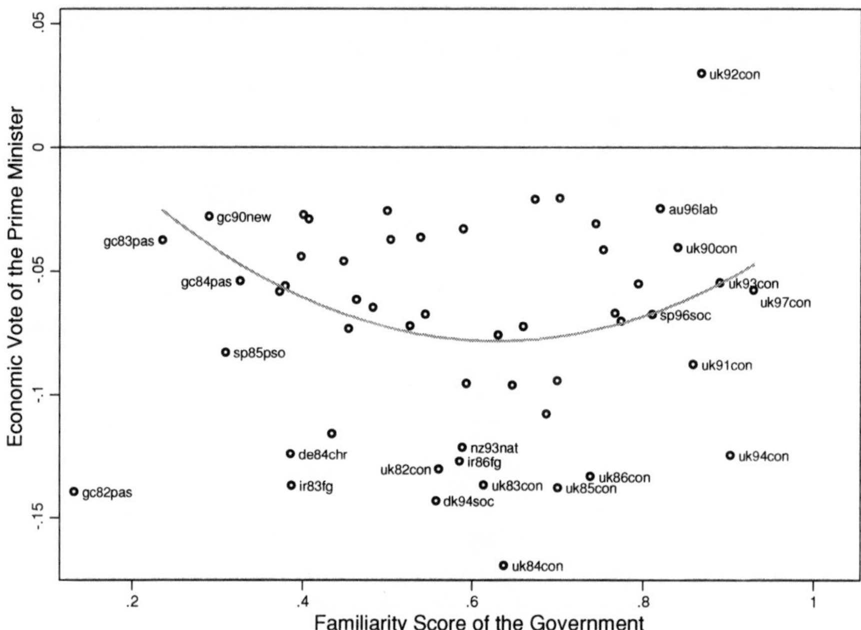

Figure 10.11. Familiarity of the incumbent government and the economic vote in noncoalitional systems. Larger negative numbers indicate a larger economic vote for the incumbent party. Fitted line excludes the Greek 1982 case.

and the return of Socialist coalitions to power in France in the early 1980s. With the partial exception of the Forza Italia government, these (admittedly few) cases of unfamiliar cabinets fit the predicted quadratic relationship. Furthermore, on the other side of the graph, the systems with the most familiar governments in our sample (the German and Dutch Christian-led coalitions in the early 1990s) have similarly depressed economic votes.

This evidence suggests that at low and high levels of familiarity, economic voting is low, and that at moderately high levels of familiarity, economic voting *may* be high, but this is not guaranteed. However, because of the relative scarcity of cases with familiarity in the range of .1 to .3, the plotted quadratic approximation does not "bend" much on the left side of the graph. Table 10.7 reports the estimates corresponding to the graphs along with specifications controlling for the extent to which the prime minister is a member of contending alternative cabinets. In the case of coalitional systems, we present not only the quadratic specification but also a linear model fit to all the cases with familiarity scores greater

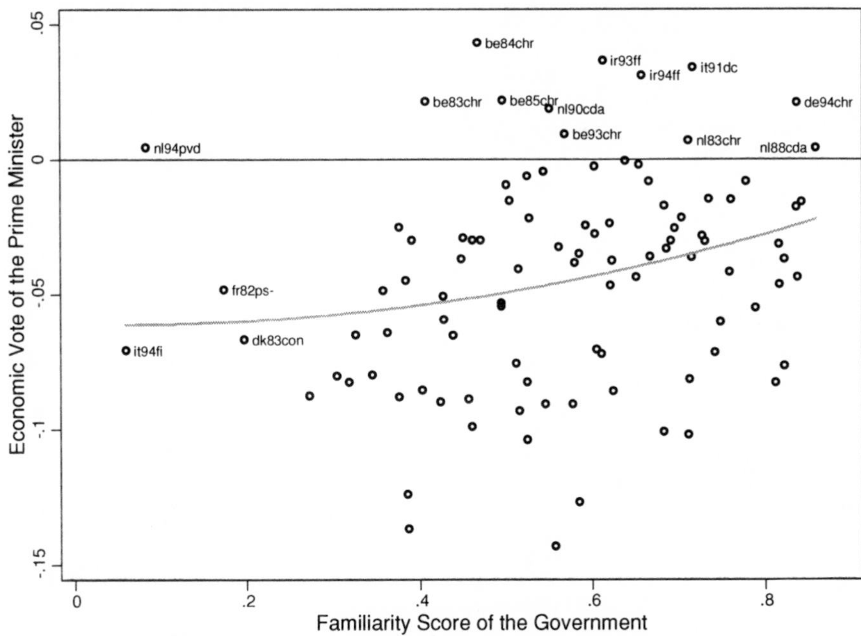

Figure 10.12. Familiarity of the incumbent government and the economic vote in coalitional systems. Larger negative numbers indicate a larger economic vote for the incumbent party.

than .2 (because we would not expect a positive linear relationship to fit the few cases with very low familiarity).

These regression results provide some support for the hypothesis in noncoalitional systems. The coefficients of the quadratic approximation are statistically different from zero in both equations, despite the "filled-in bowl" shape apparent in Figure 10.11 (and implied by the theory). In the case of coalitional systems, the evidence supports part of the hypothesis (i.e., very familiar cabinets in coalitional systems have depressed economic votes compared to those less familiar); but, because there are so few cases of unfamiliar cabinets, we cannot be very confident about our evidence for the left side of the predicted quadratic relationship.

One other thing to notice about these results is the strong positive relationship between the extent to which the prime minister is a member of contending alternative cabinets and the economic vote. This result assures us that the results in the last section that focused on this variable are robust to the inclusion to this measure of the competitiveness of the incumbent cabinet.

Table 10.7. *Familiarity of the Incumbent Government and Economic Voting*

	Noncoalitional Systems		Coalitional Systems		
Familiarity Score	−.38	−.41	−.007	.08	.06
	(−1.97)	(−1.98)	(−.06)	(2.59)	(2.25)
Familiarity Score squared	.30	.33	.061	–	–
	(1.92)	(2.01)	(0.49)	–	–
Probability of entering government in some alternative other than incumbent coalition, given incumbent does not reform (historical method)	–	.05	–	–	.04
	–	(1.60)	–	–	(5.20)
Constant	.04	.05	−.06	−.09	−.10
	(0.76)	(0.87)	−2.09	(−4.27)	(−5.27)
N	53	53	98	94	94
R^2	0.04	.06	0.06	.09	.26

Dependent variable is the *economic vote of the prime minister*. Numbers in cells are coefficients and t-ratios. All models were estimated using OLS regression with standard errors robust to heteroskedacticity and nonindependence between observations of the same party in different surveys. Similar results were obtained from models using the share of the economic vote (for coalitional systems).

A Summary Measure of the Pattern of Contention

Similar to the earlier empirical chapters on the distribution of responsibility and the quality of the competence signal, we end this chapter by developing a summary measure of overall cabinet contention that we can use (in interaction with economic perceptions) in a one-stage, individual-level model of economic voting. Any such measure needs to (1) capture those aspects of the competition for office that we have already shown are most relevant to economic voting, and (2) apply to both coalitional and noncoalitional systems. One measure that we think meets these criteria is the effective number of contenders for the office of chief executive. Although the measure does not capture all of the various aspects of competition that we have argued should matter to economic voting, it has two advantages as a summary measure. First, its focus on the competition for chief executive is consistent with the other analyses in this chapter that show that differences in the distribution of contention for the chief executive tend to have a greater impact on economic voting than differences in the distribution of contention for other roles in government. Thus, the type of contention that is most likely to be relevant to economic voting is contention among parties for the job of chief executive. Second, our theory clearly implies that economic voting in an election will be greater when incumbent parties (and those with greater responsibility) are competitive to return to power in some government (i.e., there is uncertainty as to whether they will or will not enter a new governing coalition). Because chief executive parties normally hold a large share of administrative responsibility, the extent of economic voting in the whole election should be closely tied to the extent to which the chief executive's party is competitive (as opposed to some other party).

The effective number of contenders for chief executive is calculated from our data on the historical record of service in that role. Specifically, for each month during our sample period, we calculate the percentage of months since 1960 that each party has served as chief executive and normalize this number so that it sums to 1 across all the parties competing in a country in a given month. This number then is the share of the historical record of chief executive office-holding that is held by each party in each country calculated for each month in our sample period. Thus, to get the effective number of parties competing for the office of chief executive, we simply apply the standard measure of the effective number of parties to these shares (i.e., we take the reciprocal of the sum of the squared shares). Figure 10.13 plots this measure for each country in our sample from 1980 to 2002. The measure captures the important changes in the pattern of contention that we would expect to see. For example, the most dramatic example of change is in Denmark, where the sudden viability of rightist bourgeoisie coalitions led to the emergence (over the 1980s and 1990s) of the Conservative Party as a real prime ministerial alternative to the (previously) dominant Social Democrats. Similar but less dramatic cases of increasing prime ministerial competition in this period occur in Sweden (essentially the same story as in Denmark) and France (the emergence of the Socialists Party as a viable head of government for the first time since World War II).[42] In contrast, our few cases of Norwegian data show a decline in competition that reflects the

[42] The apparent large increase in competition in Greece results from the fact that their history of democratic competition did not begin until the mid-1970s, so that although there was change in the prime ministry relatively early, this does not register in our measure until the mid-1980s when New Democracy and PASOK experienced their first alternation in power.

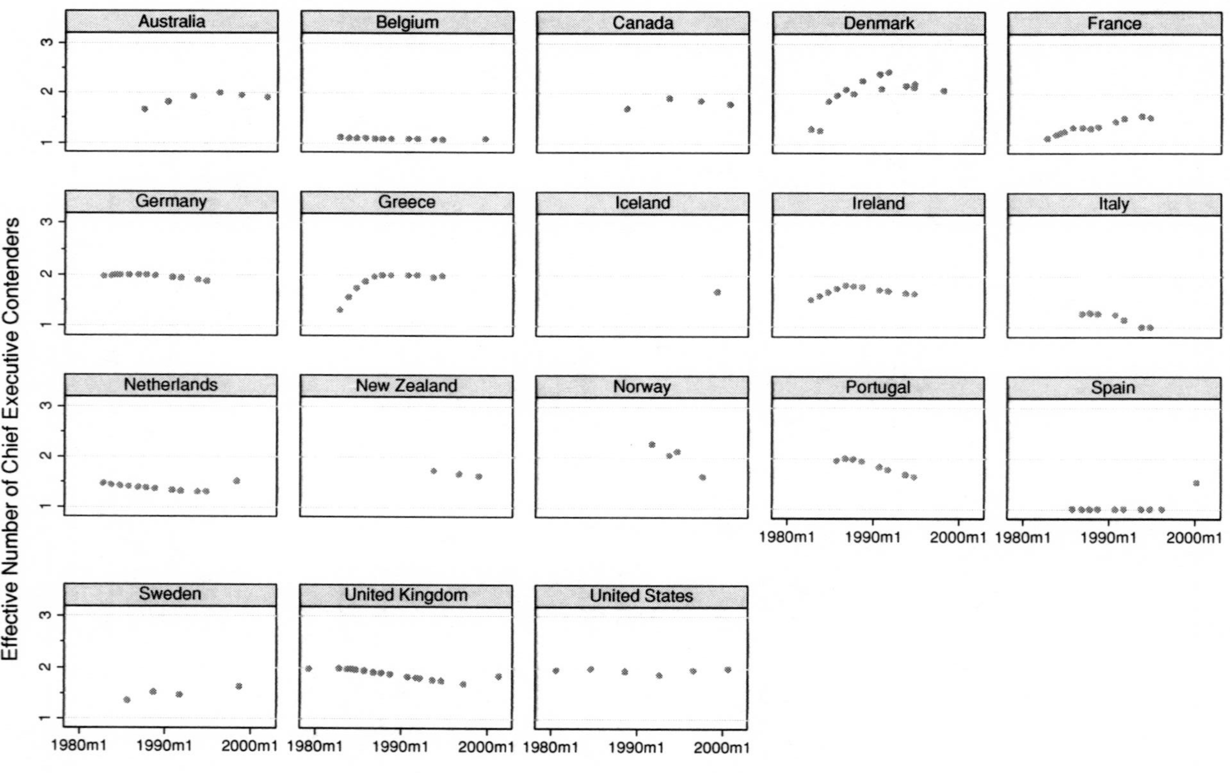

Figure 10.13. Effective number of chief executive contenders.

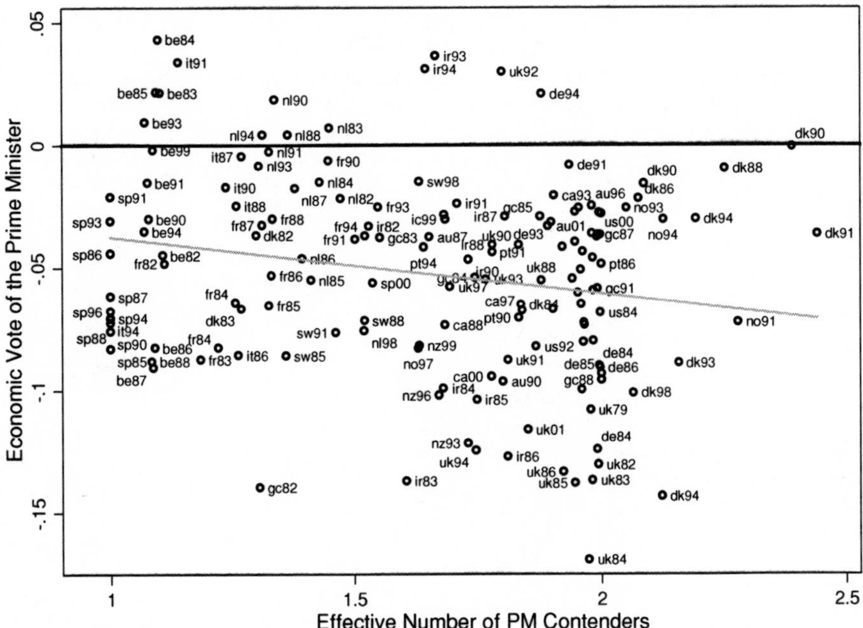

Figure 10.14. Effective number of chief executive contenders and the economic vote of the chief executive. The corresponding regression (with appropriately corrected standard errors) estimates the slope as −.023 with t-statistic of −1.48.

Norwegian Labour Party's dominance of the prime ministry between 1986 and 1997.

Figure 10.14 graphs our measure of the effective number of chief executive contenders against the economic vote of the incumbent chief executive party. Although not statistically significant, the estimated relationship is directionally consistent with our expectations. As competition for the top job in government increases (which in these countries usually means moving from one toward two contenders for the job), we see a larger economic vote.

The main advantage of constructing this measure is that it provides a single summary of much of what is most relevant about the pattern of contention for the 163 cases in our data. Thus, we can use it in a one-stage interactive model in the same way that we used similar summary measures in other chapters. We can interact this measure with individual-level perceptions of the economy after stacking all of our individual data into a single data set. Thus, the size of the economic vote will be estimated simultaneously with the impact of this feature of context.

Table 10.8. *Multilevel Model of Effective Number of PM Contenders and Economic Voting*

Left-Right Self-Placement (deviation from mean)	0.49
	(0.01)
Left-Right Self-Placement × Leftist PM (Leftist PM is an indicator variable)	−0.75
	(0.01)
Voter Perceives Economy Got Better (indicator variable)	0.45
	(0.03)
Voter Perceives Economy Got Worse (indicator variable)	−0.57
	(0.03)
Effective Number of Prime Minister Contenders	−.06
	(.08)
Voter Perceives Economy Got Better × Effective Number of Prime Minister Contenders	.34
	(.08)
Voter Perceives Economy Got Worse × Effective Number of Prime Minister Contenders	−.21
	(.09)
Size of Chief Executive's Party	5.30
	(0.24)
Constant	−2.42
	(0.07)
$\sigma^2_{\omega 1}$	0.09
$\sigma^2_{\omega 2}$	0.07
$\sigma^2_{\omega 3}$	0.10
$\sigma_{\omega 1,\omega 2}$	−0.02
$\sigma_{\omega 1,\omega 3}$	−0.04
$\sigma_{u\omega 2,\omega 3}$	−0.04
N	201,876

Standard errors listed below logit coefficients. All coefficients are statistically significant at $p < 0.1$ except the shaded cells. In the case of the United States, the dependent variable is vote for the party of the president. Congressional election studies are excluded.

As we did in Chapters 7 and 9, we also can examine the impact of this contextual variable on the economic vote in a multilevel model. The specification of the model is exactly as described in Chapter 9, except that we replace the concentration of responsibility variable described there with the effective number of contenders for the chief executive variable described previously. The results of the estimation are provided in Table 10.8. These estimates clearly support the hypothesis because all of the coefficients are statistically significant and in the expected direction. In particular, the *PM Contenders* interaction with positive economic evaluations is positive and significant, and its interaction with negative evaluations is negative and significant. Hence, an increasing effective number of *PM Contenders* results in a greater difference in incumbent vote probabilities between those with a positive versus negative evaluation of economic performance. These pooled, multilevel results tell exactly the same story as the second-stage estimates from the two-stage method – increasing the number of parties that are contenders for the chief executive position increases the *economic vote of the chief executive.*

SUMMARY

Our theory of rational economic voting stipulates that voters must believe that parties are "in contention" for significant governing responsibility in order for the economy to affect their vote for that party. This chapter makes a strong empirical case for this theoretical claim. First, we provide convincing evidence that voters have well-informed beliefs about the pattern of contention that correspond quite closely to both the predictions of empirical models of cabinet formation. Using these two measures of voter beliefs about contention, we were able to test three general hypotheses from our theory.

First, we showed that economic voting has its largest impact on those opposition parties that voters believe are most likely to replace the incumbents. This was the case when we measured voter beliefs about contention using the predictions of empirical models of cabinet formation and employing the historical record of cabinet participation.

The second hypothesis derived from our theory is that economic voting should be weaker for incumbent parties that are members of most of the viable alternative cabinets (i.e., they are perennial cabinet members). The evidence is quite convincing for prime ministerial parties. Perennial prime ministers have a smaller economic vote than prime ministerial parties who are in competition for the position. This result is especially revealing because, although consistent with our theory, it is opposite what one would expect from the more standard "clarity of responsibility" argument found in the literature (because perennial parties should be easy targets for voters seeking to attribute responsibility).

Finally, overall economic voting should be muted when the incumbent cabinet (or alternatives similar to that cabinet) is not in contention to be reselected to govern. Although the results were not as compelling as those for the other two hypotheses, they certainly were directionally correct, suggesting that when the incumbent government as a whole (or a close alternative) is either sure to be or not to be re-selected, economic voting is depressed.

Overall, this chapter makes it clear that an important piece of the explanation for contextual variation in economic voting must be the strategic environment in which parties compete for administrative responsibility. When voters are faced with a situation in which parties are continually returned to government, election after election, economic voting will be depressed. Similarly, even if there is significant competition among opposition parties, if incumbent parties are not also competitive, then the economic vote will be depressed.

PART IV

Conclusion and Summary

11

Conclusion

This book was initially motivated by a simple concern with understanding contextual variation in the economic vote. Accordingly, we set out first to describe the extent of contextual variation in the economic vote across countries, over time, and across parties. To explain this contextual variation, we develop a theoretical explanation rooted in the long tradition of rational-choice explanations of economic voting. These explanations provide a set of plausible (and testable) empirical hypotheses about the kinds of political and economic contexts that are likely to condition the economic vote. Finally, we leverage the evidence from our map of economic voting, along with measures of variation in political and economic context, to test these hypotheses. In this concluding chapter, we first summarize our results and evaluate the extent to which we have fulfilled these goals and ask what work remains to be done. Furthermore, we discuss how the lessons we have learned about economic voting in this project might speak to researchers interested in comparative political behavior more generally.

SUMMARY AND EVALUATION

Variation in the Economic Vote

Part I provides the most comprehensive and comparable description of contextual variation in individual economic voting yet available to political scientists. Our estimates of the economic vote are consistent with the limited comparative evidence already available in the literature. We also produce quite reasonable estimates of economic voting for those parties, countries, and time periods in which previous comparative work has not been available. Moreover, our empirical analyses make it clear that our estimates of economic voting do not depend, in any significant way, on the particular measurement decisions we have made or on our particular conceptualization of economic voting.[1]

Substantively, our map of economic voting confirms, clarifies, and extends the common wisdom about economic voting in Western democracies. Economic voting *is* pervasive – indeed, there is almost no variation in its broad *nature* across different contexts – that is, it is both overwhelmingly incumbency-oriented (i.e., a poor economy hurts incumbents and helps opposition parties) and more important to the party of the chief executive than to other incumbents. At the same time, however, there is significant variation in the *magnitude* of the economic vote across political and economic contexts. Thus, although worsening economic perceptions almost always lowers support for a chief executive party, the extent of this effect may be larger in some contexts and smaller in others.

Contextual Theory of the Economic Vote

A second important objective of this book is to explain this contextual variation. Accordingly, we develop a theory that identifies three broad sources of contextual influences on the magnitude of the economic vote: the extent of political (or electoral) control of the economy; the concentration and distribution of policy-making responsibility over parties; and the pattern of contention among the parties for future policy-making responsibility. Each of these effects is derived from extensions of our basic competency model of the economic vote that identify features of context that inform voters about the size of the competency signal and about strategic voting considerations.

Our theory starts with the observation that in order to understand how context might shape vote choice, one must necessarily begin with an individual-level model of vote choice and must ensure that the assumptions of that model are general enough to apply across a wide variety of political and economic contexts.[2] Our choice was to build our individual-level model of economic voting on the rich theoretical tradition that has assumed economic voting results from the actions of instrumentally

[1] That is, it does not depend on our measurement and conceptual choices from the set of plausible alternatives.

[2] This is not a trivial exercise (in our own model, this required generalizing the Alesina and Rosenthal model from two-party, winner-take-all systems to multiparty, coalitional systems), and it is one that does not receive as much attention as it should in the typical comparative study of voting behavior.

rational voters – a literature that has clearly motivated much of the previous theoretical work on the economic vote. Within the family of rational models of the economic voter, however, we rely on a selection rationale for rational economic voting rather than on the more usual sanctioning perspective. This choice was motivated by our conclusion that the selection approach was a more promising starting point for studying contextual effects than was the sanction approach. In part, we are persuaded by theoretical work, such as that by Fearon (1999), which demonstrates that selection incentives overwhelm sanctioning incentives when models of electoral selection and electoral sanction are combined formally. Specifically, when voters perceive any relevant differences between candidates in an election, it is rational for them to vote over those differences rather than to try to use their vote to discipline incumbents.[3] As we discuss here, however, our belief need not hinder others from exploring context starting from the sanction perspective. Our work here, however, should instruct any such effort by demonstrating that theoretical progress in this area is best achieved when one both clearly articulates the individual model being used and explicitly generalizes the logic of that model to apply to a wide variety of electoral contexts. Thus far, the comparative literature on economic voting that has taken a sanctioning perspective has failed in one or both of these areas.

Our theoretical development takes as a starting point Alesina and Rosenthal's (1995) model of rational retrospective voting. Like them, we assume that voters are motivated by the desire to select the most competent economic managers and voters use information about economic outcomes to assess the future economic competencies of competing candidates. The only economic outcomes that inform the vote choice in our model are those that result in unexpected shocks to the economy (either positive or negative). Voters observe shocks to the macro-economy but cannot observe the mix of exogenous and competence components that comprise these shocks. Voters do, however, know the variances of the distributions of these different kinds of shocks and so are able to solve a well-defined signal-extraction problem that produces a competence signal.

This much of the story is, of course, familiar to those readers conversant with theoretical developments in the literature on political business

[3] Recent work has argued convincingly that electoral systems must logically produce distinctions between candidates and that these distinctions are as important a part of electoral choice as any desire to ensure accountability. For example, Manin (1997: 141–142) emphasizes the inevitability of differences between politicians even when there are strong incentives for them to adopt common ideological positions.

cycles. However, we suggest a reinterpretation of the critical variance terms that comprise the competence signal that drives the model. Specifically, instead of thinking about a single exogenous or competence shock to the economy, we think of these shocks as being the sum of many smaller shocks – each associated with some economically consequential decision. As a result, we replace the usual variances of the distribution of competence and exogenous shocks with expressions for the sum of many much smaller shocks. Assuming that these smaller shocks have equal variances, the critical factor that determines the size of the overall variance terms governing competence and exogenous shocks to the economy are the number of small shocks that contribute to each sum. Furthermore, because only the decisions of electorally accountable decision makers can contribute to "competence" shocks, the overall size of the variance terms in the competence signal (and, thus, its value) is determined by the ratio of electorally accountable economic decisions to nonelectorally economic decisions. Thus, the task of identifying how political and economic institutions may impact economic voting (for this part of the model) reduces to connecting these institutions to voters' beliefs about the relative importance of electorally and nonelectorally accountable decisions on economic performance.

We then generalize the logic of this model to apply to contexts in which multiple parties compete, coalition cabinets may form, and opposition parties may share policy-making responsibility with incumbents. This generalization leads to the identification of the other two general contexts mentioned earlier – the concentration and distribution of policy-making responsibility over parties, and the pattern of contention among the parties for future policy-making responsibility. The first comes from generalizing Alesina and Rosenthal's model of rational retrospective economic voting to allow for multiparty policy making. This leads to a solution to the voter's signal-extraction problem employing what we call the responsibility augmented competency signal. It is maximized when responsibility is maximally concentrated in one party and minimized when responsibility is shared equally among them all. In addition, when we further generalize the model to allow for multiparty competition over the distribution of future policy-making authority, we show that not only will economic voting generally be more important when policy-making responsibility is more concentrated but also that that the economic vote (whatever its overall size) will be more important to the support of specific parties when they have a larger share of policy-making responsibility.

As we emphasized earlier, the predictions of this part of the model are the same as those produced by the clarity of responsibility argument.[4] Because our theory not only makes these predictions but also provides predictions about areas of context for which the clarity argument is silent, there is an opportunity for us to evaluate the added empirical content that our theory provides over the clarity approach. And, as described later, there is at least one hypothesis that stems from our theory that directly contradicts the implications of the clarity approach so provides the opportunity for a kind of critical test between them.

Given that voters in our model are instrumentally rational, our generalization of the model to multiparty contexts requires that we consider the impact of strategic voting incentives on economic voting. These considerations lead us to identify the pattern of contention for policy-making responsibility as the final general context that should impact economic voting. More specifically, we show that economic voting should have its largest impact on those opposition parties that voters believe are most likely to replace the incumbents – because they are members of the most competitive alternative cabinets. Furthermore, overall economic voting should be muted when the incumbent cabinet (or alternatives similar to that cabinet) is not in contention to be reselected to govern. As a result, when voters are faced with a situation in which parties are continually returned to government, election after election, economic voting will be depressed. Or, in the rare event that an incumbent cabinet is certain to lose an election, economic voting will also be muted. Finally, given some level of incumbent contention, the vote of any particular incumbent party's share of the economic vote will be muted relative to its partners if it is a member of many and more competitive alternative cabinets.

This last result is especially revealing because, although consistent with our theory, in the case of "perennial governing parties," it contradicts the clarity of responsibility argument. Perennial governing parties are always in government because they are members of all the viable governing coalitions (e.g., the Belgian, Dutch, and Italian Christian parties) and, as such, our theory says they should get a smaller share of the economic vote than

[4] Once again, it is worth emphasizing that the mechanism that produces these implications in our model is very different from any version of the clarity argument we have seen. In those arguments, the hurdle to economic voting created by shared responsibility stems from the voter's ignorance of who is responsible for policy making. In our model, however, voters know this information perfectly. Instead, our result comes from the fact that shared responsibility degrades the signal that economic performance can provide about the competence of incumbents.

their partners. This, of course, is exactly opposite to what one would expect from the more standard clarity of responsibility argument found in the literature (because perennial parties – particularly large ones – should be easy targets for voters seeking to attribute responsibility).

Hypotheses

The third goal of our project is to use our explanation of economic voting to provide a set of testable empirical hypotheses about the kinds of political and economic contexts that are likely to condition the economic vote. Of course, this process begins with our elaboration of the direct implications of the theoretical model that we have just reviewed. However, this is only the first step in developing our empirical hypotheses about how specific kinds of political and economic institutions should impact economic voting. Specifically, the direct implications of the theory always have the following general form: "Economic perceptions will be more important to the support of voters who believe X than they will for voters who believe Y." For example, one implication of our theory is that economic perceptions will be more important to the support of voters who believe the distribution of policy-making responsibility is concentrated than those who do not. Likewise, our theory implies that economic perceptions will be more important to the support of voters who believe the ratio of electorally accountable to nonelectorally accountable decision makers is large than those who believe this ratio is smaller.

To move from these direct implications about the beliefs of individuals on the economic vote to empirical implications about the impact of political and economic institutions on the economic vote for parties, we must supplement the implications of the theory with assumptions about how specific political and economic institutions shape the average voter's beliefs about such things as the distribution of policy-making responsibility among parties or the ratio of electorally and nonelectorally accountable decision makers. So, for example, we assume that voters believe that the distribution of policy-making responsibility is more concentrated in single-party cabinets than in coalition cabinets and so test the hypotheses that the economic vote of single-party cabinets will be larger than that of coalition cabinets. Likewise, we assume that voters believe that the ratio of electorally accountable to nonelectorally accountable decision makers is smaller in open economies than it is in more closed economies and so hypothesize that economic openness will depress the economic vote. Other such auxiliary assumptions are found in each of the main empirical chapters in Parts II and III and, when combined with the direct implications of the theory, result in the various empirical hypotheses that we test.

Evidence

Each of our empirical hypotheses relates a particular economic or political variable to the magnitude or share of the economic vote for a party or parties; and, the final goal of our book is to use our data on economic voting to test them. First, in Chapter 7, we explore a set of hypotheses about how political and economic institutions impact economic voting by changing the ratio of electorally accountable and nonelectorally accountable economic decision makers. Specifically, we assume that voters will perceive a higher ratio of nonelectorally accountable to electorally accountable decision makers in open economies than in more closed ones, and so economic voting will be less important in open economies. This comports with much of the political-economy literature, suggesting that domestic governments have declining economic policy-making latitude in open economies. A similar reasoning leads us to a more counterintuitive prediction: voters will perceive a higher ratio of politically nonaccountable to politically accountable decision makers in contexts with an expansive state sector. This, in turn, will result in a lower competency signal and lower economic voting. These two results are consistent with our theoretical argument and they predict lower levels of economic voting in contexts with open economies and with an expansive state sector – both of which turn out to be confirmed by the empirical analysis.

This result has important implications for trends in economic voting because these are characteristics of the political and economic context that (1) are changing quite dramatically over time (national economies are becoming increasingly integrated into the world economy); and (2) are increasingly distinctive cross-nationally (nations differ considerably in terms of the scope of their state sectors). We suggest how the interaction among these two trends might affect trends in economic voting and democratic accountability more generally. The net implications of globalization for the economic vote depend on whether greater exposure to the international economy occurs in a context with an extensive as opposed to more limited state sector. A larger government sector may, in fact, moderate the negative social consequences of globalization but our competency theory suggests that broadening the scope of government's involvement in the economy reinforces the negative impact that trade openness exerts on the economic vote. More specifically, increasing the size of the government sector, embracing corporatist institutions, and increasing government regulation reduce the magnitude of the incumbent's competency signal, leading voters to discount the importance of the economy in their voting decision. Paradoxically, countries that respond to increased exposure to global economic forces by privatizing their economies and adopting liberal economic policies are more likely to compensate for the decline in economic voting associated with globalization.

Second, the empirical work in Chapter 9 explores how various indicators of policy-making responsibility impact economic voting. We assume that voters believe policy-making responsibility to be less concentrated when cabinet seats are more equally divided among parties, when minority cabinets rule, and when oppositions are empowered. Our empirical evidence for each of these claims is strong. In addition to these general hypotheses about the concentration of responsibility, we also assume that voters attribute more responsibility to prime ministers than their partners, more to parties holding more seats in cabinet than to those holding less, more to parties holding the finance ministry than to those who do not, more to cabinet parties than to opposition parties, more to single-party prime ministers than to prime ministers of coalition cabinets, and (most controversially) more to single-party prime ministers than to presidents. Again, our empirical evidence strongly supports each of these predicted relationships. Indeed, there is simply no doubt that the current distribution of policy-making responsibility strongly conditions the economic vote in Western democracies.

Finally, in Chapter 10, we explore how voters' beliefs about the pattern of contention for policy-making responsibility impact the economic vote. Alhough our specific hypotheses rely on various aspects of contention – for example, whether a party is in many competitive alternative cabinets or how competitive is the incumbent cabinet as a whole – each ultimately requires that we say something about the voters' beliefs about which parties or coalitions of parties are likely to be in competition to obtain executive authority. We used two strategies (or auxiliary hypotheses) for doing this. First, we assumed that the voters' beliefs about the competitiveness of different parties or coalitions resulted from the historical record – that is, which parties or coalitions had policy-making responsibility in the past. Second, we assumed that these beliefs stemmed from the rational voter's "model" of how current observable characteristics of parties (e.g., their size or ideology) get translated into policy-making responsibility. Thus, we tested hypotheses linking a party's history of cabinet participation to the economic vote of opposition parties, as well as ones linking these parties' predicted probabilities of entering a cabinet to their economic vote – where the predicted probabilities come from a statistical model of cabinet formation. Likewise, for incumbents, we examine the connection between economic voting and the chance that cabinets similar to the current cabinet come to power. Finally, we show that the economic vote for incumbent parties that are members of competitive alternative cabinets is muted relative to their partners.

Taken together, these results provide strong support for the idea that the pattern of contention for policy-making authority has an important though previously under appreciated impact on the economic vote. Furthermore, when we examine this impact alongside measures of the current distribution of responsibility, we find that the pattern of contention has a strong independent impact on economic voting. This is seen most clearly in the case of perennial prime ministers. According to both our theory and the clarity of responsibility argument mentioned earlier, these parties should, based on their large share of policy-making responsibility, have large economic votes. However, when one adds to this the implications of the pattern of contention for the economic vote (which our theory does and the clarity argument does not), we predict that perennial prime ministers – who will be in all the cabinets that form – will actually have a depressed economic vote relative to their smaller partners. This is exactly what we find in countries such as Belgium, the Netherlands, and Italy – all cases in which the critical role of the dominant Christian parties in policy making could not have been lost on most voters, but where, nevertheless, economic voting for these parties is smaller relative to their partners than we would otherwise expect.

WHAT REMAINS TO BE DONE?

In this section, we ask what remains to be done both in extending the approach to economic voting we have developed in this book and developing the study of comparative economic voting more generally. Specifically, we think there are at least three fruitful areas in which the work begun in this book can and should be extended: (1) explorations of the assumptions of our model with the goal of improving its theoretical foundations; (2) development of alternative theoretical models so that they are both precise enough and general enough to be usefully contrasted to ours; and (3) continued empirical testing of the implications of our model that more completely capture the complex interactions implied by the theory. We discuss each of these possible areas of future work here.

Exploring Our Assumptions and Their Implications for Differences among Individuals

Although we think that our theory produces plausible empirical hypotheses about the impact of political and economic institutions on the average level of economic voting for a party or in a system, these hypotheses rest on a foundation of assumptions about the knowledge and behavior of individuals that, with some exceptions – Chapter 6 and the beginning of Chapter 10 – we have ignored empirically. In this brief section, we highlight several places in which our theory makes strong assumptions about what individuals do and do not know about their economies and political systems but that are quite amenable to future empirical exploration. Furthermore, although our focus has been on the impact of political and economic institutions on economic voting, our theory is ultimately about individuals and so we point out places in which its direct implications could be tested by looking at differences among individuals.

The first set of contextual implications that we produced from our theory rested on micro-level assumptions regarding what individuals actually know about electorally versus nonelectorally accountable decision making in different national contexts. These have not been empirically explored in this book. Is it reasonable to think that large government contexts have a smaller ratio of nonelectorally accountable to politically accountable decision makers than limited government contexts? Moreover, do voters perceive these differences? And is it reasonable to think that voters in open economies recognize that their economic outcomes are more affected by nonelectorally accountable decision makers? In general, are voters sensitive to the electoral accountability of decision makers and do they make the kind of inferences from this information that we attribute to them? We do not have definitive answers to these questions. Clearly, though, our theoretical claims regarding the impact of electorally versus nonelectorally decision making on the economic vote are contingent on the answers to these empirical questions. The importance of addressing these empirical issues goes well beyond explaining the economic vote. These empirical issues have broader implications for our understanding of democratic governance because we are proposing here a model of how citizens learn about the competency of governing elites that we believe is critical to understanding the extent to which they hold elected officials accountable for policy outcomes.

Second, economic voters, according to our theory, use the pattern of contention for policy-making responsibility in their vote choice.

Moreover, the pattern of contention may concern not just electoral contention between single parties but also the pattern of contention among potential *distributions of responsibility*. We assume that voters have knowledge about which parties or coalitions of parties are likely to form the government (or participate in policy making). They are also sensitive to how voting for a party affects the likelihood of different coalitions forming the government. Understanding the extent to which voters make these assessments, how they obtain the information necessary to do so, and how this affects their vote choice will represent an important extension of our theoretical and empirical work on the strategic economic vote reported in this book. We present, in Chapter 10, some preliminary evidence from three elections that support our assumption that voters understand which parties are likely to participate in a governing coalition and their likely roles in the cabinet. But we have not explored this across a variety of different contexts; nor have we investigated how voters actually obtain this information. It might be that media messages regarding contention are very informative in multiparty contexts and that in these contexts, voters pay close attention to them. Alternatively, the strategic economic vote may be mediated by elite activity in a fashion similar to the argument developed by Cox and Munger (1989) to explain the relationship between contention and turnout in U.S. congressional elections. Elite efforts on behalf of parties in contention for administrative responsibility may be the mechanism that mobilizes the economic vote for parties in contention for administrative responsibility. Developing and empirically evaluating these precise mechanisms will be a critical step toward confirming (or maybe challenging) the strategic economic voting results reported in Chapter 10.

Finally, because each of the aggregate-level hypotheses explored in this book stems from a more direct hypothesis about individuals, it would be worthwhile for scholars to investigate whether differences in beliefs among individuals in the same electoral context lead to the difference in economic voting at the individual level that our theory would predict. So, for example, it would be worthwhile to develop a set of survey questions that could tap the extent to which voters believe economic outcomes are the result of decisions by electorally accountable individuals or nonelectorally accountable ones. With such a measure, one could examine directly whether individuals with different beliefs about this were more or less likely to cast economic votes. Similarly, in Chapter 10, we saw one way that survey questions can be used to discover what voters believe about the competitiveness of different potential coalitions. Again, with such a measure, surveys that also included economic perceptions and vote-choice questions could test directly for the impact of difference in such beliefs on individual-level economic voting.

Alternative Models

We see no reason in principle why an alternative theoretical approach building on different micro-foundations might not follow the approach we have taken in this book and so derive alternative explanations for contextual variation in the economic vote. Alternative theoretical approaches building on conventional sanctioning models are an obvious candidate. As we noted in the introduction, Hibbs (2006) argues for a contextual theory of the economic vote that builds on the conventional retrospective punishment model and that incorporates Kramer's (1983) "error-in-variables" conception of economic evaluations as a measure of the signal-to-noise ratio regarding incumbent economic performance. Hibbs (2006) suggests that contexts in which the politically relevant portion of macro-economic outcomes is small – reflected in relatively high measurement error when overall economic evaluations are used – will be those that have a low correlation between economic evaluations and vote choice. Although it is a potentially promising theoretical approach, to our knowledge, no one has developed a fully specified contextual theory of economic voting that builds on these insights.

There are other possible micro-foundations for a contextual theory of the economic vote. A theoretical approach that builds on emotional responses to the macro-economy might be another candidate. One example is Lodge's model in which people's evaluations of candidates are "read" from a long-term tally that tracks the totality of the emotional responses that people have had to messages they have received about the candidates (Lodge et al. 1995). Some of these messages concern the economy and, if one assumes that people have a negative emotional response to the incumbent when bad economic news is received, then we would expect an association between their perceptions of the economy and their evaluations of the incumbent candidate, mediated by their tally of negative emotional responses. In Zaller's model (1992), voters also receive messages but, in his case, their evaluations of candidates are based on a random selection from the pool of messages they have received and accepted. If a voter receives and accepts negative economic messages and understands these as negative incumbent messages, then they will be more likely to sample a negative opinion of the incumbent. And Zaller (2004) has explored the application of this model to the economic vote by exploring empirically which groups in the population actually accept these negative messages regarding the economy.

Instead of thinking of sanctioning as a way that rational voters induce politicians not to shirk their responsibilities (i.e., as a moral hazard problem), we could ask how context would impact economic voting in a sanction model that invokes emotional response. This enterprise, however, would require that we have a well-specified theory of emotional response and how these responses connect to individual perceptions of aggregate economic performance. Although there has been an effort among political psychologists to develop general models of the impact of emotions on political judgments (e.g., the *Affective Intelligence Theory* proposed by Marcus, Neuman, and MacKuen [2000]), we simply know too little about what triggers specific emotional responses to predict with any confidence how variations in political and economic context are likely to affect emotional responses at the individual level (Ladd and Lenz, 2004).

Any one of these alternative modeling approaches might serve as the basis for developing explanations for the contextual variation described in Chapter 3. But, at least to our knowledge, no one has taken these alternative models of vote choice as a point of departure and then derived rigorous explanations for how the vote decisions are conditioned by context. Much of the empirical literature that examines economic voting in different political contexts (e.g., the clarity of responsibility literature) is motivated from a loose discussion of elections as devices of electoral sanction (particularly the moral hazard version of the argument). Hence, it remains to be seen whether alternative models of vote choice might provide more powerful explanations for the contextual variation in the economic vote.

Complex Causation and Alternative Ways to Explore the Implications of Our Theory

At any point in time, context will, of course, provide multiple cues to the voter regarding strategic incentives in addition to the competency signals that are central to our theory. Exploring in greater detail precisely how voters respond to these multiple, sometimes contradictory, signals will be an important extension of the research we have conducted to date. Indeed, we used the fact that voters receive different contextual signals as a critical test of our contention argument: this critical condition occurs when the voter is evaluating an incumbent party that has a high degree of administrative responsibility but one that is not in "contention" – that is, either certain to enter the governing coalition or certain not to participate in government. Our theory clearly predicts that there should be no economic vote in this situation, whereas conventional explanations, such as clarity of responsibility, suggest exactly the opposite: there should be a significant economic vote.

In fact, these juxtapositions of contextual features are likely to be most revealing about how context shapes the economic vote. So, for example, we predict little economic voting in contexts with very open economies and with an extensive state sector *even* for cases in which administrative responsibility is highly concentrated – say, in the case of single-party majority governments (which, all things being equal, contributes to a high economic vote). A more likely scenario, though, is that each of these measures – our trade/state sector index and our responsibility measure – assumes values that either moderate or exaggerate the importance of the economy in vote choice. The interesting question in this case is identifying the unique contribution of each of these contextual variables. These examples illustrate the two estimation issues that we do not address in any depth in this book but clearly are of central importance to future research in this area: determining the independent effects of each of these three contextual variables and sorting out the causal complexity of our hypothesized relationships.

First, do each of these contextual effects have independent effects on the economic vote and what are their relative magnitudes? Clearly, there will be economic votes that are exercised in contexts in which the ratio of electorally to nonelectorally accountability decision makers is high, in which a party has high administrative responsibility and in which a party is also very much in contention. Readers will note that in many of the bivariate plots presented throughout the book, there are countries that seem to have values on all of the contextual measures that are driving the economic vote in the same direction. The Netherlands, for example, is highly integrated into the global economy, has a history of a perennial incumbent prime ministerial party; and administrative responsibility is shared by a number of parties. Hence, the values of all three contextual variables for the Netherlands predict a low economic vote. In fact, it turns out that this collinearity is relatively significant in our data set. In addition, as we saw in Chapter 7, some of the country characteristics, such as trade openness, simply do not vary much over the sample. These features of the data, plus the fact that we typically have only 163 observations of the contextual variables for analysis, make it difficult to estimate these independent effects.

As the number of these voter-preference studies increases over time, we will undoubtedly get better estimates of these independent effects. In the meantime, we can obtain at least some order-of-magnitude estimates of the relative importance of these three contextual variables for the economic vote. Our goal here is simply to demonstrate that each of the three contextual variables exercises some independent effect on the economic vote. Accordingly, we present in the first three columns of Table 11.1 model specifications that pair each contextual variable with one of the other contextual variables. Combining the interaction effects of the different context variables reduces some of the interactions that we saw in the models estimated in Chapters 7, 9, and 10, in which each context effect was estimated on its own. The interaction of concentration of responsibility with positive economic evaluations is attenuated when it is included in models with the open economy/extensive state sector context interaction terms. The prime minister contender contextual variable interacted with negative economic evaluations is attenuated whenever these effects are paired with another contextual effect. But really what is important here is that all three of these contextual variables have the hypothesized effect – even when paired with each other – of exaggerating the difference in vote probabilities of individuals with positive versus negative economic evaluations.

These effects are confirmed in Model 4, which includes the three context variables and their interactions with the two economic evaluation variables. Despite the relatively high degree of collinearity among these variables, the three basic contextual effects are confirmed in this combined model. The difference in the economic vote of those with positive versus negative evaluations is significantly greater, in contexts with an open economy and an expansive state sector; when administrative responsibility is concentrated; and when there are more prime minister contenders. This results from the fact that in the case of each context interaction, at least one of the interaction terms is significant in the predicted direction (and none of the interaction effects are significant in the wrong direction). The most important consequence of combining the three context effects (compared to the estimating separate context effects) is that the interaction effects for each contextual interaction term tend to be significant in only one direction: the interaction effects for the *open economy/extensive state sector* and *PM contenders* variables are significant in interaction with the positive economic evaluation variable; whereas the *concentration of administrative responsibility* variable is significant in interaction with negative economic evaluations. Given more observations and variation on the

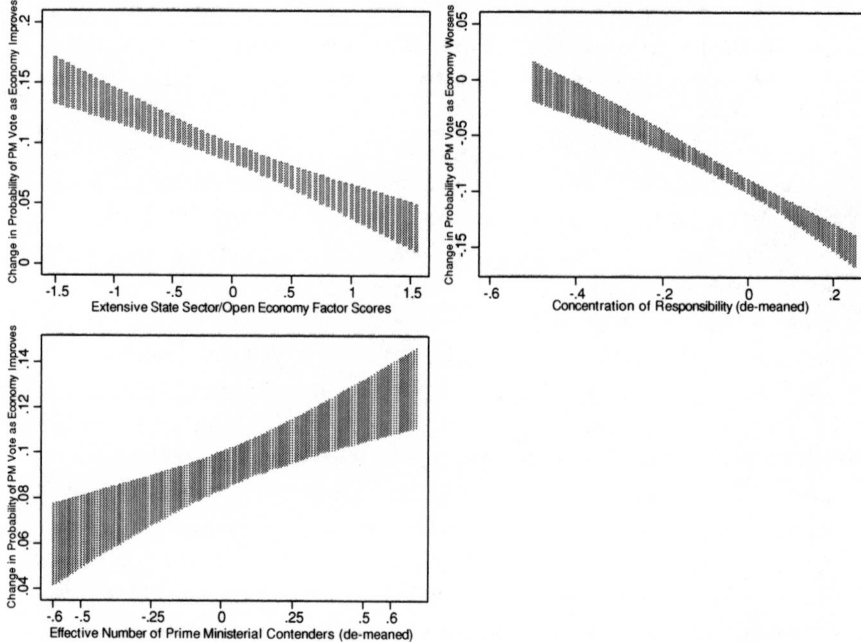

Figure 11.1. Multivariate estimates of the impact of extensive state sector/open economy, concentration of responsibility, and effective number of prime ministerial contenders (PM) on the economic vote.

contextual variables, we would likely see the same symmetric effects we saw in the individual contextual models.

Figure 11.1 illustrates the change in predicted probabilities of voting for the chief executive party associated with different values of the three contextual variables – in each case, we have plotted the direction of the economic evaluation change that matches the significance of the interaction effects in Table 11.1. The first graph illustrates how the political-economic context conditions the impact of an improving economic evaluation on the vote for the chief executive party. For countries scoring very low on the *open economy/extensive state sector* measure – that is to say, a closed economy with a limited government sector – a unit improvement in economic perceptions results in an improvement of .15 in the party's vote probabilities. At the average reading on this scale, zero, the economic vote is about 9 percent, dropping to around 4 percent for countries that have the most open economies and a large state sector. For the variable measuring the *concentration of administrative responsibility*, note that at zero, the mean value for the responsibility variable, the economic vote is

Table 11.1. *Multilevel Logistic Regression Model of Chief Executive Vote*

	Model 1	Model 2	Model 3	Model 4
Left-Right Self-Placement (deviation from mean)	0.48	0.48	0.49	0.48
	(0.01)	(0.01)	(0.01)	(0.01)
Left-Right Self-Placement × Leftist PM (Leftist PM is indicator variable)	−0.88	−0.88	−0.75	−0.88
	(0.01)	(0.01)	(0.01)	(0.01)
Voter Perceives Economy Got Better (indicator variable)	0.45	0.45	0.45	0.44
	(0.03)	(0.03)	(0.03)	(0.03)
Voter Perceives Economy Got Worse (Indicator variable)	−0.59	−0.56	−0.57	−0.59
	(0.03)	(0.04)	(0.03)	(0.03)
Open Economy/Extensive State Sector	0.07	−0.06		0.04
	(0.04)	(.04)		(0.04)
Voter Perceives Economy Got Better × Open Economy/ Extensive State Sector	−0.22	−0.18		−0.18
	(0.05)	(0.04)		(0.05)
Voter Perceives Economy Got Worse × Open Economy/ Extensive State Sector	0.09	0.19		0.09
	(0.05)	(0.05)		(0.05)
Concentration of Executive Responsibility (deviation from mean)	0.89		0.88	0.91
	(0.20)		(0.15)	(0.19)
Voter Perceives Economy Got Better × Concentration of Executive Responsibility	0.01		0.47	−0.07
	(0.22)		(0.15)	(0.21)
Voter Perceives Economy Got Worse × Concentration of Executive Responsibility	−0.78		−0.92	−0.78
	(0.21)		(0.15)	(0.22)
PM Contenders		−0.23	−.11	−0.23
		(0.09)	(.07)	(0.08)
Voter Perceives Economy Got Better × PM Contenders		0.26	.29	0.26
		(0.09)	(.08)	(0.09)
Voter Perceives Economy Got Worse × PM Contenders		−0.05	−.11	−0.01
		(0.11)	(.08)	(0.10)
Size of Chief Executive's Party	5.49	6.30	4.61	5.66
	(0.32)	(0.29)	(0.26)	(0.32)
	−2.48	−2.74	−2.21	−2.53
Constant	(0.10)	(0.09)	(0.08)	(0.10)
$\sigma^2_{\omega 1}$	0.05	0.06	0.07	0.05
$\sigma^2_{\omega 2}$	0.06	0.06	0.07	0.05
$\sigma^2_{\omega 3}$	0.06	0.08	0.07	0.06
$\sigma_{\omega 1,\omega 2}$	−0.02	−0.02	−0.03	−0.02
$\sigma_{\omega 1,\omega 3}$	−0.01	−0.02	−0.02	−0.01
$\sigma_{u\omega 2,\omega 3}$	−0.03	−0.04	−0.03	−0.03
N	201,876	201,876	201,876	201,876

Standard errors are listed below the logit coefficients. All coefficients are statistically significant at $p < 0.1$, except the shaded cells.

10 percent, whereas at the extreme value of concentration of responsibility – about 0.2 – the economic vote increases to 15 percent. The economic vote drops to zero for those cases that score very low on the measure (in the neighborhood of −0.4). In the case of our summary measure of contention – *PM contenders* – the economic vote is about 9 percent in contexts with the average value of zero, and it rises to 12 percent in contexts with high *PM contenders* score and falls to 6 percent in those with very low score. We do not want to make too much of these multivariate results for the reasons we pointed out earlier. Nevertheless, despite the data limitations here, we think the results summarized in Table 11.1 and illustrated in Figure 11.1 confirm that each of our three theoretical variables make an important independent contribution to explaining contextual variation in the economic vote. With time, of course, we will have a much larger sample of voter preferences studies that will provide the added contextual variation that we suspect will provide even stronger confirmation of the independent effect of these three contextual variables.

In presenting our empirical results, we have alluded to a second reason why the independent effects of our contextual variables may be attenuated in linear models. Our theory implies that the impact of these contexts on the economic vote should, in fact, not be independent of one another. Recall that in the equations describing the voter's utility of voting for a party, the βs, αs, Ps, λs, and σ^2s all end up in the voter's value function as multiplicative coefficients on the change in the economy. If any one of these is zero, the previous economy will fall out of the voter's value function for a party and the other contexts can have no further impact on economic voting, whatever their value. More generally, for example, this occurs when three conditions, C_1 and C_2 and C_3, jointly produce Y, so that the impact of changes in one condition on Y depends on the others. There are, in effect, multiple paths of nonoccurrence of the dependent variable such that the absence of any one condition nullifies the impact of the others. For example, with respect to our model, attribution of responsibility to a party **and** a belief that the party is in contention for the prime ministry **and** the possibility of discerning a competency signal from the background noise of economic fluctuations **produce** an economic vote for a party. If any one of these conditions is not met, then we do not expect any economic voting.[5] Furthermore, as any one variable moves toward zero, it will diminish the impact of the other three. The competency model of rational retrospective

[5] This is an estimation problem that Ragin (1987) initially identified as being particularly problematic in qualitative studies in comparative research.

economic voting suggests that economic voting will be contingent on a number of conditions being met – any of which, if absent, will sap the incentive of voters to use the retrospective economy in their vote choice.

This effect results in a triangular or wedge shape that is found in many of our graphs. We see this because the theory states that when C_1 is absent, then Y (economic voting) cannot occur. However, when C_1 is large, economic voting may occur, but whether it does or not depends on the values of C_2 and C_3. Clearly, a linear approximation to this relationship will often reveal a generally positive relationship, but if the data have this pattern, it will tend to be flattened relative to a true linear relationship because there will be cases in which C_1 is large but there is nevertheless no economic voting. We think that our bivariate graphs of context and economic voting reflect this kind of wedge-shaped structure. Hence, it is important, when we use linear models to approximate this relationship, that we do not simply run statistical models and look for statistical significance; rather, we need to examine graphs to evaluate whether we see the expected wedge shapes. Accordingly, we relied extensively on the graphical presentation of relationships throughout the book.

The hypothesis tests that we report in our empirical chapters can only be approximate because they do not account for the multiple conjunctural nature of the hypotheses developed from our theory. Although it would be ideal to test our hypotheses using techniques that do capture this causal structure, the statistical literature on multiple conjectural causation does not yet provide appropriate techniques for doing this with the kind of data we have.[6] For this reason, we did not abandon traditional techniques of examining the data. Ultimately, though, the validity of the theoretical arguments we developed here will depend on accounts for the multiple conjunctural nature of our hypotheses. Accordingly, solving the technical challenges associated with estimating statistical model that can account for multiple conjectural causation will be critical for making progress in our understanding of how context shapes vote choice.

IMPLICATIONS FOR COMPARATIVE STUDIES OF POLITICAL BEHAVIOR

Despite these challenges that remain to be addressed, we have made significant advances in understanding how context conditions the vote choice in

[6] See Braumoeller (2003) for a discussion of some of the estimation issues associated with the multiple conjectural causation that we described here.

general, even though our focus here has been on the economic vote. Two very broad insights regarding models of vote choice emerge: (1) modeling efforts that do not incorporate contextual variation are very likely wrong; and (2) theories of contextual variation in vote choice need to address the full range of contextual variation in vote choice, which is rarely the case in current research.

In estimating individual-level vote-choice models, in which the political or economic context is of consequence for the voting decision (and it is difficult to imagine when this might not be the case), contextual variation is not an option or an interesting extension of a single-case study; it is an essential part of the research design. The empirical ramifications of ignoring this maxim for the analysis of individual survey data are rarely demonstrated primarily because of small-N problems. Our project is unique in analyzing a large number of voter-preference surveys that allow us to get some insight into the consequences of ignoring context in empirical estimations. This is nicely illustrated by our empirical analysis presented in Part I of the book, in which we demonstrate that the economic vote for any particular party varies quite significantly, even from one election to the next. Our density plot of economic-vote magnitudes in Chapter 3 suggests that the estimated economic vote in about a quarter of the surveys in our sample is essentially zero. This, of course, is the logical consequence of context being important – there will be contexts in which the estimated effects will be very low or zero. Hence, to say that there is "no economic vote" in a particular context is not the same thing as saying there is no economic voting. And it certainly does not imply that voters are not rational. In fact, the absence of an economic vote in some contexts, as we demonstrate, is a testament to instrumentally rational voting. This implies, and the empirical results confirm, that there will be political parties – including the prime minister's party – that receive no economic vote with some regularity. Many – although certainly not all – of these observed zero economic votes are predicted to have this value because of the contextual factors identified in our theory.

And, even more important, it suggests that drawing conclusions about vote choice (or political behavior, more broadly) based on estimates from a single context (either in time or cross-sectionally) could very well lead to the wrong conclusion. So, for example, estimating a vote-choice model from surveys conducted in 1997 in the United Kingdom and finding an insignificant coefficient for the economic evaluations variable might lead some to conclude that there is no economic vote in the United Kingdom and that this might constitute evidence that voters are not behaving "rationally." As our theory and empirical evidence in this book strongly suggest, this would be patently wrong. But, of course, this applies to any model of vote choice – not including contextual variables, including the wrong ones, or simply drawing conclusions based on analysis from a single context, all could very likely lead to the wrong conclusions regarding the behavior of voters. A properly specified vote-choice model presumes you have properly specified contextual effects. At least in the case of individual vote-choice models, this is difficult to accomplish without samples extending over time and across national contexts.[7]

We believe that incorporating this contextual variation in individual-level models is both essential and currently feasible. As a result of almost fifty years of conducting voter-preference surveys throughout the developed world, we now have surveys from a large number of political and economic contexts. The strategy we describe in Chapter 4 for estimating contextual effects on the economic vote can easily be adapted for estimating the impact of context on other variables in the vote-choice calculus. Moreover, there are a number of factors that are widely considered to play an important role in vote choice, which means there are measures of these concepts in most voter-preference surveys – for example, ideology, postmaterialism, democratic satisfaction, partisanship, class, and so on. Hence, in our view, political scientists are well equipped with the data and the methods necessary to estimate the conditional effects of context on the factors shaping vote choice. The challenge is theoretical: developing contextual theories, as we have done in this book, that explain how these diverse factors shaping vote choice are conditioned by context.

Our findings also provide an important insight into the nature of this theoretical challenge. In particular, our results indicate that any contextual theory of vote choice that informs a well-specified model of vote choice needs to account for contextual effects that are very diverse or multidimensional in character. The analysis of variance summarized in Chapter 3 provides an important clue as to the nature of the variation in vote choice that needs to be accounted for by contextual variables. This analysis demonstrated that the economic vote can vary significantly from one voter-preference survey to the next. Although the median economic vote is around 7 percent, in any survey it could range between −20 and 8 percent. We have little doubt that this is also the case for other vote-choice models – there will be contextual variation in the "ideological

[7] One could think of experimental research designs that might represent another approach to incorporating context in empirical models of vote choice.

vote" (in fact, we document the extent of this in Chapter 3) in the "partisan vote," in the "spatial vote," and so on. What is particularly interesting about the economic vote variation we described in Chapter 3 is that much of it is survey-to-survey rather than a function of a temporal trend or cross-national effects. But to the extent that the literature addresses context at all, it tends to favor explanations grounded in temporal trends – think of "the end of class voting" or "the end of ideology" or "the decline of partisanship." Or, alternatively, the literature focuses on cross-national effects such as institutional characteristics or features of the economy that are quite static. In contrast, our examination of variation in the economic vote suggests that much of its variation is unique to each voter-preference survey. In other words, a lot of the interesting action in the data is distinct variations in the economic vote from one voter-preference study to the next within each country. Accordingly, we need theories that not only address cross-national variations in vote-choice models and temporal trends in these models but also that explain variation in vote-choice models that is unique to each voter-preference survey (or unique to each election, as the case might be). For example, we need theory that explains why ideology might be important in a Dutch vote-choice model in 2000 but much less important in 2004. Theories that are unable to address this dimension of contextual variation in vote-choice models are likely to fare quite poorly in terms of accounting for how voters factor context into their voting calculus.

This book was initially motivated by a simple concern with understanding contextual variation in the economic vote. It became clear to us – probably not as quickly as it should have – that this required that we think about a more general puzzle: How is the *vote calculus* conditioned by context? In particular, how does context condition the importance that voters accord their evaluations of government performance or their issue positions or maybe candidate personality when they make a vote decision? We have focused here on economic evaluations in the voting calculus because we believe (and have conclusively demonstrated) that this is one of the most important considerations shaping vote choice. And although it is true that our theory of context explicitly concerns economic evaluations and vote choice, we think the general theoretical and empirical approaches can inform efforts to understand how context conditions the importance of most other important factors that shape the vote decision.

Appendix A

Define a *vote total* for party $j \in \mathbf{J}$ as $v_j = \sum_{i=1}^{n} v_{ij}$, where i indexes n voters and v_{ij} is 1 if voter i votes for party j and 0 otherwise. We denote the vector of vote totals for the J parties in $\mathbf{J}$ as $\mathbf{v}_\mathrm{J} = \{v_1, v_2, \ldots, v_J\}$. We consider two different characterizations of the distribution of policy-making responsibility over parties. First, define $\lambda_k = \{\lambda_{k1}, \lambda_{k2}, \lambda_{kj}, \ldots, \lambda_{kJ}\}$ as a *distribution of responsibility* over the J parties, where $\lambda_k \in \Lambda$ is the finite set of all such distributions (of which there are K). Further, we assume that $\lambda_{kj} \geq 0$ for all λ_{kj} and that $\sum_{j \in \mathrm{J}} \lambda_{kj} = 1$.[1] Next, define $\mathbf{g}_m = \{g_{m1}, g_{m2}, g_{mj}, \ldots, g_{mJ}\}$, where $g_{mj} = 1$ if party j is a member of cabinet (or proposed cabinet) $\mathbf{g}_m$ and 0 otherwise. $\mathbf{g}_m \in \mathbf{G}$ is the finite set of all possible cabinets (of which there are M).

Define the *electoral support* associated with any distribution of responsibility λ_k as $v_{\lambda_k} = \sum_{j \in \mathrm{J}} \lambda_{kj} v_j$ and $\mathbf{v}_\Lambda = \{v_{\lambda_1}, v_{\lambda_2}, v_{\lambda_k}, \ldots, v_{\lambda_K}\}$. The impact of an increase in the vote total for party j on the electoral support for a particular distribution of responsibility is thus proportional to party j's responsibility in the proposed distribution. Thus, assuming a large enough electorate that the difference quotients for the selection function that are associated with a change in a single vote can be well approximated by derivatives, we have $\frac{\partial v_{\lambda_k}}{\partial v_j} = \lambda_{kj}$ for all J parties. Furthermore, define the *electoral support* associated with any cabinet $\mathbf{g}_m$ as $v_{\mathbf{g}_m} = \sum_{j \in \mathrm{J}} g_{mj} v_j$ and $\mathbf{v}_\mathrm{G} = \{v_{\mathbf{g}_1}, v_{\mathbf{g}_2}, v_{\mathbf{g}_m}, \ldots, v_{\mathbf{g}_M}\}$. The impact of an increase in the vote total for party j on the electoral support for a particular cabinet is thus g_{mj}, which is just 1 if the party is in the cabinet and zero otherwise.

[1] We assume that $\mathbf{\Lambda}$ is finite to avoid having to work with matrices that have an infinite number of rows and columns. Given that $\mathbf{\Lambda}$ can be as large as we like, this is not a substantive restriction.

Now define $\mathbf{s}_\Lambda = \{s_1, s_2, s_k, \ldots, s_K\}$, where $s_k = s(v_{\lambda_1}, v_{\lambda_2}, v_{\lambda_k}, \ldots, v_{\lambda_K}, \mathbf{z}_{\lambda_1}, \mathbf{z}_{\lambda_2}, \mathbf{z}_{\lambda_k}, \ldots, \mathbf{z}_{\lambda_K})$ is a *selection function* defined over the K elements of Λ. The $\mathbf{z}_{\lambda_k}$'s represent any factors associated with λ_k other than electoral support that impact the value of s_k. More compactly, we can write this selection function as: $s_k = s(\mathbf{v}_\Lambda, \mathbf{Z}_\Lambda)$, where $\mathbf{Z}_\Lambda = \{\mathbf{z}_{\lambda_1}, \mathbf{z}_{\lambda_2}, \mathbf{z}_{\lambda_k}, \ldots, \mathbf{z}_{\lambda_K}\}$.[2] We assume that s_k is everywhere differentiable with respect to $\mathbf{v}_\Lambda$, again assuming a large enough electorate that we can approximate difference quotients with derivatives.

Similarly, we can define a version of the selection function that maps electoral support for cabinets (and other factors defined over cabinets) to selection values. This is just $\mathbf{s}_G = \{s_1, s_2, s_m, \ldots, s_M\}$ with typical element $s_m = s(\mathbf{v}_G, \mathbf{Z}_G)$, where the z's are defined analogously to those given earlier and we make the same assumption of linearity between integer values of v_j.

We want to use these definitions to provide general characterizations of how a vote for party j impacts the chance that each possible cabinet or distribution of responsibility is selected to govern. To do that, we first define the derivatives of the selection functions with respect to party vote totals and then define a rule for choosing either a cabinet or a distribution of responsibility given values of the selection functions for each possible cabinet or distribution of responsibility.[3]

We want to derive $\frac{\partial \mathbf{s}_\Lambda}{\partial \mathbf{v}_J}$. Because $\mathbf{s}_\Lambda$ and $\mathbf{v}_J$ are both vectors, this is the matrix:

$$\frac{\partial \mathbf{s}_\Lambda}{\partial \mathbf{v}_J} = \begin{bmatrix} \frac{\partial s_1}{\partial v_1} & \frac{\partial s_1}{\partial v_2} & \frac{\partial s_1}{\partial v_j} & \cdots & \frac{\partial s_1}{\partial v_J} \\ \frac{\partial s_2}{\partial v_1} & \frac{\partial s_2}{\partial v_2} & & & \vdots \\ \frac{\partial s_k}{\partial v_1} & & \frac{\partial s_k}{\partial v_j} & & \\ & & & \ddots & \\ \frac{\partial s_K}{\partial v_1} & \cdots & & & \frac{\partial s_K}{\partial v_J} \end{bmatrix} \tag{A.1}$$

By definition, votes play no role in $\mathbf{Z}_\Lambda$ and we assume for convenience that $\mathbf{v}_\Lambda$ and $\mathbf{Z}_\Lambda$ appear in separable parts of the selection function and ignore $\mathbf{Z}_\Lambda$ in the discussion that follows. To find expressions for the elements of the matrix in equation (A.1), we can use the relationship between the electoral support for distributions of responsibility and party vote totals.

[2] $\mathbf{Z}_A$ is not strictly necessary but is included to remind the reader that the selection function does not only depend on electoral support.

[3] Because each v_j is just the sum of the v_{ij} over n, we need only consider the derivative of s with respect to the vote totals v_j instead of individual votes.

Specifically, from the previous definitions, we can write the relationship between $\mathbf{v}_\Lambda$ and $\mathbf{v}_\mathrm{J}$ as:

$$\mathbf{v}_\Lambda = \mathbf{A}\mathbf{v}_\mathrm{J} \tag{A.2}$$

where **A** is the Jacobean of the transformation. Consequently, using standard results on vector derivatives, we have for some possible distribution of responsibility $\lambda_{\tilde{k}}$:

$$\frac{\partial s_{\tilde{k}}}{\partial \mathbf{v}_\mathrm{J}} = \mathbf{A}\frac{\partial s_{\tilde{k}}}{\partial \mathbf{v}_\Lambda}$$

$$\left[\frac{\partial s_{\tilde{k}}}{\partial v_1}, \frac{\partial s_{\tilde{k}}}{\partial v_2}, \frac{\partial s_{\tilde{k}}}{\partial v_j}, \ldots, \frac{\partial s_{\tilde{k}}}{\partial v_J}\right]^T$$

$$= \begin{bmatrix} \lambda_{11} & \lambda_{12} & \lambda_{1j} & \cdots & \lambda_{1J} \\ \lambda_{21} & \lambda_{22} & & & \vdots \\ \lambda_{k1} & & \lambda_{kj} & & \\ \vdots & & & \ddots & \\ \lambda_{K1} & \cdots & & & \lambda_{KJ} \end{bmatrix}^T \left[\frac{\partial s_{\tilde{k}}}{\partial v_{\lambda_1}}, \frac{\partial s_{\tilde{k}}}{\partial v_{\lambda_2}}, \frac{\partial s_{\tilde{k}}}{\partial v_{\lambda_k}}, \ldots, \frac{\partial s_{\tilde{k}}}{\partial v_{\lambda_K}}\right]^T$$

$$= \left[\sum_{\lambda_k \in \Lambda} \frac{\partial s_{\tilde{k}}}{\partial v_{\lambda_k}}\lambda_{k1}, \sum_{\lambda_k \in \Lambda} \frac{\partial s_{\tilde{k}}}{\partial v_{\lambda_k}}\lambda_{k2}, \sum_{\lambda_k \in \Lambda} \frac{\partial s_{\tilde{k}}}{\partial v_{\lambda_k}}\lambda_{kj}, \ldots, \sum_{\lambda_k \in \Lambda} \frac{\partial s_{\tilde{k}}}{\partial v_{\lambda_k}}\lambda_{kJ}\right]^T \tag{A.3}$$

which are the rows of equation (A.1). The typical element of **A**, λ_{kj}, is simply the responsibility of party j in distribution of authority λ_k (where, again, there are K such distributions). If we use $\tilde{k}$ and k as separate indexes over the set $\mathbf{\Lambda}$, the whole matrix is as follows:

$$\frac{\partial \mathbf{s}_\Lambda}{\partial \mathbf{v}_\mathrm{J}} = \begin{bmatrix} \sum_{\lambda_k \in \Lambda} \frac{\partial s_1}{\partial v_{\lambda_k}}\lambda_{k1} & \sum_{\lambda_k \in \Lambda} \frac{\partial s_1}{\partial v_{\lambda_k}}\lambda_{k2} & \sum_{\lambda_k \in \Lambda} \frac{\partial s_1}{\partial v_{\lambda_k}}\lambda_{kj} & \cdots & \sum_{\lambda_k \in \Lambda} \frac{\partial s_1}{\partial v_{\lambda_k}}\lambda_{kJ} \\ \sum_{\lambda_k \in \Lambda} \frac{\partial s_2}{\partial v_{\lambda_k}}\lambda_{k1} & \sum_{\lambda_k \in \Lambda} \frac{\partial s_2}{\partial v_{\lambda_k}}\lambda_{k2} & & & \vdots \\ \sum_{\lambda_k \in \Lambda} \frac{\partial s_{\tilde{k}}}{\partial v_{\lambda_k}}\lambda_{k1} & & \sum_{\lambda_k \in \Lambda} \frac{\partial s_{\tilde{k}}}{\partial v_{\lambda_k}}\lambda_{kj} & & \\ \vdots & & & \ddots & \\ \sum_{\lambda_k \in \Lambda} \frac{\partial s_K}{\partial v_{\lambda_k}}\lambda_{k1} & \cdots & & & \sum_{\lambda_k \in \Lambda} \frac{\partial s_K}{\partial v_{\lambda_k}}\lambda_{kJ} \end{bmatrix} \tag{A.4}$$

The columns of this matrix are of the most interest for our purposes. Each column indicates how a vote for party j impacts the selection values of each possible distribution of responsibility among the parties. We assume that the selection function for λ_k never decreases when v_{λ_k} increases – so more electoral support for a particular distribution of responsibility never hurts its selection value. Because λ_{kj} is always positive, the elements of (A.4) are all nonnegative.

For cabinets, an exactly parallel argument produces:

$$\frac{\partial \mathbf{s}_{\mathbf{G}}}{\partial \mathbf{v}_{\mathbf{J}}} = \begin{bmatrix} \sum_{g_m \in G} \frac{\partial s_1}{\partial v_{g_m}} g_{m1} & \sum_{g_m \in G} \frac{\partial s_1}{\partial v_{g_m}} g_{m2} & \sum_{g_m \in G} \frac{\partial s_1}{\partial v_{g_m}} g_{mj} & \cdots & \sum_{g_m \in G} \frac{\partial s_1}{\partial v_{g_m}} g_{mJ} \\ \sum_{g_m \in G} \frac{\partial s_2}{\partial v_{g_m}} g_{m1} & \sum_{g_m \in G} \frac{\partial s_2}{\partial v_{g_m}} g_{m2} & & & \vdots \\ \sum_{g_m \in G} \frac{\partial s_{\tilde{m}}}{\partial v_{g_m}} g_{m1} & & \sum_{g_m \in G} \frac{\partial s_{\tilde{m}}}{\partial v_{g_m}} g_{mj} & & \\ \vdots & & & \ddots & \\ \sum_{g_m \in G} \frac{\partial s_M}{\partial v_{g_m}} g_{m1} & \cdots & & & \sum_{g_m \in G} \frac{\partial s_M}{\partial v_{g_m}} g_{mJ} \end{bmatrix} \tag{A.5}$$

where we use $\tilde{m}$ and m as separate indexes over the set G.

These two matrices describe how votes for parties are connected to selection values for each cabinet or distribution of executive authority. When we make assumptions about the form of these expressions, these are translatable into assumptions about the process through which cabinets get formed or, more generally, how policy-making responsibility gets distributed among parties. One assumption that we use frequently in the text to simplify the examples and explanation is that the selection function for any particular cabinet or distribution of executive authority only responds to changes in the electoral support of that cabinet or distribution of executive authority, respectively. Formally, assumption #1 is:

$$\frac{\partial s_{\tilde{m}}}{\partial v_{g_m}} = \begin{cases} \frac{\partial s_{\tilde{m}}}{\partial v_{g_{\tilde{m}}}} & \text{if } m = \tilde{m} \\ 0 & \text{otherwise} \end{cases}$$

$$\frac{\partial s_{\tilde{k}}}{\partial v_{\lambda_k}} = \begin{cases} \frac{\partial s_{\tilde{k}}}{\partial v_{\lambda_{\tilde{k}}}} & \text{if } k = \tilde{k} \\ 0 & \text{otherwise} \end{cases}$$

This means that the elements of equations (A.4) and (A.5) can be written as $\frac{\partial s_{\tilde{k}}}{\partial v_{\lambda_{\tilde{k}}}} \lambda_{\tilde{k}j}$ and $\frac{\partial s_{\tilde{m}}}{\partial v_{g_{\tilde{m}}}} g_{\tilde{m}}$, respectively.

A second assumption that we use less often but that is sometimes convenient is that the derivatives of the selection function with respect to each distribution of authority (or cabinet) are equal.[4] Specifically, we assume:

$$\frac{\partial s_{\tilde{k}}}{\partial v_{\lambda_k}} = \frac{\partial s_{\tilde{k}'}}{\partial v_{\lambda_{k'}}} \forall \tilde{k}, \tilde{k}'$$

$$\frac{\partial s_{\tilde{m}}}{\partial v_{g_{\tilde{m}}}} = \frac{\partial s_{\tilde{m}'}}{\partial v_{g_{\tilde{m}'}}} \forall \tilde{m}, \tilde{m}'$$

This assumption, which says, for example, that a small change in the *electoral support* associated with one cabinet, has the same impact on the selection value of that cabinet as the same change in the *electoral support* of another cabinet has on the selection value of that cabinet. It does not say anything about the impact of support for individual parties on selection values.

Now, continuing with our main discussion, suppose that we adopt the following simple *selection rule*: the distribution of responsibility of the cabinet with the largest selection value is always chosen to be the actual distribution of responsibility. Furthermore, we assume that the probability that more than two distributions of executive authority are tied for selection is zero. With this, we can use equations (A.4) and (A.5) to characterize how a vote for party j will impact the choice of a distribution of responsibility or cabinet, respectively.

Denote voter i's utility for the distribution of responsibility $\boldsymbol{\lambda}_k$ as $u(\boldsymbol{\lambda}_k)$ and for cabinets similarly (i.e., $u(g_m)$). Also, denote the vote totals for each party when all voters except voter i have cast their ballots as $\mathbf{v}_{J/i} = \{v_{1/i}, v_{2/i}, v_{j/i}, \ldots, v_{J/i},\}$. We first focus our attention on the two distributions of responsibility, $\lambda_{\tilde{k}}$ and $\lambda_{\tilde{k}'}$, with the highest selection values given all votes other than voter i's vote have been cast. We also assume that the selection value of the second largest of these distributions is sufficiently large relative to that of the other K-2 possible distributions that, given equation (A.4), no single vote for any of the j parties could place a different distribution of responsibility in one of the top two positions.

To simplify notation, we use $D_{\tilde{k}j}$ and $D_{\tilde{k}'j}$ to indicate the derivatives of $s_{\tilde{k}}$ and $s_{\tilde{k}'}$ with respect to v_j, evaluated at $\mathbf{v}_{J/i}$. Similarly, we use

[4] For convenience, this is stated globally but is really much less restrictive than it appears because we only ever require that this equality hold for two distributions of responsibility that are in a tie for selection (i.e., the two derivatives need only be equal when they are evaluated for a vector of electoral support in which all but one voter has voted the resulting values of the selection function are equal or can be made equal by a vote).

$s_{\bar{k},\sim i}$ and $s_{\bar{k}',\sim i}$ to refer to the value of $s_{\bar{k}}$ and $s_{\bar{k}'}$ when electoral support is $\mathbf{v}_{\mathrm{J}/i}$. Let $D_{\bar{k}j} - D_{\bar{k}'j}$ be δ_j.

Consider the case in which δ_j is positive so $D_{\bar{k}j} > D_{\bar{k}'j}$. If we assume that ties for selection are broken randomly, the difference in voter *i*'s expected utility for a vote for party $j \in \mathbf{J}$ rather than abstaining (v_0) is:

$$u(v_{ij} \mid \mathbf{v}_{\mathrm{J}/i}, \delta_j > 0) - u(v_0 \mid \mathbf{v}_{\mathrm{J}/i}, \delta_j > 0)$$
$$= \begin{cases} u(\lambda_{\bar{k}'}) - u(\lambda_{\bar{k}'}) & \text{if } s_{\bar{k}',\sim i} - s_{\bar{k},\sim i} > \delta_j \\ \frac{u(\lambda_{\bar{k}})+u(\lambda_{\bar{k}'})}{2} - u(\lambda_{\bar{k}'}) & \text{if } s_{\bar{k}',\sim i} - s_{\bar{k},\sim i} = \delta_j \\ u(\lambda_{\bar{k}}) - u(\lambda_{\bar{k}'}) & \text{if } 0 < s_{\bar{k}',\sim i} - s_{\bar{k},\sim i} < \delta_j \\ u(\lambda_{\bar{k}}) - \frac{u(\lambda_{\bar{k}})+u(\lambda_{\bar{k}'})}{2} & \text{if } s_{\bar{k}',\sim i} - s_{\bar{k},\sim i} = 0 \\ u(\lambda_{\bar{k}}) - u(\lambda_{\bar{k}}) & \text{if } s_{\bar{k}',\sim i} - s_{\bar{k},\sim i} < 0 \end{cases} \tag{A.6}$$

If we denote the probability of various electoral outcomes (before voter *i* casts her vote) with $p(\cdot)$, then we can write the expected utility difference of voting for party *j* rather than abstaining when $D_{\bar{k}j} > D_{\bar{k}'j}$ as:

$$\begin{aligned} &u(v_{ij} \mid \mathbf{v}_{\mathrm{J}/i}, \delta_j > 0) - u(v_0 \mid \mathbf{v}_{\mathrm{J}/i}, \delta_j > 0) \\ &= p(s_{\bar{k}',\sim i} - s_{\bar{k},\sim i} = \delta_j)\left[\frac{u(\lambda_{\bar{k}}) - u(\lambda_{\bar{k}'})}{2}\right] \\ &\quad + p(0 < s_{\bar{k}',\sim i} - s_{\bar{k},\sim i} < \delta_j)\left[u(\lambda_{\bar{k}}) - u(\lambda_{\bar{k}'})\right] \\ &\quad + p(s_{\bar{k}',\sim i} - s_{\bar{k},\sim i} = 0)\left[\frac{u(\lambda_{\bar{k}}) - u(\lambda_{\bar{k}'})}{2}\right] \end{aligned} \tag{A.7}$$

In large electorates in which the impact of a single vote on the selection function is likely to be quite small, we can assume that the probability of events very close to a tie for selection are the same as for a tie itself. Thus, we can rewrite equation (A.7) as:

$$u(v_{ij} \mid \mathbf{v}_{\mathrm{J}/i}, \delta_j > 0) - u(v_0 \mid \mathbf{v}_{\mathrm{J}/i}, \delta_j > 0) = 2p(s_{\bar{k}',\sim i} = s_{\bar{k},\sim i})\left[u(\lambda_{\bar{k}}) - u(\lambda_{\bar{k}'})\right] \tag{A.8}$$

We can do a similar derivation for the case in which $D_{\bar{k}j} < D_{\bar{k}'j}$. This produces:

$$u(v_{ij} \mid \mathbf{v}_{\mathrm{J}/i}, \delta_j > 0) - u(v_0 \mid \mathbf{v}_{\mathrm{J}/i}, \delta_j > 0) = 2p(s_{\bar{k}',\sim i} = s_{\bar{k},\sim i})\left[u(\lambda_{\bar{k}'}) - u(\lambda_{\bar{k}})\right] \tag{A.9}$$

Finally, when $D_{\bar{k}j} = D_{\bar{k}'j}$, a vote for *j* will necessarily leave the ordering of the selection functions for $\lambda_{\bar{k}}$ and $\lambda_{\bar{k}'}$ the same and so the utility difference of voting for party *j* or abstaining will always be zero. Expressions for cabinets rather than distributions of responsibility are exactly the same as equations (A.8) and (A.9), except replacing the $\boldsymbol{\lambda}$'s with **g**'s. These expressions follow from exactly the same argument.

Now, we are finally in a position to formally define $P_{j,\lambda\lambda'}$ and $P_{j,\mathbf{gg}'}$ from the text and to derive equations (8.10) and (8.31). Specifically, we define $P_{j,\lambda\lambda'}$ as the probability that the selection values of $\lambda_{\tilde{k}}$ and $\lambda_{\tilde{k}'}$ are tied for first place among all the potential distributions of responsibility and $D_{\tilde{k}j} > D_{\tilde{k}'j}$. Likewise, $P_{j,\lambda'\lambda}$ is the probability that the selection values of $\lambda_{\tilde{k}}$ and $\lambda_{\tilde{k}'}$ are tied for first place among all the potential distributions of responsibility and $D_{\tilde{k}j} < D_{\tilde{k}'j}$. For cabinets rather than distributions of responsibility, we define $P_{j,\mathbf{gg}'}$ as the probability that the selection values of $\mathbf{g}_{\tilde{m}}$ and $\mathbf{g}_{\tilde{m}'}$ are tied for first place among all the potential cabinets and $D_{\tilde{m}j} > D_{\tilde{m}'j}$. Likewise, $P_{j,\mathbf{g}'\mathbf{g}}$ is the probability that the selection values of $\mathbf{g}_{\tilde{m}}$ and $\mathbf{g}_{\tilde{m}'}$ are tied for first place among all the potential cabinets and $D_{\tilde{m}j} < D_{\tilde{m}'j}$.

Before using these definitions to derive the difference in expected utility of casting a vote for some party versus abstaining, we need to be somewhat more precise about what we mean when we say, for example, "the probability that the selection values of $\mathbf{g}_{\tilde{m}}$ and $\mathbf{g}_{\tilde{m}'}$ are tied for first place among all the potential cabinets and $D_{\tilde{m}j} < D_{\tilde{m}'j}$." Specifically, we invoke the probability that $D_{\tilde{m}j} < D_{\tilde{m}'j}$ not because we think the cabinet formation process that defines these derivatives is random but instead as a way to represent the voter's subjective beliefs about this aspect of the cabinet-formation process. Substantive assumptions about these derivatives are thus assumptions about what voters believe to be true about cabinet formation. The notation $P_{j,\mathbf{gg}'}$ and the like is used only as a shorthand for the joint probability $P(s_{\mathbf{g}_m,\sim i} = s_{\mathbf{g}_{m'},\sim i})P(D_{\mathbf{g}_m j} > D_{\mathbf{g}_{m'} j} \mid s_{\mathbf{g}_m,\sim i} = s_{\mathbf{g}_{m'},\sim i})$, which becomes $P(s_{\mathbf{g}_m,\sim i} = s_{\mathbf{g}_{m'},\sim i})P(D_{\mathbf{g}_m j} > D_{\mathbf{g}_{m'} j})$ under the assumption that the chance of a tie for selection between two cabinets is independent of their selection functions (which can be thought of as part of a preexisting process of cabinet selection). Another shorthand that we use when we need to make the two pieces $P_{j,\mathbf{gg}'}$ explicit is $P_{\mathbf{gg}'} = P(s_{\mathbf{g}_m,\sim i} = s_{\mathbf{g}_{m'},\sim i})$.

With these definitions, we can use equations (A.8) and (A.9) to write the difference in expected utility of casting a vote for any party versus abstaining as the sum of all the ways this vote might result in a nonzero utility difference between any two possible distributions of responsibility (or cabinets). Specifically,

$$2\sum_{\lambda\in\Lambda}\sum_{\lambda'\in\Lambda} P_{j,\lambda\lambda'}\,[u(\lambda_k) - u(\lambda_{k'})] \tag{A.10}$$

and

$$2\sum_{g\in G}\sum_{g'\in G} P_{j,gg'}\left[u(g_m) - u(g_{m'})\right] \qquad (A.11)$$

Now, define g_m as the incumbent cabinet and $g_{m'}$ and $g_{m''}$ as generic non–incumbent cabinets. Likewise, define λ_k as the "incumbent" or status quo distribution of responsibility and $\lambda_{k'}$ and $\lambda_{k''}$ as generic non–status quo distributions of responsibility. If we let **A** do double duty as the set of these alternative (i.e., nonincumbent) cabinets and the set of non–status quo distributions of responsibility, ignore the multiplication by two (which is inconsequential), and modify some of the notational conventions to match the simpler (but less precise) forms used in the text, we can rewrite the results exactly as equation (8.10) and the first lines of (8.31), respectively.

$$\begin{aligned} E[u \mid v_j] - E[u \mid v_0] = &\sum_{g'\in A} P_{j,gg'}\left(E\left[u_{g,t+1}\right] - E\left[u_{g',t+1}\right]\right) \\ &+ \sum_{g'\in A} P_{j,g'g}\left(E\left[u_{g',t+1}\right] - E\left[u_{g,t+1}\right]\right) \\ &+ \sum_{g'\in A}\sum_{g''\in A} P_{j,g'g''}\left(E\left[u_{g',t+1}\right] - E\left[u_{g'',t+1}\right]\right) \end{aligned} \qquad (A.12)$$

$$\begin{aligned} E[u \mid v_j] - E[u \mid v_0] = &\sum_{\lambda'\in\Lambda'} P_{j,\lambda\lambda'}\left(E\left[u_{\lambda,t+1}\right] - E\left[u_{\lambda',t+1}\right]\right) \\ &+ \sum_{\lambda'\in\Lambda'} P_{j,\lambda'\lambda}\left(E\left[u_{\lambda',t+1}\right] - E\left[u_{\lambda,t+1}\right]\right) \\ &+ \sum_{\lambda'\in\Lambda'}\sum_{\lambda''\in\Lambda'} P_{j,\lambda'\lambda''}\left(E\left[u_{\lambda',t+1}\right] - E\left[u_{\lambda'',t+1}\right]\right) \end{aligned} \qquad (A.13)$$

Appendix B

PROOF THAT THE MINIMUM OF THE RESPONSIBILITY AUGMENTED COMPETENCY SIGNAL IS AN EQUAL DIVISION OF RESPONSIBILITY

$$\begin{aligned}
\frac{\partial}{\partial\lambda_i}\left(\frac{\sigma_\mu^2\sum_J\lambda_{j,t}^2}{\sigma_\xi^2+\sigma_\mu^2\sum_J\lambda_{j,t}^2}\right) &= \frac{\partial}{\partial\lambda_i}\left(\sigma_\mu^2\sum_J\lambda_{j,t}^2\right)\left(\sigma_\xi^2+\sigma_\mu^2\sum_J\lambda_{j,t}^2\right)\\
&\quad -\frac{\partial}{\partial\lambda_i}\left(\sigma_\xi^2+\sigma_\mu^2\sum_J\lambda_{j,t}^2\right)\left(\sigma_\mu^2\sum_J\lambda_{j,t}^2\right)\\
&= \frac{\partial}{\partial\lambda_i}\left(\sigma_\mu^2\sum_J\lambda_{j,t}^2\right)\sigma_\xi^2+\frac{\partial}{\partial\lambda_i}\left(\sigma_\mu^2\sum_J\lambda_{j,t}^2\right)\sigma_\mu^2\sum_J\lambda_{j,t}^2\\
&\quad -\frac{\partial}{\partial\lambda_i}\left(\sigma_\mu^2\sum_J\lambda_{j,t}^2\right)\sigma_\mu^2\sum_J\lambda_{j,t}^2\\
&= \frac{\partial}{\partial\lambda_i}\left(\sigma_\mu^2\sum_J\lambda_{j,t}^2\right)\sigma_\xi^2
\end{aligned}\tag{B.1}$$

Because we have $\sum_J \lambda_{j,t} = 1$, we can rewrite $\sum_J \lambda_{j,t}$ as:

$$\begin{aligned}
&\sum_J\lambda_{j,t} = \sum_{j=1}^{J-1}\lambda_{j,t}+\left(1-\sum_{j=1}^{J-1}\lambda_{j,t}\right)\\
&\text{and}\\
&\sum_J\lambda_{j,t}^2 = \sum_{j=1}^{J-1}\lambda_{j,t}^2+\left(1-\sum_{j=1}^{J-1}\lambda_{j,t}\right)^2
\end{aligned}\tag{B.2}$$

We can now write:

$$\left(\frac{\partial\sigma_\mu^2 \sum_J \lambda_{j,t}^2}{\partial\lambda_i}\right)\sigma_\xi^2 = \left(\frac{\partial\left(\sigma_\mu^2 \sum_{j=1}^{J-1} \lambda_{j,t}^2 + \sigma_\mu^2\left(1 - \sum_{j=1}^{J-1}\lambda_{j,t}\right)^2\right)}{\partial\lambda_i}\right)\sigma_\xi^2 \tag{B.3}$$

By definition we have:

$$\sum_{j=1}^{J-1}\lambda_{j,t} = \lambda_{i,t} + \sum_{j\neq i}^{J-1}\lambda_{j,t}$$

where the sum on the right-hand side is the sum over the J−2 free $\boldsymbol{\lambda}_j$'s, not including $\boldsymbol{\lambda}_i$. Replacing this in equation (B.3) and expanding gives:

$$\begin{aligned}
&\left(\frac{\partial\sigma_\mu^2 \sum_J \lambda_{j,t}^2}{\partial\lambda_i}\right)\sigma_\xi^2 \\
&= \left(\frac{\partial\sigma_\mu^2\left(\lambda_{i,t}^2 + \sum_{j=1}^{J-1}\lambda_{j,t}^2\right) + \sigma_\mu^2 - 2\sigma_\mu^2\left(\lambda_{i,t} + \sum_{j\neq i}^{J-1}\lambda_{j,t}\right) + \sigma_\mu^2\left(\lambda_{i,t} + \sum_{j\neq i}^{J-1}\lambda_{j,t}\right)^2}{\partial\lambda_i}\right)\sigma_\xi^2 \\
&= \left(2\sigma_\mu^2\lambda_{i,t} - 2\sigma_\mu^2 + \frac{\partial\sigma_\mu^2\left(\lambda_{i,t} + \sum_{j\neq i}^{J-1}\lambda_{j,t}\right)^2}{\partial\lambda_i}\right)\sigma_\xi^2 \\
&= \left(2\sigma_\mu^2\lambda_{i,t} - 2\sigma_\mu^2 + \frac{\partial\sigma_\mu^2\left(\lambda_{i,t}^2 + 2\lambda_{i,t}\sum_{j\neq i}^{J-1}\lambda_{j,t} + \left(\sum_{j\neq i}^{J-1}\lambda_{j,t}\right)^2\right)}{\partial\lambda_i}\right)\sigma_\xi^2 \\
&= \left(2\sigma_\mu^2\lambda_{i,t} - 2\sigma_\mu^2 + 2\sigma_\mu^2\lambda_{i,t} + 2\sigma_\mu^2\sum_{j\neq i}^{J-1}\lambda_{j,t}\right)\sigma_\xi^2 \\
&= \left(4\sigma_\mu^2\lambda_{i,t} - 2\sigma_\mu^2 + 2\sigma_\mu^2\sum_{j\neq i}^{J-1}\lambda_{j,t}\right)\sigma_\xi^2 \\
&= 2\sigma_\mu^2\sigma_\xi^2\left(2\lambda_{i,t} - 1 + \sum_{j\neq i}^{J-1}\lambda_{j,t}\right)
\end{aligned} \tag{B.4}$$

Setting the last line of equation (B.4) to zero for each i defines a system of J-1 equations, each of which has the form:

$$\lambda_{i,t} + \frac{1}{2}\sum_{j\neq i}^{J-1}\lambda_{j,t} = \frac{1}{2} \tag{B.5}$$

In matrix notation, this system of equations is just:

$$\mathbf{A}\lambda = \mathbf{i}\frac{1}{2} \tag{B.6}$$

where **i** is a J−1 vector of ones and:

$$\lambda = \begin{bmatrix} \lambda_1 \\ \lambda_1 \\ \vdots \\ \lambda_{J-1} \end{bmatrix} \mathbf{A} = \begin{bmatrix} 1 & \frac{1}{2} & \cdots & \frac{1}{2} \\ \frac{1}{2} & 1 & \vdots & \vdots \\ \vdots & \cdots & \ddots & \vdots \\ \frac{1}{2} & \cdots & \cdots & 1 \end{bmatrix}$$

The solution to equation (B.6) is:

$$\lambda = \mathbf{A}^{-1}\mathbf{i}\frac{1}{2} \tag{B.7}$$

Let $k = \text{J}-1$ and define:

$$\mathbf{A}^{-1} = \begin{bmatrix} \frac{2k}{k+1} & -\frac{2}{k+1} & \cdots & -\frac{2}{k+1} \\ -\frac{2}{k+1} & \frac{2k}{k+1} & \vdots & \vdots \\ \vdots & \cdots & \ddots & \vdots \\ -\frac{2}{k+1} & \cdots & \cdots & -\frac{2k}{k+1} \end{bmatrix}$$

It follows that $\mathbf{AA}^{-1} = \mathbf{I}$, so A^{-1} is the inverse of A and, thus, solving for the $\boldsymbol{\lambda}$ that minimizes this, we get:

$$\mathbf{A}^{-1}\mathrm{i}\frac{1}{2} = \begin{bmatrix} \frac{2k}{k+1} & -\frac{2}{k+1} & \cdots & -\frac{2}{k+1} \\ -\frac{2}{k+1} & \frac{2k}{k+1} & \vdots & \vdots \\ \vdots & \cdots & \ddots & \vdots \\ -\frac{2}{k+1} & \cdots & \cdots & -\frac{2k}{k+1} \end{bmatrix} \begin{bmatrix} \frac{1}{2} \\ \vdots \\ \vdots \\ \vdots \\ \frac{1}{2} \end{bmatrix} = \begin{bmatrix} \frac{1}{k+1} \\ \vdots \\ \vdots \\ \vdots \\ \frac{1}{k+1} \end{bmatrix}$$

because $k = \text{J}-1$, and we have the sum of all shares equal to 1, this implies that for all J parties, the vector of shares that minimize the competency signal allocates all parties share 1/J.

Appendix C

DERIVATION OF EQUATION 8.34

Growth in the current period under distribution of responsibility λ is:

$$\begin{aligned} y_{\lambda,t} &= \bar{y} + \eta_{\lambda,t} \\ &= \bar{y} + \sum_{j \in J} \left\{ \lambda_{j,t}\mu_{j,t} + \lambda_{j,t-1}\mu_{j,t-1} \right\} + \xi_t \end{aligned} \tag{C.1}$$

Rearranging this gives:

$$\begin{aligned} \sum_{j \in J} \left\{ \lambda_{j,t}\mu_{j,t} \right\} + \xi_t &= y_{\lambda,t} - \bar{y} - \sum_{j \in J} \left\{ \lambda_{j,t-1}\mu_{j,t-1} \right\} \\ &= y_{\lambda,t} - \bar{y} - \mu_{\lambda,t-1} \end{aligned} \tag{C.2}$$

where everything on the right-hand side of this equality is observed and so the sum of the terms on the left is also observed, although not the individual components. Denote the sum on the left-hand side as $k_{\lambda,t} = \sum_{j \in J} \left\{ \lambda_{j,t}\mu_{j,t} \right\} + \xi_t$. Because $k_{\lambda,t}$ is observed, the voter can compute her expectation about any $\mu_{j,t}$ given $k_{\lambda,t}$. To calculate this conditional expectation, we need to know that the distribution of both $k_{\lambda,t}$ and $\mu_{j,t}$. $\mu_{j,t}$ is a normally distributed random variable with zero mean and variance σ_μ^2. Because $k_{\lambda,t} = \mu_{\lambda,t} + \xi_t = \sum_{j \in I} \{\lambda_{j,t}\mu_{j,t}\} + \xi_t$, its distribution depends on the distribution of $\mu_{\lambda,t}$, which is just:

$$\begin{aligned} \mu_{\lambda,t} = \sum_{j \in I} \lambda_{j,t}\mu_{j,t} &\sim N\left(0, \sigma_\mu^2 \sum_{j \in I} \lambda_{j,t}^2\right) \\ &\sim N(0, \sigma_{\mu_\lambda}^2) \end{aligned} \tag{C.3}$$

Thus, $k_{\lambda,t}$ is the unweighted sum of two normally distributed random variables, both with zero means and variances $\sigma^2_{\mu_\lambda}$ and σ^2_ξ, respectively. The distribution of $k_{\lambda,t}$ is thus:

$$k_{\lambda,t} = (\mu_\lambda + \xi_t) \sim N\left(0, \sigma^2_{\mu_\lambda} + \sigma^2_\xi\right) \tag{C.4}$$

Given that both, $k_{\lambda,t}$ and $\mu_{j,t}$ are distributed normally, their joint distribution is bivariate normal and the optimal forecast of $\mu_{j,t}$ given $k_{g,t}$ is just this conditional expectation, which is computed from the appropriate conditional distribution of the bivariate normal. Using standard results on the bivariate normal distribution:

$$\begin{aligned} E\left[\mu_{i,t} \mid k_{\lambda,t}\right] &= E[\mu_{i,t}] + \frac{\sigma_{\mu,k_{\lambda,t}}}{\sigma^2_{k_\lambda}}\left(y_{\lambda,t} - \bar{y} - \mu_{\lambda,t-1}\right) - E[k_{\lambda,t}] \\ &= \frac{\sigma^2_\mu \lambda_{i,t}}{\sigma^2_{\mu_\lambda} + \sigma^2_\xi}\left(y_{\lambda,t} - \bar{y} - \mu_{\lambda,t-1}\right) \end{aligned} \tag{C.5}$$

where the second line uses the fact that the covariance between $k_{\lambda,t}$ and $\mu_{i,t}$ is equal to $\sigma^2_\mu \lambda_{i,t}$. To see this:

$$\begin{aligned} \sigma_{\mu,k_{\lambda,t}} &= E\left[\left(\mu_{i,t} - E\left[\mu_{i,t}\right]\right)\left(k_{\lambda,t} - E\left[k_{\lambda,t}\right]\right)\right] \\ &= E\left[\mu_{i,t} k_{\lambda,t}\right] \\ &= E\left[\mu_{i,t}\left(\mu_{\lambda,t} + \xi_t\right)\right] \\ &= E\left[\mu_{i,t}\left(\sum_{j\in J}\left\{\lambda_{j,t}\mu_{j,t}\right\} + \xi_t\right)\right] \\ &= E\left[\mu^2_{i,t}\lambda_{i,t} + \mu_{i,t}\sum_{j\neq i\in J}\left\{\lambda_{j,t}\mu_{j,t}\right\} + \mu_{i,t}\xi_t\right] \\ &= \sigma^2_\mu \lambda_{i,t} \end{aligned}$$

where the last line follows because we assumed independence between competency draws. Finally, substituting for $\sigma^2_{\mu_\lambda}$ and noting that $E\left[\mu_{i,t} \mid k_{\lambda,t}\right] = E\left[\mu_{i,t} \mid y_{\lambda,t}\right]$, we have equation (8.34) in the text:

$$E\left[\mu_{i,t} \mid y_{\lambda,t}\right] = \frac{\sigma^2_\mu \lambda_{i,t}}{\sigma^2_\xi + \sigma^2_\mu \sum_{j\in J}\lambda^2_{j,t}}\left(y_{\lambda,t} - \bar{y} - \mu_{\lambda,t-1}\right) \tag{C.6}$$

References

Adserà, Alícia, and Carles Boix. 2002. "Trade, Democracy and the Size of the Public Sector: The Political Underpinnings of Openness." *International Organization* 56 (2): 229–262.

Alesina, Alberto, and Allan Drazen. 1991. "Why Are Stabilizations Delayed." *American Economic Review* 81(5): 1170–1188.

Alesina, A., John Londregan, and Howard Rosenthal. 1993. "A Model of the Political Economy of the United States." *American Political Science Review* 87: 12–33.

Alesina, A., and H. Rosenthal. 1995. *Partisan Politics, Divided Government, and the Economy*. Cambridge: Cambridge University Press.

Alesina, A., N. Roubini, and G. Cohen. 1997. *Political Cycles and the Macroeconomy*. Cambridge, MA: MIT Press.

Alford, Robert R. 1963. *Party and Society: The Anglo-American Democracies*. Chicago: Rand McNally.

Alt, James E. 1991. "Ambiguous Intervention: The Role of Government Action in Public Evaluation of the Economy." In Helmut Norpoth, Michael Lewis-Beck, and Jean-Dominique Lafay, eds., *Economics and Politics: The Calculus of Support*. Ann Arbor: University of Michigan Press.

Alt, James E., and K. Alec Chrystal. 1983. *Political Economics*. Berkeley, CA: Berkeley Press.

Alt, James, and David Lassen. 2006. "Transparency, Political Polarization and Political Business Cycles in OECD Countries." *American Journal of Political Science* 50(3) (July).

Alvarez, R. Michael, Antonio Cheibub, Fernando Limongi, and Adam Przeworski. 1996. "Classifying Political Regimes." *Studies in Comparative International Development* 31 (Summer): 3–36.

Alvarez, R. Michael, and Jonathan Nagler. 1995. "Economics, Issues and the Perot Candidacy: Voter Choice in the 1992 Presidential Election." *American Journal of Political Science* 39(3): 714–744.

Alvarez, R. Michael, and Jonathan Nagler. 1998a. "When Politics and Models Collide: Estimating Models of Multiparty Elections." *American Journal of Political Science* 42: 55–96.

Alvarez, R. Michael, and Jonathan Nagler. 1998b. "Economics, Entitlements and Social Issues: Voter Choice in the 1996 Presidential Election." *American Journal of Political Science* 42: 1349–1363.

Alvarez, R. Michael, Jonathan Nagler, and Jennifer R. Willette. 2000. "Measuring the Relative Impact of Issues and the Economy in Democratic Elections." *Electoral Studies* 19: 237–253.

Alvarez, R. Michael, Jonathan Nagler, and Shaun Bowler. 2000. "Issues, Economics, and the Dynamics of Multiparty Elections." *American Political Science Review* 94: 131–149.

Anderson, Cameron D. 2006. "Economic Voting and Multi-Level Governance: A Comparative Individual-Level Analysis." *American Journal of Political Science* 50(2) (April).

Anderson, Christopher J. 1995. *Blaming the Government: Citizens and the Economy in Five European Democracies.* Armonk, NY: M. E. Sharpe.

Anderson, Christopher J. 2000. "Economic Voting and Political Context: A Comparative Perspective." *Electoral Studies* 19: 151–170.

Baker, Andy. 2003. "Why Is Trade Reform So Popular in Latin America? A Consumption-Based Theory of Trade Policy Preferences." *World Politics* 55: 423–455.

Baker, Andy. 2005. "Who Wants to Globalize? Consumer Tastes and Labor Markets in a Theory of Trade Policy Beliefs." *American Journal of Political Science* 49(4): 925–939.

Barro, Robert. 1973. "The Control of Politicians: An Economic Model." *Public Choice* 14: 19–42.

Bartels, Larry M., and John Zaller. 2001. "Presidential Vote Models: A Recount." *Political Science and Politics* 34: 9–19.

Bartle, John. 2001. "The Measurement of Party Identification in Britain: Where Do We Stand Now?" In Jon Tonge, Lynn Bennie, David Denver, and Lisa Harrison (eds.), *British Elections & Parties Review, Volume 11*. London: Frank Cass.

Bartollini, S., and Peter Mair. 1990. *Identity, Competition and Electoral Availability. The Stabilisation of European Electorates 1885–1985*. Cambridge: Cambridge University Press.

Bean, Clive, and Anthony Mughan. 1989. "Leadership Effects in Parliamentary Elections in Australia and Britain." *American Political Science Review* 83: 1165–1179.

Bean, Clive. 1996. "Partisanship and Electoral Behaviour in Comparative Perspective." In M. Simms, ed., *The Paradox of Parties: Australian Political Parties in the 1990s*. Sydney: Allen and Unwin.

Bean, Clive. 2001 "Party Politics, Political Leaders and Trust in Government in Australia." *Political Science* 53: 17–27.

Beck, Nathaniel. 1991. "The Economy and Presidential Approval: An Information Theoretic Perspective." In Helmut Norpoth, Michael Lewis-Beck, and Jean-Dominique Lafay, eds., *Economics and Politics: The Calculus of Support*. Ann Arbor: University of Michigan Press.

Becker, Gary, S. 1983. "A Theory of Competition among Pressure Groups for Political Influence." *Quarterly Journal of Economics* 98: 371–400.

Begg, David K. H. 1982. *The Rational Expectations Revolution in Macroeconomics: Theories and Evidence*. Baltimore, MD: The Johns Hopkins University Press.

Bellucci, Paolo. 1985. "Economic Concerns in Italian Electoral Behavior: Toward a Rational Electorate?" In Heinz Eulau and Michael S. Lewis-Beck, eds., *Economic Conditions and Electoral Outcomes: The United States and Western Europe*. New York: Agathon.

Bellucci, Paolo. 1991. "Italian Economic Voting: A Deviant Case or Making a Case for a Better Theory? 1953–1979." In Helmut Norpoth, Michael Lewis-Beck, and Jean-Dominique Lafay, eds., *Economics and Politics: The Calculus of Support*. Ann Arbor: University of Michigan Press.

Benoit, Kenneth, and Michael Laver. 2006. *Party Policy in Modern Democracies*. London: Routledge.

Berelson, Bernard, Paul Lazarsfeld, and William McPhee. 1954. *Voting*. Chicago: University of Chicago Press.

Blais, Andre, Mathieu Turgeon, Elisabeth Gidengil, Neil Nevitte, and Richard Nadeau. 2004. "Which Matters Most? Comparing the Impact of Issues and the Economy in American, British and Canadian Elections." *British Journal of Political Science* 34: 555–564.

Bloom, Howard, and Douglas Price. 1975. "Voter Response to Short-Run Economic Conditions: The Asymmetric Effect of Prosperity and Recession." *American Political Science Review* 69: 124–154.

Boix, Carles. 1998. *Political Parties, Growth and Equality: Conservative and Social Democratic Economic Strategies in the World Economy*. Cambridge: Cambridge University Press.

Borre, Ole. 1984. "Critical Electoral Change in Scandinavia." In Russell J. Dalton, Scott C. Flannigan, and Paul Allen Beck, eds., *Electoral Change in Advanced Industrial Democracies: Realignment or Dealignment?* Princeton, NJ: Princeton University Press.

Borre, Ole. 1997. "Economic Voting in Danish Electoral Surveys 1987–1994." *Scandinavian Political Studies* 20(4): 347–365.

Bowers, Jake, and Katherine W. Drake. 2005. "EDA for HLM." *Political Analysis* (Autumn) 13(4): 301–326.

Bowler, Shaun. 1990. "Consistency and Inconsistency in Canadian Party Identifications: Toward an Institutional Approach." *Electoral Studies* 9: 133–146.

Bowler, Shaun, and Todd Donovan. 1994. "Economic Conditions and Voting on Ballot Propositions." *American Politics Quarterly* 22: 27–40.

Brady, David W. 1993. "The Causes and Consequences of Divided Government: Toward a New Theory of American Politics." *American Political Science Review* 77(2): 407–19.

Braumoeller, Bear F. 2003. "Causal Complexity and the Study of Politics." *Political Analysis* 11(3): 209–233.

Brug, Wouter van der, Cees van der Eijk, and Mark Franklin. 2007. *The Economy and the Vote: Effects of Economic Conditions on Voter Preferences and Election Outcomes in Fifteen Countries*. New York: Cambridge University Press.

Buchanan, James, and Gordon Tullock. 1962. *The Calculus of Consent: Logical Foundations of Constitutional Democracy*. Ann Arbor: University of Michigan Press.

Budge, Ian. 1994. "A New Spatial Model of Party Competition: Uncertainty, Ideology and Policy Equilibria Viewed Comparatively and Temporally." *British Journal of Political Science* 24(4): 443–467.

Budge, Ian, Ivor Crewe, and Denis Farlie, eds. 1976. *Party Identification and Beyond: Representations of Voting and Party Competition*. London: John Wiley and Sons.

Bueno De Mesquita, Bruce, and Randolph M. Siverson. 1995. "War and the Survival of Political Leaders: A Comparative Study of Regime Types and Political Accountability." *American Political Science Review* 89: 841–855.

Butler, David, and Donald Stokes. 1969. *Political Change in Britain: Forces Shaping Electoral Choice*. London: Macmillan.

Butler, David, and Donald Stokes. 1976. *Political Change in Britain*. Second College Edition. New York: St. Martin's Press.

Butler, David, and Dennis Kavanagh. 1997. *The British General Election of 1997*. London: Macmillan Press Ltd.

Cain, B. E. (1978): "Strategic Voting in Britain." *American Journal of Political Science*, 22(3): 639–655.

Callaghan, James. 1987. *Time and Chance*. London: Collins.

Cameron, David R. 1978. "The Expansion of the Public Economy: A Comparative Analysis." *American Political Science Review* 72: 1243–1261.

Campbell, A., P. E. Converse, W. E. Miller, and D. E. Stokes. 1960. *The American Voter*. New York: John Wiley.

Chaffee, Steven H., and Stacey Frank Kanihan. 1996. "How Americans Get Political Information: Print versus Broadcast News." *The Annals of the American Academy of Political and Social Science* 546: 48–58.

Chappell, Henry, and William Keech. 1985. "A New View of Political Accountability of Economic Performance." *American Political Science Review* 79: 10–27.

Chappell, Henry, and Linda G. Viega. 2000. "Economics and Elections in Western Europe: 1960–1997." *Electoral Studies* 19: 183–197.

Cheibub, Jose Antonio, and Adam Przeworski. 1999. "Democracy, Elections, and Accountability for Economic Outcomes." In Przeworski, Adam, Susan C. Stokes, and Bernard Manin, eds., *Democracy, Accountability, and Representation*. Cambridge: Cambridge University Press.

Clark, William R., Usha Reichert, Sandra Lomas, and Kevin L. Parker. 1998. "International and Domestic Constraints on Political Budget Cycles in OECD Economies." *International Organization* 52: 7–120.

Clarke, Harold, Allan Kornberg, and Peter Wearing. 2000. *A Polity on the Edge: Canada and the Politics of Fragmentation*. Toronto: Broadview Press.

Clarke, Harold D., David Sanders, Marianne C. Stewart, and Paul Whiteley. 2004. *Political Choice in Britain*. Oxford: Oxford University Press.

Clarke, Harold, and Marianne C. Stewart. 1995. "Economic Evaluations, Prime Ministerial Approval and Governing Party Support: Rival Models Considered." *British Journal of Political Science* 25: 145–170.

Clarke, Harold, and Marianne C. Stewart. 1996. "Economists and Electorates: The Subjective Economy of Governing Party Support in Canada." *European Journal of Political Research* 28: 191–214.

Clarke, Harold, Marianne C. Stewart, and Paul Whiteley. 1997. "Tory Trends: Party Identification and the Dynamics of Conservative Support since 1992." *British Journal of Political Science* 27: 299–319.

Converse, Philip. 1964. "The Nature of Belief Systems in Mass Publics." In D. Apter, ed., *Ideology and Discontent*. New York: Free Press.

Cox, Gary W. 1997. *Making Votes Count: Strategic Coordination in the World's Electoral Systems*. Cambridge: Cambridge University Press.

Cox, Gary W., and Michael Munger. 1989. "Closeness, Expenditures and Turnout in the 1982 U.S. House Elections." *American Political Science Review* 83 (March): 217–231.

Cukierman, Alex, and Allan Meltzer. 1986. "A Theory of Ambiguity, Credibility, and Inflation under Discretion and Asymmetric Information." *Econometrica* 54: 1099–1128.

Cukierman, Alex, and Allan H. Meltzer. 1989. "A Political Theory of Government Debt and Deficits in a Neo-Ricardian Framework." *American Economics Review* 79: 713–733.

Cutler, F. 2004. "Electoral Behaviour in a Federal Context: The Consequences of Confusion." *Publius* 34 (Spring): 19–38.

Dalton, Russell J. 2002. Citizen Politics: *Public Opinion and Political Parties in Advanced Industrial Democracies*. Chatham, NJ: Chatham House Publishers.

Dalton, Russell, and Martin Wattenberg, eds. 2000. *Parties without Partisans: Political Change in Advanced Industrial Democracies*. Oxford: Oxford University Press.

De Boef, Suzanna, and Paul M. Kellstedt. 2004. "The Political (and Economic) Origins of Consumer Confidence." *American Journal of Political Science* 48(4): 633–649.

Delli Carpini, Michael X., and Scott Keeter. 1996. *What Americans Know about Politics and Why It Matters*. New Haven, CT: Yale University Press.

Dow, Jay K., and James W. Endersby. 2004. "Multinomial Probit and Multinomial Logit: A Comparison of Choice Models for Voting Research." *Electoral Studies* 23: 107–122.

Downs, Anthony. 1957. *An Economic Theory of Democracy*. New York: Harper and Row.

Duch, Raymond M. 2001. "A Developmental Model of Heterogeneous Economic Voting in New Democracies." *American Political Science Review* 98(4): 895–910.

Duch, Raymond M., and Harvey Palmer. 2002a. "Heterogeneous Perceptions of Economic Conditions in Cross-National Perspective." In Han Dorussen and Michaell Taylor, eds. *Economic Voting*.

Duch, Raymond M., and Harvey Palmer. 2002b. "Strategic Voting in Post-Communist Democracy." *British Journal of Political Science* (Spring): 63–91.

Duch, Raymond M., Harvey D. Palmer, and Christopher J. Anderson. 2000. "Heterogeneity in Perceptions of National Economic Conditions." *American Journal of Political Science* 44: 635–649.

Duch, Raymond M., Randy Stevenson, and Jeff May. 2007. "Comparing Multinomial Estimation Methods." Unpublished manuscript, Nuffield College, Oxford.

Duch, Raymond M., and Randy Stevenson. 2007. "The Economy: Do Voters Get It Right?" Manuscript, Nuffield College University of Oxford, available at http://www.nuffield.ox.ac.uk/economicvoting.

Duch, Raymond M., and Randy Stevenson. 2005. "Context and the Economic Vote: A Multi-Level Analysis." *Political Analysis* 13(4): 387–409.

Duch, Raymond M., and Kaare Strom. 2004. "Liberty, Authority, and the New Politics: A Reconsideration." *Journal of Theoretical Politics* 16(3): 233–262.

Duch, Raymond M., and Michael Taylor. 1993. "Post-Materialism and the Economic Condition." *American Journal of Political Science* 37: 747–778.

Ebeid, Michael, and Jonathan Rodden. 2006. "Economic Geography and Economic Voting: Evidence from the U.S. States." *British Journal of Political Science* 36: 527–547.

Elgie, Robert. 1999. "The Politics of Semi-Presidentialism." In Robert Elgie, ed., *Semi-Presidentialism in Europe*. Oxford: Oxford University Press.

Enelow, James, and Melvin Hinich. 1984. *The Spatial Theory of Voting: An Introduction*. Cambridge: Cambridge University Press.

Erikson, Robert S. 2004. "Macro vs. Micro-Level Perspectives on Economic Voting: Is the Micro-Level Evidence Endogenously Induced?" Paper prepared for the 2004 Political Methodology Meetings, July 29–31, Stanford University.

Erikson, Robert S. 1990. "Economic Conditions and the Congressional Vote: A Review of the Macro-Level Evidence." *American Journal of Political Science* 34: 373–399.

Erikson, Robert S. 1989. "Economic Conditions and the Presidential Vote." *American Political Science Review* 83: 568–573.

Erikson, Robert S., Michael B. MacKuen, and James A. Stimson. 2000. "Bankers or Peasants Revisited: Economic Expectations and Presidential Approval." *Electoral Studies* 19: 295–312.

Erikson, Robert S., Michael B. MacKuen, and James A. Stimson. 2002. *The Macro Polity*. Cambridge: Cambridge University Press.

Evans, Geoffrey. 1999a. "Economics and Politics Revisited: Exploring the Decline in Conservative Support, 1992–1995." *Political Studies* 47: 139–151.

Evans, Geoffrey. 1999b. *The End of Class Politics? Class Voting in Comparative Context*. New York: New York University Press.

Evans, Geoffrey, and Robert Andersen. 2006. "The Political Conditioning of Economic Perceptions." *Journal of Politics* 68(1): 194–207.

Fair, Ray C. 1978. "The Effect of Economic Events on Votes for President." *Review of Economics and Statistics* 60: 159–173.

Fearon, James D. 1999. "Electoral Accountability and the Control of Politicians: Selecting Good Types versus Sanctioning Poor Performance." In Adam Przeworski, Susan C. Stokes, and Bernard Manin, eds., *Democracy, Accountability, and Representation*. Cambridge: Cambridge University Press.

Ferejohn, John. 1986. "Incumbent Performance and Electoral Control." *Public Choice* 50: 5–25.

Fey, Mark. 1997. "Stability and Coordination in Duverger's Law: A Formal Model of Preelection Polls and Strategic Voting." *American Political Science Review* 91(1): 135–147.

Fiorina, Morris P. 1978. "Economic Retrospective Voting in American National Elections: A Micro-Analysis." *American Journal of Political Science* 22: 426–443.

Fiorina, Morris P. 1981. *Retrospective Voting in American National Elections*. New Haven, CT: Yale University Press.

Fiorina, Morris P. 1992. *Divided Government*. New York: Macmillan.

Fiorina, Morris P., Samuel Abrams, and Jeremy Pope. 2003. "The 2000 U.S. Presidential Election: Can Retrospective Voting Be Saved?" *British Journal of Political Science* 33: 163–187.

Fischer, Stanley. 2003. "Globalization and Its Challenges." *American Economic Review: Papers and Proceedings* 93(2): 1–30.

Fraile Maldonado, Marta. 2001. *Does the Economy Enter the Ballot-Box? A Study of the Spanish Voters' Decisions*. Madrid: Centro de Estudios Avanzados en Ciencias Sociales.

Franklin, Mark, Tom Mackie, Henry Valen, et al. 1992. *Electoral Change: Responses to Evolving Social and Attitudinal Structures in Western Countries*. Cambridge: Cambridge University Press.

Franzese, Robert J. 2002a. *Macroeconomic Policies of Developed Democracies*. Cambridge: Cambridge University Press.

Franzese, Robert J. 2002b. "Electoral and Partisan Cycles in Economic Policies and Outcomes." *Annual Review of Political Science* 5: 369–422.

Franzese, Robert J. 2003. "Multiple Hands on the Wheel: Empirically Modeling Partial Delegation and Shared Policy Control in the Open and Institutionalized Economy." *Political Analysis* 11: 445–475.

Freeman, John. 2007. "Democracy and Markets in the Twenty-first Century: An Agenda." In Peter Nardulli, ed., *Democracy in the Twenty-first Century: International Perspectives*. Champaign, IL: University of Illinois Press.

Frey, B. 1979. "Politometrics of Government Behavior in a Democracy." *Scandinavian Journal of Economics* 81: 308–322.

Frey, Bruno S., and Hermann Garbers. 1971. "Politicio-Economics – On Estimation in Political Economy." *Political Studies* 19: 316–320.

Frieden, Jeffrey A. 1991. "Invested Interests: The Politics of National Economic Policies in a World of Global Finance." *International Organization* 45: 425–451.

Fuchs, Dieter, and Hans-Dieter Klingemann. 1989. "The Left-Right Schema." In M. Kent Jennings and J. van Deth, eds., *Continuities in Political Action*. Berlin: deGruyter.

Garrett, Geoffrey. 2000. "Capital Mobility, Exchange Rates and Fiscal Policy in the Global Economy." *Review of International Political Economy* 7: 153–170.

Garrett, Geoffery. 1998a. *Partisan Politics in the Global Economy*. Cambridge: Cambridge University Press.

Garrett, Geoffery. 1998b. "Global Markets and National Politics: Collision Course or Virtuous Circle?" *International Organization* 52(4): 787–824.

Gavin, Michael, and Ricardo Hausmann. 1996. "Sources of Macroeconomic Volatility in Developing Economies." Manuscript. Washington, DC: Inter-American Development Bank, February 1996.

Gavin, Neil, and David Sanders. 1997. "The Economy and Voting." In Pippa Norris and N. Gavin, eds., *Britain Votes*. Oxford: Oxford University Press.

Gelman, Andrew, and Gary King. 1993. "Why Are American Presidential Election Campaign Polls So Variable When Votes Are So Predictable?" *British Journal of Political Science* 23: 409–451.

Gibbard, A. 1973: "Manipulation of Voting Schemes: A General Result." *Econometrica* 41: 587–601.

Golden, Miriam. 2000. "*Is Increasing International Economic Integration Bad for Labor?*" Los Angeles: University of California, available at http://www.shelley.polisci.ucla.edu/data/papers/g98.pdf.

Golden, Miriam, Peter Lange, and Michael Wallerstein. 1995. "The End of Corporatism? Wage Setting in the Nordic and Germanic Countries." In Sanford M. Jacoby, ed., *Workers of Nations: Industrial Relations in a Global Economy*. New York: Oxford University Press.

Goldstein, H. 1995. *Multilevel Statistical Models*. 2nd edition. London: Edward Arnold.

Goldstein, H., Browne, W. J., and Rasbash, J. 2002. "Partitioning Variation in Multilevel Models." *Understanding Statistics* 1: 223–232.

Gomez, Brad T., and J. Matthew Wilson. 2006. "Cognitive Heterogeneity and Economic Voting: A Comparative Analysis of Four Democratic Electorates," *American Journal of Political Science* 50: 127–145.

Goodhart, Charles A. E., and R. J. Bhansali. 1970. "Political Economy." *Political Studies* 18: 43–106.

Greene, William H. 2003. *Econometric Analysis, Fifth Edition*. Upper Saddle River, NJ: Prentice Hall.

Gwartney, James, and Robert Lawson. 2006. *Economic Freedom of the World: 2006 Annual Report*. Vancouver, BC: Fraser Institute, available at http://www.freetheworld.com/release.html.

Hall, Peter. 1999. "The Political Economics of Europe in an Era of Interdependence." In Herbery Kitschelt, Peter Lange, Gary Marks, and John D. Stephens, eds., *Continuity and Change in Contemporary Capitalism*. Cambridge: Cambridge University Press.

Hall, Peter, ed. 1989. The *Political Power of Economic Ideas: Keynesianism across Nations*. Princeton, NJ: Princeton University Press.

Haller, Brandon H., and Helmut Norpoth. 1994. "Let the Good Times Roll: The Economic Expectations of U.S. Voters." *American Journal of Political Science* 38: 625–650.

Hallerberg, Mark. 2000. "The Role of Parliamentary Committees in the Budgetary Process within Europe." In R. Strauch and J. Von Hagen, eds., *Institutions, Politics and Fiscal Policy*. Norwell, MA: Kluwer.

Havrilesky, Thomas M. 1987. "A Partisanship Theory of Fiscal and Monetary Regimes." *Journal of Money, Credit and Banking* 19: 308–325.

Hellwig, Timothy T. 2001. "Interdependence, Government Constraints, and Economic Voting." *Journal of Politics* 63(4): 1141–1162.

Hellwig, Timothy T. 2006. "Globalization, Room to Maneuver Constraints and Vote Choice." Paper presented at the 2006 Annual Meeting of the Midwest Political Science Association, Chicago.

Hellwig, Timothy T., and David Samuels. 2007. "Electoral Accountability and the Variety of Democratic Regimes." *British Journal of Political Science* 37: 1–26.

Henisz, Witold J. 2004. "Political Institutions and Policy Volatility." *Economics and Politics* 16: 1954–1985.

Hibbs, Douglas. 1993. *Solidarity or Egoism?* Aarhus, Denmark: Aarhus University Press.

Hibbs, Douglas A. Jr. 2000. "Bread and Peace Voting in U.S. Presidential Elections." *Public Choice* 104(1–2): 149–180.

Hibbs, Douglas A., Jr. 2006. "Voting and the Macro-Economy." In Barry Weingast and Donald Whittman, eds., *The Oxford Handbook of Political Economy*. New York: Oxford University Press.

Hibbs, Douglas A., Jr., and Nicholas Vasilatos. 1981. "Economics and Politics in France: Economic Performance and Political Support for Presidents Pompidou and Giscard d'Estaing." *European Journal of Political Research* 9:133–145.

Hinich, Melvin J., and Michael C. Munger. 1997. *Analytical Politics*. New York: Cambridge University Press.

Holmberg, Soren. 1994. "Party Identification Compared across the Atlantic." In M. Kent Jennings and Thomas E. Mann, eds., *Elections at Home and Abroad*. Ann Arbor: The University of Michigan Press.

Huber, John D., and Matthew J. Gabel. 2000. "Putting Parties in Their Place: Inferring Party Left-Right Ideological Positions from Party Manifesto Data." *American Journal of Political Science* 44: 94–103.

Inglehart, Ronald. 1977. *Silent Revolution: Changing Values and Political Styles Among Western Publics*. Princeton, NJ: Princeton University Press.

Inglehart, Ronald. 1984. "The Changing Structure of Political Cleavages in Western Society." In Russell J. Dalton, Scott C. Flanagan, and Paul Allen Beck, eds., *Electoral Change in Advanced Industrial Democracies: Realignment or Dealignment?* Princeton, NJ: Princeton University Press.

International Monetary Fund. 2005. *World Economic Outlook April 2005: Globalization and External Imbalances*. Washington, DC: IMF.

Jacobson, Gary C., and Samuel Kernell. 1983. *Strategy and Choice in Congressional Elections*. 2nd Edition. New Haven, CT: Yale University Press.

Jenson, Jane. 1976. "Party Loyalty in Canada: The Question of Party Identification." *Canadian Journal of Political Science* 8: 543–553.

Johnston, Richard, Andre Blais, Henry E. Brady, and Jean Crête. 1992. *Letting the People Decide: Dynamics of a Canadian Election*. Montreal: McGill–Queen's University Press.

Jusko, Karen Long, and W. Phillips Shively. 2005. "A Two-Step Strategy for the Analysis of Cross National Public Opinion Data." *Political Analysis* (Autumn) 13(4): 327–344.

Katzenstein, P. J. 1985. *Small States in World Markets: Industrial Policy in Europe*. Ithaca, NY, and London: Cornell University Press.

Kayser, Mark A., and Christopher Wlezien. 2005. "Performance Pressure: Patterns of Partisanship and the Economic Vote." Paper presented at the Annual

Meeting of the American Political Science Association, Washington, DC, September 1–4.

Kedar, Orit. 2005a. "How Diffusion in Parliament Affects Vote Choice: Two-Step Analysis." *Political Analysis* 13(4): 410–29.

Kedar, Orit. 2005b. "When Moderate Voters Prefer Extreme Parties: Policy Balancing in Parliamentary Elections." *American Political Science Review* 99(2): 185–199.

Keech, William. 1995. *Economic Politics and the Costs of Democracy*. Cambridge: Cambridge University Press.

Key, V. O. 1966. *The Responsible Electorate*. New York: Vintage Books.

Kiewiet, D. Roderick. 1983. *Macroeconomics and Micropolitics: The Electoral Effects of Economic Issues*. Chicago: University of Chicago Press.

Kiewiet, D. Roderick, and Michael Udell. 1998. "Twenty-Five Years after Kramer: An Assessment of Economic Retrospective Voting Based upon Improved Estimates of Income and Unemployment." *Economics in Politics* 10: 219–248.

Kinder, Donald R., and D. Roderick Kiewiet. 1979. "Economic Grievances and Political Behavior: The Role of Personal Discontents and Collective Judgments in Congressional Voting." *American Journal of Political Science* 23: 495–527.

Kinder, Donald R., and D. Roderick Kiewiet. 1981. "Sociotropic Politics: The American Case." *British Journal of Political Science* 11: 129–161.

King, Gary, and Jonathan N. Katz. 1999. A Statistical Model for Multi-Party Electoral Data." *American Political Science Review* 93(1): 15–32.

King, Gary, Michael Tomz, and Jason Wittenberg. 2000. "Making the Most of Statistical Analyses: Improving Interpretation and Presentation." *American Journal of Political Science* 44(2): 341–355.

Kitschelt, Herbert. 1994. *The Transformation of European Social Democracy*. New York: Cambridge University Press.

Klingemann, Hans Dieter. 1979. "The Background of Ideological Conceptualization." In Samuel H. Barnes and M. Kaase, eds., *Political Action: Mass Participation in Five Western Democracies*. London: Sage.

Kramer, Gerald H. 1971. "Short-Term Fluctuations in U.S. Voting Behavior, 1896–1964." *American Political Science Review* 65: 131–143.

Kramer, Gerald H. 1983. "The Ecological Fallacy Revisited: Aggregate-Versus Individual-Level Findings on Economics and Elections, and Sociotropic Voting." *American Political Science Review* 77: 92–111.

Krasner, Stephen. 1984. "Approaches to the State: Alternative Conceptions and Historical Dynamics." *Comparative Politics* 16: 223–246.

Ladd, Jonathan, and Gabriel Lenz. 2004. "Emotions and Voting Behavior: A Critique." Paper presented at the Annual Meeting of the Midwest Political Science Association, Chicago, IL, April 15–18.

Lafay, Jean-Dominique. 1977. "Les conséquences électorales de la conjoncture économique: Essaie de prévision chiffrée pour Mars 1978." *Vie et Sciences Economiques* 75:1–7.

Lane, Philip R. 1997. "Inflation in Open Economies." *Journal of International Economics* 42: 327–347.

Lane, Philip R. 2001. "The New Open Economy Macroeconomics: A Survey." *Journal of International Economics* 54 (August) 235–266.

Lau, Richard R. 1994. "An Analysis of the Accuracy of 'Trial Heat' Polls During the 1992 Presidential Election." *Public Opinion Quarterly* 58(1): 2–20.
Laver, Michael, and W. Ben Hunt. 1992. *Policy and Party Competition.* New York: Routledge.
Laver, Michael, and Kenneth A. Shepsle. 1990. "Coalitions and Cabinet Government." *American Political Science Review* 84: 873–890.
Laver, Michael, and Ian Budge, eds. 1992. *Party, Policy, and Government Coalitions.* London: St. Martin's Press.
Lecaillon, J. 1981. "Popularite des Gouverments et Popularite Economique." *Consummation* 3: 17–50.
LeDuc, Lawrence. 1981. "The Dynamic Properties of Party Identification: A Four-Nation Comparison." *European Journal of Political Research* 9: 257–268.
Lehmbrunch, Gerhard, and Philippe Schmitter, eds. 1982. *Patterns of Corporatist Policy-Making.* Beverly Hills, CA: Sage Publications.
Lewis, Jeff, and Drew Linzer. 2005. "Estimating Regression Models in Which the Dependent Variable Is Based on Estimates." *Political Analysis* 13(4): 345–364.
Lewis-Beck, Michael S. 1980. "Economic Conditions and Executive Popularity: The French Experience." *American Journal of Political Science* 24: 306–323.
Lewis-Beck, Michael S. 1983. "Economics and the French Voter: A Microanalysis." *Public Opinion Quarterly* 47: 347–360.
Lewis-Beck, Michael S. 1988. *Economics and Elections: The Major Western Democracies.* Ann Arbor: University of Michigan Press.
Lewis-Beck, Michael. 1996. "Electoral Inquiry Cross-National Election Surveys: A French Pre-test." *Electoral Studies* 15(4): 513–528.
Lewis-Beck, Michael S. 1997a. "Le vote du 'porte-monnaie' en question." In D. Boy, and N. Mayer, eds., *L'Electeur a Ses Raisons.* Paris: Presses de la Fondation Naitonale des Sciences Politiques.
Lewis-Beck, Michael S. 1997b. "Who's the Chief? Economic Voting under a Dual Executive." *European Journal of Political Research* 31: 315–325.
Lewis-Beck, Michael S., B. Jerome, and V. Jerome-Speziara. 2001. *Evaluation economique et vote en France et en Allemagne, L'Opinion Europeenne.* In Dominique Reyniè and Bruno Cautrés eds., *Presses de Sciences po*, Paris, 101–122.
Lewis-Beck, Michael S., and Richard Nadeau. 2000. "French Electoral Institutions and the Economic Vote." *Electoral Studies* 19: 171–182.
Lewis-Beck, Michael S., and Glenn Mitchell. 1990. "Modelos Transnacionales de Voto Economico: Estudio de un Conjunto de Paises Europeos." *Revista del Instituto de Estudios Economicos* 4: 65–81.
Lewis-Beck, Michael S., and Heinz Eulau. 1985. "Introduction: Economic Conditions and Electoral Outcomes in Trans-National Perspective." In Heinz Eulau and Michael S. Lewis-Beck, eds., *Economic Conditions and Electoral Outcomes: The United States and Western Europe.* New York: Agathon.
Lewis-Beck, Michael S., and Tom Rice. 1992. *Forecasting Elections.* Washington, DC: Congressional Quarterly Press.
Lewis-Beck, Michael S., and Martin Paldam. 2000. "Editorial: Economic Voting: An Introduction." *Electoral Studies* 2: 113–120.

Lewis-Beck, Michael, and Richard Nadeau. 2004. "Dual Governance and Economic Votings: France and the United States. In *The French Voter Before and After the 2002 Election*, ed. Michael Lewis-Beck. New York: Palgrave MacMillan.

Lewis-Beck, Michael S., and Mary Stegmaier. 2006. "Economic Models of Voting." In Russell Dalton and Hans-Dieter Klingemann, eds. *Oxford Handbook of Political Behavior*. Oxford: Oxford University Press.

Lewis-Beck, Michael S., and Mary Stegmaier. 2000. "Economic Determinants of Electoral Outcomes." *Annual Review of Political Science* 3: 183–219.

Leyden, Kevin M., and Stephen A. Borrelli. 1995. "The Effect of State Economic Conditions on Gubernatorial Elections: Does Unified Government Make a Difference?" *Political Research Quarterly* 48: 275–300.

Lijphart, Arend. 1981. "Political Parties: Ideologies and Programs." In David Butler, Howard R. Penniman, and Austin Ranney, eds., *Democracy at the Polls: A Comparative Study of Competitive National Elections*. Washington, DC: American Enterprise Institute. Reprinted in Peter Mair, ed., 1990. *The West European Party System*. New York: Oxford University Press.

Lindbeck, A. 1975. "Business Cycles, Politics and International Economic Depedence." *Skandinaviska Enskilden Bank Quarterly Review* 2: 53–68.

Lindbeck, A. 1976. "Stabilization in Open Economies with Endogenous Politicians." *American Economics Review Papers and Proceedings* (May): 1–19.

Linz, Juan. 1990. "The Perils of Presidentialism." *Journal of Democracy* 1: 51–69.

Linz, Juan J. 1994. "Presidential versus Parliamentary Democracy: Does It Make a Difference?" In Juan Linz and Arturo Valenzuela, eds., *The Failure of Presidential Democracy, Volume 2: The Case of Latin America*. Baltimore, MD: Johns Hopkins University Press, 3–90.

Lipset, Seymour Martin, and Stein Rokkan. 1967. "Cleavage Structures, Party Systems, and Voter Alignments: An Introduction." In Seymour M. Lipset and Stein Rokkan, eds., *Party Systems and Voter Alignments: Cross-National Perspectives*. New York: Free Press.

Lockerbie, Brad. 1992. "Prospective Voting in Presidential Elections, 1956–1988." *American Politics Quarterly* 20: 308–325.

Lodge, Milton, Marco R. Steenbergen, and Shawn Brau. 1995 "The Responsive Voter: Campaign Information and the Dynamics of Candidate Evaluation." *American Political Science Review* 89 (June): 309–326.

Lowry, Robert C., James E. Alt, and Karen E. Ferree. 1998. "Fiscal Policy Outcomes and Electoral Accountability in American States." *American Political Science Review* 92: 759–774.

MacKuen, Michael B., and Steven L. Coombs. 1981. *More Than News: Media Power in Public Affairs*. Beverly Hills, CA: Sage.

MacKuen, Michael B., Robert S. Erikson, and James A. Stimson. 1992. "Peasants or Bankers?: The American Electorate and the U.S. Economy." *American Political Science Review* 86: 597–611.

Madsen, H. 1980. "Electoral Outcomes and Macro-Economic Policies: The Scandinavian Cases." In P. Whitely, ed., *Models of Political Economy*. London: Sage Publications.

Manin, Bernard. 1997. *Principles of Representative Government*. Cambridge: Cambridge University Press.

Markus, Gregory. 1988. "The Impact of Personal and National Economic Conditions on the Presidential Vote: A Pooled Cross-Sectional Analysis." *American Journal of Political Science* 32: 137–154.

Marra, Robin F., and Charles W. Ostrom. 1989. "Explaining Seat Change in the US House of Representatives, 1950–1986." *American Journal of Political Science* 33: 541–569.

Markus, Gregory. 1992. "The Impact of Personal and National Economic Conditions on the Presidential Vote: A Pooled Cross-Sectional Analysis." *American Journal of Political Science* 36: 829–834.

Marcus, George E., W. Russell Neuman, and Michael MacKuen. 2000. *Affective Intelligence and Political Judgment*. Chicago: University of Chicago Press.

Maravall, José Maria, and Adam Przeworski. 1998. "Political Reactions to the Economy: The Spanish Experience." Estudio/Working Paper 1998/127. Juan March Institute, Madrid, December.

Martin, Larry, and Randolf Stevenson. 2001. "Government Formation in Parliamentary Democracies." *American Journal of Political Science*. 45(1): 33–50.

Mayda, Anna Maria, and Dani Rodrik. 2005. "Why Are Some People (and Countries) More Protectionist Than Others?" *European Economic Review* 49(6): 1393–1430.

McKelvey, Richard, and Peter Ordeshook. 1972. "A General Theory of the Calculus of Voting." In J. F. Herndon and J. L Bernd, eds., *Mathematical Applications in Political Science*, vol. 6. Charlottesville: University Press of Virginia.

Meisel, John. 1975. *Working Papers on Canadian Politics*. 2nd edition. Montreal and Kingston: McGill–Queen's University Press.

Miller, Arthur H., and Ola Listhaug. 1985. "Economic Effects on the Vote in Norway." In Heinz Eulau and Michael S. Lewis-Beck, eds., *Economic Conditions and Electoral Outcomes: The United States and Western Europe*. New York: Agathon.

Miller, William L., and Myles Mackie. 1973. "The Electoral Cycle and the Asymmetry of Government and the Opposition Popularity: An Alternative Model of the Relationship between Economic Conditions and Political Popularity." *Political Studies* 621: 263–279.

Miller, W. E., and J. M. Shanks. (1996). *The New American Voter*. Cambridge, MA: Harvard University Press.

Miller, W. L., and R. G. Niemi. 2002. "Voting: Choice, Conditioning, and Constraint." In L. LeDuc, R. Niemi, and P. Norris, eds., *Comparing Democracies 2*. Thousand Oaks, CA: Sage.

Mueller, John. 1970. "Presidential Popularity from Truman to Johnson." *American Political Science Review* 65: 18–34.

Mundell, Robert A. 1962. "The Appropriate Use of Monetary and Fiscal Policy under Fixed Exchange Rates." *IMF Staff Paper* 9: 70–77.

Mundell, Robert A. 1963. "Capital Mobility and Stabilization Policy under Fixed and Flexible Exchange Rates." *Canadian Journal of Economics and Political Science* 29: 475–485.

Mundell, Robert A. 1964. "A Reply: Capital Mobility and Size." *Canadian Journal of Economics and Political Science* 30: 421–431.

Myerson, R. 1999. "Theoretical Comparison of Electoral Systems. 1998 Joseph Schumpeter Lecture." *European Economic Review* 43: 671–697.

Myerson, R. 1993. "Effectiveness of Electoral Systems for Reducing Government Corruption: A Game Theoretic Analysis." *Games and Economic Behaviour* 5: 118–132.

Myerson, Roger, and Robert Weber. 1993. "A Theory of Voting Equilibria." *American Political Science Review* 87: 102–114.

Nadeau, Richard, and A. Blais. 1993. "Explaining Elections Outcomes in Canada: Economy and Politics." *Canadian Journal of Political Science* 26: 775–790.

Nadeau, Richard, Richard G. Niemi, David P. Fan, and Timothy Amato. 1999. "Elite Economic Forecasts, Economic News, Mass Economic Judgments, and Presidential Approval." *Journal of Politics* 61(1): 109–135.

Nadeau Richard, and Lewis-Beck. 2004. "Dual Governance and the Economic Vote: France and the United States." in *The French Voter: Before and After the 2002 Elections*. Palgrave Macmillan.

Nadeau, Richard, and Michael S. Lewis-Beck. 2001. "National Economic Voting in U.S. Presidential Elections," *Journal of Politics* 63: 159–181.

Nadeau, Richard, Richard G. Niemi, and Antoine Yoshinaka. 2002. "A Cross-National Analysis of Economic Voting: Taking Account of the Political Context across Time and Nations." *Electoral Studies* 21: 403–423.

Nannestad, Peter and Martin Paldam. 1995. "It's the Government's Fault! A Cross-Section Study of Economic Voting in Denmark, 1990/93." *European Journal of Political Research* 28: 33–62.

Nannestad, Peter, and Martin Paldam. 1997a. "From the Pocketbook of the Welfare Man: A Pooled Cross-Section Study of Economic Voting in Denmark, 1986–1992." *British Journal of Political Science* 27: 119–137.

Nannestad, Peter, and Martin Paldam. 1997b. "The Grievance Asymmetry Revisited: A Micro Study of Economic Voting in Denmark, 1986–92." *European Journal of Political Economy* 13: 81–99.

Nannestad, Peter, and Martin Paldam. 2000. "Into Pandora's Box of Economic Evaluations. A Study of the Danish Macro VP-Function 1986–1997." *Electoral Studies* 19: 123–40.

Nickelsburg, Michael, and Helmut Norpoth. 2000. "Commander-in-Chief or Chief Economist? The President in the Eye of the Public." *Electoral Studies* 19: 313–323.

Niemi, Richard, and Herb Weisberg. 1992. *Controversies in Voting Behavior*. Cambridge: Cambridge University Press.

Norpoth, Helmut. 1985. "Politics, Economics, and the Cycle of Presidential Popularity." In Heinz Eulau and Michael S. Lewis-Beck, eds., *Economic and Electoral Outcomes*. New York: Agathon.

Norpoth, Helmut. 1987. "Guns and Butter and Government Popularity in Great Britain." *American Political Science Review* 81: 949–960.

Norpoth, Helmut. 1992. *Confidence Regained: Economics, Mrs. Thatcher, and the British Voter*. Ann Arbor: University of Michigan Press.

Norpoth, Helmut. 1996a. "The Economy." In Lawrence LeDuc, R. G. Niemi, and P. Norris, eds., *Comparing Democracies: Elections and Voting in Global Perspective*. Thousand Oaks, CA: Sage.

Norpoth, Helmut. 2001. "Divided Government and Economic Voting." *Journal of Politics* 63(2): 414–435.

Norpoth, Helmut (2002). "On a Short Leash: Term Limits and the Economic Voter." In Han Dorussen and Michaell Taylor, eds., *Economic Voting*, London: Routledge.

Norpoth, Helmut, Michael Lewis-Beck, and Jean-Dominique Lafay, eds. *Economics and Politics: The Calculus of Support and*? Arbor, MI: University of Michigan Press.

Oatley, Thomas. 1999. "How Constraining Is Mobile Capital? The Partisan Hypothesis in an Open Economy." *American Journal of Political Science* 43: 1003–1027.

OECD. 2002. *Quarterly National Accounts*. Paris: Organization for Economic Cooperation and Development.

Ogg, F. A. 1936. *English Government and Politics*. 2nd edition. New York: Macmillan.

Olson, Mancur, Jr. 1982. *The Rise and Decline of Nations: Economic Growth, Stagflation, and Social Rigidities*. New Haven, CT: Yale University Press.

Pacek, Alexander C., and Benjamin Radcliff. 1995. "Economic Voting and the Welfare State: A Cross-National Analysis." *Journal of Politics* 57(1): 44–61.

Paldam, Martin. 1986. "The distribution of Election Results and the Two Explanations of the Cost of Ruling." *European Journal of Political Economy* 2: 5–24.

Paldam, Martin. 1991. "How Robust is the Vote Function? A Study of Seventeen Nations over Four Decades." In Helmut Norpoth, Michael Lewis-Beck, and Jean-Dominique Lafay, eds., *Economics and Politics: The Calculus of Support*. Ann Arbor: University of Michigan Press.

Paldam, Martin, and Peter Nannestad. 2000. "What do Voters Know about the Economy? A Study of Danish Data, 1990–1993." *Electoral Studies* 19: 363–392.

Paldam, Martin, and F. Schneider. 1980. "The Macroeconomic Aspects of Government and Opposition Popularity in Denmark, 1957–1978." *National Okonomisk Tidsskrift* 118: 149–170.

Palfrey, Thomas. 1989. "A Mathematical Proof of Duvergen's Law." In Peter C. Crdeshook, ed., *Models of Strategic Choice in Politics*. Ann Arbor: University of Michigan Press.

Palmer, Harvey, and Raymond M. Duch. 2001. "Do Surveys Provide Representative or Whimsical Assessments of the Economy" *Political Analysis*. 9: 58–77.

Palmer, Harvey D., and Guy D. Whitten. 2000 "Government Competence, Economic Performance and Endogenous Election Dates." *Electoral Studies* 19: 413–426.

Palmer, Harvey D., and Guy D. Whitten. 2003a. "Questionable Analyses with No Theoretical Innovation: A Response to Royed, Leyden and Borrelli." *British Journal of Political Science* 33: 139–149.

Palmer, Harvey D., and Guy D. Whitten. 2003b. "Ignorance Is No Excuse: Data Mining versus Theoretical Formulation of Hypotheses." *British Journal of Political Science* 33: 159–160.

Papke, Leslie, and Jeffrey Wooldridge. 1996. "Econometric Methods for Fractional Response Variables with An Application to 401(k) Plan Participation Rates." *Journal of Applied Econometrics* (11): 619–632.

Parrish, S. 1998. "Presidential Decree Authority in Russia, 1991–1995." In J. Carey and M. Shugart, eds., *Executive Decree Authority*. New York: Cambridge University Press.

Peltzman, Sam. 1987. "Economic Conditions and Gubernatorial Election." *American Economic Review* 77(2): 293–297.

Persson, Torsten, and Guido Tabellini. 1990. *Macroeconomic Policy, Credibility, and Politics*. New York: Harwood Academic.

Persson, Torsten, and Guido Tabellini. 2000. *Political Economics: Explaining Economic Policy*. Cambridge, MA: MIT Press.

Persson, Torsten, and Guido Tabellini. 2003. *The Economic Effect of Constitutions*. Cambridge, MA: MIT Press.

Persson, Torsten, and Guido Tabellini. 2004. "Constitutional Rules and Fiscal Policy Outcomes." *American Economic Review* 94: 25–46.

Poole, Keith T., and Howard Rosenthal. 1997. *Congress: A Political-Economic History of Roll-Call Voting*. New York: Oxford University Press.

Powell, G. Bingham, Jr. 2000. *Elections as Instruments of Democracy: Majoritarian and Proportional Visions*. New Haven, CT: Yale University Press.

Powell, G. Bingham, and Guy D. Whitten. 1993. "A Cross-National Analysis of Economic Voting: Taking Account of the Political Context." *American Journal of Political Science* 37: 391–414.

Price, Simon, and David Sanders. 1995. "Economic Expectations and Voting Intentions in the UK, 1979–1987: A Pooled Cross-Section Approach." *Political Studies* 43: 451–471.

Quinn, Dennis P., and John T. Woolley. 2001. "Democracy and National Economic Performance: The Preference for Stability." *American Journal of Political Science* 45(3): 634–657.

Quinn, Kevin M., Andrew D. Martin, and Andrew B. Whitford. 1999. "Voter Choice in Multi-Party Democracies: A Test of Competing Theories and Models." *American Journal of Political Science* 43(4): 1231–1247.

Ragin, Charles C. 1987. *The Comparative Method: Moving beyond Qualitative and Quantitative Strategies*. Berkeley: University of California Press.

Rodrik, Dani. 1997a. *Has Globalization Gone Too Far?* Washington, DC: Institute for International Economics.

Rodrik, Dani. 1997b. "Democracy and Economic Performance." Available at http://ksghome.harvard.edu/~drodrik/demoecon.PDF.

Rodrik, Dani. 1998. "Why Do More Open Economies Have Larger Governments?" *Journal of Political Economy* 106(5): 997–1032.

Rogoff, Kenneth, and Sibert, Anne. 1988. "Elections and Macroeconomic Policy Cycles." *Review of Economic Studies* 55: 1–16.

Rose, Richard. 1974. *Electoral Behavior: A Comparative Handbook*. New York: The Free Press.

Rose, Richard, and Thomas Mackie. 1983. "Incumbency in Government: Asset or Liability?" In Hans Daalder and P. Mair, eds., *Western European Party Systems: Continuity and Change*. Beverly Hills, CA: Sage Publications.

Royed, Terry J., Kevin M. Leyden, and Stephen A. Borrelli. 2000. "Is 'Clarity of Responsibility' Important for Economic Voting? Revisiting Powell and Whitten's Hypothesis." *British Journal of Politics* 30: 669–698.

Rudolph, Thomas J. 2003. "Who's Responsible for the Economy? The Formation and Consequences of Responsibility Attribution." *American Journal of Political Science* 47(4): 698–713.

Sanders, David, David Marsh, and Hugh Ward. 1987. "Government Popularity and the Falklands War." *British Journal of Political Science*. 17: 281–313.

Sanders, David. 2003b. "Party Identification, Economic Perceptions, and Voting in British General Elections, 1974–97." *Electoral Studies* 22: 239–263.

Sanders, David, Jonathan Burton, and Jack Kneeshaw. 2003. "Identifying the True Identifiers: A Question Wording Experiment." *Party Politics* 8(2):193–205.

Sarno, Lucio. 2000. "Towards a Paradigm in New Open Economy Modeling: Where Do We Stand?" *Federal Reserve Bank of St. Louis Review* 83(3): 21–26.

Sartori, Giovanni. 1994. *Comparative Constitutional Analysis*. New York: New York University Press.

Satterthwaite, M. A. 1975. "Strategy-Proofness and Arrow's Conditions Existence and Correspondence Theorems for Voting Procedures and Social Welfare Functions." *Journal of Economic Theory* 10: 187–217.

Scheve, Kenneth. 2004. "Democracy and Globalization: Candidate Selection in Open Economies." Mimeograph, Yale University, May 6.

Schickler, Eric, and Donald Philip Green. 1997. "The Stability of Party Identification in Eight Western Democracies." *Comparative Political Studies* 30: 450–483.

Schmitter, Philippe, and Gerhard Lehmbrunch, eds. 1979. *Trends toward Corporatist Intermediation*. Beverley Hills, CA: Sage Publications.

Shugart, Matthew S., and John Carey. 1992. *Presidents and Assemblies: Constitutional Design and Electoral Dynamics*. Cambridge: Cambridge University Press.

Silver, Brian D., Barbara A. Anderson, and Paul R. Abramson. 1986. "Who Overreports Voting?" *American Political Science Review* 80(2): 613–624.

Snijders, Tom A. B., and Roel J. Bosker. 1999. *Multilevel Analysis: An Introduction to Basic and Advanced Multilevel Modeling*. London: Sage Publications.

Spiller, Pablo. 1990. "Politicians, Interest Groups, and Regulation: A Multiple-Principals Agency Theory of Regulation, or Let Them Be Bribed." *Journal of Law and Economics* 33: 65–101.

Stein, Robert M. 1990. "Economic Voting for Governor and U.S. Senator: The Electoral Consequences of Federalism." *Journal of Politics* 52(1): 29–53.

Stevenson, Randolph T. 2001. "Economy and Policy Preferences: A Fundamental Dynamic of Democratic Politics." *American Journal of Political Science* 45: 620–633.

Stewart, Marianne, and Harold Clarke. 1998. "The Dynamics of Party Identification in Federal Systems: The Canadian Case." *American Journal of Political Science* 42(1): 97–116.

Stigler, George J. 1973. "General Economic Conditions and National Elections." *American Economic Review* 63: 160–164.

Strom, Kaare. 1990. *Minority Government and Majority Rule*. New York: Cambridge University Press.

Thomassen, J. 1976. "Party Identification as a Cross-National Concept: Its Meaning in the Netherlands." In Ian Budge, Ivor Crewe, and Denis Farlie, eds., *Party Identification and Beyond: Representations of Voting and Party Competition*. London: John Wiley and Sons.

Train, Kenneth. 2003. *Discrete Choice Models with Simulation*. Cambridge: Cambridge University Press.

Tsebelis, George. 2002. *Veto Players: How Political Institutions Work*. Princeton, NJ: Princeton University Press.

Tucker, Joshua A. 2006. *Regional Economic Voting: Russia, Poland, Hungary, Slovakia and the Czech Republic, 1990–99*. Cambridge: Cambridge University Press.

Tufte, Edward R. 1975. "Determinants of the Outcomes of Midterm Congressional Elections." *American Political Science Review* 69: 812–826.

Tufte, Edward R. 1978. *Political Control of the Economy*. Princeton, NJ: Princeton University Press.

Verzichelli, Luca, and Maurizio Cotta. 2000. "Italy: From 'Constrained' Coalitions to Alternating Governments?" In Wolfgang C. Mueller and Kaare Strom, eds., *Coalition Governments in Western Europe*. Oxford: Oxford University Press.

Welch, S., and Hibbing, J. 1992. "Financial Conditions, Gender, and Voting in American National Elections." *Journal of Politics* 54 (Febraury): 194–213.

Whiteley, Paul F. 1986. "Macroeconomic Performance and Government Popularity in Britain: The Short-Run Dynamics." *European Journal of Political Research* 14: 45–61.

Wlezien, Christopher, Mark Franklin, and Daniel Twiggs. "Economic Perceptions and Vote Choice: Disentangling the Endogeneity." *Political Behavior* 19: 7–17.

Wolfinger, Raymond, and Steven J. Rosenstone, 1980. *Who Votes?* New Haven, CT: Yale University Press.

World Bank. 2004. *World Development Indicators*. Washington, DC: World Bank.

Zaller, John. 2004. "Floating Voters in US Presidential Elections, 1948–2000. In Paul Sniderman and W. Saris, eds., *The Issue of Belief: Essays in the Intersection of Nonattitudes and Attitude Change*. Amsterdam: University of Amsterdam Press.

Zuckerman, Alan S. 1982. "New Approaches to Political Cleavages." *Comparative Politics* 15: 131–144.

Index

(continued from page iii)

Gary W. Cox, *The Efficient Secret: The Cabinet and the Development of Political Parties in Victorian England*

Gary W. Cox, *Making Votes Count: Strategic Coordination in the World's Electoral System*

Gary W. Cox and Jonathan N. Katz, *Elbridge Gerry's Salamander. The Electoral Consequences of the Reapportionment Revolution*

Jean Ensminger, *Making a Market: The Institutional Transformation of an African Society*

David Epstein and Sharyn O'Halloran, *Delegating Powers: A Transaction Cost Politics Approach to Policy Making under Separate Powers*

Kathryn Firmin-Sellers, *The Transformation of Property Rights in the Gold Coast: An Empirical Study Applying Rational Choice Theory*

Clark C. Gibson, *Politicians and Poachers: The Political Economy of Wildlife Policy in Africa*

Stephen Haber, Armando Razo, and Noel Maurer, *The Politics of Property Rights: Political Instability, Credible Commitments, and Economic Growth in Mexico, 1876–1929*

Ron Harris, *Industrializing English Law: Entrepreneurship and Business Organization, 1720–1844*

Anna L. Harvey, *Votes without Leverage: Women in American Electoral Politics, 1920–1970*

Murray Horn, *The Political Economy of Public Administration: Institutional Choice in the Public Sector*

John D. Huber, *Rationalizing Parliament: Legislative Institutions and Party Politics in France*

Jack Knight, *Institutions and Social Conflict*

Michael Laver and Kenneth Shepsle, eds., *Cabinet Ministers and Parliamentary Government*

Michael Laver and Kenneth Shepsle, eds., *Making and Breaking Governments: Cabinets and Legislatures in Parliamentary Democracies*

Margaret Levi, *Consent, Dissent, and Patriotism*

Brian Levy and Pablo T. Spiller, eds., *Regulations, Institutions, and Commitment: Comparative Studies of Telecommunications*

Leif Lewin, *Ideology and Strategy: A Century of Swedish Politics* (English edition)

Gary Libecap, *Contracting for Property Rights*

John Londregan, *Legislative Institutions and Ideology in Chile*

Arthur Lupia and Mathew D. McCubbins, *The Democratic Dilemma: Can Citizens Learn What They Need to Know?*

C. Mantzavinos, *Individuals, Institutions, and Markets*

Mathew D. McCubbins and Terry Sullivan, eds., *Congress: Structure and Policy*

Gary J. Miller, *Managerial Dilemmas: The Political Economy of Hierarchy*

Douglass C. North, *Institutions, Institutional Change, and Economic Performance*

Elinor Ostrom, *Governing the Commons: The Evolution of Institutions for Collective Action*

J. Mark Ramseyer, *Odd Markets in Japanese History: Law and Economic Growth*

J. Mark Ramseyer and Frances Rosenbluth, *The Politics of Oligarchy: Institutional Choice in Imperial Japan*

Jean-Laurent Rosenthal, *The Fruits of Revolution: Property Rights, Litigation, and French Agriculture, 1700–1860*

Michael L. Ross, *Timber Booms and Institutional Breakdown in Southeast Asia*

Alastair Smith, *Election Timing*

Shanker Satyanath, *Globalization, Politics, and Financial Turmoil: Asia's Banking Crisis*

Norman Schofield, *Architects of Political Change: Constitutional Quandaries and Social Choice Theory*

Norman Schofield and Itai Sened, *Multiparty Democracy: Elections and Legislative Politics*

Pablo T. Spiller and Mariano Tommasi, *The Institutional Foundations of Public Policy in Argentina*

David Stasavage, *Public Debt and the Birth of the Democratic State: France and Great Britain, 1688–1789*

Charles Stewart , *Budget Reform Politics: The Design of the Appropriations Process in the House of Representatives, 1865–1921*

George Tsebelis and Jeannette Money, *Bicameralism*

Georg Vanberg, *The Politics of Constitutional Review in Germany*

Nicolas van de Walle, *African Economies and the Politics of Permanent Crisis, 1979–1999*

John Waterbury, *Exposed to Innumerable Delusions: Public Enterprise and State Power in Egypt, India, Mexico, and Turkey*

David L. Weimer, ed., *The Political Economy of Property Rights: Institutional Change and Credibility in the Reform of Centrally Planned Economies*